Annual Editions:
Physical Anthropology, 25/e

Elvio Angeloni

http://create.mheducation.com

ISBN-10: 125940031X   ISBN-13: 9781259400315

Contents

Preface

This twenty-fifth edition of *Annual Editions: Physical Anthropology* contains a variety of articles relating to human evolution. The writings were selected for their timeliness, relevance to issues not easily treated in the standard physical anthropology textbooks, and clarity of presentation.

Whereas textbooks tend to reflect the consensus within the field, *Annual Editions: Physical Anthropology* provides a forum for the controversial. We do this in order to convey to the student that the study of human development is an evolving entity in which each discovery encourages further research and each added piece of the puzzle raises new questions about the total picture.

Our final criterion for selecting articles is readability. All too often, the excitement of a new discovery or a fresh idea is deadened by the weight of a ponderous presentation. We seek to avoid that by incorporating essays written with enthusiasm and with the desire to communicate some very special ideas to the general public.

Included in this volume are a number of features that are designed to make it useful for students, researchers, and professionals in the field of anthropology. Each unit is preceded by an overview, which provides a background for informed reading of the articles and emphasizes critical issues. *Learning Outcomes* accompany each article and outline the key concepts that students should focus on as they are reading the material. *Critical Thinking* questions, found at the end of each article, allow students to test their understanding of the key points of the article. The *Internet References* section can be used to further explore the topics online.

Those involved in producing this volume wish to make the next one as useful and effective as possible. Your criticism and advice are always welcome. Any anthology can be improved. This continues to be—annually.

Editor

Elvio Angeloni received his BA from UCLA in 1963, MA in anthropology from UCLA in 1965, and MA in communication arts from Loyola Marymount University in 1976. He received the Pasadena City College Outstanding Teacher Award in 2006 and has since retired from teaching. He has produced several films, including *Little Warrior,* winner of the Cinemedia VI Best Bicentennial Theme, and *Broken Bottles,* shown on PBS. He served as an academic adviser on the instructional television series *Faces of Culture.* He is also the academic editor of *Annual Editions: Anthropology, Classic Edition Sources: Anthropology,* co-editor of *Roundtable Viewpoints Physical Anthropology,* and co-editor of *Annual Editions: Archaeology.* His primary area of interest has been indigenous peoples of the American Southwest. Contact: evangeloni@gmail.com

Academic Advisory Board

Members of the Academic Advisory Board are instrumental in the final selection of articles for the *Annual Editions* series. Their review of the articles for content, level, and appropriateness provides critical direction to the editor(s) and staff. We think that you will find their careful consideration reflected in this book.

Lauren Arenson
Pasadena City College

AnnMarie Beasley
Cosumnes River College

Donna C. Boyd
Radford University and RU Forensic Science Institute

Wendy Branwell
South Texas College

Paula Clarke
Columbia College

Gloria Everson
Lyon College

Marisa Fontana
North Central College

Shasta Gaughen
California State University San Marcos

Roberta Lenkeit
Modesto Junior College

Diane A. Lichtenstein
Baldwin-Wallace College and Cleveland Institute of Art

Joseph Lorenz
Central Washington University

Amanda Paskey
Cosumnes River College

Craig B. Stanford
University of Southern California

Unit 1

UNIT

Prepared by: Elvio Angeloni, *Pasadena City College*

Evolutionary Perspectives

As we reflect upon where the biological sciences have taken us over the past 300 years, we can see that we have been swept along a path of insight into the human condition, as well as into a heightened controversy on how to handle this potentially dangerous and/or unwanted knowledge of ourselves.

Certainly, Gregor Mendel, in the late nineteenth century, could not have anticipated that his study of pea plants would ultimately lead to the better understanding of over 3,000 genetically caused diseases, such as sickle-cell anemia, Huntington's chorea, Tay-Sachs, and hemophilia. Nor could he have foreseen the present-day controversies over matters such as cloning and genetic engineering. The significance of Mendel's work, of course, was his discovery that hereditary traits are conveyed by particular units that we now call "genes," a then-revolutionary notion that was later followed by a better understanding of how and why such units change. It is the knowledge of the process of "mutation," or alteration of the chemical structure of the gene, that is now providing us with the potential to control the genetic fate of individuals. This does not mean, however, that we should not continue to look at the role the environment plays in the development of what might be better termed as "genetically influenced conditions," such as alcoholism.

The other side of the evolutionary coin is natural selection, a concept provided by Charles Darwin and Alfred Wallace. Natural selection refers to the "weeding out" of unfavorable mutations and the perpetuation of favorable ones.

As our understanding of evolutionary processes becomes more refined, the theory of natural selection, unfortunately, continues to be poorly understood by the general public. Ever since Darwin published *On the Origin of Species* in 1859, for instance, there have been those who have embraced it as supportive of everything from communism to laissez-faire capitalism. But these interpretations say more about the theorists and their socioeconomic agenda than they do about the actual facts of human nature or even the social context in which human beings evolved. If the battle with "Social Darwinism" isn't enough, scientists throughout the same period of history have had to confront creationists with fallacies in their thinking as well as remind the rest of us why this battle is so important. There is something to be learned from these conflicts. Consider the claim of the "intelligent design theory" that nature is too orderly to have come about by a random process. What is missing from this view is the fact that natural selection is not a theory of chance, but is instead a process that results in the *appearance* of intentional design. In fact, what we see in nature is not the absolute perfection that one might expect from a purposeful god, but, rather, the somewhat orderly but less than ideal adaptation on the part of creatures that must make do with what they have. We must keep in mind that science is not simply an established and agreed-upon body of knowledge. Rather, it is a way of thinking and a method of investigation in which we seek understanding for its own sake and not for some comforting, preconceived ideas.

Article   Prepared by: Elvio Angeloni, *Pasadena City College*

Was Darwin Wrong?

DAVID QUAMMEN

Learning Outcomes

After reading this article, you will be able to:

- Define "natural selection."
- Summarize Darwin's evidence for evolution.

Evolution by natural selection, the central concept of the life's work of Charles Darwin, is a theory. It's a theory about the origin of adaptation, complexity, and diversity among Earth's living creatures. If you are skeptical by nature, unfamiliar with the terminology of science, and unaware of the overwhelming evidence, you might even be tempted to say that it's "just" a theory. In the same sense, relativity as described by Albert Einstein is "just" a theory. The notion that Earth orbits around the sun rather than vice versa, offered by Copernicus in 1543, is a theory. Continental drift is a theory. The existence, structure, and dynamics of atoms? Atomic theory. Even electricity is a theoretical construct, involving electrons, which are tiny units of charged mass that no one has ever seen. Each of these theories is an explanation that has been confirmed to such a degree, by observation and experiment, that knowledgeable experts accept it as fact. That's what scientists mean when they talk about a theory: not a dreamy and unreliable speculation, but an explanatory statement that fits the evidence. They embrace such an explanation confidently but provisionally—taking it as their best available view of reality, at least until some severely conflicting data or some better explanation might come along.

The rest of us generally agree. We plug our televisions into little wall sockets, measure a year by the length of Earth's orbit, and in many other ways live our lives based on the trusted reality of those theories.

Evolutionary theory, though, is a bit different. It's such a dangerously wonderful and far-reaching view of life that some people find it unacceptable, despite the vast body of supporting evidence. As applied to our own species, *Homo sapiens,* it can seem more threatening still. Many fundamentalist Christians and ultraorthodox Jews take alarm at the thought that human descent from earlier primates contradicts a strict reading of the Book of Genesis. Their discomfort is paralleled by Islamic creationists such as Harun Yahya, author of a recent volume titled *The Evolution Deceit,* who points to the six-day creation story in the Koran as literal truth and calls the theory of evolution "nothing but a deception imposed on us by the dominators of the world system." The late Srila Prabhupada, of the Hare Krishna movement, explained that God created "the 8,400,000 species of life from the very beginning," in order to establish multiple tiers of reincarnation for rising souls. Although souls ascend, the species themselves don't change, he insisted, dismissing "Darwin's nonsensical theory."

Other people too, not just scriptural literalists, remain unpersuaded about evolution. According to a Gallup poll drawn from more than a thousand telephone interviews conducted in February 2001, no less than 45 percent of responding U.S. adults agreed that "God created human beings pretty much in their present form at one time within the last 10,000 years or so." Evolution, by their lights, played no role in shaping us.

Only 37 percent of the polled Americans were satisfied with allowing room for both God and Darwin—that is, divine initiative to get things started, evolution as the creative means. (This view, according to more than one papal pronouncement, is compatible with Roman Catholic dogma.) Still fewer Americans, only 12 percent, believed that humans evolved from other life-forms without any involvement of a god.

The most startling thing about these poll numbers is not that so many Americans reject evolution, but that the statistical breakdown hasn't changed much in two decades. Gallup interviewers posed exactly the same choices in 1982, 1993, 1997, and 1999. The creationist conviction—that God alone, and not evolution, produced humans—has never drawn less than 44 percent. In other words, nearly half the American populace prefers to believe that Charles Darwin was wrong where it mattered most.

Why are there so many antievolutionists? Scriptural literalism can only be part of the answer. The American public certainly includes a large segment of scriptural literalists—but not *that* large, not 44 percent. Creationist proselytizers and political activists, working hard to interfere with the teaching of evolutionary biology in public schools, are another part. Honest confusion and ignorance, among millions of adult Americans, must be still another. Many people have never taken a biology course that dealt with evolution nor read a book in which the theory was lucidly explained. Sure, we've all heard of Charles Darwin, and of a vague, somber notion about struggle and survival that sometimes goes by the catchall label "Darwinism." But the main sources of information from which most Americans have drawn their awareness of this subject, it seems, are haphazard ones at best: cultural osmosis, newspaper and magazine references, half-baked nature documentaries on the tube, and hearsay.

Evolution is both a beautiful concept and an important one, more crucial nowadays to human welfare, to medical science, and to our understanding of the world than ever before. It's also deeply persuasive—a theory you can take to the bank. The essential points are slightly more complicated than most people assume, but not so complicated that they can't be comprehended by any attentive person. Furthermore, the supporting evidence is abundant, various, ever increasing, solidly interconnected, and easily available in museums, popular books, textbooks, and a mountainous accumulation of peer-reviewed scientific studies. No one needs to, and no one should, accept evolution merely as a matter of faith.

Two big ideas, not just one, are at issue: the evolution of all species, as a historical phenomenon, and natural selection, as the main mechanism causing that phenomenon. The first is a question of what happened. The second is a question of how. The idea that all species are descended from common ancestors had been suggested by other thinkers, including Jean-Baptiste Lamarck, long before Darwin published *The Origin of Species* in 1859. What made Darwin's book so remarkable when it appeared, and so influential in the long run, was that it offered a rational explanation of how evolution must occur. The same insight came independently to Alfred Russel Wallace, a young naturalist doing fieldwork in the Malay Archipelago during the late 1850s. In historical annals, if not in the popular awareness, Wallace and Darwin share the kudos for having discovered natural selection.

The gist of the concept is that small, random, heritable differences among individuals result in different chances of survival and reproduction—success for some, death without offspring for others—and that this natural culling leads to significant changes in shape, size, strength, armament, color, biochemistry, and behavior among the descendants. Excess population growth drives the competitive struggle. Because less successful competitors produce fewer surviving offspring, the useless or negative variations tend to disappear, whereas the useful variations tend to be perpetuated and gradually magnified throughout a population.

So much for one part of the evolutionary process, known as anagenesis, during which a single species is transformed. But there's also a second part, known as speciation. Genetic changes sometimes accumulate within an isolated segment of a species, but not throughout the whole, as that isolated population adapts to its local conditions. Gradually it goes its own way, seizing a new ecological niche. At a certain point it becomes irreversibly distinct—that is, so different that its members can't interbreed with the rest. Two species now exist where formerly there was one. Darwin called that splitting-and-specializing phenomenon the "principle of divergence." It was an important part of his theory, explaining the overall diversity of life as well as the adaptation of individual species.

This thrilling and radical assemblage of concepts came from an unlikely source. Charles Darwin was shy and meticulous, a wealthy landowner with close friends among the Anglican clergy. He had a gentle, unassuming manner, a strong need for privacy, and an extraordinary commitment to intellectual honesty. As an undergraduate at Cambridge, he had studied halfheartedly toward becoming a clergyman himself, before he discovered his real vocation as a scientist. Later, having established a good but conventional reputation in natural history, he spent 22 years secretly gathering evidence and pondering arguments—both for and against his theory—because he didn't want to flame out in a burst of unpersuasive notoriety. He may have delayed, too, because of his anxiety about announcing a theory that seemed to challenge conventional religious beliefs—in particular, the Christian beliefs of his wife, Emma. Darwin himself quietly renounced Christianity during his middle age, and later described himself as an agnostic. He continued to believe in a distant, impersonal deity of some sort, a greater entity that had set the universe and its laws into motion, but not in a personal God who had chosen humanity as a specially favored species. Darwin avoided flaunting his lack of religious faith, at least partly in deference to Emma. And she prayed for his soul.

In 1859 he finally delivered his revolutionary book. Although it was hefty and substantive at 490 pages, he considered *The Origin of Species* just a quick-and-dirty "abstract" of the huge volume he had been working on until interrupted by an alarming event. (In fact, he'd wanted to title it *An Abstract of an Essay on the Origin of Species and Varieties Through Natural Selection,* but his publisher found that insufficiently catchy.) The alarming event was his receiving a letter and an enclosed manuscript from Alfred Wallace, whom he knew only as a distant pen pal. Wallace's manuscript sketched out the same great idea—evolution by natural selection—that Darwin considered his own. Wallace had scribbled this paper and (unaware of Darwin's own evolutionary thinking, which so far had been kept private) mailed it to him from the Malay Archipelago, along with a request for reaction and help. Darwin was horrified. After two decades of painstaking effort, now he'd be scooped. Or maybe not quite. He forwarded Wallace's paper toward publication, though managing also to assert his own prior claim by releasing two excerpts from his unpublished work. Then he dashed off *The Origin,* his "abstract" on the subject. Unlike Wallace, who was younger and less meticulous, Darwin recognized the importance of providing an edifice of supporting evidence and logic.

The evidence, as he presented it, mostly fell within four categories: biogeography, paleontology, embryology, and morphology. Biogeography is the study of the geographical distribution of living creatures—that is, which species inhabit which parts of the planet and why. Paleontology investigates extinct life-forms, as revealed in the fossil record. Embryology examines the revealing stages of development (echoing earlier stages of evolutionary history) that embryos pass through before birth or hatching; at a stretch, embryology also concerns the immature forms of animals that metamorphose, such as the larvae of insects. Morphology is the science of anatomical shape and design. Darwin devoted sizable sections of *The Origin of Species* to these categories.

Biogeography, for instance, offered a great pageant of peculiar facts and patterns. Anyone who considers the biogeographical data, Darwin wrote, must be struck by the mysterious clustering pattern among what he called "closely allied" species—that is, similar creatures sharing roughly the same body plan. Such closely allied species tend to be found on the same continent (several species of zebras in Africa) or within the same group of oceanic islands (dozens of species of honeycreepers in Hawaii, 13 species of Galápagos finch), despite their species-by-species preferences for different habitats, food sources, or conditions of climate. Adjacent areas of South America, Darwin noted, are occupied by two similar species of large, flightless birds (the rheas, *Rhea americana* and *Pterocnemia pennata*), not by ostriches as in Africa or emus as in Australia. South America also has agoutis and viscachas (small rodents) in terrestrial habitats, plus coypus and capybaras in the wetlands, not—as Darwin wrote—hares and rabbits in terrestrial habitats or beavers and muskrats in the wetlands. During his own youthful visit to the Galápagos, aboard the survey ship *Beagle,* Darwin himself had discovered three very similar forms of mockingbird, each on a different island.

Why should "closely allied" species inhabit neighboring patches of habitat? And why should similar habitat on different continents be occupied by species that aren't so closely allied? "We see in these facts some deep organic bond, prevailing throughout space and time," Darwin wrote. "This bond, on my theory, is simply inheritance." Similar species occur nearby in space because they have descended from common ancestors.

Paleontology reveals a similar clustering pattern in the dimension of time. The vertical column of geologic strata, laid down by sedimentary processes over the eons, lightly peppered with fossils, represents a tangible record showing which species lived when. Less ancient layers of rock lie atop more ancient ones (except where geologic forces have tipped or shuffled them), and likewise with the animal and plant fossils that the strata contain. What Darwin noticed about this record is that closely allied species tend to be found adjacent to one another in successive strata. One species endures for millions of years and then makes its last appearance in, say, the middle Eocene epoch; just above, a similar but not identical species replaces it. In North America, for example, a vaguely horselike creature known as *Hyracotherium* was succeeded by *Orohippus,* then *Epihippus,* then *Mesohippus,* which in turn were succeeded by a variety of horsey American critters. Some of them even galloped across the Bering land bridge into Asia, then onward to Europe and Africa. By five million years ago they had nearly all disappeared, leaving behind *Dinohippus,* which was succeeded by *Equus,* the modern genus of horse. Not all these fossil links had been unearthed in Darwin's day, but he captured the essence of the matter anyway. Again, were such sequences just coincidental? No, Darwin argued. Closely allied species succeed one another in time, as well as living nearby in space, because they're related through evolutionary descent.

Embryology too involved patterns that couldn't be explained by coincidence. Why does the embryo of a mammal pass through stages resembling stages of the embryo of a reptile? Why is one of the larval forms of a barnacle, before metamorphosis, so similar to the larval form of a shrimp? Why do the larvae of moths, flies, and beetles resemble one another more than any of them resemble their respective adults? Because, Darwin wrote, "the embryo is the animal in its less modified state" and that state "reveals the structure of its progenitor."

Morphology, his fourth category of evidence, was the "very soul" of natural history, according to Darwin. Even today it's on display in the layout and organization of any zoo. Here are the monkeys, there are the big cats, and in that building are the alligators and crocodiles. Birds in the aviary, fish in the aquarium. Living creatures can be easily sorted into a hierarchy of categories—not just species but genera, families, orders, whole kingdoms—based on which anatomical characters they share and which they don't.

All vertebrate animals have backbones. Among vertebrates, birds have feathers, whereas reptiles have scales. Mammals have fur and mammary glands, not feathers or scales. Among mammals, some have pouches in which they nurse their tiny young. Among these species, the marsupials, some have huge rear legs and strong tails by which they go hopping across miles of arid outback; we call them kangaroos. Bring in modern microscopic and molecular evidence, and you can trace the similarities still further back. All plants and fungi, as well as animals, have nuclei within their cells. All living organisms contain DNA and RNA (except some viruses with RNA only), two related forms of information-coding molecules.

Such a pattern of tiered resemblances—groups of similar species nested within broader groupings, and all descending from a single source—isn't naturally present among other collections of items. You won't find anything equivalent if you try to categorize rocks, or musical instruments, or jewelry. Why not? Because rock types and styles of jewelry don't reflect unbroken descent from common ancestors. Biological diversity does. The number of shared characteristics between any one species and another indicates how recently those two species have diverged from a shared lineage.

That insight gave new meaning to the task of taxonomic classification, which had been founded in its modern form back in 1735 by the Swedish naturalist Carolus Linnaeus. Linnaeus showed how species could be systematically classified, according to their shared similarities, but he worked from creationist assumptions that offered no material explanation for the nested pattern he found. In the early and middle 19th century, morphologists such as Georges Cuvier and Étienne Geoffroy Saint-Hilaire in France and Richard Owen in England improved classification with their meticulous studies of internal as well as external anatomies, and tried to make sense of what the ultimate source of these patterned similarities could be. Not even Owen, a contemporary and onetime friend of Darwin's (later in life they had a bitter falling out), took the full step to an evolutionary vision before *The Origin of Species* was published. Owen made a major contribution, though, by advancing the concept of homologues—that is, superficially different but fundamentally similar versions of a single organ or trait, shared by dissimilar species.

For instance, the five-digit skeletal structure of the vertebrate hand appears not just in humans and apes and raccoons and bears but also, variously modified, in cats and bats and porpoises and lizards and turtles. The paired bones of our lower leg, the tibia and the fibula, are also represented by homologous bones in other mammals and in reptiles, and even in the long-extinct bird-reptile *Archaeopteryx*. What's the reason behind such varied recurrence of a few basic designs? Darwin, with a nod to Owen's "most interesting work," supplied the answer: common descent, as shaped by natural selection, modifying the inherited basics for different circumstances.

Vestigial characteristics are still another form of morphological evidence, illuminating to contemplate because they show that the living world is full of small, tolerable imperfections. Why do male mammals (including human males) have nipples? Why do some snakes (notably boa constrictors) carry the rudiments of a pelvis and tiny legs buried inside their sleek profiles? Why do certain species of flightless beetles have wings, sealed beneath wing covers that never open? Darwin raised all these questions, and answered them, in *The Origin of Species*. Vestigial structures stand as remnants of the evolutionary history of a lineage.

Today the same four branches of biological science from which Darwin drew—biogeography, paleontology, embryology, morphology—embrace an ever growing body of supporting data. In addition to those categories we now have others: population genetics, biochemistry, molecular biology, and, most recently, the whiz-bang field of machine-driven genetic sequencing known as genomics. These new forms of knowledge overlap one another seamlessly and intersect with the older forms, strengthening the whole edifice, contributing further to the certainty that Darwin was right.

He was right about evolution, that is. He wasn't right about *everything*. Being a restless explainer, Darwin floated a number of theoretical notions during his long working life, some of which were mistaken and illusory. He was wrong about what causes variation within a species. He was wrong about a famous geologic mystery, the parallel shelves along a Scottish valley called Glen Roy. Most notably, his theory of inheritance—which he labeled pangenesis and cherished despite its poor reception among his biologist colleagues—turned out to be dead wrong. Fortunately for Darwin, the correctness of his most famous good idea stood independent of that particular bad idea. Evolution by natural selection represented Darwin at his best—which is to say, scientific observation and careful thinking at its best.

Douglas Futuyma is a highly respected evolutionary biologist, author of textbooks as well as influential research papers. His office, at the University of Michigan, is a long narrow room in the natural sciences building, well stocked with journals and books, including volumes about the conflict between creationism and evolution. I arrived carrying a well-thumbed copy of his own book on that subject, *Science on Trial: The Case for Evolution*. Killing time in the corridor before our appointment, I noticed a blue flyer on a departmental bulletin board, seeming oddly placed there amid the announcements of career opportunities for graduate students. "Creation vs. evolution," it said. "A series of messages challenging popular thought with Biblical truth and scientific evidences." A traveling lecturer from something called the Origins Research Association would deliver these messages at a local Baptist church. Beside the lecturer's

photo was a drawing of a dinosaur. "Free pizza following the evening service," said a small line at the bottom. Dinosaurs, biblical truth, and pizza: something for everybody.

In response to my questions about evidence, Dr. Futuyma moved quickly through the traditional categories—paleontology, biogeography—and talked mostly about modern genetics. He pulled out his heavily marked copy of the journal *Nature* for February 15, 2001, a historic issue, fat with articles reporting and analyzing the results of the Human Genome Project. Beside it he slapped down a more recent issue of *Nature*, this one devoted to the sequenced genome of the house mouse, *Mus musculus*. The headline of the lead editorial announced: "HUMAN BIOLOGY BY PROXY." The mouse genome effort, according to *Nature*'s editors, had revealed "about 30,000 genes, with 99% having direct counterparts in humans."

The resemblance between our 30,000 human genes and those 30,000 mousy counterparts, Futuyma explained, represents another form of homology, like the resemblance between a five-fingered hand and a five-toed paw. Such genetic homology is what gives meaning to biomedical research using mice and other animals, including chimpanzees, which (to their sad misfortune) are our closest living relatives.

No aspect of biomedical research seems more urgent today than the study of microbial diseases. And the dynamics of those microbes within human bodies, within human populations, can only be understood in terms of evolution.

Nightmarish illnesses caused by microbes include both the infectious sort (AIDS, Ebola, SARS) that spread directly from person to person and the sort (malaria, West Nile fever) delivered to us by biting insects or other intermediaries. The capacity for quick change among disease-causing microbes is what makes them so dangerous to large numbers of people and so difficult and expensive to treat. They leap from wildlife or domestic animals into humans, adapting to new circumstances as they go. Their inherent variability allows them to find new ways of evading and defeating human immune systems. By natural selection they acquire resistance to drugs that should kill them. They evolve. There's no better or more immediate evidence supporting the Darwinian theory than this process of forced transformation among our inimical germs.

Take the common bacterium *Staphylococcus aureus*, which lurks in hospitals and causes serious infections, especially among surgery patients. Penicillin, becoming available in 1943, proved almost miraculously effective in fighting staphylococcus infections. Its deployment marked a new phase in the old war between humans and disease microbes, a phase in which humans invent new killer drugs and microbes find new ways to be unkillable. The supreme potency of penicillin didn't last long. The first resistant strains of *Staphylococcus aureus* were reported in 1947. A newer staph-killing drug, methicillin, came into use during the 1960s, but methicillin-resistant strains appeared soon, and by the 1980s those strains were widespread. Vancomycin became the next great weapon against staph, and the first vancomycin-resistant strain emerged in 2002. These antibiotic-resistant strains represent an evolutionary series, not much different in principle from the fossil series tracing horse evolution from *Hyracotherium* to *Equus*. They make evolution a very practical problem by adding expense, as well as misery and danger, to the challenge of coping with staph.

The biologist Stephen Palumbi has calculated the cost of treating penicillin-resistant and methicillin-resistant staph infections, just in the United States, at 30 billion dollars a year. "Antibiotics exert a powerful evolutionary force," he wrote last year, "driving infectious bacteria to evolve powerful defenses against all but the most recently invented drugs." As reflected in their DNA, which uses the same genetic code found in humans and horses and hagfish and honeysuckle, bacteria are part of the continuum of life, all shaped and diversified by evolutionary forces.

Even viruses belong to that continuum. Some viruses evolve quickly, some slowly. Among the fastest is HIV, because its method of replicating itself involves a high rate of mutation, and those mutations allow the virus to assume new forms. After just a few years of infection and drug treatment, each HIV patient carries a unique version of the virus. Isolation within one infected person, plus differing conditions and the struggle to survive, forces each version of HIV to evolve independently. It's nothing but a speeded up and microscopic case of what Darwin saw in the Galápagos—except that each human body is an island, and the newly evolved forms aren't so charming as finches or mockingbirds.

Understanding how quickly HIV acquires resistance to antiviral drugs, such as AZT, has been crucial to improving treatment by way of multiple drug cocktails. "This approach has reduced deaths due to HIV by severalfold since 1996," according to Palumbi, "and it has greatly slowed the evolution of this disease within patients."

Insects and weeds acquire resistance to our insecticides and herbicides through the same process. As we humans try to poison them, evolution by natural selection transforms the population of a mosquito or thistle into a new sort of creature, less vulnerable to that particular poison. So we invent another poison, then another. It's a futile effort. Even DDT, with its ferocious and long-lasting effects throughout ecosystems, produced resistant house flies within a decade of its discovery in 1939. By 1990 more than 500 species (including 114 kinds of mosquitoes) had acquired resistance to at least one pesticide. Based on these undesired results, Stephen Palumbi has commented glumly, "humans may be the world's dominant evolutionary force."

Among most forms of living creatures, evolution proceeds slowly—too slowly to be observed by a single scientist within a research lifetime. But science functions by inference, not just by direct observation, and the inferential sorts of evidence such as paleontology and biogeography are no less cogent simply because they're indirect. Still, skeptics of evolutionary theory ask: Can we see evolution in action? Can it be observed in the wild? Can it be measured in the laboratory?

The answer is yes. Peter and Rosemary Grant, two British-born researchers who have spent decades where Charles Darwin spent weeks, have captured a glimpse of evolution with their long-term studies of beak size among Galápagos finches. William R. Rice and George W. Salt achieved something similar in their lab, through an experiment involving 35 generations of the fruit fly *Drosophila melanogaster.* Richard E. Lenski and his colleagues at Michigan State University have done it too, tracking 20,000

generations of evolution in the bacterium *Escherichia coli.* Such field studies and lab experiments document anagenesis—that is, slow evolutionary change within a single, unsplit lineage. With patience it can be seen, like the movement of a minute hand on a clock.

Speciation, when a lineage splits into two species, is the other major phase of evolutionary change, making possible the divergence between lineages about which Darwin wrote. It's rarer and more elusive even than anagenesis. Many individual mutations must accumulate (in most cases, anyway, with certain exceptions among plants) before two populations become irrevocabldy separated. The process is spread across thousands of generations, yet it may finish abruptly—like a door going slam!—when the last critical changes occur. Therefore it's much harder to witness. Despite the difficulties, Rice and Salt seem to have recorded a speciation event, or very nearly so, in their extended experiment on fruit flies. From a small stock of mated females they eventually produced two distinct fly populations adapted to different habitat conditions, which the researchers judged "incipient species."

After my visit with Douglas Futuyma in Ann Arbor, I spent two hours at the university museum there with Philip D. Gingerich, a paleontologist well-known for his work on the ancestry of whales. As we talked, Gingerich guided me through an exhibit of ancient cetaceans on the museum's second floor. Amid weird skeletal shapes that seemed almost chimerical (some hanging overhead, some in glass cases) he pointed out significant features and described the progress of thinking about whale evolution. A burly man with a broad open face and the gentle manner of a scoutmaster, Gingerich combines intellectual passion and solid expertise with one other trait that's valuable in a scientist: a willingness to admit when he's wrong.

Since the late 1970s Gingerich has collected fossil specimens of early whales from remote digs in Egypt and Pakistan. Working with Pakistani colleagues, he discovered *Pakicetus,* a terrestrial mammal dating from 50 million years ago, whose ear bones reflect its membership in the whale lineage but whose skull looks almost doglike. A former student of Gingerich's, Hans Thewissen, found a slightly more recent form with webbed feet, legs suitable for either walking or swimming, and a long toothy snout. Thewissen called it *Ambulocetus natans,* or the "walking-and-swimming whale." Gingerich and his team turned up several more, including *Rodhocetus balochistanensis,* which was fully a sea creature, its legs more like flippers, its nostrils shifted backward on the snout, halfway to the blowhole position on a modern whale. The sequence of known forms was becoming more and more complete. And all along, Gingerich told me, he leaned toward believing that whales had descended from a group of carnivorous Eocene mammals known as mesonychids, with cheek teeth useful for chewing meat and bone. Just a bit more evidence, he thought, would confirm that relationship. By the end of the 1990s most paleontologists agreed.

Meanwhile, molecular biologists had explored the same question and arrived at a different answer. No, the match to those Eocene carnivores might be close, but not close enough. DNA hybridization and other tests suggested that whales had descended from artiodactyls (that is, even-toed herbivores, such as antelopes and hippos), not from meat-eating mesonychids.

In the year 2000 Gingerich chose a new field site in Pakistan, where one of his students found a single piece of fossil that changed the prevailing view in paleontology. It was half of a pulley-shaped anklebone, known as an astragalus, belonging to another new species of whale.

A Pakistani colleague found the fragment's other half. When Gingerich fitted the two pieces together, he had a moment of humbling recognition: The molecular biologists were right. Here was an anklebone, from a four-legged whale dating back 47 million years, that closely resembled the homologus anklebone in an artiodactyl. Suddenly he realized how closely whales are related to antelopes.

This is how science is supposed to work. Ideas come and go, but the fittest survive. Downstairs in his office Phil Gingerich opened a specimen drawer, showing me some of the actual fossils from which the display skeletons upstairs were modeled. He put a small lump of petrified bone, no longer than a lug nut, into my hand. It was the famous astragalus, from the species he had eventually named *Artiocetus clavis*. It felt solid and heavy as truth.

Seeing me to the door, Gingerich volunteered something personal: "I grew up in a conservative church in the Midwest and was not taught anything about evolution. The subject was clearly skirted. That helps me understand the people who are skeptical about it. Because I come from that tradition myself." He shares the same skeptical instinct. Tell him that there's an ancestral connection between land animals and whales, and his reaction is: Fine, maybe. But show me the intermediate stages. Like Charles Darwin, the onetime divinity student, who joined that round-the-world voyage aboard the *Beagle* instead of becoming a country parson, and whose grand view of life on Earth was shaped by attention to small facts, Phil Gingerich is a reverant empiricist. He's not satisfied until he sees solid data. That's what excites him so much about pulling shale fossils out of the ground. In 30 years he has seen enough to be satisfied. For him, Gingerich said, it's "a spiritual experience."

"The evidence is there," he added. "It's buried in the rocks of ages."

Critical Thinking

1. What is wrong with the argument that evolution is "just a theory"? What examples of scientific theories does the author provide?

2. What, approximately, are the current poll numbers on Americans' acceptance of evolution? How have these changed over time?

3. What reasons does the author suspect are behind American antievolutionism?

4. What is Darwin's theory of natural selection?

5. What is anagenesis? Speciation? How does speciation occur?

6. Describe Darwin's life. What was his most important work? When was it published?

7. What were the four categories of evidence presented by Darwin? List each and provide examples discussed by the author.

8. What is taxonomic classification? Who founded it (and when) in its modern form?

9. What is a homologue? Give an example and an explanation.

10. Complete and explain this statement: "There is no better or more immediate evidence supporting Darwinian theory than _____." What examples are given and discussed by the author?

11. Can evolution be observed in the wild? What examples does the author give?

12. Describe the debate (and the outcome) scientists have had about the evolution of modern day whales.

Create Central

www.mhhe.com/createcentral

Internet References

Charles Darwin on Human Origins
www.literature.org/Works/Charles-Darwin

Enter Evolution: Theory and History
www.ucmp.berkeley.edu/history/evolution.html

Quammen, David. From *National Geographic*, November 2004. Copyright © 2004 by National Geographic Society. Reprinted by permission.

Article   Prepared by: Elvio Angeloni, *Pasadena City College*

The Facts of Evolution

MICHAEL SHERMER

Learning Outcomes

After reading this article, you will be able to:

- Discuss evolution as a *historical* science.
- Summarize the evidence for evolution.

The affinities of all the beings of the same class have sometimes been represented by a great tree. I believe this simile largely speaks the truth. As buds give rise by growth to fresh buds, and these, if vigorous, branch out and overtop on all sides many a feebler branch, so by generation I believe it has been with the great Tree of Life, which fills with its dead and broken branches the crust of the earth, and covers the surface with its ever branching and beautiful ramifications.

—Charles Darwin,
On the Origin of Species, 1859

The theory of evolution has been under attack since Charles Darwin first published *On the Origin of Species* in 1859. From the start, its critics have seized on the *theory* of evolution to try to undermine its facts. But all great works of science are written in support of some particular view. In 1861, shortly after he published his new theory, Darwin wrote a letter to his colleague, Henry Fawcett, who had just attended a special meeting of the British Association for the Advancement of Science during which Darwin's book was debated. One of the naturalists had argued that *On the Origin of Species* was too theoretical, that Darwin should have just "put his facts before us and let them rest." In response, Darwin reflected that science, to be of any service, required more than list-making; it needed larger ideas that could make sense of piles of data. Otherwise, Darwin said, a geologist "might as well go into a gravelpit and count the pebbles and describe the colours." Data without generalizations are useless; facts without explanatory principles are meaningless. A "theory" is not just someone's opinion or a wild guess made by some scientist. A theory is a well-supported and well-tested generalization that explains a set of observations. Science without theory is useless.

The process of science is fueled by what I call *Darwin's Dictum*, defined by Darwin himself in his letter to Fawcett: "all observation must be for or against some view if it is to be of any service."

Darwin's casual comment nearly a hundred and fifty years ago encapsulates a serious debate about the relative roles of data and theory, or observations and conclusions, in science. In a science like evolution, in which inferences about the past must be made from scant data in the present, this debate has been exploded to encompass a fight between religion and science.

Prediction and Observation

Most essentially, *evolution is a historical science*. Darwin valued above all else prediction and verification by subsequent observation. In an act of brilliant historical science, for example, Darwin correctly developed a theory of coral reef evolution years before he developed his theory of biological evolution. He had never seen a coral reef, but during the *Beagle*'s famous voyage to the Galápagos, he had studied the types of coral reefs Charles Lyell described in *Principles of Geology*. Darwin reasoned that the different examples of coral reefs did not represent different types, each of which needed a different causal explanation; rather, the different examples represented different stages of development of coral reefs, for which only a single cause was needed. Darwin considered this a triumph of theory in driving scientific investigation: Theoretical prediction was followed by observational verification, whereby "I had therefore only to verify and extend my views by a careful examination of coral reefs." In this case, the theory came first, then the data.

The publication of the *Origin of Species* triggered a roaring debate about the relative roles of data and theory in science. Darwin's "bulldog" defender, Thomas Henry Huxley, erupted in a paroxysm against those who pontificated on science but had never practiced it themselves: "There cannot be a doubt that the method of inquiry which Mr. Darwin has adopted is not only rigorously in accord with the canons of scientific logic, but that it is the only adequate method," Huxley wrote. Those "critics exclusively trained in classics or in mathematics, who have never determined a scientific fact in their lives by induction from experiment or observation, prate learnedly about Mr.

Darwin's method," he bellowed, "which is not inductive enough, not Baconian enough, forsooth for them."

Darwin insisted that theory comes to and from the facts, not from political or philosophical beliefs, whether from God or the godfather of scientific empiricism. It is a point he voiced succinctly in his cautions to a young scientist. The facts speak for themselves, he said, advising "the advantage, at present, of being very sparing in introducing theory in your papers; let theory guide your observations, but till your reputation is well established, be sparing of publishing theory. It makes persons doubt your observations." Once Darwin's reputation was well established, he published his book that so well demonstrated the power of theory. As he noted in his autobiography, "some of my critics have said, 'Oh, he is a good observer, but has no power of reasoning.' I do not think that this can be true, for the *Origin of Species* is one long argument from the beginning to the end, and it has convinced not a few able men."

Against Some View

Darwin's "one long argument" was with the theologian William Paley and the theory Paley posited in his 1802 book, *Natural Theology: or, Evidences of the Existence and Attributes of the Deity, Collected from the Appearances of Nature.* Sound eerily familiar? The scholarly agenda of this first brand of Intelligent Design was to correlate the works of God (nature) with the words of God (the Bible). Natural theology kicked off with John Ray's 1691 *Wisdom of God Manifested in Works of the Creation,* which itself was inspired by Psalms 19:11: "The Heavens declare the Glory of the Lord and the Firmament sheweth his handy work." John Ray, in what still stands as a playbook for creationism, explains the analogy between human and divine creations: If a "curious Edifice or machine" leads us to "infer the being and operation of some intelligent Architect or Engineer," shouldn't the same be said of "the Works of nature, that Grandeur and magnificence, that excellent contrivance for Beauty, Order, use, &c. which is observable in them, wherein they do as much transcend the Efforts of human Art and infinite Power and Wisdom exceeds finite" to make us "infer the existence and efficiency of an Omnipotent and All-wise Creator"?

Paley advanced Ray's work through the accumulated knowledge of a century of scientific exploration. The opening passage of Paley's *Natural Theology* has become annealed into our culture as the winningly accessible and thus appealing "watchmaker" argument:

> In crossing a heath, suppose I pitched my foot against a stone, and were asked how the stone came to be there. I might possibly answer, that, for any thing I knew to the contrary, it had lain there forever. But suppose I had found a watch upon the ground, and it should be enquired how the watch happened to be in that place. The inference, we think, is inevitable; that the watch must have had a maker; that there must have existed, at some time and in some place or other, an artificer or artificers who formed it for the purpose which we find it actually to answer; who comprehended its construction, and designed its use.

But life is far more complex than a watch—so the design inference is even stronger!

> There cannot be design without a designer; contrivance without a contriver . . . The marks of design are too strong to be got over. Design must have had a designer. That designer must have been a person. That person is GOD.

For longer than we have had the theory of evolution, we have had theologians arguing for Intelligent Design.

From Natural Theology to Natural Selection

After abandoning medical studies at Edinburgh University, Charles Darwin entered the University of Cambridge to study theology with the goal of becoming a Church of England cleric. Natural theology provided him with a socially acceptable excuse to study natural history, his true passion. It also educated Darwin in the arguments on design popularized by Paley and others. His intimacy with their ideas was respectful, not combative. For example, in November 1859, the same month that the *Origin of Species* was published, Darwin wrote his friend John Lubbock, "I do not think I hardly ever admired a book more than Paley's 'Natural Theology.' I could almost formerly have said it by heart." Both Paley and Darwin addressed a problem in nature: the origin of the design of life. Paley's answer was to posit a top-down designer—God. Darwin's answer was to posit a bottom-up designer—natural selection. Natural theologians took this to mean that evolution was an attack on God, without giving much thought to what evolution is.

Ever since Darwin, much has been written about what, exactly, evolution is. Ernst Mayr, arguably the greatest evolutionary theorist since Darwin, offers a subtly technical definition: "evolution is change in the adaptation and in the diversity of populations of organisms." He notes that evolution has a dual nature, a "'vertical' phenomenon of adaptive change," which describes how a species responds to its environment over time, and a "'horizontal' phenomenon of populations, incipient species, and new species," which describes adaptations that break through the genetic divide. And I'll never forget Mayr's definition of a species, because I had to memorize it in my first course on evolutionary biology: "A species is a group of actually or potentially interbreeding natural populations reproductively isolated from other such populations."

Mayr outlines five general tenets of evolutionary theory that have been discovered in the years since Darwin published his revolutionary book:

1. *Evolution:* Organisms change through time. Both the fossil record of life's history and nature today document and reveal this change.
2. *Descent with modification:* Evolution proceeds through the branching of common descent. As every parent and child knows, offspring are similar to but not exact replicas of their parents, producing the necessary variation that allows adaptation to the ever-changing environment.

3. *Gradualism:* All this change is slow, steady, and stately. Given enough time, small changes within a species can accumulate into large changes that create new species; that is, macro-evolution is the cumulative effect of microevolution.

4. *Multiplication:* Evolution does not just produce new species; it produces an increasing number of new species.

And, of course,

5. *Natural selection:* Evolutionary change is not haphazard and random; it follows a selective process. Codiscovered by Darwin and the naturalist Alfred Russel Wallace, natural selection operates under five rules:

   A. Populations tend to increase indefinitely in a geometric ratio: 2, 4, 8, 16, 32, 64, 128, 256, 512, 1024 . . .

   B. In a natural environment, however, population numbers must stabilize at a certain level. The population cannot increase to infinity—the earth is just not big enough.

   C. Therefore, there must be a "struggle for existence." Not all of the organisms produced can survive.

   D. There is variation in every species.

   E. Therefore, in the struggle for existence, those individuals with variations that are better adapted to the environment leave behind more offspring than individuals that are less well adapted. This is known as *differential reproductive success.*

As Darwin said, "as more individuals are produced than can possibly survive, there must in every case be a struggle for existence, either one individual with another of the same species, or with the individuals of distinct species, or with the physical conditions of life."

The process of natural selection, when carried out over countless generations, gradually leads varieties of species to develop into new species. Darwin explained:

> It may be said that natural selection is daily and hourly scrutinising, throughout the world, every variation, even the slightest; rejecting that which is bad, preserving and adding up all that is good; silently and insensibly working, whenever and wherever opportunity offers, at the improvement of each organic being in relation to its organic and inorganic conditions of life. We see nothing of these slow changes in progress, until the hand of time has marked the long lapses of ages, and then so imperfect is our view into long past geological ages, that we only see that the forms of life are now different from what they formerly were.

The time frame is long and the changes from generation to generation are subtle. This may be one of the most important and difficult points to grasp about the theory of evolution. It is tempting to see species as they exist today as a living monument to evolution, to condense evolution into the incorrect but provocative shorthand that humans descended from chimpanzees—a shorthand that undercuts the facts of evolution.

Natural selection is the process of organisms struggling to survive and reproduce, with the result of propagating their genes into the next generation. As such, it operates primarily at the local level. The Oxford evolutionary biologist Richard Dawkins elegantly described the process as "random mutation plus non-random cumulative selection," emphasizing the non-random. Evolution is not the equivalent of a warehouse full of parts randomly assorting themselves into a jumbo jet, as the creationists like to argue. If evolution were truly random there would be no biological jumbo jets. Genetic mutations and the mixing of parental genes in offspring may be random, but the selection of genes through the survival of their hosts is anything but random. Out of this process of self-organized directional selection emerge complexity and diversity.

Natural selection is a description of a process, not a force. No one is "selecting" organisms for survival or extinction, in the benign sense of dog breeders selecting for desirable traits in show breeds, or in the malignant sense of Nazis selecting prisoners at Auschwitz-Birkenau. Natural selection, and thus evolution, is unconscious and nonprescient—it cannot look forward to anticipate what changes are going to be needed for survival. The evolutionary watchmaker is blind, says Dawkins, *pace* Paley.

By way of example, once when my young daughter asked how evolution works, I used the polar bear as an example of a "transitional species" between land mammals and marine mammals, because although they are land mammals they spend so much time in the water that they have acquired many adaptations to an aquatic life. But this is not correct. It implies that polar bears are *on their way* (in transition) to becoming marine mammals. They aren't. Polar bears are not "becoming" anything. Polar bears are well adapted for their lifestyle. That's all. If global warming continues, perhaps polar bears will adapt to a full-time aquatic existence, or perhaps they will move south and become smaller brown bears, or perhaps they will go extinct. Who knows? No one.

Where Are All the Fossils?

Evolution is a historical science, and historical data—fossils—are often the evidence most cited for and against it. In the creationist textbook, *Of Pandas and People*—one of the bones of contention in the 2005 Intelligent Design trial of *Kitzmiller et al. v. Dover Area School District,* in Dover, Pennsylvania—the authors state: "Design theories suggest that various forms of life began with their distinctive features already intact: fish with fins and scales, birds with feathers and wings, mammals with fur and mammary glands . . . Might not gaps exist . . . not because large numbers of transitional forms mysteriously failed to fossilize, but because they never existed?"

Darwin himself commented on this lack of transitional fossils, asking, "Why then is not every geological formation and every stratum full of such intermediate links?" In contemplating the answer, he turned to the data and noted that "geology assuredly does not reveal any such finely graduated organic chain; and this, perhaps, is the gravest objection which can be urged against my theory." So where *are* all the fossils?

One answer to Darwin's dilemma is the exceptionally low probability of any dead animal's escaping the jaws and stomachs of predators, scavengers, and detritus feeders, reaching the stage of fossilization, and then somehow finding its way back to the surface through geological forces and unpredictable events to be discovered millions of years later by the handful of paleontologists looking for its traces. Given this reality, it is remarkable that we have as many fossils as we do.

There is another explanation for the missing fossils. Ernst Mayr outlines the most common way that a species gives rise to a new species: when a small group (the "founder" population) breaks away and becomes geographically—and thus reproductively— isolated from its ancestral group. As long as it remains small and detached, the founder group can experience fairly rapid genetic changes, especially relative to large populations, which tend to sustain their genetic homogeneity through diverse interbreeding. Mayr's theory, called *allopatric speciation,* helps to explain why so few fossils would exist for these animals.

The evolutionary theorists Niles Eldredge and Stephen Jay Gould took Mayr's observations about how new species emerge and applied them to the fossil record, finding that gaps in the fossil record are not missing evidence of gradual changes; they are extant evidence of punctuated changes. They called this theory *punctuated equilibrium.* Species are so static and enduring that they leave plenty of fossils in the strata while they are in their stable state (equilibrium). The change from one species to another, however, happens relatively quickly on a geological time scale, and in these smaller, geographically isolated population groups (punctuated). In fact, species change happens so rapidly that few "transitional" carcasses create fossils to record the change. Eldredge and Gould conclude that "breaks in the fossil record are real; they express the way in which evolution occurs, not the fragments of an imperfect record." Of course, the small group will also be reproducing, following the geometric increases that are observed in all species, and will eventually form a relatively large population of individuals that retain their phenotype for a considerable time—and leave behind many well-preserved fossils. Millions of years later this process results in a fossil record that records mostly the equilibrium. The punctuation is in the blanks.

The Evidence of Evolution

In August 1996, NASA announced that it discovered life on Mars. The evidence was the Allan Hills 84001 rock, believed to have been ejected out of Mars by a meteor impact millions of years ago, which then fell into an orbit that brought it to Earth. On the panel of NASA experts was paleobiologist William Schopf, a specialist in ancient microbial life. Schopf was skeptical of NASA's claim because, he said, the four "lines of evidence" claimed to support the find did not converge toward a single conclusion. Instead, they pointed to several possible conclusions.

Schopf's analysis of "lines of evidence" reflects a method of science first described by the nineteenth-century philosopher of science William Whewell. To prove a theory, Whewell believed, one must have more than one induction, more than a single generalization drawn from specific facts. One must have multiple inductions that converge upon one another, independently but in conjunction. Whewell said that if these inductions "jump together" it strengthens the plausibility of a theory: "Accordingly the cases in which inductions from classes of facts altogether different have thus jumped together, belong only to the best established theories which the history of science contains. And, as I shall have occasion to refer to this particular feature in their evidence, I will take the liberty of describing it by a particular phrase; and will term it the Consilience of Inductions." I call it a *convergence of evidence.*

Just as detectives employ the convergence of evidence technique to deduce who most likely committed a crime, scientists employ the method to deduce the likeliest explanation for a particular phenomenon. Cosmologists reconstruct the history of the universe through a convergence of evidence from astronomy, planetary geology, and physics. Geologists reconstruct the history of the planet through a convergence of evidence from geology, physics, and chemistry. Archaeologists piece together the history of civilization through a convergence of evidence from biology (pollen grains), chemistry (kitchen middens), physics (potsherds, tools), history (works of art, written sources), and other site-specific artifacts.

As a historical science, evolution is confirmed by the fact that so many independent lines of evidence converge to its single conclusion. Independent sets of data from geology, paleontology, botany, zoology, herpetology, entomology, biogeography, comparative anatomy and physiology, genetics and population genetics, and many other sciences each point to the conclusion that life evolved. This is a convergence of evidence. Creationists can demand "just one fossil transitional form" that shows evolution. But evolution is not proved through a single fossil. It is proved through a convergence of fossils, along with a convergence of genetic comparisons between species, and a convergence of anatomical and physiological comparisons between species, and many other lines of inquiry. For creationists to disprove evolution, they need to unravel all these independent lines of evidence, as well as construct a rival theory that can explain them better than the theory of evolution. They have yet to do so.

The Tests of Evolution

Creationists like to argue that evolution is not a science because no one was there to observe it and there are no experiments to run today to test it. The inability to observe past events or set up controlled experiments is no obstacle to a sound science of cosmology, geology, or archaeology, so why should it be for a sound science of evolution? The key is the ability to test one's hypothesis. There are a number of ways to do so, starting with the broadest method of how we know evolution happened.

Consider the evolution of our best friend, the dog. With so many breeds of dogs popular for so many thousands of years, one would think that there would be an abundance of transitional fossils providing paleontologists with copious data from which to reconstruct their evolutionary ancestry. Not so. In fact, according to Jennifer A. Leonard of the National Museum of Natural History in Washington, D.C., "the fossil record from wolves to dogs is pretty sparse." Then how do we know the origin of dogs? In a 2002 issue of *Science,* Leonard and her colleagues report that mitochrondrial DNA (mtDNA) data from early dog remains "strongly support the hypothesis that ancient American and Eurasian domestic dogs share a common origin from Old World gray wolves." In the same issue of *Science,* Peter Savolainen from the Royal Institute of Technology in Stockholm and his colleagues note that the fossil record is problematic "because of the difficulty in discriminating between small wolves and domestic dogs," but their study of mtDNA sequence variation among 654 domestic dogs from around the world "points to an origin of the domestic dog in East Asia ~15,000 yr B.P." from a single gene pool of wolves. Finally, Brian Hare from Harvard and his colleagues describe the results of their study in which they found that domestic dogs are more skillful than wolves at using human communicative signals indicating the location of hidden food, but that "dogs and wolves do not perform differently in a non-social memory task, ruling out the possibility that dogs outperform wolves in all human-guided tasks." Therefore, "dogs' social-communicative skills with humans were acquired during the process of domestication." Although no single fossil proves that dogs came from wolves, the convergence of evidence from archaeological, morphological, genetic, and behavioral "fossils"reveals the ancestor of all dogs to be the East Asian wolf.

The tale of human evolution is revealed in a similar manner (although here we do have an abundance of transitional fossil riches), as it is for all ancestors in the history of life. One of the finest compilations of evolutionary convergence is Richard Dawkins's magnum opus, *The Ancestor's Tale,* 673 pages of convergent science recounted with literary elegance. Dawkins traces innumerable "transitional fossils" (what he calls "concestors"— the "point of rendezvous" of the last common ancestor shared by a set of species) from *Homo sapiens* back four billion years to the origin of replicating molecules and the emergence of evolution. No one concestor proves that evolution happened, but together they reveal a majestic story of a process over time. We know human evolution happened because innumerable bits of data from myriad fields of science conjoin to paint a rich portrait of life's pilgrimage.

But the convergence of evidence is just the start. The *comparative method* allows us to infer evolutionary relationships using data from a wide variety of fields. Luigi Luca Cavalli-Sforza and his colleagues, for example, compared fifty years of data from population genetics, geography, ecology, archaeology, physical anthropology, and linguistics to trace the evolution of the human races. Using both the convergence and comparative methods led them to conclude that "the major stereotypes, all based on skin color, hair color and form, and facial traits, reflect superficial differences that are not confirmed by deeper analysis with more reliable genetic traits."

By comparing surface (physical) traits—the phenotype of individuals—with genetic traits—the genotype—they teased out the relationship between different groups of people. Most interesting, they found that the genetic traits disclosed "recent evolution mostly under the effect of climate and perhaps sexual selection." For example, they discovered that Australian aborigines are genetically more closely related to southeast Asians than they are to African blacks, which makes sense from the perspective of the evolutionary timeline: The migration pattern of humans out of Africa would have led them first to Asia and then to Australia.

Dating techniques provide evidence of the timeline of evolution. The dating of fossils, along with the earth, moon, sun, solar system, and universe, are all tests of evolutionary theory, and so far they have passed all the tests. We know that the earth is approximately 4.6 billion years old because of the convergence of evidence from several methods of dating rocks: Uranium Lead, Rubidium Strontium, and Carbon-14. Further, the age of the earth, the age of the moon, the age of the sun, the age of the solar system, and the age of the universe are consistent, maintaining yet another consilience. If, say, the earth was dated at 4.6 billion years old but the solar system was dated at one million years old, the theory of evolution would be in trouble. But Uranium Lead, Rubidium Strontium, and Carbon-14 have not provided any good news for the so-called Young Earth creationists.

Better yet, the fossils and organisms speak for themselves. *Fossils do show intermediate stages,* despite their rarity. For example, there are now at least eight intermediate fossil stages identified in the evolution of whales. In human evolution, there are at least a dozen known intermediate fossil stages since hominids branched off from the great apes six million years ago. *And geological strata consistently reveal the same sequence of fossils.* A quick and simple way to debunk the theory of evolution would be to find a fossil horse in the same geological stratum as a trilobite. According to evolutionary theory, trilobites and mammals are separated by hundreds of millions of years. If such a fossil juxtaposition occurred, and it was not the product of some geological anomaly (such as uplifted, broken, bent, or even flipped strata—all of which occur but are traceable), it would mean that there was something seriously wrong with the theory of evolution.

Evolution also posits that *modern organisms should show a variety of structures from simple to complex, reflecting an evolutionary history rather than an instantaneous creation.* The human eye, for example, is the result of a long and complex pathway that goes back hundreds of millions of years. Initially a simple eyespot with a handful of light-sensitive cells that provided information to the organism about an important source of the light, it developed into a recessed eyespot, where a small surface indentation filled with light-sensitive cells provided additional data on the direction of light; then into a deep recession eyespot, where additional cells at greater depth provide more accurate information about the environment; then into a pinhole camera eye that is able to focus an image on the back of a deeply recessed layer of light-sensitive cells; then into a pinhole lens eye that is able to focus the image; then into a complex eye found in such modern mammals as humans. All of these structures are expressed in modern eyes.

Further, *biological structures show signs of natural design.* The anatomy of the human eye, in fact, shows anything but "intelligence" in its design. It is built upside down and backwards, requiring photons of light to travel through the cornea, lens, aqueous fluid, blood vessels, ganglion cells, amacrine cells, horizontal cells, and bipolar cells before they reach the light-sensitive rods and cones that transduce the light signal into neural impulses—which are then sent to the visual cortex at the back of the brain for processing into meaningful patterns. For optimal vision, why would an intelligent designer have built an eye upside down and backwards? This "design" makes sense only if natural selection built eyes from available materials, and in the particular configuration of the ancestral organism's preexisting organic structures. The eye shows the pathways of evolutionary history, not of intelligent design.

Additionally, *vestigial structures stand as evidence of the mistakes, the misstarts, and, especially, the leftover traces of evolutionary history.* The cretaceous snake *Pachyrhachis problematicus,* for example, had small hind limbs used for locomotion that it inherited from its quadrupedal ancestors, gone in today's snakes. Modern whales retain a tiny pelvis for hind legs that existed in their land mammal ancestors but have disappeared today. Likewise, there are wings on flightless birds, and of course humans are replete with useless vestigial structures, a distinctive sign of our evolutionary ancestry. A short list of just ten vestigial structures in humans leaves one musing: Why would an Intelligent Designer have created these?

1. *Male nipples.* Men have nipples because females need them, and the overall architecture of the human body is more efficiently developed in the uterus from a single developmental structure.

2. *Male uterus.* Men have the remnant of an undeveloped female reproductive organ that hangs off the prostate gland for the same reason.

3. *Thirteenth rib.* Most modern humans have twelve sets of ribs, but 8 percent of us have a thirteenth set, just like chimpanzees and gorillas. This is a remnant of our primate ancestry: We share common ancestors with chimps and gorillas, and the thirteenth set of ribs has been retained from when our lineage branched off six million years ago.

4. *Coccyx.* The human tailbone is all that remains from our common ancestors' tails, which were used for grasping branches and maintaining balance.

5. *Wisdom teeth.* Before stone tools, weapons, and fire, hominids were primarily vegetarians, and as such we chewed a lot of plants, requiring an extra set of grinding molars. Many people still have them, despite the smaller size of our modern jaws.

6. *Appendix.* This muscular tube connected to the large intestine was once used for digesting cellulose in our largely vegetarian diet before we became meat eaters.

7. *Body hair.* We are sometimes called "the naked ape"; however, most humans have a layer of fine body hair,

again left over from our evolutionary ancestry from thick-haired apes and hominids.

8. *Goose bumps.* Our body hair ancestry can also be inferred from the fact that we retain the ability of our ancestors to puff up their fur for heat insulation, or as a threat gesture to potential predators. Erector pili— "goose bumps"—are a telltale sign of our evolutionary ancestry.

9. *Extrinsic ear muscles.* If you can wiggle your ears you can thank our primate ancestors, who evolved the ability to move their ears independently of their heads as a more efficient means of discriminating precise sound directionality and location.

10. *Third eyelid.* Many animals have a nictitating membrane that covers the eye for added protection; we retain this "third eyelid" in the corner of our eye as a tiny fold of flesh.

Evolutionary scientists can provide dozens more examples of vestigial structures—let alone examples of how we know evolution happened from all of these other various lines of historical evidence. Yet as a science, evolution depends primarily on the ability to test a hypothesis. How can we ever test an evolutionary hypothesis if we cannot go into a lab and create a new species naturally?

I once had the opportunity to help dig up a dinosaur with Jack Horner, the curator of paleontology at the Museum of the Rockies in Bozeman, Montana. As Horner explains in his book *Digging Dinosaurs,* "paleontology is not an experimental science; it's a historical science. This means that paleontologists are seldom able to test their hypotheses by laboratory experiments, but they can still test them." Horner discusses this process of historical science at the famous dig in which he exposed the first dinosaur eggs ever found in North America. The initial stage of the dig was "getting the fossils out of the ground." Unsheathing the bones from the overlying and surrounding stone is backbreaking work. As you move from jackhammers and pickaxes to dental tools and small brushes, historical interpretation accelerates as a function of the rate of bone unearthed. Then, in the second phase of a dig, he gets "to look at the fossils, study them, make hypotheses based on what we saw and try to prove or disprove them."

When I arrived at Horner's camp I expected to find the busy director of a fully sponsored dig barking out orders to his staff. I was surprised to come upon a patient historical scientist, sitting cross-legged before a cervical vertebra from a 140-million-year-old *Apatosaurus* (formerly known as *Brontosaurus*), wondering what to make of it. Soon a reporter from a local paper arrived inquiring of Horner what this discovery meant for the history of dinosaurs. Did it change any of his theories? Where was the head? Was there more than one body at this site? Horner's answers were those of a cautious scientist: "I don't know yet." "Beats me." "We need more evidence." "We'll have to wait and see." It was historical science at its best.

After two long days of exposing nothing but solid rock and my own ineptness at seeing bone within stone, one of the paleontologists pointed out that the rock I was about to toss away was a piece of bone that appeared to be part of a rib. If it was a rib, then the bone should retain its riblike shape as more of the overburden was chipped away. This it did for about a foot, until it suddenly flared to the right. Was it a rib, or something else? Horner moved in to check. "It could be part of the pelvis," he suggested. If it was part of the pelvis, then it should also flare out to the left when more was uncovered. Sure enough, Horner's prediction was verified by further digging.

In science, this process is called the *hypothetico-deductive method,* in which one forms a hypothesis based on existing data, deduces a prediction from the hypothesis, then tests the prediction against further data. For example, in 1981 Horner discovered a site in Montana that contained approximately thirty million fossil fragments of approximately ten thousand *Maiasaurs* in a bed measuring 1.25 miles by .25 miles. His hypothesizing began with a question: "What could such a deposit represent?" There was no evidence that predators had chewed the bones, yet many were broken in half lengthwise. Further, the bones were all arranged from east to west—the long dimension of the bone deposit. Small bones had been separated from bigger bones, and there were no bones of baby *Maiasaurs,* only those of individuals between nine and twenty-three feet long. What would cause the bones to splinter lengthwise? Why would the small bones be separated from the big bones? Was this one giant herd, all killed at the same time, or was it a dying ground over many years?

An early hypothesis—that a mud flow buried the herd alive—was rejected because "it didn't make sense that even the most powerful flow of mud could break bones lengthwise . . . nor did it make sense that a herd of living animals buried in mud would end up with all their skeletons disarticulated." Horner constructed another hypothesis. "It seemed that there had to be a twofold event," he reasoned, "the dinosaurs dying in one incident and the bones being swept away in another." Since there was a layer of volcanic ash 1.5 feet above the bone bed, volcanic activity was implicated in the death of the herd. Horner then deduced that only fossil bones would split lengthwise, and therefore the damage to the bones had occurred long after the dying event. His hypothesis and deduction led to his conclusion that the herd was "killed by the gases, smoke and ash of a volcanic eruption. And if a huge eruption killed them all at once, then it might have also killed everything else around." Then perhaps there was a flood, maybe from a breached lake, carrying the rotting bodies downstream, separating the big bones from the small, lighter bones, and giving the bones a uniform orientation.

A paleontological dig is a good example of how hypothetico-deductive reasoning and historical sciences can make predictions based on initial data that are then verified or rejected by later historical evidence. Evolutionary theory is rooted in a rich array of data from the past that, while nonreplicable in a laboratory, are nevertheless valid sources of information that can be used to piece together specific events and test general hypotheses. While the specifics of evolution—how quickly it happens, what triggers species change, at which level of the organism it occurs—are still being studied and unraveled, the general theory of evolution is the most tested in science over the past century and a half. Scientists agree: Evolution happened.

Critical Thinking

1. What is the point Shermer is trying to make in this article?
2. What was Darwin's contribution to our understanding of coral reefs?
3. Who was Darwin's "one long argument" with? What was his view? How was it different from the Darwinian one?
4. What did Ernst Mayr mean when he asserted that evolution has both "horizontal" and "vertical" dimensions?
5. What five tenets of evolution does Mayr outline? Describe each.
6. What, according to Shermer, is "one of the most important and difficult points to grasp about evolution?" Why do you think this is?
7. What are the random and non-random processes in evolution as identified by Richard Dawkins? What makes them random and non-random respectively?
8. What was wrong with Shermer's example of a "polar bear" as a transitional species when he was talking to his daughter?
9. Why are fossils so difficult to come by?
10. Why is it that genetic change can occur more quickly in small groups? Why is this important for the evolution of new species?
11. What does Shermer mean by the "convergence of evidence"?
12. How long ago did the domestic dog "evolve"? Why does Shermer use this as an example of the way science works?
13. What is the "comparative method"?
14. What other lines of evidence mentioned by Shermer support the evolution?
15. What human vestigial structures does he mention? What is the evolutionary reason for their existence? Discuss the likely original function of at least four of these supposedly meaningless features.

Create Central

www.mhhe.com/createcentral

Internet References

American Anthropologist Association
www.aaanet.org
Charles Darwin on Human Origins
www.literature.org/Works/Charles-Darwin
Enter Evolution: Theory and History
www.ucmp.berkeley.edu/history/evolution.html
Fossil Hominids FAQ
www.talkorigins.org/faqs/homs
Harvard Dept. of MCB–Biology Links
http://mcb.harvard.edu/BioLinks.html

Article Prepared by: Elvio Angeloni, *Pasadena City College*

Evolution in Action

Finches, monkeyflowers, sockeye salmon, and bacteria are changing before our eyes.

JONATHAN WEINER

Learning Outcomes

After reading this article, you will be able to:

- Explain the ways in which human ecological pressure is bringing about "evolution in action" in wildlife.
- Discuss the various ways in which evolution is being observed and documented.

Charles Darwin's wife, Emma, was terrified that they would be separated for eternity, because she would go to heaven and he would not. Emma confessed her fears in a letter that Charles kept and treasured, with his reply to her scribbled in the margin: "When I am dead, know that many times, I have kissed and cryed over this."

Close as they were, the two could hardly bear to talk about Darwin's view of life. And today, those of us who live in the United States, by many measures the world's leading scientific nation, find ourselves in a house divided. Half of us accept Darwin's theory, half of us reject it, and many people are convinced that Darwin burns in hell. I find that old debate particularly strange, because I've spent some of the best years of my life as a science writer peering over the shoulders of biologists who actually watch Darwin's process in action. What they can see casts the whole debate in a new light—or it should.

Darwin himself never tried to watch evolution happen. "It may metaphorically be said," he wrote in the *Origin of Species,*

> that natural selection is daily and hourly scrutinizing, throughout the world, the slightest variations; rejecting those that are bad, preserving and adding up all that are good; silently and insensibly working, whenever and wherever opportunity offers. . . . We see nothing of these slow changes in progress, until the hand of time has marked the lapse of ages.

Darwin was a modest man who thought of himself as a plodder (one of his favorite mottoes was, "It's dogged as does it"). He thought evolution plodded too. If so, it would be more boring

to watch evolution than to watch drying paint. As a result, for several generations after Darwin's death, almost nobody tried. For most of the twentieth century the only well-known example of evolution in action was the case of peppered moths in industrial England. The moth had its picture in all the textbooks, as a kind of special case.

Then, in 1973, a married pair of evolutionary biologists, Peter and Rosemary Grant, now at Princeton University, began a study of Darwin's process in Darwin's islands, the Galápagos, watching Darwin's finches. At first, they assumed that they would have to infer the history of evolution in the islands from the distribution of the various finch species, varieties, and populations across the archipelago. That is pretty much what Darwin had done, in broad strokes, after the *Beagle*'s five-week survey of the islands in 1835. But the Grants soon discovered that at their main study site, a tiny desert island called Daphne Major, near the center of the archipelago, the finches were evolving rapidly. Conditions on the island swung wildly back and forth from wet years to dry years, and finches on Daphne adapted to each swing, from generation to generation. With the help of a series of graduate students, the Grants began to spend a good part of every year on Daphne, watching evolution in action as it shaped and reshaped the finches' beaks.

At the same time, a few biologists began making similar discoveries elsewhere in the world. One of them was John A. Endler, an evolutionary biologist at the University of California, Santa Barbara, who studied Trinidadian guppies. In 1986 Endler published a little book called *Natural Selection in the Wild,* in which he collected and reviewed all of the studies of evolution in action that had been published to that date. Dozens of new field projects were in progress. Biologists finally began to realize that Darwin had been too modest. Evolution by natural selection can happen rapidly enough to watch.

Now the field is exploding. More than 250 people around the world are observing and documenting evolution, not only in finches and guppies, but also in aphids, flies, grayling, monkeyflowers, salmon, and sticklebacks. Some workers are even documenting pairs of species—symbiotic insects and plants—that have recently found each other, and observing the pairs as they drift off into their own world together like lovers in a novel by D.H. Lawrence.

The Grants' own study gets more sophisticated every year. A few years ago, a group of molecular biologists working with the Grants nailed down a gene that plays a key role in shaping the beaks of the finches. The gene codes for a signaling molecule called bone morphogenic protein 4 (BMP4). Finches with bigger beaks tend to have more BMP4, and finches with smaller beaks have less. In the laboratory, the biologists demonstrated that they could sculpt the beaks themselves by adding or subtracting BMP4. The same gene that shapes the beak of the finch in the egg also shapes the human face in the womb.

Some of the most dramatic stories of evolution in action result from the pressures that human beings are imposing on the planet. As Stephen Palumbi, an evolutionary biologist at Stanford University, points out, we are changing the course of evolution for virtually every living species everywhere, with consequences that are sometimes the opposite of what we might have predicted, or desired.

Take trophy hunting. Wild populations of bighorn mountain sheep are carefully managed in North America for hunters who want a chance to shoot a ram with a trophy set of horns. Hunting permits can cost well into the six figures. On Ram Mountain, in Alberta, Canada, hunters have shot the biggest of the bighorn rams for more than thirty years. And the result? Evolution has made the hunters' quarry scarce. The runts have had a better chance than the giants of passing on their genes. So on Ram Mountain the rams have gotten smaller, and their horns are proportionately smaller yet.

Or take fishing, which is economically much more consequential. The populations of Atlantic cod that swam for centuries off the coasts of Labrador and Newfoundland began a terrible crash in the late 1980s. In the years leading up to the crash, the cod had been evolving much like the sheep on Ram Mountain. Fish that matured relatively fast and reproduced relatively young had the better chance of passing on their genes; so did the fish that stayed small. So even before the population crashed, the average cod had been shrinking.

We often seem to lose out wherever we fight hardest to control nature. Antibiotics drive the evolution of drug-resistant bacteria at a frightening pace. Sulfonamides were introduced in the 1930s, and resistance to them was first observed a decade later. Penicillin was deployed in 1943, and the first penicillin resistance was observed in 1946. In the same way, pesticides and herbicides create resistant bugs and weeds.

Palumbi estimates that the annual bill for such unintended human-induced evolution runs to more than $100 billion in the U.S. alone. Worldwide, the pressure of global warming, fragmented habitats, heightened levels of carbon dioxide, acid rain, and the other myriad perturbations people impose on the chemistry and climate of the planet—all change the terms of the struggle for existence in the air, in the water, and on land. Biologists have begun to worry about those perturbations, but global change may be racing ahead of them.

To me, the most interesting news in the global evolution watch concerns what Darwin called "that mystery of mysteries, the origin of species."

The process whereby a population acquires small, inherited changes through natural selection is known as microevolution. Finches get bigger, fish gets smaller, but a finch is still a finch and a fish is still a fish. For people who reject Darwin's theory, that's the end of the story: no matter how many small, inherited changes accumulate, they believe, natural selection can never make a new kind of living thing. The kinds, the species, are eternal.

Darwin argued otherwise. He thought that many small changes could cause two lines of life to diverge. Whenever animals and plants find their way to a new home, for instance, they suffer, like emigres in new countries. Some individuals fail, others adapt and prosper. As the more successful individuals reproduce, Darwin maintained, the new population begins to differ from the ancestral one. If the two populations diverge widely enough, they become separate species. Change on that scale is known as macroevolution.

In *Origin,* Darwin estimated that a new species might take between ten thousand and fourteen thousand generations to arise. Until recently, most biologists assumed it would take at least that many, or maybe even millions of generations, before microevolutionary changes led to the origin of new species. So they assumed they could watch evolution by natural selection, but not the divergence of one species into separate, reproductively isolated species. Now that view is changing too.

Not long ago, a young evolution-watcher named Andrew Hendry, a biologist at McGill University in Montreal, reported the results of a striking study of sockeye salmon. Sockeye tend to reproduce either in streams or along lake beaches. When the glaciers of the last ice age melted and retreated, about ten thousand years ago, they left behind thousands of new lakes. Salmon from streams swam into the lakes and stayed. Today their descendants tend to breed among themselves rather than with sockeyes that live in the streams. The fish in the lakes and streams are reproductively isolated from each other. So how fast did that happen?

In the 1930s and 1940s, sockeye salmon were introduced into Lake Washington, in Washington State. Hundreds of thousands of their descendants now live and breed in Cedar River, which feeds the lake. By 1957 some of the introduced sockeye also colonized a beach along the lake called Pleasure Point, about four miles from the mouth of Cedar River.

Hendry could tell whether a full-grown, breeding salmon had been born in the river or at the beach by examining the rings on its otoliths, or ear stones. Otolith rings reflect variations in water temperature while a fish embryo is developing. Water temperatures at the beach are relatively constant compared with the river temperatures. Hendry and his colleagues checked the otoliths and collected DNA samples from the fish—and found that more than a third of the sockeye breeding at Pleasure Point had grown up in the river. They were immigrants.

With such a large number of immigrants, the two populations at Pleasure Point should have blended back together. But they hadn't. So at breeding time many of the river sockeye that swam over to the beach must have been relatively unsuccessful at passing on their genes.

Hendry could also tell the stream fish and the beach fish apart just by looking at them. Where the sockeye's breeding waters are swift-flowing, such as in Cedar River, the males tend to be slender. Their courtship ritual and competition with other males requires them to turn sideways in strong current—an awkward maneuver for a male with a deep, roundish body. So in strong current, slender males have the better chance of passing on their genes. But in still waters, males with the deepest bodies have the best chance of getting mates. So beach males tend to be rounder—their dimensions greater from the top of the back to the bottom of the belly—than river males.

What about females? In the river, where currents and floods are forever shifting and swirling the gravel, females have to dig deep nests for their eggs. So the females in the river tend to be bigger than their lake-dwelling counterparts, because bigger females can dig deeper nests. Where the water is calmer, the gravel stays put, and shallower nests will do.

So all of the beachgoers, male and female, have adapted to life at Pleasure Point. Their adaptations are strong enough that reproductive isolation has evolved. How long did the evolution take? Hendry began studying the salmon's reproductive isolation in 1992. At that time, the sockeyes in the stream and the ones at Pleasure Point had been breeding in their respective habitats for at most thirteen generations. That is so fast that, as Hendry and his colleagues point out, it may be possible someday soon to catch the next step, the origin of a new species.

And it's not just the sockeye salmon. Consider the three-spined stickleback. After the glaciers melted at the end of the last ice age, many sticklebacks swam out of the sea and into new glacial lakes—just as the salmon did. In the sea, sticklebacks wear heavy, bony body armor. In a lake they wear light armor. In a certain new pond in Bergen, Norway, during the past century, sticklebacks evolved toward the lighter armor in just thirty-one years. In Loberg Lake, Alaska, the same kind of change took only a dozen years. A generation for sticklebacks is two years. So that dramatic evolution took just six generations.

Dolph Schluter, a former finch-watcher from the Galápagos and currently a biologist at the University of British Columbia in Vancouver, has shown that, along with the evolution of new body types, sticklebacks also evolve a taste for mates with the new traits. In other words, the adaptive push of sexual selection is going hand-in-hand with natural selection. Schluter has built experimental ponds in Vancouver to observe the phenomenon under controlled conditions, and the same patterns he found in isolated lakes repeat themselves in his ponds. So adaptation can sometimes drive sexual selection and accelerate reproductive isolation.

There are other developments in the evolution watch, too many to mention in this small space. Some of the fastest action is microscopic. Richard Lenski, a biologist at Michigan State University in East Lansing, watches the evolution of *Escherichia coli*. Because one generation takes only twenty minutes, and billions of *E. coli* can fit in a petri dish, the bacteria make ideal subjects for experimental evolution. Throw some *E. coli* into a new dish, for instance, with food they haven't encountered before, and they will evolve and adapt—quickly

at first and then more slowly, as they refine their fit with their new environment.

And then there are the controversies. Science progresses and evolves by controversy, by internal debate and revision. In the United States these days one almost hates to mention that there are arguments among evolutionists. So often, they are taken out of context and hyperamplified to suggest that nothing about Darwinism is solid—that Darwin is dead. But research is messy because nature is messy, and fieldwork is some of the messiest research of all. It is precisely here at its jagged cutting edge that Darwinism is most vigorously alive.

Not long ago, one of the most famous icons of the evolution watch toppled over: the story of the peppered moths, familiar to anyone who remembers biology 101. About half a century ago, the British evolutionist Bernard Kettlewell noted that certain moths in the British Isles had evolved into darker forms when the trunks of trees darkened with industrial pollution. When the trees lightened again, after clean air acts were passed, the moths had evolved into light forms again. Kettlewell claimed that dark moths resting on dark tree trunks were harder for birds to see; in each decade, moths of the right color were safer.

But in the past few years, workers have shown that Kettlewell's explanation was too simplistic. For one thing, the moths don't normally rest on tree trunks. In forty years of observation, only twice have moths been seen resting there. Nobody knows where they do rest. The moths did evolve rapidly, but no one can be certain why.

To me what remains most interesting is the light that studies such as Hendry's, or the Grants', may throw on the origin of species. It's extraordinary that scientists are now examining the very beginnings of the process, at the level of beaks and fins, at the level of the genes. The explosion of evolution-watchers is a remarkable development in Darwin's science. Even as the popular debate about evolution in America is reaching its most heated moment since the trial of John Scopes, evolutionary biologists are pursuing one of the most significant and surprising voyages of discovery since the young Darwin sailed into the Galápagos Archipelago aboard Her Majesty's ship *Beagle*.

Not long ago I asked Hendry if his studies have changed the way he thinks about the origin of species. "Yes," he replied without hesitation, "I think it's occurring all over the place."

Critical Thinking

1. Did Darwin ever see evolution in action? Why or why not?
2. Who are Rosemary and Peter Grant? What did they study? Where? How did they show that natural selection occurs?
3. How many people around the world are documenting evolution now?
4. What recent advance has been found in the Grants' research?
5. How have trophy hunting and fishing impacted the evolution of species according to the research presented by Weiner?

6. When was penicillin first deployed? How soon did resistance show up?

7. What is "microevolution"?

8. How many generations did Darwin think it would take for a new species to arise? Did more recent scholars agree with this? Was Darwin right, too optimistic, or too pessimistic?

9. What happened with the sockeye salmon? What did they show about the number of generations these changes took?

10. What selection pressure drove differences in morphology (body shape and size) between males and females of the river and lake types?

11. How do the stickleback findings show that "adaptations sometimes drive sexual selection and accelerate reproductive isolation"?

12. Why does Weiner say "in the United States these days one almost hates to mention that there are arguments among evolutionists"?

13. What is the classic story about the peppered moths? Why has this icon been "toppled"?

Create Central

www.mhhe.com/createcentral

Internet References

American Anthropologist Association
www.aaanet.org

Charles Darwin on Human Origins
www.literature.org/Works/Charles-Darwin

Enter Evolution: Theory and History
www.ucmp.berkeley.edu/history/evolution.html

Harvard Dept. of MCB–Biology Links
http://mcb.harvard.edu/BioLinks.html

JONATHAN WEINER began writing about evolution in 1990, when he met Peter and Rosemary Grant, who observe evolution firsthand in finch populations in the Galápagos. Weiner's book *The Beak of the Finch* (Alfred A. Knopf) won a Pulitzer Prize in 1994. He is a professor in the Graduate School of Journalism at Columbia University, in New York City. He is also working on a book about human longevity for Ecco Press.

Article   Prepared by: Elvio Angeloni, *Pasadena City College*

America's Science Problem

SHAWN LAWRENCE OTTO

Learning Outcomes

After reading this article, you will be able to:

• Discuss science as the preeminent force driving the U.S. economy.

• Explain "anti-science" and its effect on politics and science in the United States.

It is hard to know exactly when it became acceptable for U.S. politicians to be anti-science. For some two centuries science was a preeminent force in American politics, and scientific innovation has been the leading driver of U.S. economic growth since World War II. Kids in the 1960s gathered in school cafeterias to watch moon launches and landings on televisions wheeled in on carts. Breakthroughs in the 1970s and 1980s sparked the computer revolution and a new information economy. Advances in biology, based on evolutionary theory, created the biotech industry. New research in genetics is poised to transform the understanding of disease and the practice of medicine, agriculture and other fields.

The Founding Fathers were science enthusiasts. Thomas Jefferson, a lawyer and scientist, built the primary justification for the nation's independence on the thinking of Isaac Newton, Francis Bacon and John Locke—the creators of physics, inductive reasoning and empiricism. He called them his "trinity of three greatest men." If anyone can discover the truth by using reason and science, Jefferson reasoned, then no one is naturally closer to the truth than anyone else. Consequently, those in positions of authority do not have the right to impose their beliefs on other people. The people themselves retain this inalienable right. Based on this foundation of science—of knowledge gained by systematic study and testing instead of by the assertions of ideology—the argument for a new, democratic form of government was self-evident.

Yet despite its history and today's unprecedented riches from science, the U.S. has begun to slip off of its science foundation. Indeed, in this election cycle, some 236 years after Jefferson penned the Declaration of Independence, several major party contenders for political office took positions that can only be described as "antiscience": against evolution, human-induced climate change, vaccines, stem cell research, and more. A former Republican governor even warned that his own political party was in danger of becoming "the antiscience party."

Such positions could typically be dismissed as nothing more than election-year posturing except that they reflect an anti-intellectual conformity that is gaining strength in the U.S. at precisely the moment that most of the important opportunities for economic growth, and serious threats to the well-being of the nation, require a better grasp of scientific issues. By turning public opinion away from the antiauthoritarian principles of the nation's founders, the new science denialism is creating an existential crisis like few the country has faced before.

In late 2007 growing concern over this trend led six of us to try to do something about it. Physicist Lawrence M. Krauss, science writer and film director Matthew Chapman (who is Charles Darwin's great-great-grandson), science philosopher Austin Dacey, science writer Chris Mooney, marine biologist Sheril Kirshenbaum and I decided to push for a presidential science debate. We put up a Web site and began reaching out to scientists and engineers. Within weeks 38,000 had signed on, including the heads of several large corporations, a few members of Congress from both parties, dozens of Nobel laureates, many of the nation's leading universities and almost every major science organization. Although presidential hopefuls Barack Obama and John McCain both declined a debate on scientific issues, they provided written answers to the 14 questions we asked, which were read by millions of voters.

In 2012 we developed a similar list, called "The Top American Science Questions," that candidates for public office should be answering [see "Science in an Election Year," for a report card by Scientific American's editors measuring how President Obama and Governor Mitt Romney did]. The presidential candidates' complete answers, as well as the responses provided by key congressional leaders to a subset of those questions, can be found at www.ScientificAmerican.com/nov2012/science-debate and at www.sciencedebate.org/debate2.

These efforts try to address the problem, but a larger question remains: What has turned so many Americans against science—the very tool that has transformed the quality and quantity of their lives?

A Call to Reason

Today's denial of inconvenient science comes from partisans on both ends of the political spectrum. Science denialism among Democrats tends to be motivated by unsupported suspicions of hidden dangers to health and the environment. Common examples include the belief that cell phones cause brain cancer (high school physics shows why this is impossible) or that vaccines cause autism (science has shown no link whatsoever). Republican science denialism tends to be motivated by antiregulatory fervor and fundamentalist concerns over control of the reproductive cycle. Examples are the conviction that global warming is a hoax (billions of measurements show it is a fact) or that we should "teach the controversy" to schoolchildren over whether life on the planet was shaped by evolution over millions of years or an intelligent designer over thousands of years (scientists agree evolution is real). Of these two forms of science denialism, the Republican version is more dangerous because the party has taken to attacking the validity of science itself as a basis for public policy when science disagrees with its ideology.

It gives me no pleasure to say this. My family founded the Minnesota Republican Party. But much of the Republican Party has adopted an authoritarian approach that demands ideological conformity, even when contradicted by scientific evidence, and ostracizes those who do not conform. It may work well for uniform messaging, but in the end it drives diverse thinkers away—and thinkers are what we need to solve today's complex problems.

This process has left a large, silent body of voters who are fiscally conservative, who believe in science and evidence-based policies, and who are socially tolerant but who have left the party. In addition, Republican attacks on settled scientific issues—such as anthropogenic climate change and evolution—have too often been met with silence or, worse, appeasement by Democrats.

Governor Romney's path to endorsement exemplifies the problem. "I don't speak for the scientific community, of course, but I believe the world is getting warmer," Romney told voters in June 2011 at a town hall meeting after announcing his candidacy. "I can't prove that, but I believe based on what I read that the world is getting warmer, and number two, I believe that humans contribute to that." Four days later radio commentator Rush Limbaugh blasted Romney on his show, saying, "Bye-bye nomination. Bye-bye nomination, another one down. We're in the midst here of discovering that this is all a hoax. The last year has established that the whole premise of man-made global warming is a hoax! And we still have presidential candidates who want to buy into it."

By October 2011 Romney had done an about-face. "My view is that we don't know what's causing climate change on this planet, and the idea of spending trillions and trillions of dollars to try and reduce CO_2 emissions is not the right course for us," he told an audience in Pittsburgh, then advocated for aggressive oil drilling. And on the day after the Republican National Convention, he tacked back toward his June 2011 position when he submitted his answers to ScienceDebate.org.

Romney is not alone in appreciating the political necessity of embracing antiscience views. House Speaker John A. Boehner, who controls the flow of much legislation through Congress, once argued for teaching creationism in science classes and asserted on national television that climate scientists are suggesting that carbon dioxide is a carcinogen. They are

not. Representative Michele Bachmann of Minnesota warned in 2011 during a Florida presidential primary debate that "innocent little 12-year-old girls" were being "forced to have a government injection" to prevent infection with human papillomavirus (HPV) and later said the vaccine caused "mental retardation." HPV vaccine prevents the main cause of cervical cancer. Religious conservatives believe this encourages promiscuity. There is no evidence of a link to mental retardation.

In a separate debate, Republican candidate Jon Huntsman was asked about comments he had made that the Republican Party is becoming the antiscience party. "All I'm saying," he replied, "is that for the Republican Party to win, we can't run from science." Republican primary voters apparently disagreed. Huntsman, the lone candidate to actively embrace science, finished last in the polls.

In fact, candidates who began to lag in the GOP presidential primaries would often make antiscience statements and would subsequently rise in the polls. Herman Cain, who is well respected in business circles, told voters that "global warming is poppycock." Newt Gingrich, who supported doubling the budget of the National Institutes of Health and who is also a supporter of ScienceDebate.org, began describing stem cell research as "killing children in order to get research material." Candidates Rick Perry and Ron Paul both called climate change "a hoax." In February, Rick Santorum railed that the left brands Republicans as the antiscience party. "No. No, we're not," he announced. "We're the truth party."

Antiscience reproductive politics surfaced again in August, this time in one of the most contested U.S. Senate races. Todd Akin, who is running in Missouri against Claire McCaskill, said that from what he understood from doctors, pregnancy from rape is extremely rare because "if it's a legitimate rape, the female body has ways to try to shut that whole thing down." Akin sits on the House Committee on Science, Space, and Technology, which is responsible for much of the U.S. federal science enterprise, so he should be aware of what science actually says about key policy issues. In fact, studies suggest that women are perhaps twice as likely to become pregnant from rape, and, in any event, there is no biological mechanism to stop pregnancy in the case of rape. Akin's views are by no means unusual among abortion foes, who often seek to minimize what science says to politically justify a no-exception antiabortion stance, which has since become part of the 2012 national GOP platform.

A look at down-ticket races suggests that things may get worse. The large crop of antiscience state legislators elected in 2010 are likely to bring their views into mainstream politics as they eventually run for Congress. In North Carolina this year the state legislature considered House Bill No. 819, which prohibited using estimates of future sea-level rise made by most scientists when planning to protect low-lying areas. (Increasing sea level is a predicted consequence of global warming.) The proposed law would have permitted planning only for a politically correct rise of eight inches instead of the three to four feet that scientists predict for the area by 2100.

Virginia Republicans took similar action in June, banning the use of the term "sea-level rise" from a government-commissioned study and instead requiring use of the phrase "recurrent flooding" because "sea-level rise" is considered "a left-wing term," according to one of the legislators.

The Evolution of American Science Denialism

The American antiscience movement did not travel from the fringe to the center of society overnight. Its roots can be traced back a century to three-time Democratic candidate for president William Jennings Bryan, who ran fundamentalist campaigns against the theory of evolution, which he argued was causing moral decay in the nation's youth by undermining the authority of the Bible.

Bryan lost to proscience Republicans William McKinley and William Howard Taft, but he continued to campaign throughout the South, working to banish the scientific theory from American classrooms. Eventually Tennessee passed a law prohibiting the teaching of "any theory that denies the Story of the Divine Creation of man as taught in the Bible, and to teach instead that man has descended from a lower order of animals." The coverage of the resulting Scopes "monkey trial" in 1925 turned the American public against religious fundamentalism for a generation, and the persistent campaigns against evolution drove most scientists into the Republican Party.

When World War II broke out, science gained new luster. President Franklin D. Roosevelt turned to science as an intellectual weapon to help win the war. FDR asked Vannevar Bush, who led what is now known as the Carnegie Institution for Science, to marshal the U.S. science enterprise. Bush's efforts succeeded, leading to the development of radar, artificial rubber, the mass production of penicillin and the atomic bomb. After the war, he convinced President Harry S. Truman that continued federal investment in science could make the U.S. into a world leader.

The investment paid off, but the steady flow of federal funding had an unanticipated side effect. Scientists no longer needed to reach out to the public or participate in the civic conversation to raise money for research. They consequently began to withdraw from the national public dialogue to focus more intently on their work and private lives. University tenure systems grew up that provided strong disincentives to public outreach, and scientists came to view civics and political involvement as a professional liability.

As the voice of science fell silent, the voice of religious fundamentalism was resurging. Moral disquietude over the atomic bomb caused many to predict the world would soon end, and a new wave of fundamentalist evangelists emerged. "All across Europe, people know that time is running out," a charismatic young preacher named Billy Graham said in 1949. "Now that Russia has the atomic bomb, the world is in an armament race driving us to destruction."

Increasing control over the reproductive process widened the split in the following years. Religious conservatives felt that humans should not interfere in God's plan, denouncing the growing popularity of the birth-control pill in the 1960s and debating in the 1970s whether "test-tube babies," produced by in vitro fertilization, would have souls. They redefined pregnancy to begin at fertilization, rather than implantation in the uterine wall, and argued that abortion was murder.

Science's black eye grew with the broader public as well. In the 1950s children played in the fog of DDT as trucks sprayed neighborhoods, but with the 1962 publication of Rachel Carson's *Silent Spring*, we learned it was toxic. This pattern repeated over and over again as unforeseen health and environmental consequences of quickly commercialized science came to light. Similar scandals erupted over the effects of scores of industrial applications, ranging from sulfur dioxide and acid rain, to certain aerosols and the hole in the ozone layer, to leaded gas and cognitive impairment, to the granddaddy of them all, fossil fuels and global climate change.

Industrial mishaps led to new health and environmental regulatory science. The growing restrictions drove the older industries in the chemical, petroleum and pharmaceutical fields to protect their business interests by opposing new regulations. Proponents of this view found themselves in a natural alliance with the burgeoning religious fundamentalists who opposed the teaching of evolution. Industrial money and religious foot soldiers soon formed a new basis for the Republican Party: "In this present crisis, government is not the solution to our problem," President Ronald Reagan argued in his 1981 inaugural address. "Government is the problem." This antiregulatory-antiscience alliance largely defines the political parties today and helps to explain why, according to a 2009 survey, nine out of 10 scientists who identified with a major political party said they were Democrats.

This marriage of industrial money with fundamentalist values gave fundamentalism renewed power in the public debate, and efforts to oppose the teaching of evolution in public schools have returned in several states. Tennessee, South Dakota and Louisiana have all recently passed legislation that encourages unwarranted criticisms of evolution to be taught in the states' public schools. Evangelical state legislators and school board members mounted similar efforts this year in Oklahoma, Missouri, Kansas, Texas and Alabama, and the Texas Republican Party platform opposes "the teaching of . . . critical thinking skills and similar programs that . . . have the purpose of challenging the student's fixed beliefs and undermining parental authority."

An Antiscience Philosophy

If both Democrats and Republicans have worn the antiscience mantle, why not just wait until the pendulum swings again and denialism loses its political potency? The case for action rests on the realization that for the first time since the beginning of the Enlightenment era in the mid-17th century, the very idea of science as a way to establish a common book of knowledge about the world is being broadly called into question by heavily financed public relations campaigns.

Ironically, the intellectual tools currently being used by the political right to such harmful effect originated on the academic left. In the 1960s and 1970s a philosophical movement called postmodernism developed among humanities professors displeased at being deposed by science, which they regarded as right-leaning. Postmodernism adopted ideas from cultural anthropology and relativity theory to argue that truth is relative and subject to the assumptions and prejudices of the observer. Science is just one of many ways of knowing, they argued, neither more nor less valid than others, like those of Aborigines, Native Americans or women. Furthermore, they defined science as the way of knowing among Western white men and a tool of cultural oppression. This argument resonated with many feminists and civil-rights activists and became widely adopted, leading to the "political correctness" justifiably hated by Rush Limbaugh and the "mental masturbation" lampooned by Woody Allen.

Acceptance of this relativistic world-view undermines democracy and leads not to tolerance but to authoritarianism. John Locke, one of Jefferson's "trinity of three greatest men," showed why almost three centuries ago. Locke watched the arguing factions of Protestantism, each claiming to be the one true religion, and asked: How do we know something to be true? What is the basis of knowledge? In 1689 he defined what knowledge is and how it is grounded in observations of the physical world in *An Essay Concerning Human Understanding*. Any claim that fails this test is "but faith, or opinion, but not knowledge." It was this idea—that the world is knowable and that objective, empirical knowledge is the most equitable basis for public policy—that stood as Jefferson's foundational argument for democracy.

By falsely equating knowledge with opinion, postmodernists and antiscience conservatives alike collapse our thinking back to a pre-Enlightenment era, leaving no common basis for public policy. Public discourse is reduced to endless warring opinions, none seen as more valid than another. Policy is determined by the loudest voices, reducing us to a world in which might makes right—the classic definition of authoritarianism.

Postmodernism infiltrated a generation of American education programs, as Allan Bloom first pointed out in *The Closing of the American Mind*. It also infected journalism, where the phrase "there is no such thing as objectivity" is often repeated like a mantra.

Reporters who agree with this statement will not dig to get to the truth and will tend to simply present "both sides" of contentious issues, especially if they cannot judge the validity of scientific evidence. This kind of false balance becomes a problem when one side is based on knowledge and the other is merely an opinion, as often occurs when policy problems intersect with science. If the press corps does not strive to report objective reality, for which scientific evidence is our only reliable guide, the ship of democracy is set adrift from its moorings in the well-informed voter and becomes vulnerable once again to the tyranny that Jefferson feared.

An Existential Crisis

"Facts," John Adams argued, "are stubborn things; and whatever may be our wishes, our inclinations, or the dictates of our passion, they cannot alter the state of facts and evidence." When facts become opinions, the collective policymaking process of democracy begins to break down. Gone is the common denominator—knowledge—that can bring opposing sides together. Government becomes reactive, expensive and late at solving problems, and the national dialogue becomes mired in warring opinions.

In an age when science influences every aspect of life—from the most private intimacies of sex and reproduction to the most public collective challenges of climate change and the economy—and in a time when democracy has become the dominant form of government on the planet, it is important that the voters push elected officials and candidates of all parties to explicitly state their views on the major science questions facing the nation. By elevating these issues in the public dialogue, U.S. citizens gain a fighting chance of learning whether those who would lead them have the education, wisdom and courage necessary to govern in a science-driven century and to preserve democracy for the next generation.

Critical Thinking

1. How is it that science has been the preeminent force in driving the U.S. economy for two centuries and in establishing our democratic form of government?
2. Describe the growing trend toward "antiscience." Concerning the two ends of the political spectrum, which antiscience movement is more dangerous and why?
3. Be familiar with the most important antiscience claims, the relevant scientific evidence regarding them and the "political necessity" behind them.
4. How have antiscience attitudes affected actual legislation?
5. How did World War II affect the U.S. science enterprise? Why did the "voice of science" subsequently fall silent? How did religious fundamentalism fill the vacuum and why?
6. How did science's black eye grow with the broader public as well?
7. Explain the rise of the antiregulatory–antiscience coalition and its consequences.
8. How did the "postmodernism" of the left lead to the antiscience movement and authoritarianism?
9. When does "false balance" result in the "ship of democracy" being set adrift?
10. What must citizens do to correct this problem, according to the author?

Create Central

www.mhhe.com/createcentral

Internet References

American Anthropologist Association
    www.aaanet.org
American Institute of Biological Sciences
    www.actionbioscience.org
National Center for Science Education
    www.natcenscied.org

SHAWN LAWRENCE OTTO is co-founder of ScienceDebate.org and author of *Fool Me Twice: Fighting the Assault on Science in America*. He is recipient of IEEE-USA's Award for Distinguished Public Service and writes for the Huffington Post and blogs at Neorenaissance.org.

Otto, Shawn Lawrence. From *Scientific American*, Vol. 307, No. 5, November, 2012, pp. 62–71. Copyright © 2012 by Scientific American, a division of Nature America, Inc.

Article   Prepared by: Elvio Angeloni, *Pasadena City College*

Why Should Students Learn Evolution?

BRIAN J. ALTERS AND SANDRA M. ALTERS

Learning Outcomes

After reading this article, you will be able to:

- Give some examples of why students should learn about evolution.

- Discuss evolution as the unifying theory that provides context for all of the biological sciences.

> "When you combine the lack of emphasis on evolution in kindergarten through 12th grade, with the immense popularity of creationism among the public, and the industry discrediting evolution, it's easy to see why half of the population believes humans were created 10,000 years ago and lived with dinosaurs. It is by far the biggest failure of science education from top to bottom."
>
> —Randy Moore, Editor, *The American Biology Teacher*

> "This is an important area of science, with particular significance for a developmental psychologist like me. Unless one has some understanding of the key notions of species, variation, natural selection, adaptation, and the like (and how these "have been discovered"), unless one appreciates the perennial struggle among individuals (and populations) for survival in a particular ecological niche, one cannot understand the living world of which we are a part."
>
> —Howard Gardner, Professor, Harvard Graduate School of Education

With all of the controversy over the teaching of evolution reported in the media, with parents confronting their children's science teachers on this issue, and with students themselves confronting their instructors in high schools and colleges, would it be best—and easiest—to just delete the teaching of evolution in the classroom? Can't students attain a well-rounded background in science without learning this controversial topic? The overwhelming consensus of biologists in the scientific community is "no." Why, then, should science students learn about evolution?

A simple answer is that evolution is the basic context of all the biological sciences. Take away this context, and all that is left is disparate facts without the thread that ties them all together. Put another way, evolution is the explanatory framework, the unifying theory. It is indispensable to the study of biology, just as the atomic theory is indispensable to the study of chemistry. The characteristics and behavior of atoms and their subatomic particles form the basis of this physical science. So, too, biology can be understood fully only in an evolutionary context. In explaining how the organisms of today got to be the way they are, evolution helps make sense out of the history of life and explains relationships among species. It is a useful and often essential framework within which scientists organize and interpret observations and make predictions about the living world.

But this simple answer is not the entire reason why students should learn evolution. There are other considerations as well. Evolutionary explanations answer key questions in the biological sciences such as why organisms across species have so many striking similarities yet are tremendously diverse. These key questions are the *why* questions of biology. Much of biology explains *how* organisms work . . . how we breathe, how fish swim, or how leopard frogs produce thousands of eggs at one time . . . but it is up to evolution to explain the why behind these mechanisms. In answering the key *why* questions of biology, evolutionary explanations become an important lens through which scientists interpret data, whether they are developmental biologists, plant physiologists, or biochemists, to mention just a few of the many foci of those who study life.

Understanding evolution also has practical considerations that affect day-to-day life. Without an understanding of natural selection, students cannot recognize and understand problems based on this process, such as insect resistance to pesticides or microbial resistance to antibiotics. In a report released in June, 2000, Dr. Gro Harlem Brunddand, Director-General of the World Health Organization, stated that the world is at risk of losing drugs that control many infectious diseases because of increasing antimicrobial resistance. The report goes on to give examples, stating that 98% of strains of gonorrhea in Southeast Asia are now resistant to penicillin. Additionally, 14,000 people die each year from drug-resistant infections acquired in hospitals in the United States. And in New Delhi, India, typhoid drugs are no longer effective against this disease. Such problems face every person on our planet, and an understanding of natural selection will help students realize how important their behavior is in either contributing to or helping stem this crisis in medical progress.

Evolution not only enriches and provides a conceptual foundation for biological sciences such as ecology, genetics, developmental biology, and systematics, it provides a framework for scientific disciplines with historical aspects, such as anthropology, astronomy, geology, and paleontology. Evolution is therefore a unifying theme among many sciences, providing students with a framework by which to understand the natural world from many perspectives.

As scientists search for evolutionary explanations to the many questions of life, they develop methods and formulate concepts that are being applied in other fields, such as molecular biology, medicine, and statistics. For example, scientists studying molecular evolutionary change have developed methods to distinguish variations in gene sequences within and among species. These methods not only add to the toolbox of the molecular biologist but also will have likely applications in medicine by helping to identify variations that cause genetic diseases. In characterizing and analyzing variation, evolutionary biologists have also developed statistical methods, such as analysis of variance and path analysis, which are widely used in other fields. Thus, methods and concepts developed by evolutionary biologists have wide relevance in other fields and influence us all daily in ways we cannot realize without an understanding of this important and central idea.

Evolution is not only a powerful and wide-reaching concept among the pure and applied sciences, it also permeates other disciplines such as philosophy, psychology, literature, and the arts. Evolution by means of natural selection, articulated amidst controversy in the mid-nineteenth century, has reached the twenty-first century having had an extensive and expansive impact on human thought. An important intellectual development in the history of ideas, evolution should hold a central place in science teaching and learning.

Why is evolution—the context of the biological sciences—a unifying theory?

First, how does evolution take place? A key idea is that some of the individuals within a population of organisms possess measurable changes in inheritable characteristics that favor their survival. (These characteristics can be morphological, physiological, behavioral, or biochemical.) These individuals are more likely to live to reproductive age than are individuals not possessing the favorable characteristics. These reproductively advantageous traits (called *adaptive traits* or *adaptations*) are passed on from surviving individuals to their offspring. Over time, the individuals carrying these traits will increase in numbers within the population, and the nature of the population as a whole will gradually change. This process of survival of the most reproductively fit organisms is called *natural selection.*

The process of evolutionary change explains that the organisms of today got to be the way they are, at least in part, as the result of natural selection over billions of years and even billions more generations. Organisms are related to one another, some more distantly, branching from a common ancestor long ago, and some more recently, branching from a common ancestor

closer to the present day. The fact that diverse organisms have descended from common ancestors accounts for the similarities exhibited among species. Since biology is the story of life, then evolution is the story of biology and the relatedness of all life.

How do evolutionary explanations answer key questions in the biological sciences?

Evolution answers the question of the unity and similarity of life by its relatedness and shared history. But what about its diversity? And how does evolution answer other key questions in the biological sciences? What are these questions and how does evolution answer the *why* question inherent in each?

Evolution explains the diversity of life in the same way that it explains its unity. As mentioned in the preceding paragraphs, some individuals within a population of organisms possess measurable changes in inheritable characteristics that favor their survival. These adaptive traits are passed on from surviving individuals to their offspring. Over time, as populations inhabit different ecological niches, the individuals carrying adaptive traits in each population increase in numbers, and the nature of each population gradually changes. Such divergent evolution, the splitting of single species into multiple, descendant species, accounts for variation. There are different modes, or patterns, of divergence, and various reproductive isolating mechanisms that contribute to divergent evolution. However, the result is the same: Populations split from common ancestral populations and their genetic differences accumulate.

What are some other key questions in biology that are answered by evolution? One key question asks why form is adapted to function. Evolutionary theory tells us that more organisms that have parts of their anatomy (a long, slender beak, for instance) better adapted to certain functions (such as capturing food that lives deep within holes in rotting tree trunks) will live to reproductive age in greater numbers than those with less-well-adapted beaks. Therefore, the organisms with better-adapted beaks will pass on the genes for these features to greater numbers of off-spring. Eventually, after numerous generations, natural selection will result in a population that has long slender beaks adapted to procuring food. Thus, anatomical, behavioral, or biochemical traits (the "forms") fit their functions because form fitting function is adaptive. But this idea leads us to yet another important question: Why do organisms have a variety of nonadaptive features that coexist amidst those that are adaptive?

During the course of evolution, traits that no longer confer a reproductive advantage do not disappear in the population unless they are reproductively disadvantageous. A population of beige beach birds that escaped predation because of protective coloration will not change coloration if this population becomes geographically isolated to a grasslands environment, unless the now useless beige coloration allows the birds to be hunted and killed more easily. In other words, if beige coloration is not a liability in the new environment, the genes that code for this trait will be passed on by all surviving birds in this grasslands niche. Even as the population of birds changes over generations, the genes for beige feathers will be retained in the population as long as this trait confers no reproductive disadvantage (and as long as mutation and genetic drift do not result in such a change).

These preceding examples do not cover all the key questions of biology (of course), but do show that such key questions are really questions about evolution and its mechanisms. Only evolutionary theory can answer the *why* questions inherent in these themes of life.

How does understanding evolution help us understand processes that affect our health and our day-to-day life? and How are evolutionary methods applied to other fields?
As mentioned earlier, without an understanding of natural selection, students cannot recognize and understand problems based on this process, such as insect resistance to pesticides or microbial resistance to antibiotics. Additionally, it is only through such understanding that scientists can hope to find solutions to these serious situations. Scientists know that the underlying cause of microbial resistance to antibiotics is improper use of these drugs. As explained in the World Health Organization report *Overcoming Antimicrobial Resistance,* in poor countries antibiotics are often used in ways that encourage the development of resistance. Unable to afford the full course of treatment, patients often take antibiotics only until their symptoms go away—killing the most susceptible microbes while allowing those more resistant to survive and reproduce. When these most resistant pathogens infect another host, antibiotics are less effective against the more resistant strains. In wealthy countries such as the United States, antibiotics are overused, being prescribed for viral diseases for which they are ineffective and being used in agriculture to treat sick animals and promote the growth of those that are well. Such misuse and overuse of antibiotics speeds the process whereby less resistant strains of bacteria are wiped out and more resistant strains flourish.

In addition to developing resistance to antibiotics and other therapies, pathogens can evolve resistance to the body's natural defenses. The virulence of pathogens (the ease with which they cause disease) can also evolve rapidly. Understanding the co-evolution of the human immune system and the pathogens that attack it help scientists track and predict disease outbreaks.

Understanding evolution also helps researchers understand the frequency, nature, and distribution of genetic disease. Gene frequencies in populations are affected by selection pressures, mutation, migration, and random genetic drift. Studying genetic diseases from an evolutionary standpoint helps us see that even lethal genes can remain in a population if there is a reproductive advantage in the heterozygote, as in the case of sickle-cell anemia and malaria.

Sickle-cell anemia is one of the most common genetic disorders among African Americans, having arisen in their African ancestors. It has been observed in persons whose ancestors came from the Mediterranean basin, the Indian subcontinent, the Caribbean, and parts of Central and South America (particularly Brazil). The sickle-cell gene has persisted in these populations, even though the disease eventually kills its victims, because carriers who inherit a single defective gene are resistant to malaria. Those with the sickle-cell gene have a survival advantage in regions of the world in which malaria is prevalent, which are the regions of the ancestral populations listed previously. Although many of these peoples have since migrated from these areas, this ancestral gene still persists within their populations.

Scientists are also working to identify gene variations that cause genetic diseases. Molecular evolutionary biologists have developed methods to distinguish between variations in gene sequences that affect reproductive fitness and variations that do not. To do this, scientists analyze human DNA sequences and DNA sequences among closely related species. The Human Genome Project, a worldwide effort to map the positions of all the genes and to sequence the over 3 billion DNA base pairs of the human genome, is providing much of the data for this effort and also is allowing scientists to study the relationships between the structure of genes and the proteins they produce. (On June 26, 2000, scientists announced the completion of the "working draft," of the human genome. The working draft covers 85% of the genome's coding regions in rough form.)

Some diseases are caused by interaction between genes and environment (lifestyle) factors. Genetic factors may predispose a person to a disease. For example, America's number one killers, cardiovascular disease and cancer, have both genetic and environmental causes. However, the complex interplay between genes and environmental factors in the development of these diseases makes it difficult for scientists to study the genetics of these diseases. Nevertheless, using evolutionary principles and approaches, scientists have developed a technique called *gene tree analysis* to discover genetic markers that are predictive of certain diseases. (Genetic markers are pairs of alleles whose inheritance can be traced through a pedigree [family tree].) Analyses of gene trees can help medical researchers identify the mutations in genes that cause certain diseases. This knowledge helps medical researchers understand the cause of the diseases to which these genes are linked and can help them develop treatments for such illnesses.

How is evolution indispensable to the subdisciplines of biology? and How does it enrich them?
Organizing life, for example, a process on which Linnaeus worked as he grouped organisms by morphological characteristics, continues today with processes that reflect evolutionary relationships. Systematics, the branch of biology that studies the classification of life, does so in the context of evolutionary relationships. Cladistics, the predominant method used in systematics today, classifies organisms with respect to their phylogenetic relationships—those based on their evolutionary history. Therefore, students who do not understand evolution cannot understand modern methods of classification.

Developmental biology is another example of a biological subdiscipline enriched by an evolutionary perspective. In fact, some embryological phenomena can be understood only in the light of evolutionary history. For example, why terrestrial salamanders go through a larval stage with gills and fins that are never used is a question answered by evolution. During evolution, as new species (e.g., terrestrial salamanders) evolve from ancestral forms (e.g., aquatic ancestors), their new developmental instructions are often added to developmental instructions already in place. Thus, patterns of development in groups of organisms were built over the evolutionary history of those groups, thus retaining ancestral instructions. This process results in the embryonic stages of particular vertebrates reflecting the embryonic stages of those vertebrates' ancestors.

The study of animal behavior is enriched by an evolutionary perspective as well. Behavioral traits also evolve, and like morphological traits they are often most similar among closely related species. Phylogenetic studies of behavior have provided examples of how complex behaviors such as the courtship displays of some birds have evolved from simpler ancestral behaviors. Likewise, the study of human behavior can be enhanced by an evolutionary perspective. Evolutionary psychologists seek to uncover evolutionary reasons for many human behaviors, searching through our ancestral programming to determine how natural selection has resulted in a species that behaves as it does.

There are many sciences with significant historical aspects, such as anthropology, astronomy, geology, and paleontology. Geology, for example, is the study of the history of the earth, especially as recorded in the rocks. Paleontology is the study of fossils. Inherent in the work of the geologist and the paleontologist are questions about the relationships of modern animals and plants to ancestral forms, and about the chronology of the history of the earth. Evolution provides the framework within which these questions can be answered.

What do science and education societies say about the study of evolution?

Instructors often look to scientific societies for answers to many questions regarding their teaching. There is one aspect of teaching on which the scientific societies agree and are emphatic. Evolution is key to scientific study, and should be taught in the science classroom. The National Research Council, part of the National Academy of Science, identified evolution as a major unifying idea in science that transcends disciplinary boundaries. Its publication *National Science Education Standards* lists biological evolution as one of the six content areas in the life sciences that are important for all high school students to study. Likewise, the American Association for the Advancement of Science identified the evolution of life as one of six major areas of study in the life sciences in its publication *Benchmarks for Scientific Literacy*. The National Science Teachers Association, the largest organization in the world committed to promoting excellence and innovation "in science teaching and learning," published a position statement on the teaching of evolution in 1997, which states that "evolution is a major unifying concept of science and should be included as part of K—College science frameworks and curricula." The National Association of

Biology Teachers, a leading organization in life science education, also issued a position statement on the teaching of evolution in 1997, which states that evolution has a "central, unifying role . . . in nature, and therefore in biology. Teaching biology in an effective and scientifically honest manner requires classroom discussions and laboratory experiences on evolution." Evolution has been identified as the unifying theme of biology by almost all science organizations that focus on the biological sciences.

So why should students learn evolution? Eliminating evolution from the education of students removes the context and unifying theory that underpins and permeates the biological sciences. Students thus learn disparate facts in the science classroom without the thread that ties them together, and they miss the answers to its underlying *why* questions. Without an understanding of evolution, they cannot understand processes based on this science, such as insect resistance to pesticides and microbial resistance to antibiotics. Students will not come to understand evolutionary connections to other scientific fields, nor will they fully understand the world of which we are a part. Evolution is, in fact, one of the most important concepts in attaining scientific literacy.

Critical Thinking

1. Why does evolution provide the basic context of all the biological sciences?

2. Be aware of each of the following reasons students should learn evolution: answering the *why* questions; dealing with problems of everyday life; providing a conceptual foundation for the biological sciences; applications in medicine.

3. Why is evolution—in the context of the biological sciences—a unifying theory?

4. How do evolutionary explanations answer key questions in the biological sciences?

5. How does understanding evolution help us understand processes that affect our health and our day-to-day life? How are evolutionary methods applied to other fields?

6. How is evolution indispensable to the subdisciplines of biology and how does it enrich them?

7. What do science and education societies say about the study of evolution?

Create Central

www.mhhe.com/createcentral

Internet References

American Institute of Biological Sciences
 www.actionbioscience.org
Enter Evolution: Theory and History
 www.ucmp.berkeley.edu/history/evolution.html
National Center for Science Education
 www.natcenscied.org

Unit 2

UNIT

Prepared by: Elvio Angeloni, *Pasadena City College*

Primates

Primates are fun. They are active, intelligent, colorful, emotionally expressive, and unpredictable. Because, in some ways, they are very much like us, observing them is like holding up an opaque mirror to ourselves. The image may not be crystal-clear or, indeed, what some would consider flattering, but it is certainly familiar enough to be illuminating.

Primates are, of course, one of the many orders of mammals that adaptively radiated into the variety of ecological niches, which were vacated at the end of the Age of Reptiles about 65 million years ago. Whereas some mammals took to the sea (cetaceans), and some took to the air (chiroptera, or bats), primates took to the trees and are characterized by an arboreal or forested adaptation. While some mammals can be identified by their food-getting habits, such as the meat-eating carnivores, primates have a penchant for eating almost anything and are best described as omnivorous. After ascending into the trees, primates did not simply develop a full-blown set of distinguishing characteristics that set them off easily from other orders of mammals, the way the rodent order can be readily identified by its gnawing set of front teeth. Rather, each primate seems to represent degrees of anatomical, biological, and behavioral characteristics on a continuum of change, in the direction of the particular traits in which we humans happen to be interested.

None of this is meant to imply, of course, that the living primates are our ancestors. Because the prosimians, monkeys, and apes are contemporaries, they are no more our ancestors than we are theirs, and, as living end-products of evolution, we have all descended from a common stock in the distant past. So, if we are interested primarily in our own evolutionary past, why study primates at all? Because, by the criteria we have set up as significant milestones in the evolution of humanity, an inherent reflection of our own bias, primates have not evolved as far as we have. They and their environments, therefore, may provide a glimmer of the evolutionary stages and ecological circumstances through which our own ancestors may have gone. What we stand to gain, for instance, is an educated guess as to how our own ancestors might have appeared and behaved as semi-erect creatures before becoming bipedal. Aside from being

a pleasure to observe, then, living primates can teach us something about our past.

The kind of answers obtained in doing research on primates depend upon the kind of questions asked, and so we have to be very careful in making inferences about the motivations of any given species of primate, including humans, based on limited study. This goes for theory as well. Ever since Darwin published *On the Origin of Species* in 1859, for instance, some prominent economists have embraced it as supportive of laissez-faire capitalism. This interpretation, however, says more about the theorists and their socioeconomic agenda than it does about the actual facts of human nature or even the social context in which human beings evolved.

Still another benefit of primate field research is that it provides us with perspectives that the bones and stones of the fossil hunters will never reveal: a sense of the richness and variety of social patterns that must have existed in the primate order for many tens of millions of years.

Even if we had the physical remains of the earliest hominids in front of us, which we do not, there is no way such evidence could thoroughly answer the questions that physical anthropologists care most deeply about: How did these creatures move about and get their food? Did they cooperate and share? At what levels did they think and communicate? Did they have a sense of family, let alone a sense of self? But what sets off the study of our closest relatives from other aspects of anthropology is how primatologists attempt to deal with these matters head-on, even in the absence of direct fossil evidence. Thus, the finding that chimpanzees cooperatively hunt for meat and share food indicates that at least some aspects of "hominization" (the acquisition of humanlike qualities) may have actually begun while our own ancestors were still in the African rain forest rather than in the dry savanna, as has been proposed usually.

Although extrapolating from primate behavior to that of humans may seem like a reach may generate irreconcilable differences among theorists, a readiness to entertain new ideas should be welcomed for what it is—a stimulus for more intensive and meticulous research.

Article   Prepared by: Elvio Angeloni, *Pasadena City College*

No Alpha Males Allowed

STEVE KEMPER

Learning Outcomes

After reading this article, you will be able to:

- Discuss Karen Strier's findings in her study of the Muriqui monkeys and how it contrasts with primatology's traditional emphasis upon aggression.

- Contrast the muriqui "alternative life style" with other primate societies.

It's 9 o'clock on a June morning in a muggy tropical forest not far from Brazil's Atlantic coast and brown howler monkeys have been roaring for an hour. But the muriquis—the largest primates in the Americas after human beings, and the animals that the anthropologist Karen Strier and I have huffed uphill to see—are still curled high in the crooks of trees, waiting for the morning sun to warm them.

As they begin to stir, the adults scratch, stretch, and watch the suddenly frisky youngsters without moving much themselves. A few languidly grab leaves for breakfast. They are striking figures, with fur that varies between gray, light brown, and russet. Their black faces inspired the Brazilian nickname "charcoal monkey," after the sooty features of charcoal makers.

Strier knows these faces well. At age 54, the University of Wisconsin-Madison professor has been observing muriquis here for three decades. One of the longest-running studies of its kind, it has upended conventional wisdom about primates and may have a surprising thing or two to say about human nature.

"Louise!" Strier says, spotting one of her old familiars. Louise belongs to Strier's original study group of 23—clássicos, Strier's Brazilian students call them. "She's the only female who's never had a baby," says Strier. "Her friends are some of the old girls."

Above us, two youngsters frolic near their mother. "That's Barbara," says Strier, "and her three-year-old twins Bamba and Beleco." Female muriquis typically emigrate out of their natal group at about age 6, but Barbara has never left hers, the Matão study group, named after a valley that bisects this part of the forest. Even today, more than two years after I visited Brazil, Barbara remains in the group.

Strier first came to this federally protected reserve in 1982, at the invitation of Russell Mittermeier, now president of Conservation International and chairman of the primate specialist group of the International Union for Conservation of Nature's Species Survival Commission, who had been conducting a survey of primates in eastern Brazil. The reserve at the time held only about 50 muriquis, and Strier, a Harvard graduate student, was smitten with the lanky creatures cavorting in the canopy.

"As soon as I saw the muriquis," says Strier, "I said, 'This is it.'" She stayed for two months and then returned for 14 more.

In those days, to reach this patch of forest, she rode a bus almost 40 miles from the nearest town and walked the last mile to a simple house without electricity. Often alone, she rose before dawn to look for the monkeys and didn't leave the forest until they had settled down at dusk. She cut her own network of footpaths, collecting data on births, relationships, diets, dispositions, daily locations, and emigrations. At night, she sorted the data by the light of gas lanterns.

"As my contact with the animals increased, they introduced me to new species of food that they ate, and allowed me to witness new behaviors," Strier wrote in her 1992 book *Faces in the Forest*, now a classic of primatology. As a personal account of a field biologist's extraordinary, often lonely efforts to become acquainted with a wild primate, Strier's work has been compared to Jane Goodall's *In the Shadow of Man* and Dian Fossey's *Gorillas in the Mist*.

When Strier was first getting to know the muriquis, primatology was still largely focused on just a handful of species that had adapted to life on the ground, including baboons, or that had close evolutionary relationships with humans, such as apes. This emphasis came to shape public perception of primates as essentially aggressive. We picture chest-beating, teeth-flashing dominant male gorillas competing to mate with any female they choose. We picture, as Goodall had witnessed beginning in 1974, chimpanzees invading other territories, biting and beating other chimps to death. Primates, including possibly the most violent one of all—us—seemed to be born ruffians.

In reality, as Strier's work would underscore, the primates are a varied group, with diverse social structures and far more complex behavior. Descended from a tree-dwelling ancestor living some 55 million years ago in Africa or Asia, the group includes tarsiers, lemurs, lorises, monkeys, apes (such as gorillas, chimps, bonobos, and gibbons), and hominids. Monkeys, characterized by long tails and flat, hairless faces, are generally divided into two types: Old World monkeys, such as baboons and macaques, live in Asia and Africa. New World monkeys, including muriquis, are descended from ancestors that found their way from Africa to South America perhaps 35 million years ago.

For a long time, New World monkeys were the second-class citizens of primatology. "New World primates were considered not so smart, not so interesting, and not so relevant to human evolution," says Frans de Waal, director of the Living Links Center at Emory University's Yerkes National Primate Research Center. "They were sidelined—totally inappropriately, as Karen has demonstrated."

Strier's research introduced the world to an alternative primate lifestyle. Female muriquis mate with a lot of males and males don't often fight. Though bonobos, known for their casual sex, are often called the "hippie" primates, the muriquis in Strier's study site are equally deserving of that reputation. They are peace-loving and tolerant. Strier also showed that the muriquis turn out to be incredibly cooperative, a characteristic that may be just as important in primate societies as vicious rivalry.

Strier's ideas shook up primatology, making her an influential figure in the field. Her widely used textbook, *Primate Behavioral Ecology*, is in its fourth edition and "has no peers," according to the American Society of Primatologists. In 2005, at age 45, Strier was elected to the National Academy of Sciences, a rare honor. The University of Wisconsin recently recognized her with an endowed professorship. The money is being used to support her research in Brazil, where the muriquis she knows so well continue to surprise her.

Lately, they've been doing something arboreal primates aren't supposed to do. In an unusual behavioral twist, they're coming down out of the trees.

Muriquis are acrobats, spending much of the day swinging through the treetops in search of food. They ride branches down and scurry across vines like tightrope walkers. Hanging fully extended, muriquis appear 5 feet tall but weigh only 20 pounds, an elongated physique allowing for quick and astonishingly nimble movement.

As Strier and I walk through the forest, the muriquis sound like a herd of horses flying overhead. They neigh to maintain long-distance contact. A staccato hnk hnk hnk keeps them out of one another's way, and an excited chirp summons the others when a monkey has found a fruiting tree.

Muriquis' cooperative behaviors are often on display when they're eating. A few days into my visit, Strier and I watch nine males demonstrate their manners as they eat pods in a legume tree. When one monkey scoots past another on a branch, it pauses to hug its neighbor, as if to say, "Pardon, so sorry."

Muriquis almost never fight over food with members of their own group. They will chase howler monkeys or capuchins out of fruiting trees, and they loudly protest incursions by muriquis from other parts of the forest. But males and females, young and old, behave toward members of their own group in ways that can fairly be described as considerate.

Some of the muriquis in the legume tree exchange little pats as they brush by each other. Two of them, on a short break from eating, sit haunch to haunch, one resting his hand on top of the other's head. Before they resume picking pods, they hug.

Affectionate gestures, including full-body face-to-face embraces, are common. It's not unusual to see five or more muriquis in a tangled furry cuddle. Strier says that some males become more popular as they age, and younger males seek the company of the elders and solicit hugs during times of tension. Squabbles are rare. "Maybe their drive for social cohesion and conformity is much stronger than their aggression," says Strier.

They also tend to be easygoing about the other big activity that agitates almost all other primates: sex. Unlike chimpanzees and baboons, male muriquis don't attack rivals to keep them from females, Strier says. There are no alphas in these societies, so muriqui twosomes don't have to sneak off to evade punishment by jealous suitors. What's more, female muriquis don't need to form coalitions to protect infants from murderous males. Strier has called muriqui mating a "passive affair." Males don't chase down females or bully them into sexual submission. Instead, a male waits for an invitation from a female, who selects her partners and copulates openly. Instead of battling each other for access to females, males bond into extensive brotherhoods, and Strier suspects they have replaced fighting with "sperm competition." In proportion to their slight frames, muriquis have oversized testicles. It may be that the male producing the most sperm has the most tickets in the reproductive raffle.

When Strier first observed these behaviors, she thought muriquis were anomalies in the primate world. But as research documented the behaviors of a broader range of primates, Strier realized that there was actually a lot of variation—more than was generally acknowledged. In 1994, she wrote a paper titled "Myth of the Typical Primate" that urged her colleagues to reconsider the emphasis on aggression as a mediator of primate relationships, which "prevailed despite repeated efforts to demonstrate the limitations of such arguments." She contended that the roots of primate social behavior, including that of people, might be more accurately reflected in the flexibility, tolerance, cooperation, and affection that predominate among most primates and that these qualities are at least as recognizably human as aggressiveness, competition, and selfishness. Strier's paper was pivotal in initiating a new way of thinking about primate behavior.

"We have this idea that competition is good," says Robert Sussman, professor of anthropology at Washington University in St. Louis and co-author of *Man the Hunted: Primates, Predators, and Human Evolution*, "that everybody is out for themselves and that the people at the top are by nature superior. But there's now lots of evidence that competition among primates only occurs when the environment changes because of outside influence. The ultimate goal of evolution is to reach an ecological equilibrium and avoid competition and aggression, a very different point of view. Karen Strier has become one of the leaders in this alternative paradigm about the evolution of cooperation."

So as not to influence the behavior of the muriquis themselves, Strier decided at the start only to observe them and not interact with them. She has never trapped or tranquilized a monkey to take a blood sample or to affix a radio collar, and she won't use feeding stations to lure them to convenient spots for observations, as some researchers studying chimps in the wild have been known to do. For years she has collected hormone data on individual females by positioning herself to catch falling feces. She says they smell like cinnamon.

Though Strier maintains a kind of clinical detachment from the muriquis in the field that doesn't mean she's uninvolved. She has in fact become their impassioned advocate. No matter how cooperative they are, they can't by themselves overcome the forces at work to destroy them.

Once called woolly spider monkeys, muriquis occur in two closely related species that scientists didn't officially split until 2000: northern (Brachyteles hypoxanthus) and southern (Brachyteles arachnoides). Both species live only in Brazil, in scattered remnants of the once-vast Atlantic coastal forest, now greatly reduced by clearing for pasture and agricultural land. Because of extensive habitat fragmentation, both muriqui species are classified as endangered, the northern one critically: Only 1,000 of them survive, spread across about a dozen patches of forest, one of which is Strier's study site. Early in Strier's career, colleagues asked her why she wanted to study monkey behavior in such an altered habitat. But Strier didn't see the environment as an obstacle; she wanted to know how the monkeys adapt.

Born in New Jersey, Strier grew up in southern California, western New York, and then Maryland. She enjoyed the outdoors, hiking, and backpacking with friends, but she doesn't trace her deep fascination with primates to any childhood "aha" moment, unlike Jane Goodall, who recalls receiving a toy chimpanzee as a youngster. As an undergraduate studying biology and anthropology at Swarthmore College, Strier actually thought she might go on to conduct research on bears in the United States. But during her junior year she was offered the opportunity to work on the Amboseli Baboon Project in Kenya. She had never taken a course in primatology.

"It was a catharsis," she says. "Everything about who I was and what I liked came together—the outdoors, the animals, science." It was in graduate school that her adviser connected her with Mittermeier, who connected her with the muriquis. "She's one of the great leaders in primatology today," says Mittermeier. "She's had a huge influence in Brazil. She has trained some of the key people there, the richest country on earth for primates."

Her research is situated in the 2,365-acre federally protected Reserva Particular do Patrimônio Natural Feliciano Miguel Abdala, named after the coffee farmer who owned the land. After Abdala's death in 2000, his heirs followed his wishes and put the forest into permanent trust as a reserve. More than four dozen Brazilian students have conducted research there under Strier, with pairs and trios rotating in and out every 14 months. Strier typically spends about a month each year at the reserve, conversing with the students and making quips in Portuguese, which she studied for one semester but largely picked up during her fieldwork. She spends the rest of her time in Madison, where she lives with her husband and their cats. She prefers dogs, but her travel schedule makes caring for them difficult.

Acting on her profound concern for the muriquis' future, she has discussed in public lectures and scientific papers the need for national and international investment in wildlife preservation and for educational programs and employment opportunities that get the local community involved. She is a key member of the committee that advises the Brazilian government on its plans for muriqui conservation. Largely thanks to her efforts, the muriquis have become something of a cause célèbre of conservation in Brazil, featured on T-shirts and postage stamps. In June, the city of Caratinga, Brazil, not far from the reserve, made Strier an honorary citizen, and used her project's thirtieth anniversary to announce a new long-term sustainability program.

Though northern muriquis are critically endangered, the population in Strier's study site, which is protected from further deforestation and hunting, has increased. There are now 335 individuals in four groups, a sixfold increase since Strier started her study.

That's a development worth celebrating, but it's not without consequences. The monkeys appear to be outgrowing the reserve and, in response to this population pressure, altering millennia of arboreal behavior. These tree-dwellers, these born aerialists, are spending more and more time on the ground. At first, the behavior was surprising. Over time, though, Strier made some sense of it. "They're on an island, with no place to go but up or down. When humans didn't have enough food, they invented intensive agriculture. Monkeys come to the ground. It makes me think of how hominids had to eke out an existence in a hostile environment. Our ancestors would have brought to that challenge the plasticity we're seeing here."

Initially the muriquis descended only briefly and only for necessities, Strier says. Now they're staying down for up to four hours—playing, resting, and even mating. One of Strier's students shot a video of a big group of monkeys lounging on the ground, leaning against each other, and casually hugging, as if they're at a picnic. "Next they'll lose their tails," jokes Carla Possamai, a Brazilian postdoctoral researcher who's been working with Strier at the reserve for a decade.

One day we watch muriquis eat white berries on low bushes. At first the monkeys hang from their tails above the bushes, but soon they drop to the ground and stand there like customers at a pick-your-own patch. Upright but awkward, they are out of their element. "You're watching an animal whose body is adapted for something else, using it in new ways," says Strier.

In another unexpected break with predictable behavior, five female muriquis emigrated to another forest on the far side of 200 yards of bare pasture. Two of these adventurers made the dangerous trip back into the reserve, where it's suspected that one of them mated before again crossing the open ground to the new forest.

Eking out a living on the ground might sound like a radical departure with no real consequences, but it makes the muriquis more vulnerable to predators. Camera traps have captured images of ocelots and a family of cougars in the reserve, and feral dogs and other carnivores are known to roam the pastures.

"Basically they're telling us they need more space," Strier says. To give it to them, Preserve Muriqui, the Abdala family foundation that runs the reserve, is working with local ranchers and landowners to connect the forest to the archipelago of small forest fragments on the reserve's periphery.

Strier wonders about the potential for other changes. What will peaceful, egalitarian primates do if crowding becomes more severe and resources run short? "I predict a cascade of effects and demographic changes," she says. Will the monkeys become more aggressive and start to compete for food and other essentials the way chimps and baboons do? Will the clubby camaraderie between males fall apart? Will the social fabric tear or will the muriquis find new ways to preserve it? Strier has learned that there is no fixed behavior; instead, it's driven by circumstances and environmental conditions. Context matters.

"Nature is designing my experiment: the effects of population growth on wild primates," she says. Among the many unknowns there's one certainty: The muriquis will try to adapt. "It's not surprising that long-lived, intelligent, socially complex primates are capable of great behavioral plasticity," says Strier. "It gives me hope. After watching this group for 30 years," she adds, "I think anything is possible."

Critical Thinking

1. Explain primatology's emphasis on aggression before Karen Strier published her work.
2. Explain why New World monkeys were considered second-class citizens of primatology.
3. Describe the muriquis "alternative lifestyle."
4. Be familiar with muriqui social life and behavior, especially in contrast to other primates.
5. Discuss "sperm competition."
6. Why does Strier believe that muriqui behavior is not an anomaly among primates?
7. How has Strier been able to avoid influencing the behavior of the muriquis?
8. Why are the muriquis spending more time on the ground? What further changes might this involve, according to Strier?

Create Central

www.mhhe.com/createcentral

Internet References

Electronic Zoo/NetVet-Primate Page
http://netvet.wustl.edu/primates.htm

National Primate Research Center
http://pin.primate.wisc.edu/factsheets

Article   Prepared by: Elvio Angeloni

Love in the Time of Monkeys

Eduardo Fernandez-Duque and Benjamin Finkel

Learning Outcomes

After reading this article, you will be able to:

- Discuss the rarity of monogamy among mammals.
- Discuss the relationship between monogamy, territoriality, and the distribution of food resources among owl monkeys.

Even though there is great diversity in the organization of human societies, we all fall in love. Many of us maintain long relationships with the person we love romantically—or, as biologists state it, establish pair bonds—and together we form families and raise children, albeit with different levels of paternal involvement. Although we cannot pinpoint when a predisposition for pair bonding and monogamy evolved, it was surely long ago, well before we organized ourselves with religion, law, government, and complex technology. Most likely love and pair bonding evolved due to the influence of a specific set of ecological and biological factors. We know this because we see it in other primates, nonhuman primates that allow us to examine the biological basis of monogamy without the influences of language, religion, and technology.

Monogamy comes in different shapes and sizes. Researchers have described it in taxa as diverse as amphibians, birds, shrimp, and termites, but monogamy is relatively rare in mammals—only about 10 percent of mammalian species and 25 percent of primates organize around a breeding adult pair. Why is monogamy so uncommon among mammals? First, because mammalian fertilization is internal, a "father" may risk investing time, energy, and resources in a baby that he cannot be sure he has sired. Even more important, a female mammal is reproductively limited by pregnancy and lactation, whereas a male is unfettered by these time and energy constraints. To illustrate the point, one can contrast the most reproductively prolific woman, Valentina Vassilyeva of eighteenth-century Russia, credited with the birth of 69 children (including many twins, triplets, and even quadruplets), with the most reproductively prolific man, the Emperor of Morocco, Moulay Ismael (1672–1727), who allegedly had 888 children. Given that male and female mammals have such different reproductive potentials, how then did a mating strategy evolve that, without the guarantee of paternity, limits the male to breed with a single female?

Nearly two decades ago, I set off for Argentina in the hope of answering that question. I had just finished my doctoral dissertation investigating monogamy in titi monkeys (*Callicebus cupreus*) at the University of California, Davis, and was eager to study monogamous monkeys in the wild. My wife and I, along with our two young sons, moved to the rainforests of northeastern Argentina with a small grant from the Leakey Foundation and lots of dreams. To establish a field site and balance research with family life was a labor of love: my wife, Claudia Valeggia, a biological anthropologist as well, was beginning her field research on the reproductive ecology of the Toba-Qom indigenous communities of northern Argentina. We had to juggle our incipient projects with two kids attending school, along with a large number of volunteers and assistants in need of logistical (and emotional) support in the field. Some days, I would start at four or five o'clock in the morning, racing between home and the rainforest. Other times, it was more efficient to stay in the forest for several days at once. And so I started to study Azara's owl monkeys (*Aotus azarae*), known to locals as mirikiná, a species believed to find a partner, establish a monogamous pair bond, and share parental duties quite evenly.

In Argentina, owl monkeys live only in the eastern portion of the Formosa and Chaco provinces in the northern tip of the country. Both provinces are part of the South American Gran Chaco, a vast expanse of flat land that includes forests growing along rivers (gallery forests), savannas, and patches of forest immersed in those savannas. Most of the region is privately owned, and the main activity is raising cattle that graze on the open savannas. It was with the help of gauchos (Argentine cowboys) at Estancia Guaycolec, a 62,000-acre cattle ranch, that I was able to establish a research camp, carving out nearly ten miles of trails through 170 acres of forest. The owl monkey's habitat—a hot, dense and often mosquito-swarmed atmosphere—has earned the name el Infierno Verde, the Green Hell. Yet the Chaco's outstanding biodiversity is worth the effort, with more armadillo species than any other place in the world; a host of large mammals, including capybara, tapir, and puma; and two species of monkeys, the black and gold howler monkey (*Alouatta caraya*) and the owl monkey.

Owl monkeys are arboreal and relatively small primates, weighing roughly three pounds, which poses some challenges for detailed observation of their distant, scurrying bodies. To our eyes they are sexually mono-morphic: body size and coloring are identical between males and females. A lack of obvious differences between the sexes tends to be associated with pair-living species, as in the case of gibbons in southeast Asia, titi monkeys in the Amazon, and a number of lemurs in Madagascar. Fortunately, though, while the other 11 owl monkey species in Central and South America are nocturnal, the Azara's owl monkeys of the Chaco are cathemeral, with a mix of diurnal and nocturnal activity that allowed us to observe them in the daylight.

Early in my research, we made little progress in understanding the social behavior of owl monkeys, because this required the identification of individuals, their age, and their sex. Four years into the project, a description of a group would still frequently read, "3 adult-size individuals, 2 smaller, 1 dependent infant." Even so, we had begun to fill in our image of owl monkey life. We learned that their social lives centered on tightly affiliated and territorial units that consisted of two reproducing adults and one to three nonreproducing individuals. We suspected that these could be a pair of breeding adults and their offspring, but could not precisely define the relatedness between group members. Occasionally, a few animals looked distinctive to us. In 1998, we spotted an individual with a ten-inch tail, rather than the typical fifteen inches, and Cola Corta ("short tail" in Spanish) became easy to identify; he lived at least 14 years and sired five infants. Sometimes we classified individuals as female if we saw them nursing. Nonetheless, it became clear that we had to capture and mark the animals, examine their genitalia, measure them, and obtain genetic samples if we were going to have a groundbreaking project on primate monogamy. The project needed new tools.

A breakthrough came in 1999, once we were able to use radio collars and telemetry receivers to track individuals. The efficiency and reliability of locating the monkeys via telemetry was what finally let us address the questions about monogamy that had taken me to Argentina in the first place. As of today, we have tagged 166 individuals. My colleagues and I have found a surprising amount of biparental care. Mom is always around, but her main interaction with the infant is limited to nursing.

Males often play with and carry the infants, with equal or perhaps greater doggedness than the mother. When owl monkey males (presumed fathers) skitter through the trees, their young typically go along for the ride.

We also gathered valuable information on the relationships between pair bonding, monogamy, paternal care, and life-history traits. Owl monkeys have a remarkably slow life history for being so small: infants are wholly dependent until six months of age, and following weaning, both males and females continue to grow until four years of age, at which time they tend to disperse from their natal groups. Reproducing for the first time when they are at least six years old, individuals may produce in a lifetime four to six offspring, one at a time. Although our study has not lasted long enough to establish their lifespan conclusively, we estimate that some individuals have lived as long as 15 years.

So why are the mirikiná socially monogamous? We believe that the answer lies partly in how food is distributed in the forest. Their habitat is a subtropical forest where seasonal variation in both temperature and rainfall creates periods of food abundance and scarcity. There are sharp peaks in the abundance of preferred food items for owl monkeys and, conversely, lulls, which may constitute critical periods when the monkeys struggle to meet nutritional demands. We collaborated with botanists to examine the owl monkeys' feeding ecology: we created large plots within the forest to survey the production of leaves, flowers, and fruits, and we assembled a database detailing the forest structure, including the distribution and size of tree species. Since 2003, we have collected monthly data on food availability from 425 trees in those plots. We learned that owl monkey foods are not laid out in continuous buffets, but are distributed in smaller plates throughout the forest. While there are many dishes, they are separated, and each "plate" can only sustain a single female. Therefore, the distribution of food separates females who disperse into their individual plates, or territories. What are males to do given this spacious distribution of females? If a male wants to be close to one female, he will necessarily be far away from any other. In other words, the distribution of females may make it impossible for the male to control more than one of them.

Yet, this would only explain why there is social monogamy, not why the males are committed to the care of infants they may or may not have fathered. Just because a male stays with a female doesn't mean he will help with parenting. So why are male owl monkeys exceptionally good fathers? Genetic monogamy is a reasonable explanation. Social monogamy refers to the structure of groups, groups that only include one adult male and one adult female. Genetic, or reproductive, monogamy is about fidelity; it is about who has offspring with whom. This is a crucial distinction when attempting to understand the evolution of paternal care and monogamy, because what counts in evolution is the offspring produced.

Are male owl monkeys guaranteed of their parentage? For an answer, we examined jealousy and mate guarding in male and female owl monkeys. Absolute control of a mate's reproduction can be a behavioral mechanism to ensure fidelity. If one partner constantly watches out for and fends off competition, there won't be an opportunity for the other to mate outside of the pair; there won't be "extra-pair copulation." We have learned that owl monkeys are territorial, each group not only occupying a well-defined space within the forest, but actively defending a portion of it as well. Both adults take part in protecting the group from intruders who attempt to supplant one of them. Their young too will rally against the intruder, with serious consequences. When an intruder approaches the group and a fight ensues, sometimes one of the individuals may die in the aggressive encounter. Furthermore, when we examined demographic records from eighteen groups over 10 years, we discovered that owl monkeys that succeed in preserving their monogamous relationship produce 25 percent more offspring than those who are forced to take on a new partner. In other words, there are significant costs and benefits of this extreme mate guarding, and both sexes appear to be preserving their bond with equal stake. Such behavioral and demographic data supported the critical importance of monogamy to the mirikinás, but genetic data was still the Holy Grail to definitively confirm whether owl monkeys are reproductively monogamous and faithful in practice, not just in appearance.

Modern technology provided us much-needed answers. These days, a droplet of blood, a single baby hair, or a little saliva from a pacifier are enough to run a paternity test. The biological samples we had collected from 166 individuals during ten years allowed us to examine paternity relationships in owl monkeys. One of our first and most significant findings using genetic data was to confirm that the socially monogamous groups of owl monkeys are not always "families" of biological parents and offspring. We suspected this from the demographic data showing changes in the adult composition of these groups—many intruders were indeed successful. But the genetic data provided conclusive proof that intruders sometimes supplanted biological parents as stepparents, and the intense territoriality we observed was justified by legitimate threats. Still, the question remained: did a pair bond guarantee the father paternity of the offspring in his group?

To answer that question we examined the genetic relationships between 35 infants and 35 male and female pairs. In 100 percent of cases, the male in the group was the biological father of the infant. Combined with the absence of any observations of extra-pair copulation in 17 years, these findings strongly indicate that owl monkey mates are always faithful, making them socially and genetically monogamous. They are socially monogamous because of ecological issues that limit their chances of having multiple partners, and intolerance toward competitors protects the couple and keeps them genetically monogamous. Owl monkeys are the first primate species, and only the fifth mammal, for which there is substantial evidence of genetic monogamy. Our analyses show that, once social monogamy has evolved, paternal care, and potentially close bonds as well, may facilitate the evolution of genetic monogamy. This helps to explain why males play an unusually dominant role in parenting. With biparental care, the female can recover more easily from pregnancy; having two attentive parents increases an infant's chances of survival; and the male gets a better guarantee of replicating his own genes.

The study of monogamy, pair bonding, and alloparental care is of special interest to anthropologists and evolutionary biologists because pair bonding was likely a fundamental adaptation of our early ancestors. In human societies everywhere, couples develop relationships that are qualitatively different from the relationships they have with other adults. Psychologists, anthropologists, behavioral ecologists, economists, historians, and poets have all testified to this ubiquitous phenomenon: a pair bond, attachment, or love that develops between a couple with a commitment to share space, time, resources, offspring, and labor. As the research continues, under the auspices of the Owl Monkey Project of Argentina, we will continue to take advantage of one of the few primate models in which we can explore the interactions between behavior, ecology, demography, and genetics, in shaping primate behavior and life history.

Critical Thinking

1. Why is monogamy rare among mammals?
2. Why are owl monkeys monogamous?

Internet References

African Primates at Home
www.indiana.edu/~primate/primates.html
Living Links
www.emory.edu/LIVING_LINKS/dewaal.html
National Primate Research Center
http://pin.primate.wisc.edu/factsheets
Primate Society of Great Britain
http://www.psgb.org/

Article   Prepared by: Elvio Angeloni, *Pasadena City College*

The 2% Difference

Now that scientists have decoded the chimpanzee genome, we know that 98 percent of our DNA is the same. So how can we be so different?

ROBERT SAPOLSKY

Learning Outcomes

After reading this article, you will be able to:

- Discuss the similarities and differences between chimps and humans.
- Explain why we humans are so different from chimpanzees even though we share 98% of our DNA with them.

If you find yourself sitting close to a chimpanzee, staring face to face and making sustained eye contact, something interesting happens, something that is alternately moving, bewildering, and kind of creepy. When you gaze at this beast, you suddenly realize that the face gazing back is that of a sentient individual, who is recognizably kin. You can't help but wonder, What's the matter with those intelligent design people?

Chimpanzees are close relatives to humans, but they're not identical to us. We are not chimps. Chimps excel at climbing trees, but we beat them hands down at balance-beam routines; they are covered in hair, while we have only the occasional guy with really hairy shoulders. The core differences, however, arise from how we use our brains. Chimps have complex social lives, play power politics, betray and murder each other, make tools, and teach tool use across generations in a way that qualifies as culture. They can even learn to do logic operations with symbols, and they have a relative sense of numbers. Yet those behaviors don't remotely approach the complexity and nuance of human behaviors, and in my opinion there's not the tiniest bit of scientific evidence that chimps have aesthetics, spirituality, or a capacity for irony or poignancy.

What makes the human species brainy are huge numbers of standard-issue neurons.

What accounts for those differences? A few years ago, the most ambitious project in the history of biology was carried out: the sequencing of the human genome. Then just four months ago, a team of researchers reported that they had likewise sequenced the complete chimpanzee genome. Scientists have long known that chimps and humans share about 98 percent of their DNA. At last, however, one can sit down with two scrolls of computer printout, march through the two genomes, and see exactly where our 2 percent difference lies.

Given the outward differences, it seems reasonable to expect to find fundamental differences in the portions of the genome that determine chimp and human brains—reasonable, at least, to a brainocentric neurobiologist like me. But as it turns out, the chimp brain and the human brain differ hardly at all in their genetic underpinnings. Indeed, a close look at the chimp genome reveals an important lesson in how genes and evolution work, and it suggests that chimps and humans are a lot more similar than even a neurobiologist might think.

DNA, or deoxyribonucleic acid, is made up of just four molecules, called nucleotides: adenine (A), cytosine (C), guanine (G), and thymine (T). The DNA codebook for every species consists of billions of these letters in a precise order. If, when DNA is being copied in a sperm or an egg, a nucleotide is mistakenly copied wrong, the result is a mutation. If the mutation persists from generation to generation, it becomes a DNA difference—one of the many genetic distinctions that separate one species (chimpanzees) from another (humans). In genomes involving billions of nucleotides, a tiny 2 percent difference translates into tens of millions of ACGT differences. And that 2 percent difference can be very broadly distributed. Humans and chimps each have somewhere between 20,000 and 30,000 genes, so there are likely to be nucleotide differences in every single gene.

To understand what distinguishes the DNA of chimps and humans, one must first ask: What is a gene? A gene is a string of nucleotides that specify how a single distinctive protein should be made. Even if the same gene in chimps and humans differs by an A here and a T there, the result may be of no consequence. Many nucleotide differences are neutral—both the mutation and the normal gene cause the same protein to be made. However, given the right nucleotide difference between the same gene in the two species, the resulting proteins may differ slightly in construction and function.

One might assume that the differences between chimp and human genes boil down to those sorts of typographical errors: one nucleotide being swapped for a different one and altering the gene it sits in. But a close look at the two codebooks reveals very few such instances. And the typos that do occasionally occur follow a compelling pattern. It's important to note that genes don't act alone. Yes, each gene regulates the construction of a specific protein. But what tells that gene *when* and *where* to build that protein? Regulation is everything: It's important not to start up genes related to puberty during, say, infancy, or to activate genes that are related to eye color in the bladder.

In the DNA code list, that critical information is contained in a short stretch of As and Cs and Gs and Ts that lie just before each gene and act as a switch that turns the gene on or off. The switch, in turn, is flicked on by proteins called transcription factors, which activate certain genes in response to certain stimuli. Naturally, every gene is not regulated by its own distinct transcription factor; otherwise, a codebook of as many as 30,000 genes would require 30,000 transcription factors—and 30,000 more genes to code for them. Instead, one transcription factor can flick on an array of functionally related genes. For example, a certain type of injury can activate one transcription factor that turns on a bunch of genes in your white blood cells, triggering inflammation.

Accurate switch flickers are essential. Imagine the consequences if some of those piddly nucleotide changes arose in a protein that happened to be a transcription factor: Suddenly, instead of activating 23 different genes, the protein might charge up 21 or 25 of them—or it might turn on the usual 23 but in different ratios than normal. Suddenly, one minor nucleotide difference would be amplified across a network of gene differences. (And imagine the ramifications if the altered proteins are transcription factors that activate the genes coding for still other transcription factors!) When the chimp and human genomes are compared, some of the clearest cases of nucleotide differences are found in genes coding for transcription factors. Those cases are few, but they have far-ranging implications.

The genomes of chimps and humans reveal a history of other kinds of differences as well. Instead of a simple mutation, in which a single nucleotide is copied incorrectly, consider an insertion mutation, where an extra A, C, G, or T is dropped in, or a deletion mutation, whereby a nucleotide drops out. Insertion or deletion mutations can have major consequences: Imagine the deletion mutation that turns the sentence "I'll have the mousse for dessert" into "I'll have the mouse for dessert," or the insertion mutation implicit in "She turned me down for a date after I asked her to go bowling with me." Sometimes, more than a single nucleotide is involved; whole stretches of a gene may be dropped or added. In extreme cases, entire genes may be deleted or added.

More important than how the genetic changes arise—by insertion, deletion, or straight mutation—is where in the genome they occur. Keep in mind that, for these genetic changes to persist from generation to generation, they must convey some evolutionary advantage. When one examines the 2 percent difference between humans and chimps, the genes in question turn out to be evolutionarily important, if banal. For example, chimps have a great many more genes related to olfaction than we do; they've got a better sense of smell because we've lost many of those genes. The 2 percent distinction also involves an unusually large fraction of genes related to the immune system, parasite vulnerability, and infectious diseases: Chimps are resistant to malaria, and we aren't; we handle tuberculosis better than they do. Another important fraction of that 2 percent involves genes related to reproduction—the sorts of anatomical differences that split a species in two and keep them from interbreeding.

That all makes sense. Still, chimps and humans have very different brains. So which are the brain-specific genes that have evolved in very different directions in the two species? It turns out that there are hardly any that fit that bill. This, too, makes a great deal of sense. Examine a neuron from a human brain under a microscope, then do the same with a neuron from the brain of a chimp, a rat, a frog, or a sea slug. The neurons all look the same: fibrous dendrites at one end, an axonal cable at the other. They all run on the same basic mechanism: channels and pumps that move sodium, potassium, and calcium around, triggering a wave of excitation called an action potential. They all have a similar complement of neurotransmitters: serotonin, dopamine, glutamate, and so on. They're all the same basic building blocks.

The main difference is in the sheer number of neurons. The human brain has 100 million times the number of neurons a sea slug's brain has. Where do those differences in quantity come from? At some point in their development, all embryos—whether human, chimp, rat, frog, or slug—must have a single first cell committed toward generating neurons. That cell divides and gives rise to 2 cells; those divide into 4, then 8, then 16. After a dozen rounds of cell division, you've got roughly enough neurons to run a slug. Go another 25 rounds or so and you've got a human brain. Stop a couple of rounds short of that and, at about one-third the size of a human brain, you've got one for a chimp. Vastly different outcomes, but relatively few genes regulate the number of rounds of cell division in the nervous system before calling a halt. And it's precisely some of those genes, the ones involved in neural development, that appear on the list of differences between the chimp and human genomes.

That's it; that's the 2 percent solution. What's shocking is the simplicity of it. Humans, to be human, don't need to have evolved unique genes that code for entirely novel types of neurons or neurotransmitters, or a more complex hippocampus (with resulting improvements in memory), or a more complex frontal cortex (from which we gain the ability to postpone gratification). Instead, our braininess as a species arises from having humongous numbers of just a few types of off-the-rack neurons and from the exponentially greater number of interactions between them. The difference is sheer quantity: Qualitative distinctions emerge from large numbers. Genes may have something to do with that quantity, and thus with the complexity of the quality that emerges. Yet no gene or genome can ever tell us what sorts of qualities those will be. Remember that when you and the chimp are eyeball to eyeball, trying to make sense of why the other seems vaguely familiar.

Critical Thinking

1. What are the similarities and differences between chimps and humans?

2. How much of our DNA differs from chimps? How do these differences come about?

3. What is the structure of DNA? How much of this material is different between chimps and humans, given the 2% overall difference between us?

4. What does Sapolsky mean when he says "genes don't act alone"?

5. What is a transcription factor? Is every gene regulated by its own transcription factor?

6. Where are "some of the clearest cases of nucleotide differences" between chimps and humans found?

7. What is the difference between a "simple mutation," an "insertion mutation," and a "deletion mutation"?

8. What type of genes do chimps have more of than we do? What other types of genes are disproportionately impacted by the 2% difference? What are four areas of difference?

9. How are chimp brains and human brains similar and how are they different?

10. What is shocking about the "2% solution"?

Create Central

www.mhhe.com/createcentral

Internet References

Electronic Zoo/NetVet-Primate Page
  http://netvet.wustl.edu/primates.htm
Laboratory Primate Newsletter
  www.brown.edu/Research/Primate/other.html
Wellcome Trust Sanger Institute
  www.sanger.ac.uk/research/projects/humanevolution
Max Planck Institute for Evolutionary Biology
  wwwstaff.eva.mpg.de/~paabo

Article   Prepared by Elvio Angeloni, *Pasadena City College*

Got Culture?

CRAIG STANFORD

Learning Outcomes

After reading this article, you will be able to:

- Discuss the implications of tool use, social hunting, and food sharing by the Ivory Coast chimpanzees for human evolution.

- Determine if chimpanzees' behavioral patterns should be classified as "cultural."

On my first trip to east Africa in the early 1990s, I stood by a dusty, dirt road hitchhiking. I had waited hours in rural Tanzania for an expected lift from a friend who had never shown up, leaving me with few options other than the kindness of strangers. I stood with my thumb out, but the cars and trucks roared by me, leaving me caked in paprika-red dust. I switched to a palm-down gesture I had seen local people using to get lifts. Voilà; on the first try a truck pulled over and I hopped in. A conversation in Kiswahili with the truck driver ensued and I learned my mistake. Hitchhiking with your thumb upturned may work in the United States, but in Africa the gesture can be translated in the way that Americans understand the meaning of an extended, declarative middle finger. Not exactly the best way to persuade a passing vehicle to stop. The universally recognized symbol for needing a lift is not so universal.

Much of culture is the accumulation of thousands of such small differences. Put a suite of traditions together—religion, language, ways of dress, cuisine and a thousand other features—and you have a culture. Of course cultures can be much simpler too. A group of toddlers in a day care center possesses its own culture, as does a multi-national corporation, suburban gardeners, inner-city gang members. Many elements of a culture are functional and hinged to individual survival: thatched roof homes from the tropics would work poorly in Canada, nor would harpoons made for catching seals be very useful in the Sahara. But other features are purely symbolic. Brides in Western culture wear white to symbolize sexual purity. Brides in Hindu weddings wear crimson, to symbolize sexual purity. Whether white or red is more pure is nothing more than a product of the long-term memory and mindset of the two cultures. And the most symbolic of cultural traditions, the one that has always been considered the bailiwick of humanity only, is language. The words "white" and "red" have an entirely arbitrary relationship to the colors themselves. They are simply code names.

Arguing about how to define culture has long been a growth industry among anthropologists. We argue about culture the way the Joint Chiefs of Staff argue about national security: as though our lives depended on it. But given that culture requires symbolism and some linguistic features, can we even talk about culture in other animals?

In 1996 I was attending a conference near Rio de Janeiro when the topic turned to culture.[1] As a biological anthropologist with a decade of field research on African great apes, I offered my perspective on the concept of culture. Chimpanzees, I said with confidence, display a rich cultural diversity. Recent years have shown that each wild chimpanzee population is more than just a gene pool. It is also a distinct culture, comprising a unique assortment of learned traditions in tool use, styles of grooming and hunting, and other features of the sort that can only be seen in the most socially sophisticated primates. Go from one forest to another and you will run into a new culture, just as walking between two human villages may introduce you to tribes who have different ways of building boats or celebrating marriages.

At least that's what I meant to say. But I had barely gotten the word "culture" past my lips when I was made to feel the full weight of my blissful ignorance. The cultural anthropologists practically leaped across the seminar table to berate me for using the words "culture" and "chimpanzee" in the same sentence. I had apparently set off a silent security alarm, and the culture-theory guards came running. How dare you, they said, use a human term like "cultural diversity" to describe what chimpanzees do? Say "behavioral variation," they demanded. "Apes are mere animals, and culture is something that only the human animal can claim. Furthermore, not only can humans alone claim culture, culture alone can explain humanity." It became clear to me that culture, as understood by most anthropologists, is a human concept, and many passionately want it to stay that way. When I asked if this was not just a semantic difference—what are cultural traditions if not learned behavioral variations?—they replied that culture is symbolic, and what animals do lacks symbolism.

When Jane Goodall first watched chimpanzees make simple stick tools to probe into termite mounds, it became clear that tool cultures are not unique to human societies. Of course many animals use tools. Sea otters on the California coast forage for abalones, which they place on their chests and hammer open with stones. Egyptian vultures use stones to break the eggs of ostriches. But these are simple, relatively inflexible lone behaviors. Only among chimpanzees do we see elaborate forms of tools made and used in variable ways, and also see distinct chimp tool cultures across Africa. In Gombe National Park in Tanzania, termite mounds of red earth rise 2 meters high and shelter millions of the almond-colored insects. Chimpanzees pore over the mounds, scratching at plugged tunnels until they find portals into the mound's interior. They will gently insert a twig or blade of grass into a tunnel until the soldier termites latch onto the tools with their powerful mandibles, then they'll withdraw the probe from the mound. With dozens of soldier and worker termites clinging ferociously to the twig, the chimpanzee draws the stick between her lips and reaps a nutritious bounty.

Less than 100 kilometers away from Gombe's termite-fishing apes is another culture. Chimpanzees in Mahale National Park live in a forest that is home to most of the same species of termites, but they practically never use sticks to eat them. If Mahale chimpanzees forage for termites at all, they use their fingers to crumble apart soil and pick out their insect snacks. However, Mahale chimpanzees love to eat ants. They climb up the straight-sided trunks of great trees and poke Gombe-like probes into holes to obtain woodboring species. As adept as Gombe chimpanzees are at fishing for termites, they practically never fish for these ants, even though both the ants and termites occur in both Gombe and Mahale.[2]

Segue 2,000 kilometers westward, to a rainforest in Côte d'Ivoire. In a forest filled with twigs, chimpanzees do not use stick tools. Instead, chimpanzees in Taï National Park and other forests in western Africa use hammers made of rock and wood. Swiss primatologists Christophe and Hedwige Boesch and their colleagues first reported the use of stone tools by chimpanzees twenty years ago.[3] Their subsequent research showed that Taï chimpanzees collect hammers when certain species of nut-bearing trees are in fruit. These hammers are not modified in any way as the stone tools made by early humans were; they are hefted, however, and appraised for weight and smashing value before being carried back to the nut tree. A nut is carefully positioned in a depression in the tree's aboveground root buttresses (the anvil) and struck with precision by the tool-user. The researchers have seen mothers instructing their children on the art of tool use, by assisting them in placing the nut in the anvil in the proper way.

So chimpanzees in East Africa use termite- and ant-fishing tools, and West African counterparts use hammers, but not vice versa. These are subsistence tools; they were almost certainly invented for food-getting. Primatologist William McGrew of Miami University of Ohio has compared the tool technologies of wild chimpanzees with those of traditional human hunter-gatherer societies. He found that in at least some instances, the gap between chimpanzee technology and human technology is not wide. The now-extinct aboriginal Tasmanians, for example, possessed no complex tools or weapons of any kind. Though they are an extreme example, the Tasmanians illustrate that human culture need not be technologically complex.[4]

As McGrew first pointed out, there are three likeliest explanations for the differences we see among the chimpanzee tool

industries across Africa.[5] The first is genetic: perhaps there are mutations that arise in one population but not others that govern tool making. This seems extremely unlikely, just as we would never argue that Hindu brides wear red while Western brides wear white due to a genetic difference between Indians and Westerners. The second explanation is ecological: maybe the environment in which the chimpanzee population lives dictates patterns of tool use. Maybe termite-fishing sticks will be invented in places where there are termites and sticks but not rocks and nuts, and hammers invented in the opposite situation. But a consideration of each habitat raises doubts. Gombe is a rugged, rock-strewn place where it is hard to find a spot to sit that is not within arm's reach of a few stones, but Gombe chimpanzees do not use stone tools. The West African chimpanzees who use stone tools live, by contrast, in lowland rainforests that are nearly devoid of rocks. Yet they purposely forage to find them. The tool-use pattern is exactly the opposite of what we would expect if environment and local availability accounted for differences among chimpanzee communities in tool use.

British psychologist Andrew Whiten and his colleagues recently conducted the first systematic survey of cultural differences in tool use among the seven longest-term field studies, representing more than a century and a half of total observation time. They found thirty-nine behaviors that could not be explained by environmental factors at the various sites.[6] Alone with humans in the richness of their behavior repertoire, chimpanzee cultures show variations that can only be ascribed to learned traditions. These traditions, passed from one generation to the next through observation and imitation, are a simple version of human culture.

But wait. I said earlier that human culture must have a symbolic element. Tools that differ in form and function, from sticks to hammers to sponges made of crushed leaves, are all utterly utilitarian. They tell us much about the environment in which they are useful but little about the learned traditions that led to their creation. Human artifacts, on the other hand, nearly always contain some purely symbolic element, be it the designs carved into a piece of ancient pottery or the "Stanley" logo on my new claw hammer. Is there anything truly symbolic in chimpanzee culture, in the human sense of an object or behavior that is completely detached from its use?

Male chimpanzees have various ways of indicating to a female that they would like to mate. At Gombe, one such courtship behavior involves rapidly shaking a small bush or branch several times, after which a female in proximity will usually approach the male and present her swelling to him. But in Mahale, males have learned to use leaves in their courtship gesture. A male plucks a leafy stem from a nearby plant and noisily uses his teeth and fingers to tear off its leaves. Leaf-clipping is done mainly in the context of wanting to mate with a particular female, and appears to function as a purely symbolic signal of sexual desire (it could also be a gesture of frustration). A second leafy symbol is leaf-grooming. Chimpanzees pick leaves and intently groom them with their fingers, as seriously as though they were grooming another chimpanzee. And this may be the function; leaf-grooming may signal a desire for real grooming from a social partner. Since the signal for grooming involves grooming, albeit of another object, this gesture is not symbolic in the sense that leaf-clipping is. But its distribution across Africa is equally spotty; leaf-grooming is commonly practiced in East African chimpanzee cultures but is largely absent in western Africa.[7]

These two cases of potentially symbolic behavior may not seem very impressive. After all, the briefest consideration of human culture turns up a rich array of symbolism, from language to the arts. But are all human cultures highly symbolic? If we use language and other forms of symbolic expression as the criterion for culture, then how about a classroom full of two-year-old toddlers in a day care center? They communicate by a very simple combination of gestures and half-formed sentences. Toddlers have little symbolic communication or appreciation for art and are very little different from chimpanzees in their cultural output. We grant them human qualities because we know they will mature into symbol-using, linguistically expert adults, leaving chimpanzees in the dust. But this is no reason to consider them on a different plane from the apes when both are fifteen months old.

Chimpanzee societies are based on learned traditions passed from mother to child and from adult males to eager wannabe males. These traditions vary from place to place. This is culture. Culture is not limited, however, to those few apes that are genetically 99 percent human. Many primates show traditions. These are usually innovations by younger members of a group, which sweep rapidly through the society and leave it just slightly different than before. Japanese primatologists have long observed such traditions among the macaques native to their island nation. Researchers long ago noticed that a new behavior had arisen in one population of Japanese macaque monkeys living on Koshima Island just offshore the mainland. The monkeys were regularly tossed sweet potatoes, rice and other local treats by the locals. One day Imo, a young female in the group, took her potato and carried it to the sea, where she washed it with salty brine before eating it. This behavior rapidly spread throughout the group, a nice example of innovation happening in real time so that researchers could observe the diffusion. Later, other monkeys invented the practice of scooping up rice offered them with the beach sand it was scattered on, throwing both onto the surf and then scraping up the grains that floated while the sand sank.

At a supremely larger scale, such innovations are what human cultural differences are all about. Of course, only in human cultures do objects such as sweet potatoes take on the kind of symbolic meaning that permits them to stand for other objects and thus become a currency. Chimpanzees lack the top-drawer cognitive capacity needed to invent such a currency. Or do they? Wild chimpanzees hunt for a part of their living. All across equatorial Africa, meat-eating is a regular feature of chimpanzee life, but its style and technique vary from one forest to another. In Taï National Park in western Africa, hunters are highly cooperative; Christophe Boesch has reported specific roles such as ambushers and drivers as part of the apes' effort to corral colobus monkeys in the forest canopy.[8] At Gombe in East Africa, meanwhile, hunting is like a baseball game; a group sport performed on an individual

basis. This difference may be environmentally influenced; perhaps the high canopy rain forest at Taï requires cooperation more than the broken, low canopy forest at Gombe. There is a culture of hunting in each forest as well, in which young and eager male wannabes copy the predatory skills of their elders. At Gombe, for instance, chimpanzees relish wild pigs and piglets in addition to monkeys and small antelope. At Taï, wild pigs are ignored even when they stroll in front of a hunting party.

There is also a culture of sharing the kill. Sharing of meat is highly nepotistic at Gombe; sons who make the kill share with their mothers and brothers but snub rival males. They also share preferentially with females who have sexual swellings, and with high-ranking females. At Taï, the captor shares with the other members of the hunting party whether or not they are allies or relatives; a system of reciprocity seems to be in place in which the golden rule works. I have argued that since the energy and time that chimpanzees spend hunting is rarely paid back by the calories, protein and fat gotten from a kill, we should consider hunting a social behavior done at least partly for its own sake.[9] When chimpanzees barter a limited commodity such as meat for other services—alliances, sex, grooming—they are engaging in a very simple and primitive form of a currency exchange. Such an exchange relies on the ability of the participants to remember the web of credits and debts owed one another and to act accordingly. It may be that the two chimpanzee cultures 2,000 kilometers apart have developed their distinct uses of meat as a social currency. In one place meat is used as a reward for cooperation, in the other as a manipulative tool of nepotism. Such systems are commonplace in all human societies, and their roots may be seen in chimpanzees' market economy, too.[10]

I have not yet considered one obvious question. If tool use and other cultural innovations can be so valuable to chimpanzees, why have they not arisen more widely among primates and other big-brained animals? Although chimpanzees are adept tool-users, their very close relatives the bonobos are not. Bonobos do a number of very clever things—dragging their hands beside them as they wade through streams to catch fish is one notable example—but they are not accomplished technicians. Gorillas don't use tools at all, and orangutans have only recently been observed to occasionally use sticks as probing tools in their rainforest canopy world.[11]

Other big-brained animals fare even worse. Wild elephants don't use their wonderfully dexterous trunks to manipulate tools in any major way, although when you're strong enough to uproot trees you may not have much use for a pokey little probe. Dolphins and whales, cognitively gifted though they may be, lack the essential anatomical ingredient for tool manufacture—a pair of nimble hands. Wild bottlenose dolphins have been observed to carry natural sponges about on their snouts to ferret food from the sea bottom, the only known form of cetacean tool use.[12] But that may be the limit of how much a creature that lacks any grasping appendages can manipulate its surroundings.

So to be a cultural animal, it is not enough to be big-brained. You must have the anatomical prerequisites for tool cultures to develop. Even if these are in place, there is no guarantee that a species will generate a subsistence culture in the form of tools. Perhaps environmental necessity dictates which ape species use tools and which don't, except it is hard to imagine that bonobos have much less use for tools than chimpanzees do. There is probably a strong element of chance involved. The chance that a cultural tradition—tool use, hunting style or grooming technique—will develop may be very small in any given century or millennium. Once innovated, the chance that the cultural trait will disappear—perhaps due to the death of the main practitioners from whom everyone learned the behavior—may conversely be great. Instead of a close fit between the environment and the cultural traditions that evolve in it—which many scholars believe explains cultural diversity in human societies—the roots of cultural variation may be much more random. A single influential individual who figures out how to make a better mousetrap, so to speak, can through imitation spread his mousetrap through the group and slowly into other groups.

We tend to think of cultural traditions as highly plastic and unstable compared to biological innovation. It takes hundreds of generations for natural selection to bring about biological change, whereas cultural change can happen in one lifetime, even in a few minutes. Because we live in a culture in which we buy the newest cell phone and the niftiest handheld computer—we fail to appreciate how conservative traditions like tool use can be. *Homo erectus,* with a brain nearly the size of our own, invented a teardrop-shaped stone tool called a hand axe 1.5 million years ago. It was presumably used for butchering carcasses, though some archaeologists think it may have also been a weapon. Whatever its purpose, more than a million years later those same stone axes were still being manufactured and used. Fifty thousand generations passed without a significant change in the major piece of material culture in a very big-brained and intelligent human species. *That's* conservatism and it offers us two lessons. First, if it ain't broke don't fix it: when a traditional way of making a tool works and the environment is not throwing any curves your way, there may be no pressure for a change. Second, we see a human species vastly more intelligent than an ape (*Homo erectus'* neocortical brain volume was a third smaller than a modern human's, but two and a half times larger than a chimpanzee's) whose technology didn't change at all. This tells us that innovations, once made, may last a very long time without being either extinguished or improved upon. It suggests that chimpanzee tool cultures may have been in place for all of the 5 million years since their divergence from our shared ancestor.

The very word *culture,* as William McGrew has pointed out, was invented for humans, and this has long blinded cultural theorists to a more expansive appreciation of the concept. Whether apes have culture or not is not really the issue. The heart of the debate is whether scholars who study culture and consider it their intellectual territory will accept a more expansive definition. In purely academic arguments like this one, the power lies with the party who owns the key concepts of the discipline. They define concepts however they choose, and the choice is usually aimed at fencing off their intellectual turf from all others.

Primatologists are latecomers to the table of culture, and they have had to wait their turn before being allowed to sit. We should be most interested in what the continuum of intelligence tells us about the roots of human behavior, not whether what apes do or don't do fits any particular, rigid definition of culture. When it comes to human practices, from building boats to weddings to choosing mates, we should look at the intersections of our biology and our culture for clues about what has made us who we are.

Notes

1. *Changing Views of Primate Societies: The Role of Gender and Nationality,* June 1996, sponsored by the Wenner-Gren Foundation for Anthropological Research.

2. For an enlightening discussion of cross-cultural differences in chimpanzee tool use, see almost anything William McGrew has written, but especially McGrew (1992).

3. See Boesch and Boesch (1989).

4. Again, see McGrew (1992).

5. McGrew (1979).

6. Whiten *et al.* (1999) combined data from seven long-term chimpanzees studies to produce the most systematic examination of cultural variation in these apes.

7. For further discussion of chimpanzee symbolic behavior in the wild, see Goodall (1986), Wrangham *et al.* (1994), and McGrew et al. (1996).

8. See Boesch and Boesch (1989).

9. See Stanford (1999, 2001).

10. See de Waal (1996) and Stanford (2001).

11. For the first report of systematic tool use by wild orangutans, see van Schaik *et al.* (1996).

12. See Smolker *et al.* (1997).

Critical Thinking

1. Be aware of the fact that a culture may consist of a suite of traditions and it may be simple, symbolic, or even arbitrary, as with language.

2. What were the cultural anthropologists' objections to the author's use of culture to describe chimpanzee behavior?

3. How does the author distinguish chimpanzee tool behavior from that of otters and Egyptian vultures?

4. What is the difference between Gombe chimps and Mahale chimps with regard to tool use and ant/termite eating?

5. What kinds of tools do the Taï chimps use and for what purpose? What kind of instruction is involved?

6. Why does McGrew conclude that, at least in some instances, the gap between chimpanzee technology and human technology is not wide?

7. How does the author assess the three likeliest explanations for the differences among chimpanzee tool industries across Africa in light of the evidence?

8. Do other primates show traditions that vary from place to place? How do the Japanese macaques serve as an example?

9. How does hunting and meat sharing vary among chimps? In what sense do they engage in a form of currency exchange?

10. Why does the author think that chimpanzee tool cultures may have existed for all the 5 million years since our shared ancestry?

11. What is really the issue, according to the author? In what should we be most interested?

Create Central

www.mhhe.com/createcentral

Internet References

Great Ape Survival Project: United Nations
www.unep.org/grasp/ABOUT_GRASP/index.asp

National Primate Research Center
http://pin.primate.wisc.edu/factsheets

Article   Prepared by Elvio Angeloni, *Pasadena City College*

Dim Forest, Bright Chimps

In the rain forest of Ivory Coast, chimpanzees meet the challenge of life by hunting cooperatively and using crude tools.

CHRISTOPHE BOESCH AND HEDWIGE BOESCH-ACHERMANN

Learning Outcomes

After reading this article, you will be able to:

- Discuss the implications of tool use, social hunting, and food sharing by the Ivory Coast chimpanzees for human evolution.

- Discuss the environmental circumstances that may have caused the common ancestor of apes and humans to divergence into two separate evolutionary paths.

Taï National Park, Ivory Coast, December 3, 1985. Drumming, barking, and screaming, chimps rush through the undergrowth, little more than black shadows. Their goal is to join a group of other chimps noisily clustering around Brutus, the dominant male of this seventy-member chimpanzee community. For a few moments, Brutus, proud and self-confident, stands fairly still, holding a shocked, barely moving red colobus monkey in his hand. Then he begins to move through the group, followed closely by his favorite females and most of the adult males. He seems to savor this moment of uncontested superiority, the culmination of a hunt high up in the canopy. But the victory is not his alone. Cooperation is essential to capturing one of these monkeys, and Brutus will break apart and share this highly prized delicacy with most of the main participants of the hunt and with the females. Recipients of large portions will, in turn, share more or less generously with their offspring, relatives, and friends.

In 1979, we began a long-term study of the previously unknown chimpanzees of Taï National Park, 1,600 square miles of tropical rain forest in the Republic of the Ivory Coast (Côte d'Ivoire). Early on, we were most interested in the chimps' use of natural hammers—branches and stones—to crack open the five species of hard-shelled nuts that are abundant here. A sea otter lying on its back, cracking an abalone shell with a rock, is a familiar picture, but no primate had ever before been observed in the wild using stones as hammers. East Africa's savanna chimps, studied for decades by Jane Goodall in Gombe, Tanzania, use twigs to extract ants and termites from their nests or honey from a bees' nest, but they have never been seen using hammerstones.

As our work progressed, we were surprised by the many ways in which the life of the Taï forest chimpanzees differs from that of their savanna counterparts, and as evidence accumulated, differences in how the two populations hunt proved the most intriguing. Jane Goodall had found that chimpanzees hunt monkeys, antelope, and wild pigs, findings confirmed by Japanese biologist Toshida Nishida, who conducted a long-term study 120 miles south of Gombe, in the Mahale Mountains. So we were not surprised to discover that the Taï chimps eat meat. What intrigued us was the degree to which they hunt cooperatively. In 1953 Raymond Dart proposed that group hunting and cooperation were key ingredients in the evolution of *Homo sapiens*. The argument has been modified considerably since Dart first put it forward, and group hunting has also been observed in some social carnivores (lions and African wild dogs, for instance), and even some birds of prey. Nevertheless, many anthropologists still hold that hunting cooperatively and sharing food played a central role in the drama that enabled early hominids, some 1.8 million years ago, to develop the social systems that are so typically human.

We hoped that what we learned about the behavior of forest chimpanzees would shed new light on prevailing theories of human evolution. Before we could even begin, however, we had to habituate a community of chimps to our presence. Five long years passed before we were able to move with them on their daily trips through the forest, of which "our" group appeared to claim some twelve square miles. Chimpanzees are alert and shy animals, and the limited field of view in the rain forest—about sixty-five feet at best—made finding them more difficult. We had to rely on sound, mostly their vocalizations and drumming on trees. Males often drum regularly while moving through the forest: pant-hooting, they draw near a big buttress tree; then, at full speed they fly over the buttress, hitting it repeatedly with their hands and feet. Such drumming may resound more than half a mile in the forest. In the beginning, our ignorance about how they moved and who was drumming led to failure more often than not, but eventually we learned that the dominant males drummed during the day to let other group members know the direction of travel. On some days, however, intermittent drumming about dawn was the only signal for the whole day. If we were out of earshot at the time, we were often reduced to guessing.

During these difficult early days, one feature of the chimps' routine proved to be our salvation: nut cracking is a noisy business. So noisy, in fact, that in the early days of French colonial rule, one officer apparently even proposed the theory that some unknown tribe was forging iron in the impenetrable and dangerous jungle.

Guided by the sounds made by the chimps as they cracked open nuts, which they often did for hours at a time, we were gradually able to get within sixty feet of the animals. We still seldom saw the chimps themselves (they fled if we came too close), but even so, the evidence left after a session of nut cracking taught us a great deal about what types of nuts they were eating, what sorts of hammer and anvil tools they were using, and—thanks to the very distinctive noise a nut makes when it finally splits open—how many hits were needed to crack a nut and how many nuts could be opened per minute.

After some months, we began catching glimpses of the chimpanzees before they fled, and after a little more time, we were able to draw close enough to watch them at work. The chimps gather nuts from the ground. Some nuts are tougher to crack than others. Nuts of the *Panda oleosa* tree are the most demanding, harder than any of the foods processed by present-day hunter-gatherers and breaking open only when a force of 3,500 pounds is applied. The stone hammers used by the Taï chimps range from stones of ten ounces to granite blocks of four to forty-five pounds. Stones of any size, however, are a rarity in the forest and are seldom conveniently placed near a nut-bearing tree. By observing closely, and in some cases imitating the way the chimps handle hammerstones, we learned that they have an impressive ability to find just the right tool for the job at hand. Taï chimps could remember the positions of many of the stones scattered, often out of sight, around a panda tree. Without having to run around rechecking the stones, they would select one of appropriate size that was closest to the tree. These mental abilities in spatial representation compare with some of those of nine-year-old humans.

To extract the four kernels from inside a panda nut, a chimp must use a hammer with extreme precision. Time and time again, we have been impressed to see a chimpanzee raise a twenty-pound stone above its head, strike a nut with ten or more powerful blows, and then, using the same hammer, switch to delicate little taps from a height of only four inches. To finish the job, the chimps often break off a small piece of twig and use it to extract the last tiny fragments of kernel from the shell. Intriguingly, females crack panda nuts more often than males, a gender difference in tool use that seems to be more pronounced in the forest chimps than in their savanna counterparts.

After five years of fieldwork, we were finally able to follow the chimpanzees at close range, and gradually, we gained insights into their way of hunting. One morning, for example, we followed a group of six male chimps on a three-hour patrol that had taken them into foreign territory to the north. (Our study group is one of five chimpanzee groups more or less evenly distributed in the Taï forest.) As always during these approximately monthly incursions, which seem

to be for the purpose of territorial defense, the chimps were totally silent, clearly on edge and on the lookout for trouble. Once the patrol was over, however, and they were back within their own borders, the chimps shifted their attention to hunting. They were after monkeys, the most abundant mammals in the forest. Traveling in large, multi-species groups, some of the forest's ten species of monkeys are more apt than others to wind up as a meal for the chimps. The relatively sluggish and large (almost thirty pounds) red colobus monkeys are the chimps' usual fare. (Antelope also live in the forest, but in our ten years at Taï, we have never seen a chimp catch, or even pursue, one. In contrast, Gombe chimps at times do come across fawns, and when they do, they seize the opportunity—and the fawn.)

The six males moved on silently, peering up into the vegetation and stopping from time to time to listen for the sound of monkeys. None fed or groomed; all focused on the hunt. We followed one old male, Falstaff, closely, for he tolerates us completely and is one of the keenest and most experienced hunters. Even from the rear, Falstaff set the pace; whenever he stopped, the others paused to wait for him. After thirty minutes, we heard the unmistakable noises of monkeys jumping from branch to branch. Silently, the chimps turned in the direction of the sounds, scanning the canopy. Just then, a diana monkey spotted them and gave an alarm call. Dianas are very alert and fast; they are also about half the weight of colobus monkeys. The chimps quickly gave up and continued their search for easier, meatier prey.

Shortly after, we heard the characteristic cough of a red colobus monkey. Suddenly Rousseau and Macho, two twenty-year-olds, burst into action, running toward the cough. Falstaff seemed surprised by their precipitousness, but after a moment's hesitation, he also ran. Now the hunting barks of the chimps mixed with the sharp alarm calls of the monkeys. Hurrying behind Falstaff, we saw him climb up a conveniently situated tree. His position, combined with those of Schubert and Ulysse, two mature chimps in their prime, effectively blocked off three of the monkeys' possible escape routes. But in another tree, nowhere near any escape route and thus useless, waited the last of the hunters, Kendo, eighteen years old and the least experienced of the group. The monkeys, taking advantage of Falstaff's delay and Kendo's error, escaped.

The six males moved on and within five minutes picked up the sounds of another group of red colobus. This time, the chimps approached cautiously, nobody hurrying. They screened the canopy intently to locate the monkeys, which were still unaware of the approaching danger. Macho and Schubert chose two adjacent trees, both full of monkeys, and started climbing very quietly, taking care not to move any branches. Meanwhile, the other four chimps blocked off anticipated escape routes. When Schubert was halfway up, the monkeys finally detected the two chimps. As we watched the colobus monkeys take off in literal panic, the appropriateness of the chimpanzees' scientific name—*Pan* came to mind: with a certain stretch of the imagination, the fleeing monkeys could be shepherds and shepherdesses frightened at the sudden appearance of Pan, the wild Greek god of the woods, shepherds, and their flocks.

Taking off in the expected direction, the monkeys were trailed by Macho and Schubert. The chimps let go with loud hunting barks. Trying to escape, two colobus monkeys jumped into smaller trees lower in the canopy. With this, Rousseau and Kendo, who had been watching from the ground, sped up into the trees and tried to grab them. Only a third of the weight of the chimps, however, the monkeys managed to make it to the next tree along branches too small for their pursuers. But Falstaff had anticipated this move and was waiting for them. In the following confusion, Falstaff seized a juvenile and killed it with a bite to the neck. As the chimps met in a rush on the ground, Falstaff began to eat, sharing with Schubert and Rousseau. A juvenile colobus does not provide much meat, however, and this time, not all the chimps got a share. Frustrated individuals soon started off on another hunt, and relative calm returned fairly quickly: this sort of hunt, by a small band of chimps acting on their own at the edge of their territory, does not generate the kind of high excitement that prevails when more members of the community are involved.

So far we have observed some 200 monkey hunts and have concluded that success requires a minimum of three motivated hunters acting cooperatively. Alone or in pairs, chimps succeed less than 15 percent of the time, but when three or four act as a group, more than half the hunts result in a kill. The chimps seem well aware of the odds; 92 percent of all the hunts we observed were group affairs.

Gombe chimps also hunt red colobus monkeys, but the percentage of group hunts is much lower: only 36 percent. In addition, we learned from Jane Goodall that even when Gombe chimps do hunt in groups, their strategies are different. When Taï chimps arrive under a group of monkeys, the hunters scatter, often silently, usually out of sight of one another but each aware of the others' positions. As the hunt progresses, they gradually close in, encircling the quarry. Such movements require that each chimp coordinate his movements with those of the other hunters, as well as with those of the prey, at all times.

Coordinated hunts account for 63 percent of all those observed at Taï but only 7 percent of those at Gombe. Jane Goodall says that in a Gombe group hunt, the chimpanzees typically travel together until they arrive at a tree with monkeys. Then, as the chimps begin climbing nearby trees, they scatter as each pursues a different target. Goodall gained the impression that Gombe chimps boost their success by hunting independently but simultaneously, thereby disorganizing their prey; our impression is that the Taï chimps owe their success to being organized themselves.

Just why the Gombe and Taï chimps have developed such different hunting strategies is difficult to explain, and we plan to spend some time at Gombe in the hope of finding out. In the meantime, the mere existence of differences is interesting enough and may perhaps force changes in our understanding of human evolution. Most currently accepted theories propose that some three million years ago, a dramatic climate change in Africa east of the Rift Valley turned dense forest into open, drier habitat. Adapting to the difficulties of life under these new conditions, our ancestors supposedly evolved into cooperative hunters and began sharing food they caught. Supporters of this idea point out that plant and animal remains indicative of dry, open environments have been found at all early hominid excavation sites in Tanzania, Kenya, South Africa, and Ethiopia. That the large majority of apes in Africa today live west of the Rift Valley appears to many anthropologists to lend further support to the idea that a change in environment caused the common ancestor of apes and humans to evolve along a different line from those remaining in the forest.

Our observations, however, suggest quite another line of thought. Life in dense, dim forest may require more sophisticated behavior than is commonly assumed: compared with their savanna relatives, Taï chimps show greater complexity in both hunting and tool use. Taï chimps use tools in nineteen different ways and have six different ways of making them, compared with sixteen uses and three methods of manufacture at Gombe.

Anthropologist colleagues of mine have told me that the discovery that some chimpanzees are accomplished users of hammerstones forces them to look with a fresh eye at stone tools turned up at excavation sites. The important role played by female Taï chimps in tool use also raises the possibility that in the course of human evolution, women may have been decisive in the development of many of the sophisticated manipulative skills characteristic of our species. Taï mothers also appear to pass on their skills by actively teaching their offspring. We have observed mothers providing their young with hammers and then stepping in to help when the inexperienced youngsters encounter difficulty. This help may include carefully showing how to position the nut or hold the hammer properly. Such behavior has never been observed at Gombe.

Similarly, food sharing, for a long time said to be unique to humans, seems more general in forest than in savanna chimpanzees. Taï chimp mothers share with their young up to 60 percent of the nuts they open, at least until the latter become sufficiently adept, generally at about six years old. They also share other foods acquired with tools, including honey, ants, and bone marrow. Gombe mothers share such foods much less often, even with their infants. Taï chimps also share meat more frequently than do their Gombe relatives, sometimes dividing a chunk up and giving portions away, sometimes simply allowing beggars to grab pieces.

Any comparison between chimpanzees and our hominid ancestors can only be suggestive, not definitive. But our studies lead us to believe that the process of hominization may have begun independently of the drying of the environment. Savanna life could even have delayed the process; many anthropologists have been struck by how slowly hominid-associated remains, such as the hand ax, changed after their first appearance in the Olduvai age.

Will we have the time to discover more about the hunting strategies or other, perhaps as yet undiscovered abilities of these forest chimpanzees? Africa's tropical rain forests, and their inhabitants, are threatened with extinction by extensive logging, largely to provide the Western world with tropical timber and such products as coffee, cocoa, and rubber. Ivory Coast has lost 90 percent of its original forest, and less than 5 percent of the remainder can be considered pristine. The climate has changed dramatically. The harmattan, a cold, dry wind from the Sahara previously unknown in the forest, has now swept through the Taï forest every year since 1986. Rainfall has diminished; all the rivulets in our study region are now dry for several months of the year.

In addition, the chimpanzee, biologically very close to humans, is in demand for research on AIDS and hepatitis vaccines. Captive-bred chimps are available, but they cost about twenty times more than wild-caught animals. Chimps taken from the wild for these purposes are generally young, their mothers having been shot during capture. For every chimp arriving at its sad destination, nine others may well have died in the forest or on the way. Such priorities—cheap coffee and cocoa and chimpanzees—do not do the economies of Third World countries any good in the long run, and they bring suffering and death to innocent victims in the forest. Our hope is that Brutus, Falstaff, and their families will survive, and that we and others will have the opportunity to learn about them well into the future. But there is no denying that modern times work against them and us.

Critical Thinking

1. To what extent does cooperation and sharing of food exist among the Ivory Coast chimpanzees?

2. What were the researchers interested in at first? What was unique about it? What did they find that was not surprising? What was surprising?

3. What is the purpose of drumming?

4. How do the authors describe the chimps' mental abilities with regard to hammerstones? What manual skills are required? In what respect is there a gender difference in tool use?

5. What is the purpose of the "patrol" into foreign territories?

6. What is their favorite hunting target and why?

7. Describe the hunting strategies. What is the minimum number for success? In what ways do these chimps contrast with the Gombe chimps and what is the partial explanation given?

8. How did chimps and humans diverge, according to most currently accepted theories?

9. How do comparisons between forest-dwelling chimps and the savanna-dwelling Gombe chimps lead the authors to different conclusions from the above? (Include in this the important role of females in tool use and food sharing.)

10. In what ways are chimpanzee populations threatened?

Create Central

www.mhhe.com/createcentral

Internet References

Great Ape Survival Project: United Nations
    www.unep.org/grasp/ABOUT_GRASP/index.asp
Jane Goodall Institute for Wildlife Research, Education, and Conservation
    www.janegoodall.org

Article Prepared by: Elvio Angeloni, *Pasadena City College*

Earthly Delights

Is man only a blunder of God? Or is God only a blunder of man?

—Friedrich Nietzsche[1]

FRANS DE WAAL

Learning Outcomes

After reading this article, you will be able to:

- Discuss the existence of animal empathy.
- Discuss whether human morality derives from science, religion, or our basic nature.

I was born in Den Bosch, the Dutch city after which Hieronymus Bosch named himself.[2] This doesn't make me an expert on the painter, but having grown up with his statue on the market square, I have always been fond of his surrealist imagery, his symbolism, and how it relates to humanity's place in the universe under a waning influence of God.

His famous triptych in which naked figures frolic around, *The Garden of Earthly Delights,* is a tribute to paradisiacal innocence. The middle tableau is far too happy and relaxed to fit the interpretation of depravity and sin advanced by puritan experts. It shows humanity free from guilt and shame either before the Fall or without any Fall at all. For a primatologist like myself, the nudity, the allusions to sex and fertility, the plentiful birds and fruits, and the moving about in groups are thoroughly familiar, and hardly in need of a religious or moral interpretation. Bosch seems to have depicted us in our natural state, while reserving his moralistic outlook for the right-hand panel, in which he punishes not the frolickers from the middle panel but monks, nuns, gluttons, gamblers, warriors, and drunkards. Bosch was no fan of the clergy and their avarice, which explains a small detail in which a man resists signing his fortune away to a pig veiled like a Dominican nun. The poor figure is said to be the painter himself.

Five centuries later, we remain embroiled in debates about the place of religion in society. As in Bosch's day, the central theme is morality. Can we envision a world without God? Would this world be good? Don't think for one moment that the current battle lines between fundamentalist Christianity and science are determined by evidence. One has to be pretty immune to data to doubt evolution, which is why books and documentaries aimed at convincing the skeptics are a waste of effort.

They are helpful for those prepared to listen, but fail to reach their target audience. The debate is less about the truth than about how to handle it. For those who believe that morality comes straight from God the creator, acceptance of evolution would open a moral abyss. Listen to the Reverend Al Sharpton debating the late atheist firebrand Christopher Hitchens: "If there is no order to the universe, and therefore some being, some force that ordered it, then who determines what is right or wrong? There is nothing immoral if there's nothing in charge."[3] Similarly, I have heard people echo Dostoevsky's Ivan Karamazov, exclaiming, "If there is no God, I am free to rape my neighbor!"

Perhaps it's just me, but I am wary of any persons whose belief system is the only thing standing between them and repulsive behavior. Why not assume that our humanity, including the self-control needed for a livable society, is built into us? Does anyone truly believe that our ancestors lacked social norms before they had religion? Did they never assist others in need, or complain about an unfair deal? Humans must have worried about the functioning of their communities well before current religions arose, which occurred only a couple of millennia ago. Biologists are unimpressed by that kind of timescale.

The Dalai Lama's Turtle

The above introduced a blog entitled *Morals without God?* on the *New York Times'* website, in which I argued that morality antedates religion and that much can be learned about its origin by considering our fellow primates.[4] Contrary to the customary blood-soaked view of nature, animals are not devoid of tendencies that we morally approve of, which to me suggests that morality is not as much of a human innovation as we like to think.

This being the topic of the present book, let me lay out its themes by describing the week that followed my blog's publication, including a trip to Europe. Right before this, however, I attended a meeting between science and religion at Emory University, in Atlanta, where I work. The occasion was a forum with the Dalai Lama on his favorite theme: compassion. Being compassionate seems to me an excellent recommendation for life; hence I welcomed the message of our honorable guest. As the first discussant, I was seated next to him surrounded by a sea of red and yellow chrysanthemums. I had been instructed to address him as "your holiness," but to speak of him to others as "his holiness," which I found sufficiently confusing that I avoided all forms of address. One of the most admired men on the planet dropped his shoes and folded his legs under him in his chair, put on a huge baseball cap color-matched to his orange robe, while an audience of over three thousand people hung on his every word. Before my presentation, I had been appropriately deflated by the organizers' reminding me that no one had come to hear me speak, and that all those people were there only for his pearls of wisdom.

In my remarks, I reviewed the latest evidence for animal altruism. For example, apes will voluntarily open a door to offer a companion access to food, even if they lose part of it in the process. And capuchin monkeys are prepared to seek rewards for others, as we see when we place two of them side by side, while one of them barters with us with differently colored tokens. One token rewards only the monkey itself, whereas the other rewards both monkeys. Soon, the monkeys prefer the "prosocial" token. This is not out of fear, because dominant monkeys (who have least to fear) are in fact the most generous.

Good deeds also occur spontaneously. An old female, Peony, spends her days outdoors with other chimpanzees at the Yerkes Primate Center's field station. On bad days, when her arthritis is flaring up, she has trouble walking and climbing, but other females help her out. Peony may be huffing and puffing to get up into the climbing frame in which several apes have gathered for a grooming session. But an unrelated younger female moves behind her, placing both hands on her ample behind to push her up with quite a bit of effort, until Peony has joined the rest.

We have also seen Peony get up and slowly move toward the water spigot, which is at quite a distance. Younger females sometimes run ahead of her, take in some water, then return to Peony and give it to her. At first, we had no idea what was going on, since all we saw was one female placing her mouth close to Peony's, but after a while the pattern became clear: Peony would open her mouth wide, and the younger female would spit a jet of water into it.

Such observations fit the emerging field of animal empathy, which deals not only with primates but also with canines, elephants, and even rodents. A typical example is how chimpanzees console distressed parties, hugging and kissing them, which is so predictable that we have documented literally thousands of cases. Mammals are sensitive to each other's emotions and react to those in need. The whole reason people fill their homes with furry carnivores, and not with, say, iguanas and turtles, is that mammals offer something no reptile ever will. They give affection, they want affection, and they respond to our emotions the way we do to theirs.

Up to this point, the Dalai Lama had listened attentively, but now he lifted his cap to interrupt me. He wanted to hear more about turtles. These animals are a favorite of his, because they supposedly carry the world on their backs. The Buddhist leader wondered whether turtles, too, know empathy. He described how the female sea turtle crawls onto land to look for the best spot to lay her eggs, thus showing concern for future young. How would the mother behave if she ever encountered her offspring?

the Dalai Lama wondered. To me, the process suggests that turtles have been preprogrammed to seek out the best environment for incubation. The turtle digs a hole in the sand above the tide line, deposits her eggs and covers them, packing the sand tight with her rear flippers, and then leaves the nest behind. The hatchlings emerge a few months later to rush to the ocean under the moonlight. They never get to know their mother.

Empathy requires awareness of the other and sensitivity to the other's needs. It probably started with parental care, like that found in the mammals, but there is also evidence for bird empathy. I once visited the Konrad Lorenz Research Station, in Grünau, Austria, which keeps ravens in large aviaries. These are impressive birds, especially when they sit on your shoulder with their powerful black beak right next to your face! It brought back memories of the tame jackdaws I had kept as a student: much smaller birds from the same corvid (crow) family. In Grünau, scientists follow spontaneous fights among the ravens and have seen bystanders respond to distress. Losers can count on some cozy preening or beak-to-beak nudging from their friends. At the same station, free-ranging descendants of Lorenz's flock of geese have been equipped with transmitters to measure their heart rate. Since every adult goose has a mate, that offers a window on empathy. If one bird confronts another in a fight, its partner's heart starts racing. Even if the partner is in no way involved, its heart betrays concern about the quarrel. Birds, too, feel each other's pain.

If both birds and mammals have some measure of empathy, that capacity probably goes back to their reptilian ancestors. Not just any reptiles, though, because most lack parental care. One of the surest signs of a caring attitude, according to Paul MacLean, the American neuroscientist who named the limbic system the seat of the emotions, is the "lost call" of young animals. Young monkeys do it all the time: left behind by mom, they call until she returns. They look miserable, sitting all alone on a tree limb, giving a long string of plaintive "coo" calls with pouted lips directed at no one in particular. MacLean noted the absence of the "lost call" in most reptiles, such as snakes, lizards, and turtles.

In a few reptiles, however, the young do call when upset or in danger, so that mom will take care of them. Have you ever held a baby alligator? Be careful, because they have a good set of teeth, but they also utter throaty barks when upset, which may bring the cow (mother) flying out of the water. That will teach you to doubt reptilian feelings!

I mentioned this to the Dalai Lama, saying that we expect empathy only in animals with attachments, and that few reptiles qualify. I am not sure this satisfied him, because of course he wanted to know about turtles, which look so much cuter than those ferocious toothy monsters of the Crocodilian family. Appearances are deceptive, though. Some members of this family gently transport their young in their big jaws or on their backs and defend them against danger. They sometimes even let them snatch pieces of meat from their mouth. The dinosaurs, too, cared for their young, and plesiosaurs—giant marine reptiles—may even have been viviparous, giving birth to a single live offspring in the water, as whales do today. From everything we know, the smaller the number of offspring an animal produces, the better it will take care of them, which is why plesiosaurs are thought to have been doting parents. So, by the way, are birds, which science regards as feathered dinosaurs.

Pressing me even further, the Dalai Lama jumped to butterflies and asked about their empathy, upon which I couldn't resist joking, "They don't have time, they live just one day!" The short life of butterflies is actually a myth, but whatever these insects feel about each other, I doubt it has much to do with empathy. This is not to minimize the larger thrust behind the Dalai Lama's question, which was that all animals do what is best for themselves and their offspring. In this sense, all life is caring, perhaps not consciously caring, but caring nonetheless. He was getting at the idea that compassion goes to the root of what life is all about.

Greeting Mama

After this, the forum moved on to other topics, such as how to measure compassion in the brains of Buddhist monks who have meditated on it all their lives. Richard Davidson from the University of Wisconsin related how monks straight from Tibet balked at his invitation to submit to neuroscience since, clearly, compassion didn't take place in the brain but in the heart! Everyone felt this was hilarious, and the monks in the audience shrieked with laughter. But the monks had a point. Davidson subsequently discovered the connection between mind and heart: compassion meditation brings about a quicker heart rate upon hearing sounds of human suffering.

I had to think of the geese. But I also sat there wondering at this auspicious meeting of minds. In 2005, the Dalai Lama himself had spoken about the need to integrate science and religion, telling thousands of scientists at the annual meeting of the Society for Neuroscience, in Washington, how much trouble society has in keeping up with their groundbreaking research: "It is all too evident that our moral thinking simply has not been able to keep pace with such rapid progress in our acquisition of knowledge and power."[5] What a refreshing departure from attempts to drive a wedge between religion and science!

This topic was on my mind as I prepared for Europe. I had barely received a blessing and a khata (a long white silk scarf) around my neck, and seen the Dalai Lama off in his limousine with heavily armed guards, and I was on my way to Ghent, a beautiful old city in the Flemish part of Belgium. This region is culturally closer to the southern part of the Netherlands, where I am from, than the part to the north that we call Holland. All of us speak the same language, but Holland is Calvinist, whereas the southern provinces were kept Catholic in the sixteenth century by the Spanish, who brought us the Duke of Alva and the Inquisition. Not the silly "Nobody expects the Spanish Inquisition!" of *Monty Python,* but one that would put actual thumbscrews on you if you so much as doubted Mary's virginity. Not allowed to draw blood, the inquisitors loved the *strappado,* or reverse hanging, in which a victim is hung by wrists tied behind his back and a weight is attached to his ankles. This treatment is sufficiently debilitating that one soon abandons any preconceived notions about the link between sex and conception. Lately, the Vatican has been on a campaign to soften the Inquisition's image—they did not kill *every* heretic, they followed Standard Operating Procedures—but the Jesuits in charge surely could have used some compassion training.

This ancient history also explains, by the way, why one will look in vain for Bosch paintings in the lowlands. Most hang in the Prado, in Madrid. It is thought that the Iron Duke obtained *The Garden* when, in 1568, he declared the Prince of Orange an outlaw and confiscated all of his properties. The duke then left the masterpiece to his son, from whom it went to the Spanish state. The Spanish adore the painter they call El Bosco, whose imagery inspired Joan Miró and Salvador Dalí. On my first visit to the Prado, I could not really enjoy Bosch's work, since all I could think was "Colonial plunder!" To its credit, the museum has now digitized the popular painting at an incredibly high resolution so that everyone can "own" it through Google Earth.

After my lecture in Ghent, fellow scientists took me on an impromptu visit to the world's oldest zoo collection of bonobos, which started at Antwerp Zoo and is now located in the animal park of Planckendael. Given that bonobos are native to a former Belgian colony, their presence in Planckendael is hardly surprising. Bringing specimens from Africa, dead or alive, was another kind of colonial plunder, but without it we might never have learned of this rare ape. The discovery took place in 1929, in a museum not far from here, when a German anatomist dusted off a small round skull labeled as that of a young chimp, which he recognized as an adult with an unusually small head. He quickly announced a new subspecies. Soon his claim was overshadowed, however, by the even more momentous pronouncement by an American anatomist that we had an entirely new species on our hands, one with a strikingly humanlike anatomy. Bonobos are more gracefully built and have longer legs than any other ape. The species was put in the same genus, Pan, as the chimpanzee. For the rest of their long lives, both scientists illustrated the power of academic rivalry by never agreeing on who had made this historic discovery. I was in the room when the American stood up in the midst of a symposium on bonobos to declare, in a voice quavering with indignation, that he had been "scooped" half a century before.

The German scientist had written in German and the American in English, so guess whose story is most widely cited? Many languages feel the pinch of the rise of English, but I was happily chatting in Dutch, which despite decades abroad still crosses my lips a fraction of a second faster than any other language. While a young bonobo swung on a rope in and out of view, getting our attention by hitting the glass each time he passed, we commented on how much his facial expression resembled human laughter. He was having fun, especially if we jumped back from the window, acting scared. We now find it impossible to imagine that the two Pan species were once mixed up. There is a famous photograph of the American expert Robert Yerkes, with two young apes on his lap, both of whom he considered chimps. This was before the bonobo was known. Yerkes did remark how one of those two apes was far more sensitive and empathic than any other he knew, and perhaps also smarter. Calling him an "anthropoid genius," he wrote his book *Almost Human* largely about this "chimpanzee," not knowing that he was in fact dealing with one of the first live bonobos to have reached the West.

The Planckendael colony shows the difference with chimpanzees right away, because it is led by a female. The biologist Jeroen Stevens told me how the atmosphere in the group had turned more relaxed since their longtime alpha female, who had been a real iron lady, had been sent off to another zoo. She had terrified most other bonobos, especially the males. The new alpha has a nicer character. The exchange of females between zoos is a new and commendable trend that fits the natural bonobo pattern. In the wild, sons stay with their mothers through adulthood, whereas daughters migrate to other places. For years, zoos had been moving males around, thus causing disaster upon disaster, because male bonobos get hammered in the absence of their mom. Those poor males often ended up in isolation in an off-display area of zoos in order to protect their lives. A lot of problems are being avoided by keeping males with their mothers and respecting their bond.

During human evolution, bipedal locomotion demanded longer legs. Of all the apes, the arm-to-leg ratio of bonobos most resembles that of our ancestor *Ardipithecus*.

This goes to show that bonobos are no angels of peace. But it also indicates how much the males are "mama's boys," something not everyone approves of. Some men feel affronted by matriarchal apes with "wimpy" males. After a lecture in Germany, a famous old professor in my audience barked, "Was ist vrong with those males?!" It is the fate of the bonobo to have burst on the scientific scene at a time when anthropologists and biologists were busy emphasizing violence and warfare, hence scarcely interested in peaceful primate kin. Since no one knew what to do with them, bonobos quickly became the black sheep of the human evolutionary literature. An American anthropologist went so far as to recommend that we simply ignore them, given that they are close to extinction anyway.[6]

Holding a species' imminent demise against it is extraordinary. Is something the matter with bonobos? Are they ill adapted? Extinction says nothing about initial adaptiveness, though. The dodo was doing fine until sailors landed on Mauritius and found these flightless birds an easy (if repugnant) meal. Similarly, all of our ancestors must have been well adapted at some point, even though none of them is around anymore. Should we stop paying attention to them? But we never stop. The media go crazy each time a minuscule trace of our past is discovered, a reaction encouraged by personalized fossils with names like Lucy and Ardi.

I welcome bonobos precisely because the contrast with chimpanzees enriches our view of human evolution. They show that our lineage is marked not just by male dominance and xenophobia but also by a love of harmony and sensitivity to others. Since evolution occurs through both the male and the female lineage, there is no reason to measure human progress purely by how many battles our men have won against other hominins.[7] Attention to the female side of the story would not hurt, nor would attention to sex. For all we know, we did not conquer other groups, but bred them out of existence through love rather than war. Modern humans carry Neanderthal DNA, and I wouldn't be surprised if we carry other hominin genes as well. Viewed in this light, the bonobo way doesn't seem so alien.

Leaving those gentle apes behind, I next stopped at the Arnhem Zoo, in the Netherlands, where I began my career with the other *Pan* species. The German professor would love chimpanzees, since males rule supremely and are constantly vying for position, so much so that I wrote an entire book, *Chimpanzee Politics,* on their schmoozing and scheming. As a student,

I began to read Niccolò Machiavelli to gain insights that biology textbooks couldn't offer me. One of the central male characters of that tumultuous period, now four decades in the past, was murdered while I was still there, an event that continues to haunt me, not least because of the gruesome removal of his testicles by the attackers. The other male characters have all died over the years, but the colony still includes their adult sons, who not only look unnervingly like their fathers but also sound like them when they hoot or scream. Chimps have distinctive voices: I used to be able to tell all twenty-five of them apart by their calls alone. I feel very much at home with these primates and consider them absolutely fascinating, but I never have any illusions about how "nice" they are, even if they look like it to most people. They take their power games very seriously and are ready to kill their rivals. That they sometimes kill humans, or bite off their face, as has happened with pet chimps in the United States, is what you can expect if you keep a wild animal in a situation in which sexual jealousy and its dominance drive risk being aroused by our own feeble species. A single adult male chimpanzee has such muscle power (not to mention his daggerlike canine teeth and four "hands") that even a team of five hefty men would never be able to hold him down. Chimps raised around people know this all too well.

The females I knew in Arnhem are still around, however, especially the impressive matriarch of the colony, named Mama. She was never like a bonobo matriarch, who rules the place, but has been alpha among the females for as long as I remember. In her heyday, Mama was an active player in male power struggles. She would rally female support for one male or another, who would be in her debt if he managed to get to the top. This male would do well to stay on her good side, because if Mama turned against him, his career might be over. Mama went so far as to punish females who dared side with males she did not approve of, acting like a party whip. Chimpanzee males physically dominate females, but it is not as if females know nothing about politics or stay out of it. Females in wild communities often do, but on the island in Arnhem this isn't an option. The result is a reduced power gap between the sexes. Since all females are present all the time, actively supporting each other, it is impossible for any male to get around the female power block.

I have always been close to Mama, who greets me with a mixture of respect and affection each time she sees me. She did so already all those years ago, and still does so each time she detects my face in a crowd of visitors. I have been to the zoo every couple of years, and sometimes engage in a bit of friendly grooming with her, but this time I arrived with almost one hundred people in tow, attendees of a symposium at the zoo's convention center. As we walked up to the chimp island, both Mama and another old female, Jimmy, hurried forward to greet me: they gave a series of low grunts, and Mama stretched out a hand to me from a distance. Females typically use this "come here" gesture when they are about to move and want their offspring to jump on their back. I made the same gesture back at her and later helped the caretaker feed the chimpanzees by throwing fruit across the water moat, making sure that Mama, who walks slowly and isn't as skilled as the others at plucking flying oranges out of the air, got enough.

Jealousy was on display right then and there, because Mama's adult daughter, Moniek, snuck up on us to lob a heavy stone from a distance of about forty feet. Moniek's parabolic launch would have hit me in the head had I not kept an eye on her. I caught the rock in the air. Moniek was born while I still worked at the zoo, and I have seen many times how she hates her mother's attention for me. She probably doesn't remember me, hence has no clue why Mama greets this stranger like an old friend. Better throw something at him! Since aimed throwing is viewed by some scholars as a human specialization related to language evolution, I have invited proponents of this theory to experience firsthand what chimps are capable of, but never had any volunteers. Perhaps they realize that stones may be replaced by smelly body products.

Moved by the reunion between Mama and myself, the symposium participants wondered how well chimpanzees recognize us and how well we recognize them. For me, ape faces are as distinct as human faces, even though both species have a bias for their own kind. This bias was ignored not too long ago when only humans were considered good at face recognition. Apes had done poorly on the same tests as applied to humans with the same stimuli, which meant that the apes had been tested on human faces. I call this the "anthropocentric bias" in ape research, which is responsible for much misinformation. When one of my co-workers in Atlanta, Lisa Parr, used the hundreds of photographs I had shot in Arnhem to test chimpanzees on portraits of their own species, they excelled at it. Seeing the portraits on a computer screen, they were even able to tell which juveniles were offspring of which females, doing so without personally knowing the pictured chimps. In the same way, leafing through a photo album, we can tell from the faces alone which humans are blood relatives.

We live in a time of increasing acceptance of our kinship with the apes. True, humanity never runs out of claims of what sets it apart, but it is a rare uniqueness claim that holds up for over a decade. If we consider our species without letting ourselves be blinded by the technical advances of the last few millennia, we see a creature of flesh and blood with a brain that, albeit three times larger than a chimpanzee's, doesn't contain any new parts. Even our vaunted prefrontal cortex turns out to be of rather typical size compared with that of other primates. No one doubts the superiority of our intellect, but we have no basic wants or needs that are not also present in our close relatives. Just like us, monkeys and apes strive for power, enjoy sex, want security and affection, kill over territory, and value trust and cooperation. Yes, we have computers and airplanes, but our psychological makeup remains that of a social primate.

This is why we had an entire symposium at the zoo on what health care professionals and social scientists might learn from primatology. I was the primatologist, of course, but learned something myself from a discussion on the side. We were talking about where morality gets its justification. If the weight behind it doesn't come from above, who or what provides it? A colleague noted that while the Dutch had become quite secular over the past few decades, there is a growing problem with moral authority. No one publicly corrects anyone anymore, and people have become less civilized as a result. I saw heads nodding around the table. Was this just a frustrated rant by the older generation, always ready to complain about the younger one? Or was there a pattern? Secularization is all around us in Europe, but its moral implications are poorly understood. Even the German political philosopher Jürgen Habermas—an atheist Marxist if there ever was one—has come to regard the loss of religion as perhaps not altogether beneficial, stating that "something was lost when sin became guilt."[8]

The Atheist Dilemma

I am not convinced that morality needs to get its weight from above, though. Can't it come from within? This would certainly work for compassion, but perhaps also for our sense of fairness. A few years ago, we demonstrated that primates will happily perform a task for cucumber slices until they see others getting grapes, which taste so much better. The cucumber eaters become agitated, throw down their veggies, and go on strike. A perfectly fine food has become unpalatable as a result of seeing a companion get something better. We labeled it *inequity aversion*, a topic since investigated in other animals, including dogs. A dog will repeatedly perform a trick without rewards, but refuse as soon as another dog gets pieces of sausage for the same trick.

Such findings have implications for human morality. According to most philosophers, we reason ourselves toward moral truths. Even if they don't invoke God, they're still proposing a top-down process in which we formulate the principles and then impose them on human conduct. But do moral deliberations really take place at such an elevated plane? Don't they need to be anchored in who and what we are? Would it be realistic, for example, to urge people to be considerate of others if we didn't already have a natural inclination to be so? Would it make sense to appeal to fairness and justice if we didn't have powerful reactions to their absence? Imagine the cognitive burden if every decision we took had to be vetted against handed-down logic. I am a firm believer in David Hume's position that reason is the slave of the passions. We started out with moral sentiments and intuitions, which is also where we find the greatest continuity with other primates. Rather than having developed morality from scratch through rational reflection, we received a huge push in the rear from our background as social animals.

At the same time, however, I am reluctant to call a chimpanzee a "moral being." This is because sentiments do not suffice. We strive for a logically coherent system and have debates about how the death penalty fits arguments for the sanctity of life, or whether an unchosen sexual orientation can be morally wrong. These debates are uniquely human. There is little evidence that other animals judge the appropriateness of actions that do not directly affect themselves. The great pioneer of morality research, the Finnish anthropologist Edward Westermarck, explained that moral emotions are disconnected from one's immediate situation. They deal with good and bad at a more abstract, disinterested level. This is what sets human morality apart: a move toward universal standards combined with an elaborate system of justification, monitoring, and punishment.

At this point, religion comes in. Think of the narrative support for compassion, such as the parable of the good Samaritan, or the challenge to our sense of fairness, such as the parable of the workers in the vineyard with its famous conclusion "The last will be first, and the first will be last." Add to this an almost Skinnerian fondness of reward and punishment—from the virgins to be met in heaven to the hellfire awaiting sinners—and the exploitation of our desire to be "praiseworthy," as Adam Smith called it. Humans are in fact so sensitive to public opinion that we only need to see a picture of two eyes glued to the wall to respond with good behavior. Religion understood this long ago and uses the image of an all-seeing eye to symbolize an omniscient God.

But even assigning such a modest role to religion is anathema for some. Over the past few years, we have gotten used to a strident atheism arguing that God is not great (Christopher Hitchens) or is a delusion (Richard Dawkins). The neo-atheists call themselves "brights," thus implying that believers are not as bright. They have replaced Saint Paul's view that non-believers live in darkness by its opposite: non-believers are the only ones to have seen the light. Urging trust in science, they wish to root ethics in the naturalistic worldview. I do share their skepticism regarding religious institutions and their "primates"—popes, bishops, megapreachers, ayatollahs, and rabbis—but what good could possibly come from insulting the many people who find value in religion? And more pertinently, what alternative does science have to offer? Science is not in the business of spelling out the meaning of life and even less in telling us how to live our lives. The British philosopher John Gray put it as follows: ". . . science is not sorcery. The growth of knowledge enlarges what humans can do. It cannot reprieve them from being what they are."[9] We scientists are good at finding out why things are the way they are, or how they work, and I do believe that biology helps us understand why morality looks the way it does. But to go from there to offering moral advice is a stretch.

Even the staunchest atheist growing up in Western society cannot avoid having absorbed the basic tenets of Christianity. The increasingly secular northern Europeans, whose cultures I know firsthand, consider themselves largely Christian in outlook. Everything humans have accomplished anywhere—from architecture to music, from art to science—developed hand in hand with religion, never separately. It is impossible, therefore, to know what morality would look like without religion. It would require a visit to a human culture that is not now and never was religious. That such cultures do not exist should give us pause.

Bosch struggled with the same issue—not with being an atheist, which was not an option, but with science's place in society. The little figures in his paintings with inverted funnels on their heads or the background buildings in the form of distillation bottles and furnaces reference chemical equipment. However we view science now, it is good to realize that it didn't start out as a very rational enterprise. Alchemy was gaining ground in Bosch's days, yet mixed with the occult and full of charlatans and quacks, which the painter depicted with great humor in front of their gullible audiences. Alchemy turned into empirical science only when it liberated itself from these influences and developed self-correcting procedures. But how science might contribute to a moral society remained unclear.

Notes

1. Friedrich Nietzsche (1889), p. 5.
2. Also known as s'Hertogenbosch, the city is a twelfth-century provincial capital in the south of the Netherlands. At the time of Bosch's life (from circa 1450 until 1516), it was the second-largest city of the country, after Utrecht.
3. In 2007, Al Sharpton and Christopher Hitchens debated religion at the New York Public Library. See www.fora.tv.
4. The blog was posted on "The Stone," on 17 October 2010, available at http://opinionator.blogs.nytimes.com/2010/10/17/morals-without-god.
5. Marc Kaufman, "Dalai Lama gives talk on science," Washington Post, 13 November 2005.
6. Advocating attention to chimpanzees rather than to bonobos, Melvin Konner (2002), p. 199, wrote, "And in any case, chimps have done far better than bonobos, which are very close to extinction."
7. "Hominin" is the new label for humans and their bipedal ancestors; previously it was "hominid."
8. Jürgen Habermas (2001) in his acceptance speech as recipient of the Peace Prize of the German Book Trade. The German text uses the word "Schuld," which means both blameworthy and being guilty: "Als sich Sünde in Schuld verwandelte, ging etwas verloren." Translated at www.csudh.edu/dearhabermas/habermas11.htm.
9. John Gray (2011), p. 235.

Critical Thinking

1. Discuss the notion that morality antedates religion.
2. Explain the existence of animal empathy and why it seems to have originated with parental care.
3. Discuss the differences between bonobos and chimpanzees and what these differences have to do with relative amounts of empathy and violence among them.
4. Discuss "inequity aversion" as it appears in some animal species.
5. Explain the difference between the moral sentiments and intuitions that we have in common with some animals versus the more abstract and disinterested human morality that involves universal standards.
6. Discuss the role of religion in support of human morality.
7. Explain why science alone cannot be the basis of human morality.
8. Discuss the author's view of the origin of human morality.

Create Central

www.mhhe.com/createcentral

Internet References

African Primates at Home
www.indiana.edu/~primate/primates.html
Living Links
www.emory.edu/LIVING_LINKS/dewaal.html
National Primate Research Center
http://pin.primate.wisc.edu/factsheets
Primate Society of Great Britain
www.psgb.org

Article   Prepared by: Elvio Angeloni

One for All

Our ability to cooperate in large societies has deep evolutionary roots in the animal kingdom.

FRANS DE WAAL

Learning Outcomes

After reading this article, you will be able to:

- Discuss the traditional scenario as to how humanity became the dominant form of life and why it is unlikely.

- Discuss the findings of recent studies of primate cooperation.

Traditional discussions of how humanity became the dominant form of life, with a population of more than seven billion and counting, have focused on competition. Our ancestors seized land, so the story goes, wiped out other species—including our brethren the Neandertals—and hunted big predators to extinction. We conquered nature, red in tooth and claw.

Overall, however, this is an unlikely scenario. Our forebears were too small and vulnerable to rule the savanna. They must have lived in constant fear of pack-hunting hyenas, 10 different kinds of big cats and other dangerous animals. We probably owe our success as a species more to our cooperativeness than our capacity for violence.

Our propensity to cooperate has old evolutionary roots. Yet only humans organize into groups capable of achieving colossal feats. Only humans have a complex morality that emphasizes responsibilities to others and is enforced through reputation and punishment. And sometimes we do incredible things that put a lie to the idea of humans as purely self-interested actors.

Consider this scene that unfolded last year in a Metrorail station in Washington, D.C. A passenger's motorized wheelchair malfunctioned, and the man ended up sprawled on the tracks. Within seconds, multiple bystanders jumped down to bring him back up before the next train. An even more dramatic rescue occurred in 2007 in the New York City subway, when Wesley Autrey, a 50-year-old construction worker, saved a man who had fallen in front of an approaching train. Too late to pull him up, Autrey jumped between the tracks and lay on top of the other man while five cars rolled overhead. Afterward, he downplayed his heroism: "I don't feel like I did something spectacular."

What he did was spectacular, of course. But what propelled him to put his own life in jeopardy to help a fellow stranger in the subway? For answers to this question and to how we came to cooperate in other ways, we must first look at similar behavior in our evolutionary cousins, particularly our closest living relatives: chimpanzees and bonobos.

Primate Cooperation

I regularly watch less dramatic cases of selfless cooperation in these animals at the Yerkes National Primate Research Center at Emory University. My office overlooks a large, grassy enclosure, in which an aging female, Peony, spends her days in the sun with other chimpanzees. Whenever her arthritis flares up, she has trouble walking and climbing. But while Peony is huffing and puffing to get up into the climbing frame, an unrelated younger female may move behind her, place both hands on her ample behind and push her up. We have also seen others bring water to Peony, for whom the walk to the spigot is strenuous. When she starts out in that direction, others run ahead to pick up a mouthful of water, then stand in front of the old lady, who opens her mouth to let them spit a jet of water into it.

A host of recent studies have carefully documented primate cooperation, reaching three main conclusions. First, cooperation does not require family ties. Even though these animals favor kin, they do not limit their cooperation to family. DNA extracted from chimpanzee feces collected in the African forest has allowed field-workers to examine which animals hunt and travel together. Most close partnerships in the forest involve unrelated individuals. Friends mutually groom one another, warn each other of predators and share food. We know the same is true for bonobos.

Second, cooperation is often based on reciprocity. Experiments indicate that chimpanzees remember received favors. One study measured grooming in a captive colony in the morning before feeding time. On introduction of sharable food, such as watermelons, the few lucky possessors would be surrounded by beggars holding out a hand, whimpering and whining. Researchers found that an individual that earlier in the day had groomed another was more likely to obtain a share from this partner later on.

Third, cooperation may be motivated by empathy, a characteristic of all mammals, from rodents to primates. We identify with others in need, pain or distress. This identification arouses emotions that tend to prompt helping action. Scientists now believe that primates, in particular, go further and care about the well-being of others. In a typical experiment, two monkeys are placed side by side, while one of them selects a token based on color. One color rewards only the monkey itself but the other rewards both of them. After a few rounds, the choosing monkey opts most often for the "prosocial" token. This preference is not based on fear of the other monkey, because dominant monkeys (which have the least to fear) are the most generous.

Sometimes caring about others costs primates nothing, such as in the above test, but they also help one another at a substantial cost, such as when they lose half their food in the process. In nature, chimpanzees are known to adopt orphans or defend others against leopards—both extremely costly forms of altruism.

Deeper Roots of Helping

These caring tendencies in primates probably evolved from the obligatory maternal care demanded of all mammals. Whether a mouse or an elephant, mothers need to respond to their young's signals of hunger, pain or fear—otherwise the infants might perish. This sensitivity (and the neural and hormonal processes that support it) was then co-opted for other relationships, helping to enhance emotional bonding, empathy and cooperation within the larger society.

Cooperation affords substantial benefits, so it is not surprising that it was co-opted in these ways. The most ubiquitous form in the animal kingdom is known as mutualistic cooperation and is presumably so widespread because it produces immediate payoffs, such as providing food or defending against predators. It is marked by working together toward an obvious goal that is advantageous to all—say when hyenas bring down a wildebeest together or when a dozen pelicans in a semicircle drive fish together with their feet in a shallow lake, which allows them to simultaneously scoop up mouthfuls of prey. Such cooperation rests on well-coordinated action and shared payoffs.

This kind of cooperation can spawn more subtle cooperative behaviors such as sharing. If one hyena or one pelican were to monopolize all rewards, the system would collapse. Survival depends on sharing, which explains why both humans and animals are exquisitely sensitive to fair divisions. Experiments show that monkeys, dogs and some social birds reject rewards inferior to those of a companion performing the same task; chimpanzees and humans go even further by moderating their share of joint rewards to prevent frustration in others. We owe our sense of fairness to a long history of mutualistic cooperation.

The Human Difference

Humans provide sharp examples of how sharing is linked with survival. Lamaleran whale hunters in Indonesia roam the open ocean in large canoes, from which a dozen men capture whales almost bare-handed. The hunters row toward the whale, the harpoonist jumps onto its back to thrust his weapon into it, and then the men stay nearby until the leviathan dies of blood loss. With entire families tied together around a life-threatening activity, their men being literally in the same boat, distribution of the food bonanza is very much on their mind. Not surprisingly, the Lamalera people are the champions of fairness, as measured by anthropologists using a tool called the Ultimatum Game, which measures preferences for equitable offers. In societies with greater self-sufficiency, such as those in which every family tends its own plot of land, equity is less important.

One oft-mentioned difference between humans and other primates is that we are the only species to cooperate with outsiders and strangers. Although our willingness to cooperate depends on the circumstances (after all, we may also kill those who do not belong to our group), primates in nature are mostly competitive between groups. The way human communities allow outsiders to travel through their territories, share meals with them, exchange goods and gifts, or band together against common enemies is not a typical primate pattern.

Yet this openness does not need a special evolutionary explanation, as some have argued. Most likely, cooperation among strangers is an extension of tendencies that arose for in-group use. In nature, it is not unusual for existing capacities to be applied outside their original context, a bit the way primates use hands (which evolved for tree climbing) to cling to their mothers. Experiments in which capuchin monkeys and bonobos interact with unfamiliar outsiders have shown them capable of exchanging favors and sharing food. In other words, the potential for cooperating with outsiders is present in other species even if they rarely encounter situations in nature that prompt them to do so.

One way we may be truly unique, though, is in the highly organized nature of our cooperativeness. We have the capacity to create hierarchical collaborations that can execute large-scale projects of a complexity and magnitude not found elsewhere in nature. Consider the terraced rice paddies of the Mekong Delta—or the technology that went into CERN's Large Hadron Collider.

Most animal cooperation is self-organized in that individuals fulfill roles according to their capacities and the "slots" open to them. Sometimes animals divide roles and closely coordinate, such as when synchronized killer whales make a wave that washes a seal off an ice floe or when several chimpanzee males organize as drivers and blockers to chase a group of monkeys through the canopy, as if they agreed on their roles beforehand. We do not know how the shared intentions and goals of this kind of cooperation are established and communicated, but they do not seem to be orchestrated from above by leaders, as is typical of humans.

Humans also have ways of enforcing cooperation that thus far have not been documented in other animals. Through repeated interactions, we build reputations as reliable friends, or poor ones, and may get punished if our efforts fall short. The potential for punishment also discourages individuals from cheating the system. In the laboratory, humans punish freeloaders, even at a cost to themselves, a practice that, in the long run, would tend to promote cooperation in a population. There is much debate about how typical such punishment is in real life, outside the lab, but we do know that our moral systems include expectations about cooperation and that we are hypersensitive to public opinion. In one experiment, people donated more money to a good cause if a picture of two eyes were mounted on the wall to watch them. Feeling observed, we worry about our reputation.

These concerns over reputation could have been the primordial glue that enabled early *Homo sapiens* to stick together in ever larger societies. During much of human prehistory, our ancestors lived nomadic lives much like current hunter-gatherers. These modern peoples demonstrate a robust potential for peace and trade between communities, which suggests that early *H. sapiens* had these traits, too.

Without denying our violent potential, I am convinced that it is these cooperative tendencies that have brought us as far as we have come. Building on tendencies that evolved in nonhuman primates, we have been able to shape our societies into complex networks of individuals who cooperate with one another in all kinds of ways.

Critical Thinking

1. Why are caring tendencies rooted in primate maternal care and what are the substantial benefits afforded by cooperation?

2. In comparison to other primates, how are humans unique with respect to cooperation?

More to Explore

The Human Potential for Peace. Douglas P. Fry. Oxford University Press, 2005.

The Age of Empathy. Frans de Waal. Harmony Books, 2009.

Prosocial Primates: Selfish and Unselfish Motivations. Frans B. M. de Waal and Malini Suchak in Philosophical Transactions of the Royal Society B, Vol. 365, No. 1553, pages 2711–2722; September 12, 2010.

From our Archives

Why We Help. Martin A. Nowak; July 2012. scientificamerican.com/magazine/sa

In Brief

Human beings have a unique ability to cooperate in large, well-organized groups and employ a complex morality that relies on reputation and punishment.

But much of the foundation for this cooperation—including empathy and altruism—can also be observed in our primate cousins.

Homo sapiens' unique cooperative abilities are what have allowed the species to become the dominant one on the earth.

Internet References

Electronic Zoo/NetVet-Primate Page
http://netvet.wustl.edu/primates.htm

Living Links
www.emory.edu/LIVING_LINKS/dewaal.html

National Primate Research Center
http://pin.primate.wisc.edu/factsheets

FRANS DE WAAL is C. H. CANDLER Professor of Primate Behavior at Emoiy University and director of the Living Links Center at the Yerkes National Primate Research Center. His books include Our Inner Ape (Riverhead, 2005) and The Bonobo and the Atheist (W. W. Norton, 2013).

Article   Prepared by: Elvio Angeloni

Friends with Benefits

LAUREN BRENT

Learning Outcomes

After reading this article, you will be able to:

- Discuss the benefits of having friends.

- Describe and explain the genetic, neurological, and hormonal factors involving friendship, health, and prosocial behavior.

We need friends. They have a positive impact on our health, wealth and mental well-being. Social isolation, on the other hand, creates feelings akin to physical pain and leaves us stressed and susceptible to illness. In fact, our bodies react to a lack of friends as if a crucial biological need is going unfulfilled. This is not surprising. For us humans, friends are not an optional extra—we have evolved to rely on them.

But friendship comes at a cost; time spent socialising could be used in other activities key to survival such as preparing food, having sex and sleeping. Besides, just because something is good for us, doesn't mean we will necessarily do it. That's why evolution has equipped us with the desire to make friends and spend time with them. Like sex, eating or anything a species needs to survive, friendship is driven by a system of reinforcement and reward. In other words, being friendly is linked with the release of various neurotransmitters in the brain and biochemicals in the body that make us feel good.

Understanding what motivates friendship begins in a seemingly unlikely place—with lactation. As a baby suckles, a neuropeptide called oxytocin is released from the mother's pituitary gland. This causes muscles in the breast to contract, allowing milk to flow, but it also reduces anxiety, blood pressure and heart rate. For mothers and babies, the relaxed feeling produced by oxytocin encourages suckling and helps create a strong and loving bond. This occurs in all mammals, but in humans and the few other species that make friends the system has been co-opted and expanded. Rather than reinvent the wheel, evolution has economised and oxytocin has become associated with relationships beyond the mother-child bond. You release it in response to many types of positive physical contact with another person, including hugs, light touches and massage. The resulting pleasant feeling is your reward for the interaction and encourages you to see that person again. A budding friendship is born.

Of course, most interactions between friends do not involve physical contact but oxytocin works in other ways too. It promotes prosocial decisions, increases feelings of trust and encourages generosity. And, while important, it is not the only chemical driver of friendship. Another key player is a group of opioid chemicals called endorphins. Also produced by the pituitary gland, they are released in response to mild pain, such as exercise, and act as neurotransmitters in the brain to create a feeling of well-being. All vertebrates produce endorphins, so they must have evolved early on, but like oxytocin, they have come to play a role in motivating friendship. Endorphins also make physical contact feel good, but they underpin another aspect of friendship too.

Robin Dunbar and his colleagues at the University of Oxford asked people to row a boat, either alone or in pairs, and measured their endorphin levels before and after. What they found was striking. Despite exerting the same physical effort, people who rowed as a synchronous pair released more endorphins than those who rowed alone. One of the major components of friendship is behavioural synchrony—friends must be in the same place at the same time to establish and maintain a relationship. Endorphins seem to promote friendships by making synchrony feel good.

The flip side of this is how bad it feels to be socially isolated. Lonely people have elevated levels of the stress hormone cortisol. Chronic stress damages your health, which probably explains why social isolation increases the risk of cardiovascular diseases and susceptibility to infection. But stress can be useful. The stress response is produced by activation of a system known as the hypothalamic-pituitary-adrenal axis. This activation acts as a warning that homeostasis—the body's maintenance of stable internal conditions—has been disrupted. So stress prompts us to behave in ways that restore homeostasis, including resting when tired and seeking shade when hot. Perhaps it also motivates us to seek out social contact when we are lonely. The fact that we produce less cortisol in a stressful situation if we have a friend with us suggests that friends either help us to restore homeostasis or prevent its disruption in the first place.

To select, acquire and maintain friends we need to gather social information. Again, this is something we enjoy. Even before babies can speak, they prefer looking at faces rather than other visual stimuli. We find social information intrinsically rewarding because it triggers reward-related areas of the brain. When Dar Meshi of the Free University in Berlin, Germany, showed people in an MRI scanner pictures from their Facebook accounts, he found strong activity in the nucleus accumbens, a brain region associated with drug addiction. Interestingly, people with the greatest response were the most frequent social media users.

Although the neural and biochemical processes that underlie friendship are the same in everyone, some people are friendlier than others. These people may simply be better at making friends, but Meshi's results hint that they are also more motivated to do so because it gives them a bigger kick. Friendlier people are more sociable, in part, because their genes make them that way. James Fowler at the University of California, San Diego, and Nicholas Christakis at Harvard University compared the social networks of identical twins, who share all their genes, and paternal twins, who share 50 percent on average. They found that genetic factors accounted for 46 percent of differences in how popular among their peers individuals were.

Even social butterflies aren't friends with everyone. Of the many people we encounter, how do we pick a select few? The answer, at first, seems quite simple—we are friends with people who are similar to us, whether they are the same age, gender or profession. But it turns out that this tendency for "like" to associate with "like", termed homophily, also has a basis in our genes. Fowler and Christakis found that people are as genetically similar to their non-kin friends as they would be to fourth cousins. One of the mysteries of friendship has been why we would cooperate so readily with complete strangers. In evolutionary terms, you should cooperate with kin rather than kindred spirits because your genetic similarity to relatives allows you to reap indirect benefits. In other words, you succeed by proxy if they pass on more of the genes they share with you to future generations. But if friends are more genetically similar than we would expect by chance, perhaps we should think of them not so much as strangers than as "facultative relatives".

So, your genome may help determine not only how friendly you are, but also who you choose for your friends. No one knows how we recognise people who are genetically similar. It could be similarities in facial features, voice, gestures or smell. Our tendency to befriend people who share our traits may even hold an answer. Your personality is shaped in part by your genes

so, if you choose friends with a similar personality, they will probably have genes in common with you. Whatever attracts us to certain people, one thing is certain, befriending them will be rewarding. Because if there's one thing we all know about friendship, it's that it feels good.

1 Do We Really Need Friends?

Yes. People with weak social relationships are 50 per cent more likely to die in a given period than those with strong social ties. Social isolation is as bad for you as drinking or smoking—by some estimates equivalent to smoking 15 cigarettes per day—and worse than inactivity or obesity.

Friendships also contribute to happiness—although quality, not quantity, is what counts. A study of 423 college students found that the quality of friendships had a big impact on how happy people were, whereas the number of friends they had made no difference.

However, the benefits of friendship probably vary from person to person, which would explain why some people say they feel happiest when alone.

2 What Makes a Good Friendship?

We forge friendships with people who are similar to ourselves. The six most important criteria are language, profession, world view (political, moral and religious), sense of humour, local identity and education. Personality appears to be less important than cultural preferences—the bands you like, the books you enjoy, the jokes you find funny. In fact, the best predictor of how well you will get on with a stranger is whether you like the same music.

3 Why Do Some People Have More Friends Than Others?

It may be in their biology. Neuroimaging studies have found that people with more grey matter in areas such as the amygdalae—which are associated with memory and emotional processing—tend to have more friends. But it is not clear whether this is cause or effect. There are also cultural influences: people from big, extended families tend to have fewer non-kin friends than those from small families.

4 Can Straight Men and Women Be "Just Friends"?

Yes, but that doesn't mean they aren't attracted to each other. Numerous studies show that attraction is a frequent component of cross-gender friendships. A survey of US college students found that half had had sex with an otherwise platonic friend.

Young men tend to be more attracted to their female friends than the other way round. They are also more likely to become friends with a woman because they are attracted to her, and to overestimate how attractive their female friends find them.

Women are more interested in protection. They are also more likely than men to secretly test whether their opposite-sex friends fancy them. Researchers have identified 158 such tests, the most common are attempts to make a friend jealous, tests of fidelity and temporary physical separation.

5 Do Male and Female Friendships Differ?

Women are more likely to have a best friend, whereas men more often hang out with a group. Women tend to consider friendships more in terms of emotional connection. By contrast, men think about how much time they spend together or how long they have known each other.

Female-female friendships tend to be more intimate, and women make friends with similarly physically attractive women. That is a good mating strategy—their friends attract men who are likely to find them attractive too—but it also leads to competition.

6 Are All Friendships Good for You?

No. Relationships with "frenemies" can actually damage your health. These are people who bring us down but who we put up with anyway. About half of the people in your social networks are likely to be frenemies—most of them family members. Interacting with unreliable friends is stressful. Your blood pressure is likely to be more elevated when you are with a frenemy than it is with someone you do not like at all.

7 Does Friendship Change as We Age?

Yes. Small children only really need one close friend—we don't develop the ability to juggle large numbers until our early 20s. Teenagers are hugely influenced by their friends, especially in behaviours such as substance use, violence and suicide.

The strongest and most enduring friendships are forged in our late teens and early 20s, possibly via intense, shared emotional experiences. Adults often find their friendships change as they get older. That is because friends reflect cultural preferences including music, books and jokes, and our tastes in these change.

Middle-aged adults tend to have fewer opposite-sex friends than young adults, possibly because they spend time with same sex friends through circumstances such as motherhood. Older people tend to be involved in more group activities with casual friends but they continue to exchange confidences with close friends.

Men have fewer friends as they age and less desire for close friendships. The same is not true for women.

8 How do Facebook Friends Compare with Real-life Ones?

The size of human social groups is naturally about 150, according to Robin Dunbar at the University of Oxford. Dunbar's number is in the right ballpark online as well. Facebook allows up to 5000 friends, but most users have between 150 and 250—although many of these will be acquaintances and some will be strangers.

There is little evidence that social media is damaging real-life friendships. People with more Facebook friends also tend to have greater numbers of friends in their in-person social networks.

9 Is There a Formula for Maintaining Friendships?

According to Dunbar, you need to be in contact with very close friends about every other day and your next five closest pals about once a week—whether face-to-face or electronically.

Once a month is enough for the next 15. For the next 50 it's about every six months, and for the rest of your 150 or so personal connections, once a year. Less often than that and friends will quickly fall through the layers of your social networks.

The exception is close friendships forged in your late teens/early 20s you can often pick these relationships up exactly where you left off, even after decades.

Critical Thinking

1. Why do people need friends?
2. What makes a good friend?
3. Why do some people have more friends than others?

Internet References

National Primate Research Center
   http://pin.primate.wisc.edu/factsheets
Primate Info Net
   http://pin.primate.wisc.edu/

Article   Prepared by: Elvio Angeloni

The "It" Factor

The capacity to engage in shared tasks such as hunting large game and building cities may be what separated modern humans from our primate cousins.

GARY STIX

Learning Outcomes

After reading this article, you will be able to:

- Discuss how the ability to engage in shared tasks separated modern humans from our primate cousins.

- Explain how selective forces, acting on human physical traits cannot explain the emergence of complex tools, language, mathematics, and elaborate social institutions.

- Discuss the "shared brain hypothesis": as a way of explaining human achievements that go far beyond what any animals can do.

A t a psychology laboratory in Leipzig, Germany, two toddlers eye gummy bears that lie on a board beyond their reach. To get the treats, both tots must pull in tandem on either end of a rope. If only one child pulls, the rope detaches, and they wind up with nothing.

A few miles away, in a plexiglass enclosure at Pongoland, the ape facility at the Leipzig Zoo, researchers repeat the identical experiment, but this time with two chimpanzees. If the primates pass the rope-and-board test, each one gets a fruit treat.

By testing children and chimps in this way, investigators hope to solve a vexing puzzle: Why are humans so successful as a species? *Homo sapiens* and *Pan troglodytes* share almost 99 percent of their genetic material. Why, then, did humans come to populate virtually every corner of the planet—building the Eiffel Tower, Boeing 747s and H-bombs along the way? And why are chimps still foraging for their supper in the dense forests of equatorial Africa, just as their ancestors did seven or so million years ago, when archaic humans and the great apes separated into different species?

As with any event that occurred on the time scale of evolution—hundreds of thousands or millions of years in the making—scientists may never reach a consensus on what really happened. For years the prevailing view was that only humans make and use tools and are capable of reasoning using numbers and other symbols. But that idea fell by the wayside as we learned more about what other primates are capable of. A chimp, with the right coach, can add numbers, operate a computer and light up a cigarette.

At present, the question of why human behavior differs from that of the great apes, and how much, is still a matter of debate. Yet experiments such as the one in Leipzig, under the auspices of the Max Planck Institute for Evolutionary Anthropology, have revealed a compelling possibility, identifying what may be a unique, but easy to overlook, facet of the human cognitive apparatus. From before their first birthday—a milestone some psychologists term "the nine-month revolution"—children begin to show an acute awareness of what goes on inside their mother's and father's heads. They evince this new ability by following their parents' gaze or looking where they point. Chimps can also figure out what is going on in a companion's mind to some degree, but humans take it one step further: infant and elder also have the ability to put their heads together to focus on what must be done to carry out a shared task. The simple act of adult and infant rolling a ball back and forth is enabled by this subtle cognitive advantage.

Some psychologists and anthropologists think that this melding of minds may have been a pivotal event that occurred hundreds of thousands of years ago and that shaped later human evolution. The ability of small bands of hunter-gatherers to work together in harmony ultimately set off a cascade of cognitive changes that led to the development of language and the spread of diverse human cultures across the globe.

This account of human psychological evolution, synthesized from bits and pieces of research on children and chimps, is speculative, and it has its doubters. But it provides perhaps the most impressively broad-ranging picture of the origins of cognitive abilities that make humans special.

The Ratchet Effect

The Max Planck Institute maintains the world's largest research facility devoted to examining the differences in behavior between humans and the great apes. Dozens of studies may be running at any one time. Researchers can draw subjects from a database of more than 20,000 children and recruit chimpanzees or members of any of the other great ape species—orangutans, bonobos and gorillas—from the Wolfgang Köhler Primate Research Center at the Leipzig Zoo a few miles away.

The institute began 17 years ago, seven years after the reunification of Germany. Founding the institute required coming to grips with the tarnished legacy of German anthropology—and its association with Nazi racial theories and, in particular, the grisly human experiments performed in Auschwitz by Josef Mengele, who was a physician with a doctorate in anthropology. The institute's organizers went out of their way to recruit group leaders for genetics, primatology, linguistics and other disciplines who were not native Germans.

One of them was Michael Tomasello, a tall, bearded psychologist and primatologist. Now 64, he grew up in a small citrus-growing city at the epicenter of the Florida peninsula. He began his academic career at the University of Georgia with a dissertation on the way toddlers acquire language. While he was doing his doctorate in the 1970s, linguists and psychologists often cited language as exhibit number one for human exceptionalism in the animal world.

Tomasello's doctoral thesis chronicled how his almost two-year-old daughter learned her first verbs. The emergence of proto words—"play play" or "ni ni"—revealed a natural inclination of the young child to engage in trial-and-error testing of language elements, an exercise that gradually took on the more conventional structuring of grammar and syntax. This learning process stood in contrast to the ideas of Noam Chomsky and other linguists who contended that grammar is somehow genetically hardwired in our brains—an explanation that struck Tomasello as reductionist. "Language is such a complicated thing that it couldn't have evolved like the opposable thumb," he says.

His work on language broadened his thinking about the relation between culture and human evolution. Tomasello realized that selective forces alone, acting on physical traits, could not explain the emergence of complex tools, language, mathematics and elaborate social institutions in the comparatively brief interval on the evolutionary time line since humans and chimps parted ways. Some innate mental capacity displayed

by hominins (modern humans and our extinct relatives) but absent in nonhuman primates must have enabled our forebears to behave in ways that vastly hastened the ability to feed and clothe themselves and to flourish in any environment, no matter how forbidding.

When Tomasello moved to a professorship at Emory University during the 1980s, he availed himself of the university's Yerkes primate research center to look for clues to this capacity in studies comparing the behaviors of children with those of chimps. The move set in motion a multidecade quest that he has continued at Max Planck since 1998.

In his studies of chimp learning, Tomasello noticed that apes do not ape each other the way humans imitate one another. One chimp might emulate another chimp using a stick to fetch ants out of a nest. Then others in the group might do the same. As Tomasello looked more closely, he surmised that chimps were able to understand that a stick could be used for "ant dipping," but they were unconcerned with mimicking one technique or another that might be used in hunting for the insects. More important, there was no attempt to go beyond the basics and then do some tinkering to make a new and improved ant catcher.

In human societies, in contrast, this type of innovation is a distinguishing characteristic that Tomasello calls a "ratchet effect." Humans modify their tools to make them better and then pass this knowledge along to their descendants, who make their own tweaks—and the improvements ratchet up. What starts as a lobbed stone projectile invented to kill a mammoth evolves over the millennia into a slingshot and then a catapult, a bullet, and finally an intercontinental ballistic missile.

This cultural ratchet provides a rough explanation for humans' success as a species but leads to another question: What specific mental processes were involved in transmitting such knowledge to others? The answer has to begin with speculations about changes in hominin physiology and behavior that may have taken place hundreds of thousands of years ago. One idea—the social brain hypothesis, put forward by anthropologist Robin Dunbar of the University of Oxford—holds that group size, and hence cultural complexity, scales up as brains get bigger. And scientists know that by 400,000 years ago, *Homo heidelbergensis*, probably our direct ancestor, had a brain almost as large as ours.

Tomasello postulates that, equipped with a bigger brain and confronted with the need to feed a growing population, early hominins began careful strategizing to track and outwit game. The circumstances exerted strong selection pressures for cooperation: any member of a hunting party who was not a team player—taking on a carefully defined role when tracking and cornering an animal—would have been excluded from future outings and so might face an unremittingly bleak future. If one hunter was a bad partner, Tomasello notes, the rest of the group would then decide: "We won't do this again." In his view, what separated modern humans from the hominin pack was an evolutionary adaptation for hypersociality.

The paleoarchaeological record of bones and artifacts is too scant to provide support for Tomasello's hypothesis. He draws his evidence from a comparison of child and chimp—matching our closest primate relative with a toddler who has yet to master a language or be exposed to formal schooling. The untutored child allows researchers to assess cognitive skills that have yet to be fully shaped by cultural influences and so can be considered to be innate.

Studies in Leipzig during the past decade or so have uncovered more similarities than differences between humans and chimps, but they also highlight what Tomasello calls "a small difference that made a big difference." One immense research undertaking, led by Esther Herrmann of the developmental and comparative psychology department at the Max Planck Institute under Tomasello's tutelage, ran from 2003 until its publication in *Science* in 2007. It entailed administering multiple cognitive tests to 106 chimpanzees at two African wildlife sanctuaries, 32 orangutans in Indonesia and 105 toddlers, aged two and a half years, in Leipzig.

The investigators set out to determine whether humans' bigger brain meant the children were smarter than great apes and, if so, what being smarter meant, exactly. The three species were tested on spatial reasoning (such as looking for a hidden reward), an ability to discriminate whether quantities were large or small, and an understanding of cause-and-effect relationships. It turned out that the toddlers and the chimpanzees scored almost identically on these tests (orangutans did not perform quite as well).

When it came to social skills, though, there was no contest. Toddlers bested both chimps and orangutans on tests (adapted for nonverbal apes) that examined the ability to communicate, learn from others, and evaluate another being's perceptions and wishes. The researchers interpreted the results as showing that human children are not born with a higher IQ (general reasoning capacities) but rather come equipped with a special set of abilities—"cultural intelligence," as the *Science* study put it—that prepares them for learning later from parents, teachers and playmates. "It was really the first time that it was shown that social-cognitive abilities are the key skills that make us special in comparison to other animals," Herrmann says.

Digging deeper required probing for the specific psychological processes that underlie humans' ultrasocial tendencies. Tomasello's research showed that at about nine months of age, parent and child engage in a figurative form of mind reading. Each has what psychologists call a "theory of mind." Each is aware of what the other one knows when they look together at a ball or block and play a little game with it. Each carries a mental image of these items in the same way a group of

H. heidelbergensis would have all visualized a deer intended as dinner. This capacity to engage with another person to play a game or achieve a common goal is what Tomasello calls shared intentionality (a term he borrowed from philosophy). In Tomasello's view, shared intentionality is an evolutionary adaptation unique to humans—a minute difference with momentous consequences, rooted in an inherited predisposition for a degree of cooperative social interactions that is absent in chimps or any other species.

The Benefits of Mind Reading

The institute researchers noted that chimps, too, can read one another's minds to some degree. But their natural inclination is to use whatever they learn in that way to outcompete one another in the quest for food or mates. The chimp mind, it appears, is involved in a kind of Machiavellian mental scheming—"If I do this, will he do that?"—as Tomasello explains it. "It is inconceivable," he said in an October 2010 talk at the University of Virginia, "that you would ever see two chimpanzees carrying a log together."

The Leipzig researchers formally demonstrated the differences that separate the two species in the rope-and-board experiment, in which two chimpanzees at the Leipzig Zoo could get a snack of fruit only if they both pulled a rope attached to a board. If food was placed at both ends of the board, the apes took the fruit closest to them. If the treats were placed in the middle, however, the more dominant ape would grab the food, and after a few trials, the subordinate simply stopped playing. In the institute's child lab, the children worked together, whether the gummy bears were placed in the middle or at the ends of the board. When the treat was in the middle, the three-year-olds negotiated so that each would get an equal share.

Ancestral humans' mutual understanding of what was needed to get the job done laid the basis for the beginnings of social interactions and a culture based on cooperation, Tomasello argues. This "common ground," as he calls it, in which members of a group know much of what others know, may have opened the way for development of new forms of communication.

An ability to devise and perceive shared goals—and to intuit immediately what a hunting partner was thinking—apparently allowed our hominin ancestors to make cognitive strides in other ways, such as developing more sophistication in communicative uses of gesturing than our ape relatives possess.

The basic gestural repertoire of our hominin kin may have once been similar to that of the great apes. Archaic humans may have pointed, as chimpanzees do today, to convey commands—"Give me this" or "Do that"—a form of communication centered on an individual's needs. Chimps, perhaps reminiscent of humans in a primeval past, still make no attempt to use these gestures for teaching or passing along information.

For humans, gesturing took on new meaning as their mental-processing abilities got better. A hunter would point to a glade in the forest to indicate where a deer was grazing, an action immediately understood by a nearby companion. The way such pointing can take on new meanings is evident in modern life. "If I point to indicate 'Let's go have a cup of coffee over there,' it's not in the language," Tomasello says. "The meaning of 'that café' is in the finger, not in the language."

Young children understand this type of pointing, but chimps do not. This difference became evident in one study in which the experimenter repeatedly put blocks on a plate that the child needed for building a tower, which the child then used. At a certain juncture, there were no objects left when needed, and so the infant started pointing to the now empty plate, indicating that she wanted one of the blocks that were no longer there. The child knew that the adult would make the correct inference—the ability to refer to an absent entity is, in fact, a defining characteristic of human language. At the zoo, chimps put through a similar exercise—with food substituted for blocks—did not lift a finger when facing a vacant plate.

Only slightly older children start to understand gestures that pantomime an action—moving a hand to one's mouth to represent hunger or thirst. Chimps seeing these gestures during a study remain clueless. An ape will understand what is happening when a human applies a hammer to a nut to get the meat but is befuddled when that same person makes a pounding motion on the hand to convey the idea of carrying out the same action.

This type of gesturing—an extension of humans' cognitive capacity for shared intentionality—may have been the basis for communicating abstract ideas needed to establish more elaborate social groups, whether they be a tribe or a nation. Pantomiming would have enabled people to create story lines, such as conveying "the antelope grazes on the other side of the hill" by holding both hands in a V pattern on the top of one's head to signify the animal and then raising and lowering the hands to depict the hill. These scenarios derive from comparative experiments demonstrating that toddlers have an intuitive understanding of iconic gestures for many familiar activities but that chimpanzees do not.

Some of this gesturing occurred perhaps not just through moving the hands but also through vocalizations intended to represent specific objects or actions. These guttural noises may have evolved into speech, further enhancing the ability to manage complex social relationships as populations continued to grow—and rivalries arose among tribal groups. A group adept at working together would outcompete those that bickered among themselves.

Humans' expanding cognitive powers may have promoted specific practices for hunting, fishing, plant gathering or marriage that turned into cultural conventions—the way "we" do things—that the group as a whole was expected to adopt. A collection of social norms required each individual to gain awareness of the values shared by the group—a "group-mindedness" in which every member conformed to an expected role. Social norms produced a set of moral principles that eventually laid a foundation for an institutional framework—governments, armies, legal and religious systems—to enforce the rules by which people live. The millennial journey that began with a particular mind-set needed by bands of hunters now scaled up to entire societies.

Chimps and other great apes never got started down this path. When chimps hunt together to prey on colobus monkeys in Ivory Coast, this activity, as Tomasello interprets it, entails every chimp trying to run down the monkey first to get the most meat, whereas human hunter-gatherers, even in contemporary settings, cooperate closely as they track game and later share the spoils equitably. Tomasello concludes that ape societies and those of other foragers such as lions may appear to cooperate, but the dynamics at play within the group are still fundamentally competitive in nature.

The Great Debate

Tomasello's version of an evolutionary history is not universally accepted, even within the institution. One floor up from his office, in the department of primatology, Catherine Crockford talks me though a video her graduate student Liran Samuni made in March. It shows a young chimpanzee in the Taï National Park in Ivory Coast near the Liberian border.

The chimp the researchers call Shogun has just caught a large, black-and-white colobus monkey. Shogun is having trouble eating his still alive and squirming catch and issues a series of sharp "recruitment screams" to summon help from two elder hunters lodged in the tree canopy. Kuba, one of the two, arrives on the scene shortly, and Shogun calms down a bit and takes his first real bite. But then Shogun continues to scream until the other hunter, Ibrahim, shows up. The younger ape puts his finger in Ibrahim's mouth as a "reassurance gesture," a mannerism that ensures that all is well. Ibrahim gives the sought-for emotional support by not biting Shogun's finger. The three then share the meal. "It's interesting that he's recruiting these two dominant males that could take this whole monkey from him," Crockford says. "But as you can see, they're not taking it from him. He's still allowed to eat it."

Crockford argues that it is still too early to draw conclusions about the extent to which chimps cooperate. "I don't think we know the limits of what chimps are doing," she says. "I think [Tomasello's] arguments are brilliant and really clear in terms of our current knowledge, but I think that with new tools that we're taking to the field, we'll find out whether the current limits are the limits of what chimps can do or not." Crockford is working with several other researchers to develop tests that would identify the social-bonding hormone oxytocin in chimpanzee urine. Some studies have shown that the hormone rises when chimps share food, a sign that the animals may cooperate when feeding.

Crockford did her doctoral studies at the institute in Leipzig, with both Tomasello and Christophe Boesch, head of the Max Planck Institute's department of primatology. Boesch has argued against Tomasello's conclusions by highlighting his own extensive research in the Taï National Park showing that chimps have a highly collaborative social structure—one chimp steers the monkey prey in the desired direction; others block its path along the way or take on yet additional roles. Boesch's views on chimp cooperation are similar to those of Frans de Waal of the Yerkes National Primate Research Center at Emory. Still others criticize Tomasello from a diametrically opposing viewpoint. Daniel Povinelli of the University of Louisiana at Lafayette contends that Tomasello overstates chimps' cognitive capacities in suggesting that they have some ability to understand the psychological state of others in the group.

For his part, Tomasello seems to enjoy being in the midst of this academic jousting, saying: "In my mind, Boesch and de Waal are anthropomorphizing apes, and Povinelli is treating them like rats, and they're neither." He adds, jokingly, "We're in the middle. Since we're getting attacked equally from both sides, we must be right."

Condemnation from some quarters is tempered by a deep respect from others. "I used to think that humans were very similar to chimps," says Jonathan Haidt, a leading social scientist at the New York University Stern School of Business. "Over the years, thanks in large part to Tomasello's work, I've come to believe that the small difference he has studied and publicized—the uniquely human ability to do shared intentionality—took us over the river to a new shore, where social life is radically different."

Resolving these debates will require more research from zoo, lab and field station—perhaps through new studies on the extent to which chimps have a theory of mind about others. Still other research already under way by Tomasello's group is intended to determine whether the conclusions about human behavior, drawn from tests on German children, carry over if similar tests are performed on children in Africa or Asia. One study asks whether German preschoolers share their collective sense of what is right or wrong with the Samburu, a semi-nomadic people in northern Kenya.

There may also be room to look more deeply at human-ape differences. One of Tomasello's close longtime colleagues, Josep Call, who heads the Wolfgang Köhler Center, thinks that shared intentionality alone may not suffice to explain what makes humans special. Other cognitive capacities, he says, may also differentiate humans from other primates—one example may be "mental time travel"—our ability to imagine what may happen in the future.

More perspective on the overlap between humans and chimps may come from looking inside the human brain—an endeavor that is ongoing on yet another floor at Max Planck.

More to Explore

Cultural Origins of Human Cognition. Michael Tomasello. Harvard University Press, 1999.

Humans Have Evolved Specialized Skills of Social Cognition: The Cultural Intelligence Hypothesis. Esther Herrmann, Josep Call, Maria Victoria Hemàndez-Lloreda. Brian Hare and Michael Tomasello in Science, Vol. 317, pages 1360–1366; September 7, 2007.

A Natural History of Human Thinking. Michael Tomasello. Harvard University Press, 2014.

From our Archives

The Morning of the Modern Mind. Kate Wong; June 2005.
scientificamerican.com/magazine/sa

In Brief

Humans—it was once thought—differed from other animals by their use of tools and their overall superiority in a range of cognitive abilities. Close observation of the behaviors of chimpanzees and other great apes has proved these ideas to be wrong.

Chimpanzees score as highly as young children on tests of general reasoning abilities but lack many of the social skills that come naturally to their human cousins. Unlike humans, chimps do not collaborate in the large groups needed to build complex societies.

Comparison of human and chimp psychology reveals that an essential source of the differences in humans may be the evolution of the ability to intuit what another person is thinking so that both can work toward a shared goal.

Cross-Species IQ Testing
Smart as a Chimp?

One widely held hypothesis suggests that, overall, humans are more intelligent than other primates. A study by the Leipzig researchers showed that chimps and young children (though not orangutans) perform equally on tests of capacities measured by conventional IQ tests (top), such as spatial and quantitative abilities. But children do better on cognitive tests related to social skills, such as learning from others.

Svante Pääbo, who led a team that finished an initial sequencing of the Neandertal genome in 2010, conjectures in a recent book that Tomasello's ideas about the uniqueness of human thinking may ultimately be tested through genetic analyses.

When those studies begin, a logical place to start would be to fuse research on chimp and human behaviors with the quixotic journey to understand the interactions among the hundreds of genes involved in autism. Children with the disorder, not unlike chimps, have difficulty understanding social cues. Comparing the genes in children with autism with those in unaffected children—and then with the DNA of chimps and perhaps even Neandertals, our closest evolutionary cousins—may yield a better understanding of a genetic basis for human sociality.

These investigations may also help explain why, over millennia, we progressed from bands of foragers to societies that not only provide food and shelter more efficiently than chimps do but also offer unceasing opportunities for social dealings—chances to move to any corner of the planet within a day's time or to convey messages to Tucson or Timbuktu as fast as a thought comes to mind.

Critical Thinking

1. How did the ability to engage in shared tasks separate modern humans from our primate cousins?

2. How does the "ratchet effect" explain human cultural success?

3. Why is it that selective forces acting on human physical traits cannot explain the emergence of complex tools, language, mathematics, and elaborate social institutions?

4. What is the significance of the "theory of mind" and "shared intentionality" with respect to human evolution?

5. What is the relationship between the ability to communicate abstract ideas and the "group mindedness" of human societies?

Internet References

American Anthropological Association Children and Childhood Interest Group
http://aaacig.usu.edu/

National Primate Research Center
http://pin.primate.wisc.edu/factsheets

Primate Society of Great Britain
http://www.psgb.org/

Society for Neuroscience
http://www.sfn.org/public-outreach/brainfacts-dot-org

GARY STIX is a senior editor at *Scientific American.*

Unit 3

UNIT

Prepared by: Elvio Angeloni, *Pasadena City College*

Sex and Gender

Any account of hominid evolution would be remiss if it did not attempt to explain that which is the most mystifying of all human experiences—our sexuality. No other aspect of humanity—whether it be upright posture, tool-making ability, or intelligence in general—seems to elude our intellectual grasp at least as much as it dominates our subjective consciousness. While we are a long way from reaching a consensus as to why it arose and what it is all about, there is widespread agreement that our very preoccupation with sex is, in itself, one of the hallmarks of being human. Even as we experience it and analyze it, we exalt it and condemn it. Beyond seemingly irrational fixations, however, there is the further tendency to project our own values onto the observations we make and the data we collect.

There are many who argue quite reasonably that the anthropological bias has been too male-oriented and that the recent "feminization" of the field has resulted in new kinds of research and refreshingly new theoretical perspectives. Not only should we consider the source when evaluating the old theories, but we should also welcome the source when considering the new.

One reason for studying the sexual and social lives of primates is that they allow us to test certain notions too often taken for granted. For instance, are primate males always dominant over females? Is it always the adolescent females that leave the group in which they were born? Does sexual exclusivity always result from pair-bonding between males and females? Are males always larger than females within a species? Primate research has shown that the answers to these questions are not as simple and straightforward as some have thought—that primates vary in their behavior just as humans do, depending upon the particular circumstances of their lives.

Finally, it should be noted that the study of primate social and sexual lives enables us to better comprehend our own. The more we know about why they do as they do in the context of their particular adaptations, the more insight we gain as why we may be similar to them, often because we are trying to solve similar problems, or differ from them, because our circumstances are not the same as theirs. It is these kinds of comparisons and contrasts, in other words, that help us to understand who we are.

Article   Prepared by: Elvio Angeloni, *Pasadena City College*

What Are Friends For?

Among East African baboons, friendship means companions, health, safety . . . and, sometimes, sex.

Barbara Smuts

Learning Outcomes

After reading this article, you will be able to:

- Explain why friendship is important to olive baboons and determine the implications for the origin of pair-bonding.

- Discuss the circumstances in which long-term male-female bonds form.

Virgil, a burly adult male olive baboon, closely followed Zizi, a middle-aged female easily distinguished by her grizzled coat and square muzzle. On her rump Zizi sported a bright pink swelling, indicating that she was sexually receptive and probably fertile. Virgil's extreme attentiveness to Zizi suggested to me—and all rival males in the troop—that he was her current and exclusive mate.

Zizi, however, apparently had something else in mind. She broke away from Virgil, moved rapidly through the troop, and presented her alluring sexual swelling to one male after another. Before Virgil caught up with her, she had managed to announce her receptive condition to several of his rivals. When Virgil tried to grab her, Zizi screamed and dashed into the bushes with Virgil in hot pursuit. I heard sounds of chasing and fighting coming from the thicket. Moments later Zizi emerged from the bushes with an older male named Cyclops. They remained together for several days, copulating often. In Cyclops's presence, Zizi no longer approached or even glanced at other males.

Primatologists describe Zizi and other olive baboons (*Papio cynocephalus anubis*) as promiscuous, meaning that both males and females usually mate with several members of the opposite sex within a short period of time. Promiscuous mating behavior characterizes many of the larger, more familiar primates, including chimpanzees, rhesus macaques, and gray langurs, as well as olive, yellow, and chacma baboons, the three subspecies of savanna baboon. In colloquial usage, promiscuity often connotes wanton and random sex, and several early studies of primates supported this stereotype. However, after years of laboriously recording thousands of copulations under natural conditions, the Peeping Toms of primate fieldwork have shown that, even in promiscuous species, sexual pairings are far from random.

Some adult males, for example, typically copulate much more often than others. Primatologists have explained these differences in terms of competition: the most dominant males monopolize females and prevent lower-ranking rivals from mating. But exceptions are frequent. Among baboons, the exceptions often involve scruffy, older males who mate in full view of younger, more dominant rivals.

A clue to the reason for these puzzling exceptions emerged when primatologists began to question an implicit assumption of the dominance hypothesis—that females were merely passive objects of male competition. But what if females were active arbiters in this system? If females preferred some males over others and were able to express these preferences, then models of mating activity based on male dominance alone would be far too simple.

Once researchers recognized the possibility of female choice, evidence for it turned up in species after species. The story of Zizi, Virgil, and Cyclops is one of hundreds of examples of female primates rejecting the sexual advances of particular males and enthusiastically cooperating with others. But what is the basis for female choice? Why might they prefer some males over others?

This question guided my research on the Eburru Cliffs troop of olive baboons, named after one of their favorite sleeping sites, a sheer rocky outcrop rising several hundred feet above the floor of the Great Rift Valley, about 100 miles northwest of Nairobi, Kenya. The 120 members of Eburru Cliffs spent their days wandering through open grassland studded with occasional acacia thorn trees. Each night they retired to one of a dozen sets of cliffs that provided protection from nocturnal predators such as leopards.

Most previous studies of baboon sexuality had focused on females who, like Zizi, were at the peak of sexual receptivity. A female baboon does not mate when she is pregnant or lactating, a period of abstinence lasting about eighteen months. The female then goes into estrus, and for about two weeks out of every thirty-five-day cycle, she mates. Toward the end of this two-week period she may ovulate, but usually the female undergoes four or five estrous cycles before she conceives. During pregnancy, she once again resumes a chaste existence. As a result, the typical female baboon is sexually active for less than 10 percent of her adult life. I thought that by focusing on the other 90 percent, I might learn something new. In particular, I suspected that routine, day-to-day relationships between males and pregnant or lactating (nonestrous) females might provide clues to female mating preferences.

Nearly every day for sixteen months, I joined the Eburru Cliffs baboons at their sleeping cliffs at dawn and traveled several miles with them while they foraged for roots, seeds, grass, and occasionally, small prey items, such as baby gazelles or hares (see "Predatory Baboons of Kekopey," *Natural History,* March 1976). Like all savanna baboon troops, Eburru Cliffs functioned as a cohesive unit organized around a core of related females, all of whom were born in the troop. Unlike the females, male savanna baboons leave their natal troop to join another where they may remain for many years, so most of the Eburru Cliffs adult males were immigrants. Since membership in the troop remained relatively constant during the period of my study, I learned to identify each individual. I relied on differences in size, posture, gait, and especially, facial features. To the practiced observer, baboons look as different from one another as human beings do.

As soon as I could recognize individuals, I noticed that particular females tended to turn up near particular males again and again. I came to think of these pairs as friends. Friendship among animals is not a well-documented phenomenon, so to convince skeptical colleagues that baboon friendship was real, I needed to develop objective criteria for distinguishing friendly pairs.

I began by investigating grooming, the amiable simian habit of picking through a companion's fur to remove dead skin and ectoparasites (see "Little Things That Tick Off Baboons," *Natural History,* February 1984). Baboons spend much more time grooming than is necessary for hygiene, and previous research had indicated that it is a good measure of social bonds.

Although eighteen adult males lived in the troop, each nonestrous female performed most of her grooming with just one, two, or occasionally, three males. For example, of Zizi's twenty-four grooming bouts with males, Cyclops accounted for thirteen, and a second male, Sherlock, accounted for all the rest. Different females tended to favor different males as grooming partners.

Another measure of social bonds was simply who was observed near whom. When foraging, traveling, or resting, each pregnant or lactating female spent a lot of time near a few males and associated with the others no more often than expected by chance. When I compared the identities of favorite grooming partners and frequent companions, they overlapped almost completely. This enabled me to develop a formal definition of friendship: any male that scored high on both grooming and proximity measures was considered a friend.

Virtually all baboons made friends; only one female and three males who had most recently joined the troop lacked such companions. Out of more than 600 possible adult female–adult male pairs in the troop, however, only about one in ten qualified as friends; these really were special relationships.

Several factors seemed to influence which baboons paired up. In most cases, friends were unrelated to each other, since the male had immigrated from another troop. (Four friendships, however, involved a female and an adolescent son who had not yet emigrated. Unlike other friends, these related pairs never mated.) Older females tended to be friends with older males; younger females with younger males. I witnessed occasional May–December romances, usually involving older females and young adult males. Adolescent males and females were strongly rule-bound, and with the exception of mother-son pairs, they formed friendships only with one another.

Regardless of age or dominance rank, most females had just one or two male friends. But among males, the number of female friends varied greatly from none to eight. Although high-ranking males enjoyed priority of access to food and sometimes mates, dominant males did not have more female friends than low-ranking males. Instead it was the older males who had lived in the troop for many years who had the most friends. When a male had several female friends, the females were often closely related to one another. Since female baboons spend a lot of time near their kin, it is probably easier for a male to maintain bonds with several related females at once.

When collecting data, I focused on one nonestrous female at a time and kept track of her every movement toward or away from any male; similarly, I noted every male who moved toward or away from her. Whenever the female and male moved close enough to exchange intimacies, I wrote down exactly what happened. When foraging together, friends tended to remain a few yards apart. Males more often wandered away from females than the reverse, and females, more often than males, closed the gap. The female behaved as if she wanted to keep the male within calling distance, in case she needed his protection. The male, however, was more likely to make approaches that brought them within actual touching distance. Often, he would plunk himself down right next to his friend and ask her to groom him by holding a pose with exaggerated stillness. The female sometimes responded by grooming, but more often, she exhibited the most reliable sign of true intimacy: she ignored her friend and simply continued whatever she was doing.

In sharp contrast, when a male who was not a friend moved close to a female, she dared not ignore him. She stopped whatever she was doing and held still, often glancing surreptitiously at the intruder. If he did not move away, she sometimes lifted her tail and presented her rump. When a female is not in estrus, this is a gesture of appeasement, not sexual enticement. Immediately after this respectful acknowledgement of his presence, the female would slip away. But such tense interactions with nonfriend males were rare, because females usually moved away before the males came too close.

These observations suggest that females were afraid of most of the males in their troop, which is not surprising: male baboons are twice the size of females, and their canines are longer and sharper than those of a lion. All Eburru Cliffs males directed both mild and severe aggression toward females. Mild aggression, which usually involved threats and chases but no body contact, occurred most often during feeding competition or when the male redirected aggression toward a female after losing a fight with another male. Females and juveniles showed aggression toward other females and juveniles in similar circumstances and occasionally inflicted superficial wounds. Severe aggression by males, which involved body contact and sometimes biting, was less common and also more puzzling, since there was no apparent cause.

An explanation for at least some of these attacks emerged one day when I was watching Pegasus, a young adult male, and his friend Cicily, sitting together in the middle of a small clearing. Cicily moved to the edge of the clearing to feed, and a higher-ranking female, Zora, suddenly attacked her. Pegasus stood up and looked as if he were about to intervene when both females disappeared into the bushes. He sat back down, and I remained with him. A full ten minutes later, Zora appeared at the edge of the clearing; this was the first time she had come into view since her attack on Cicily. Pegasus instantly pounced on Zora, repeatedly grabbed her neck in his mouth and lifted her off the ground, shook her whole body, and then dropped her. Zora screamed continuously and tried to escape. Each time, Pegasus caught her and continued his brutal attack. When he finally released her five minutes later she had a deep canine gash on the palm of her hand that made her limp for several days.

This attack was similar in form and intensity to those I had seen before and labeled "unprovoked." Certainly, had I come upon the scene after Zora's aggression toward Cicily, I would not have understood why Pegasus attacked Zora. This suggested that some, perhaps many, severe attacks by males actually represented punishment for actions that had occurred some time before.

Whatever the reasons for male attacks on females, they represent a serious threat. Records of fresh injuries indicated that Eburru Cliffs adult females received canine slash wounds from males at the rate of one for every female each year, and during my study, one female died of her injuries. Males probably pose an even greater threat to infants. Although only one infant was killed during my study, observers in Botswana and Tanzania have seen recent male immigrants kill several young infants.

Protection from male aggression, and from the less injurious but more frequent aggression of other females and juveniles, seems to be one of the main advantages of friendship for a female baboon. Seventy times I observed an adult male defend a female or her offspring against aggression by another troop member, not infrequently a high-ranking male. In all but six of these cases, the defender was a friend. Very few of these confrontations involved actual fighting; no male baboon, subordinate or dominant, is anxious to risk injury by the sharp canines of another.

Males are particularly solicitous guardians of their friends' youngest infants. If another male gets too close to an infant or if a juvenile female plays with it too roughly, the friend may intervene. Other troop members soon learn to be cautious when the mother's friend is nearby, and his presence provides the mother with a welcome respite from the annoying pokes and prods of curious females and juveniles obsessed with the new

baby. Male baboons at Gombe Park in Tanzania and Amboseli Park in Kenya have also been seen rescuing infants from chimpanzees and lions. These several forms of male protection help to explain why females in Eburru Cliffs stuck closer to their friends in the first few months after giving birth than at any other time.

The male–infant relationship develops out of the male's friendship with the mother, but as the infant matures, this new bond takes on a life of its own. My co-worker Nancy Nicolson found that by about nine months of age, infants actively sought out their male friends when the mother was a few yards away, suggesting that the male may function as an alternative caregiver. This seemed to be especially true for infants undergoing unusually early or severe weaning. (Weaning is generally a gradual, prolonged process, but there is tremendous variation among mothers in the timing and intensity of weaning. See "Mother Baboons," *Natural History,* September 1980). After being rejected by the mother, the crying infant often approached the male friend and sat huddled against him until its whimpers subsided. Two of the infants in Eburru Cliffs lost their mothers when they were still quite young. In each case, their bond with the mother's friend subsequently intensified, and—perhaps as a result—both infants survived.

A close bond with a male may also improve the infant's nutrition. Larger than all other troop members, adult males monopolize the best feeding sites. In general, the personal space surrounding a feeding male is inviolate, but he usually tolerates intrusions by the infants of his female friends, giving them access to choice feeding spots.

Although infants follow their male friends around rather than the reverse, the males seem genuinely attached to their tiny companions. During feeding, the male and infant express their pleasure in each other's company by sharing spirited, antiphonal grunting duets. If the infant whimpers in distress, the male friend is likely to cease feeding, look at the infant, and grunt softly, as if in sympathy, until the whimpers cease. When the male rests, the infants of his female friends may huddle behind him, one after the other, forming a "train," or, if feeling energetic, they may use his body as a trampoline.

When I returned to Eburru Cliffs four years after my initial study ended, several of the bonds formed between males and the infants of their female friends were still intact (in other cases, either the male or the infant or both had disappeared). When these bonds involved recently matured females, their long-time male associates showed no sexual interest in them, even though the females mated with other adult males. Mothers and sons, and usually maternal siblings, show similar sexual inhibitions in baboons and many other primate species.

The development of an intimate relationship between a male and the infant of his female friend raises an obvious question: Is the male the infant's father? To answer this question definitely we would need to conduct genetic analysis, which was not possible for these baboons. Instead, I estimated paternity probabilities from observations of the temporary (a few hours or days) exclusive mating relationships, or consortships, that estrous females form with a series of different males. These estimates were apt to be fairly accurate, since changes in the female's sexual swelling allow one to pinpoint the timing of conception to within a few days. Most females consorted with only two or three males during this period, and these males were termed likely fathers.

In about half the friendships, the male was indeed likely to be the father of his friend's most recent infant, but in the other half he was not—in fact, he had never been seen mating with the female. Interestingly, males who were friends with the mother but not likely fathers nearly always developed a relationship with her infant, while males who had mated with the female but were not her friend usually did not. Thus friendship with the mother, rather than paternity, seems to mediate the development of male–infant bonds. Recently, a similar pattern was documented for South American capuchin monkeys in a laboratory study in which paternity was determined genetically.

These results fly in the face of a prominent theory that claims males will invest in infants only when they are closely related. If males are not fostering the survival of their own genes by caring for the infant, then why do they do so? I suspected that the key was female choice. If females preferred to mate with males who had already demonstrated friendly behavior, then friendships with mothers and their infants might pay off in the future when the mothers were ready to mate again.

To find out if this was the case, I examined each male's sexual behavior with females he had befriended before they resumed estrus. In most cases, males consorted considerably more often with their friends than with other females. Baboon females typically mate with several different males, including both friends and nonfriends, but prior friendship increased a male's probability of mating with a female above what it would have been otherwise.

This increased probability seemed to reflect female preferences. Females occasionally overtly advertised their disdain for certain males and their desire for others. Zizi's behavior, described above, is a good example. Virgil was not one of her friends, but Cyclops was. Usually, however, females expressed preferences and aversions more subtly. For example, Delphi, a petite adolescent female, found herself pursued by Hector, a middle-aged adult male. She did not run away or refuse to mate with him, but whenever he wasn't watching, she looked around for her friend Homer, an adolescent male. When she succeeded in catching Homer's eye, she narrowed her eyes and flattened her ears against her skull, the friendliest face one baboon can send another. This told Homer she would rather be with him. Females expressed satisfaction with a current consort partner by staying close to him, initiating copulations, and not making advances toward other males. Baboons are very sensitive to such cues, as indicated by an experimental study in which rival hamadryas baboons rarely challenged a male–female pair if the female strongly preferred her current partner. Similarly, in Eburru Cliffs, males were less apt to challenge consorts involving a pair that shared a long-term friendship.

Even though females usually consorted with their friends, they also mated with other males, so it is not surprising that friendships were most vulnerable during periods of sexual activity.

In a few cases, the female consorted with another male more often than with her friend, but the friendship survived nevertheless. One female, however, formed a strong sexual bond with a new male. This bond persisted after conception, replacing her previous friendship. My observations suggest that adolescent and young adult females tend to have shorter, less stable friendships than do older females. Some friendships, however, last a very long time. When I returned to Eburru Cliffs six years after my study began, five couples were still together. It is possible that friendships occasionally last for life (baboons probably live twenty to thirty years in the wild), but it will require longer studies, and some very patient scientists to find out.

By increasing both the male's chances of mating in the future and the likelihood that a female's infant will survive, friendship contributes to the reproductive success of both partners. This clarifies the evolutionary basis of friendship-forming tendencies in baboons, but what does friendship mean to a baboon? To answer this question we need to view baboons as sentient beings with feelings and goals not unlike our own in similar circumstances. Consider, for example, the friendship between Thalia and Alexander.

The affair began one evening as Alex and Thalia sat about fifteen feet apart on the sleeping cliffs. It was like watching two novices in a singles bar. Alex stared at Thalia until she turned and almost caught him looking at her. He glanced away immediately, and then she stared at him until his head began to turn toward her. She suddenly became engrossed in grooming her toes. But as soon as Alex looked away, her gaze returned to him. They went on like this for more than fifteen minutes, always with split-second timing. Finally, Alex managed to catch Thalia looking at him. He made the friendly eyes-narrowed, ears-back face and smacked his lips together rhythmically. Thalia froze, and for a second she looked into his eyes. Alex approached, and Thalia, still nervous, groomed him. Soon she calmed down, and I found them still together on the cliffs the next morning. Looking back on this event months later, I realized that it marked the beginning of their friendship. Six years later, when I returned to Eburru Cliffs, they were still friends.

If flirtation forms an integral part of baboon friendship, so does jealousy. Overt displays of jealousy, such as chasing a friend away from a potential rival, occur occasionally, but like humans, baboons often express their emotions in more subtle ways. One evening a colleague and I climbed the cliffs and settled down near Sherlock, who was friends with Cybelle, a middle-aged female still foraging on the ground below the cliffs. I observed Cybelle while my colleague watched Sherlock, and we kept up a running commentary. As long as Cybelle was feeding or interacting with females, Sherlock was relaxed, but each time she approached another male, his body would stiffen, and he would stare intently at the scene below. When Cybelle presented politely to a male who had recently tried to befriend her, Sherlock even made threatening sounds under his breath. Cybelle was not in estrus at the time, indicating that male baboon jealousy extends beyond the sexual arena to include affiliative interactions between a female friend and other males.

Because baboon friendships are embedded in a network of friendly and antagonistic relationships, they inevitably lead to repercussions extending beyond the pair. For example, Virgil once provoked his weaker rival Cyclops into a fight by first attacking Cyclops's friend Phoebe. On another occasion, Sherlock chased Circe, Hector's best friend, just after Hector had chased Antigone, Sherlock's friend.

In another incident, the prime adult male Triton challenged Cyclops's possession of meat. Cyclops grew increasingly tense and seemed about to abandon the prey to the younger male. Then Cyclops's friend Phoebe appeared with her infant Phyllis. Phyllis wandered over to Cyclops. He immediately grabbed her, held her close, and threatened Triton away from the prey. Because any challenge to Cyclops now involved a threat to Phyllis as well, Triton risked being mobbed by Phoebe and her relatives and friends. For this reason, he backed down. Males frequently use the infants of their female friends as buffers in this way. Thus, friendship involves costs as well as benefits because it makes the participants vulnerable to social manipulation or redirected aggression by others.

Finally, as with humans, friendship seems to mean something different to each baboon. Several females in Eburru Cliffs had only one friend. They were devoted companions. Louise and Pandora, for example, groomed their friend Virgil and no other male. Then there was Leda, who, with five friends, spread herself more thinly than any other female. These contrasting patterns of friendship were associated with striking personality differences. Louise and Pandora were unobtrusive females who hung around quietly with Virgil and their close relatives. Leda seemed to be everywhere at once, playing with infants, fighting with juveniles, and making friends with males. Similar differences were apparent among the males. Some devoted a great deal of time and energy to cultivating friendships with females, while others focused more on challenging other males. Although we probably will never fully understand the basis of these individual differences, they contribute immeasurably to the richness and complexity of baboon society.

Male–female friendships may be widespread among primates. They have been reported for many other groups of savanna baboons, and they also occur in rhesus and Japanese Macaques, capuchin monkeys, and perhaps in bonobos (pygmy chimpanzees). These relationships should give us pause when considering popular scenarios for the evolution of male–female relationships in humans. Most of these scenarios assume that, except for mating, males and females had little to do with one another until the development of a sexual division of labor, when, the story goes, females began to rely on males to provide meat in exchange for gathered food. This, it has been argued, set up new selection pressures favoring the development of long-term bonds between individual males and females, female sexual fidelity, and as paternity certainty increased, greater male investment in the offspring of these unions. In other words, once women began to gather and men to hunt, presto—we had the nuclear family.

This scenario may have more to do with cultural biases about women's economic dependence on men and idealized views of the nuclear family than with the actual behavior of our hominid ancestors. The nonhuman primate evidence challenges this story in at least three ways.

First, long-term bonds between the sexes can evolve in the absence of a sexual division of labor of food sharing. In our primate relatives, such relationships rest on exchanges of social, not economic, benefits.

Second, primate research shows that highly differentiated, emotionally intense male–female relationships can occur without sexual exclusivity. Ancestral men and women may have experienced intimate friendships long before they invented marriage and norms of sexual fidelity.

Third, among our closest primate relatives, males clearly provide mothers and infants with social benefits even when they are unlikely to be the fathers of those infants. In return, females provide a variety of benefits to the friendly males, including acceptance into the group and, at least in baboons, increased mating opportunities in the future. This suggests that efforts to reconstruct the evolution of hominid societies may have overemphasized what the female must supposedly do (restrict her mating to just one male) in order to obtain male parental investment.

Maybe it is time to pay more attention to what the male must do (provide benefits to females and young) in order to obtain female cooperation. Perhaps among our ancestors, as in baboons today, sex and friendship went hand in hand. As for marriage—well, that's another story.

Critical Thinking

1. How have primatologists typically described the sexual behavior of olive baboons? In what sense is this description a stereotype?

2. How have primatologists explained the fact that some males copulate more than others? What has been the explicit assumption? How does the alternative view help to explain the apparent exceptions?

3. Why did the author choose not to focus simply upon females in estrus?

4. How does the author describe the typical baboon troop? How does she measure friendship? What proportion of the possible relationships actually constituted friendship?

5. What factors influenced friendship?

6. Describe the behavior patterns of friends.

7. Why are females afraid of most males in their troop?

8. What advantages does friendship bring to females and to their infants?

9. Does paternity have anything to do with a male's relationship with his female friend's infant? Explain.

10. According to Smuts, why do males care for the infants of their female friends?

11. In what ways do females express preference for certain male friends? Do other males tend to honor this preference?

12. Which baboons tend to have shorter, less stable friendships?

13. How does friendship increase the reproductive success of both partners?

14. Discuss flirtation and jealousy among baboons.

15. Why does the author say that friendship involves a network of relationships that result in repercussions extending beyond the pair?

16. To what extent is friendship something different to each baboon?

17. What has been the assumption of popular scenarios regarding the evolution of male–female relationships? In what ways does the author challenge this story?

Create Central

www.mhhe.com/createcentral

Internet References

American Scientist
www.americanscientist.org
Primate Society of Great Britain
www.psgb.org

Smuts, Barbara. From *Natural History*, February 1987, pp. 36, 38–44. Copyright © 1987 by Natural History Magazine. Reprinted by permission.

Article   Prepared by Elvio Angeloni, *Pasadena City College*

What's Love Got to Do with It?

Sex among Our Closest Relatives Is a Rather Open Affair

MEREDITH F. SMALL

Learning Outcomes

After reading this article, you will be able to:

- Discuss how the study of bonobo sexual behavior helps us understand human evolution.
- Discuss the pros and cons of the theory of "hidden heat."
- Explain how social bonds help provide protection against abusive male apes for female apes.

M aiko and Lana are having sex. Maiko is on top, and Lana's arms and legs are wrapped tightly around his waist. Lina, a friend of Lana's, approaches from the right and taps Maiko on the back, nudging him to finish. As he moves away, Lina enfolds Lana in her arms, and they roll over so that Lana is now on top. The two females rub their genitals together, grinning and screaming in pleasure.

This is no orgy staged for an X-rated movie. It doesn't even involve people—or rather, it involves them only as observers. Lana, Maiko, and Lina are bonobos, a rare species of chimplike ape in which frequent couplings and casual sex play characterize every social relationship—between males and females, members of the same sex, closely related animals, and total strangers. Primatologists are beginning to study the bonobos' unrestrained sexual behavior for tantalizing clues to the origins of our own sexuality.

In reconstructing how early man and woman behaved, researchers have generally looked not to bonobos but to common chimpanzees. Only about 5 million years ago human beings and chimps shared a common ancestor, and we still have much behavior in common: namely, a long period of infant dependency, a reliance on learning what to eat and how to obtain food, social bonds that persist over generations, and the need to deal as a group with many everyday conflicts. The assumption has been that chimp behavior today may be similar to the behavior of human ancestors.

Bonobo behavior, however, offers another window on the past because they, too, shared our 5-million-year-old ancestor, diverging from chimps just 2 million years ago. Bonobos have been less studied than chimps for the simple reason that they are difficult to find. They live only on a small patch of land

in Zaire, in central Africa. They were first identified, on the basis of skeletal material, in the 1920s, but it wasn't until the 1970s that their behavior in the wild was studied, and then only sporadically.

Bonobos, also known as pygmy chimpanzees, are not really pygmies but welterweights. The largest males are as big as chimps, and the females of the two species are the same size. But bonobos are more delicate in build, and their arms and legs are long and slender.

On the ground, moving from fruit tree to fruit tree, bonobos often stand and walk on two legs—behavior that makes them seem more like humans than chimps. In some ways their sexual behavior seems more human as well, suggesting that in the sexual arena, at least, bonobos are the more appropriate ancestral model. Males and females frequently copulate face-to-face, which is an uncommon position in animals other than humans. Males usually mount females from behind, but females seem to prefer sex face-to-face. "Sometimes the female will let a male start to mount from behind," says Amy Parish, a graduate student at the University of California at Davis who's been watching female bonobo sexual behavior in several zoo colonies around the world. "And then she'll stop, and of course he's really excited, and then she continues face-to-face." Primatologists assume the female preference is dictated by her anatomy: her enlarged clitoris and sexual swellings are oriented far forward. Females presumably prefer face-to-face contact because it feels better.

Like humans but unlike chimps and most other animals, bonobos separate sex from reproduction. They seem to treat sex as a pleasurable activity, and they rely on it as a sort of social glue, to make or break all sorts of relationships. "Ancestral humans behaved like this," proposes Frans de Waal, an ethologist at the Yerkes Regional Primate Research Center at Emory University. "Later, when we developed the family system, the use of sex for this sort of purpose became more limited, mainly occurring within families. A lot of the things we see, like pedophilia and homosexuality, may be leftovers that some now consider unacceptable in our particular society."

Depending on your morals, watching bonobo sex play may be like watching humans at their most extreme and perverse. Bonobos seem to have sex more often and in more combinations than the average person in any culture, and most of the time bonobo sex has nothing to do with making babies. Males mount females and females sometimes mount them back; females rub against other females just for fun; males stand rump to rump and press their scrotal areas together. Even juveniles participate by rubbing their genital areas against adults, although ethologists don't think that males actually insert their penises into juvenile females. Very young animals also have sex with each other: little males suck on each other's penises or French-kiss. When two animals initiate sex, others freely join in by poking their fingers and toes into the moving parts.

One thing sex does for bonobos is decrease tensions caused by potential competition, often competition for food. Japanese primatologists observing bonobos in Zaire were the first to notice that when bonobos come across a large fruiting tree or encounter piles of provisioned sugarcane, the sight of food triggers a binge of sex. The atmosphere of this sexual free-for-all is decidedly friendly, and it eventually calms the group down. "What's striking is how rapidly the sex drops off," says Nancy Thompson-Handler of the State University of New York at Stony Brook, who has observed bonobos at a site in Zaire called Lomako. "After ten minutes, sexual behavior decreases by fifty percent." Soon the group turns from sex to feeding.

But it's tension rather than food that causes the sexual excitement. "I'm sure the more food you give them, the more sex you'll get," says de Waal. "But it's not really the food, it's competition that triggers this. You can throw in a cardboard box and you'll get sexual behavior." Sex is just the way bonobos deal with competition over limited resources and with the normal tensions caused by living in a group. Anthropologist Frances White of Duke University, a bonobo observer at Lomako since 1983, puts it simply: "Sex is fun. Sex makes them feel good and therefore keeps the group together."

Sex is fun. Sex makes them feel good and keeps the group together.

Sexual behavior also occurs after aggressive encounters, especially among males. After two males fight, one may reconcile with his opponent by presenting his rump and backing up against the other's testicles. He might grab the penis of the other male and stroke it. It's the male bonobo's way of shaking hands and letting everyone know that the conflict has ended amicably.

Researchers also note that female bonobo sexuality, like the sexuality of female humans, isn't locked into a monthly cycle. In most other animals, including chimps, the female's interest in sex is tied to her ovulation cycle. Chimp females sport pink swellings on their hind ends for about two weeks, signaling their fertility, and they're only approachable for sex during that time. That's not the case with humans, who show no outward signs that they are ovulating, and can mate at all phases of the cycle. Female bonobos take the reverse tack, but with similar results. Their large swellings are visible for weeks before and after their

fertile periods, and there is never any discernibly wrong time to mate. Like humans, they have sex whether or not they are ovulating.

What's fascinating is that female bonobos use this boundless sexuality in all their relationships. "Females rule the business—sex and food," says de Waal. "It's a good species for feminists, I think." For instance, females regularly use sex to cement relationships with other females. A genital-genital rub, better known as GG-rubbing by observers, is the most frequent behavior used by bonobo females to reinforce social ties or relieve tension. GG-rubbing takes a variety of forms. Often one female rolls on her back and extends her arms and legs. The other female mounts her and they rub their swellings right and left for several seconds, massaging their clitorises against each other. GG-rubbing occurs in the presence of food because food causes tension and excitement, but the intimate contact has the effect of making close friends.

Females rule the business. It's a good species for feminists, I think.

Sometimes females would rather GG-rub with each other than copulate with a male. Parish filmed a 15-minute scene at a bonobo colony at the San Diego Wild Animal Park in which a male, Vernon, repeatedly solicited two females, Lisa and Loretta. Again and again he arched his back and displayed his erect penis—the bonobo request for sex. The females moved away from him, tactfully turning him down until they crept behind a tree and GG-rubbed with each other.

Unlike most primate species, in which males usually take on the dangerous task of leaving home, among bonobos females are the ones who leave the group when they reach sexual maturity, around the age of eight, and work their way into unfamiliar groups. To aid in their assimilation into a new community, the female bonobos make good use of their endless sexual favors. While watching a bonobo group at a feeding tree, White saw a young female systematically have sex with each member before feeding. "An adolescent female, presumably a recent transfer female, came up to the tree, mated with all five males, went into the tree, and solicited GG-rubbing from all the females present," says White.

Once inside the new group, a female bonobo must build a sister-hood from scratch. In groups of humans or chimps, unrelated females construct friendships through the rituals of shopping together or grooming. Bonobos do it sexually. Although pleasure may be the motivation behind a female-female assignation, the function is to form an alliance.

These alliances are serious business, because they determine the pecking order at food sites. Females with powerful friends eat first, and subordinate females may not get any food at all if the resource is small. When times are rough, then, it pays to have close female friends. White describes a scene at Lomako in which an adolescent female, Blanche, benefited from her established friendship with Freda. "I was following Freda and her boyfriend, and they found a tree that they didn't expect to

Hidden Heat

Standing upright is not a position usually—or easily—associated with sex. Among people, at least, anatomy and gravity prove to be forbidding obstacles. Yet our two-legged stance may be the key to a distinctive aspect of human sexuality: the independence of women's sexual desires from a monthly calendar.

Males in the two species most closely related to us, chimpanzees and bonobos, don't spend a lot of time worrying, "Is she interested or not?" The answer is obvious. When ovulatory hormones reach a monthly peak in female chimps and bonobos, and their eggs are primed for fertilization, their genital area swells up, and both sexes appear to have just one thing on their mind. "These animals really turn on when this happens. Everything else is dropped," says primatologist Frederick Szalay of Hunter College in New York.

Women, however, don't go into heat. And this departure from our relatives' sexual behavior has long puzzled researchers. Clear signals of fertility and the willingness to do something about it bring major evolutionary advantages: ripe eggs lead to healthier pregnancies, which leads to more of your genes in succeeding generations, which is what evolution is all about. In addition, male chimps give females that are waving these red flags of fertility first chance at high-protein food such as meat.

So why would our ancestors give this up? Szalay and graduate student Robert Costello have a simple explanation. Women gave heat up, they say, because our ancestors stood up. Fossil footprints indicate that somewhere around 3.5 million years ago hominids—non-ape primates—began walking on two legs. "In hominids, something dictated getting up. We don't know what it was," Szalay says. "But once it did, there was a problem with the signaling system." The problem was that it didn't work. Swollen genital areas that were visible when their owners were down on all fours became hidden between the legs. The mating signal was lost.

"Uprightness meant very tough times for females working with the old ovarian cycle," Szalay says. Males wouldn't notice them, and the swellings themselves, which get quite large, must have made it hard for two-legged creatures to walk around.

Those who found a way out of this quandary, Szalay suggests, were females with small swellings but with a little less hair on their rears and a little extra fat. It would have looked a bit like the time-honored mating signal. They got more attention, and produced more offspring. "You don't start a completely new trend in signaling," Szalay says. "You have a little extra fat, a little nakedness to mimic the ancestors. If there was an ever-so-little advantage because, quite simply, you look good, it would be selected for."

And if a little nakedness and a little fat worked well, Szalay speculates, then a lot of both would work even better. "Once you start a trend in sexual signaling, crazy things happen," he notes. "It's almost like: let's escalate, let's add more. That's what happens in horns with sheep. It's a particular part of the body that brings an advantage." In a few million years human ancestors were more naked than ever, with fleshy rears not found in any other primate. Since these features were permanent, unlike the monthly ups and downs of swellings, sex was free to become a part of daily life.

It's a provocative notion, say Szalay's colleagues, but like any attempt to conjure up the past from the present, there's no real proof of cause and effect. Anthropologist Helen Fisher of the American Museum of Natural History notes that Szalay is merely assuming that fleshy buttocks evolved because they were sex signals. Yet their mass really comes from muscles, which chimps don't have, that are associated with walking. And anthropologist Sarah Blaffer Hrdy of the University of California at Davis points to a more fundamental problem: our ancestors may not have had chimplike swellings that they needed to dispense with. Chimps and bonobos are only two of about 200 primate species, and the vast majority of those species don't have big swellings. Though they are our closest relatives, chimps and bonobos have been evolving during the last 5 million years just as we have, and swollen genitals may be a recent development. The current unswollen human pattern may be the ancestral one.

"Nobody really knows what happened," says Fisher. "Everybody has an idea. You pays your money and you takes your choice."

—Joshua Fischman

be there. It was a small tree, heavily in fruit with one of their favorites. Freda went straight up the tree and made a food call to Blanche. Blanche came tearing over—she was quite far away—and went tearing up the tree to join Freda, and they GG-rubbed like crazy."

Alliances also give females leverage over larger, stronger males who otherwise would push them around. Females have discovered there is strength in numbers. Unlike other species of primates, such as chimpanzees or baboons (or, all too often, humans), where tensions run high between males and females, bonobo females are not afraid of males, and the sexes mingle peacefully. "What is consistently different from chimps," says Thompson-Handler, "is the composition of parties. The vast majority are mixed, so there are males and females of all different ages."

Female bonobos cannot be coerced into anything, including sex. Parish recounts an interaction between Lana and a male called Akili at the San Diego Wild Animal Park. "Lana had just been introduced into the group. For a long time she lay on the grass with a huge swelling. Akili would approach her with a big erection and hover over her. It would have been easy for him to do a mount. But he wouldn't. He just kept trying to catch her eye, hovering around her, and she would scoot around the ground, avoiding him. And then he'd try again. She went around full circle." Akili was big enough to force himself on her. Yet he refrained.

In another encounter, a male bonobo was carrying a large clump of branches. He moved up to a female and presented his erect penis by spreading his legs and arching his back. She rolled onto her back and they copulated. In the midst of their joint ecstasy, she reached out and grabbed a branch from the male. When he pulled back, finished and satisfied, she moved away, clutching the branch to her chest. There was no tension between them, and she essentially traded copulation for food. But the key here is that the male allowed her to move away with the branch—it didn't occur to him to threaten her, because their status was virtually equal.

Although the results of sexual liberation are clear among bonobos, no one is sure why sex has been elevated to such a high position in this species and why it is restricted merely to reproduction among chimpanzees. "The puzzle for me," says de Waal, "is that chimps do all this bonding with kissing and embracing, with body contact. Why do bonobos do it in a sexual manner?" He speculates that the use of sex as a standard way to underscore relationships began between adult males and adult females as an extension of the mating process and later spread to all members of the group. But no one is sure exactly how this happened.

It is also unclear whether bonobo sexually became exaggerated only after their split from the human lineage or whether the behavior they exhibit today is the modern version of our common ancestor's sex play. Anthropologist Adrienne Zihlman of the University of California at Santa Cruz, who has used the evidence of fossil bones to argue that our earliest known non-ape ancestors, the australopithecines, had body proportions similar to those of bonobos, says, "The path of evolution is not a straight line from either species, but what I think is important is that the bonobo information gives us more possibilities for looking at human origins."

Some anthropologists, however, are reluctant to include the details of bonobo life, such as wide-ranging sexuality and a strong sisterhood, into scenarios of human evolution. "The researchers have all these commitments to male dominance [as in chimpanzees], and yet bonobos have egalitarian relationships," says de Waal. "They also want to see humans as unique, yet bonobos fit very nicely into many of the scenarios, making humans appear less unique."

Our divergent, non-ape path has led us away from sex and toward a culture that denies the connection between sex and social cohesion. But bonobos, with their versatile sexuality, are here to remind us that our heritage may very well include a primordial urge to make love, not war.

Critical Thinking

1. How long ago did humans and chimps share a common ancestor? What kinds of behavior do we still have in common?

2. When did bonobos diverge from chimps? How do they differ from chimps? How do primatologists explain the female preference for face-to-face sex?

3. In what respects do bonobos, like humans, separate sex from reproduction?

4. How does bonobo sexual behavior contrast with that of most humans?

5. What is the "one thing" that sex does for bonobos? Why is this not just connected with food?

6. How is sexual behavior related to aggression?

7. In what way is female bonobo sexuality similar to that of female humans and different from that of chimps? How is it also different from humans?

8. How do females use sex? How is "GG-rubbing" related to the fact that females are the ones to leave the group? What are the parallels in humans and chimps? Why are such alliances "serious business"? How does this affect the relationship between the sexes and how is this different from chimps?

9. Can female bonobos be coerced into sex?

10. How do the methods of bonding contrast between chimps and bonobos? Do we know why this is so?

11. Do we know if bonobo sexuality became exaggerated before or after their split from the human lineage? Why are some anthropologists reluctant to include the details of bonobo life in scenarios of human evolution, according to de Waal?

12. Discuss the pros and cons of Szalay and Costello's theory of "hidden heat."

Create Central

www.mhhe.com/createcentral

Internet References

Sexuality Studies
https://sxs.sfsu.edu/ https://sxs.sfsu.edu
Sexuality Studies.net
http://sexualitystudies.net/programs

Article   Prepared by Elvio Angeloni, *Pasadena City College*

The Double Life of Women

The invisible turns of the reproductive cycle shape the everyday behavior of women and men. A woman's cycle influences not just her preference in a partner, but her personality as well.

Annie Murphy Paul

Learning Outcomes

After reading this article, you will be able to:

- Discuss the three principal theories regarding human female ovulation.

- Explain how and why a woman's reproductive cycle affects her preferences, perceptions, and behavior with respect to men.

Step into any bar or party and it won't take you long to spot her. She's the woman with the ringing laugh, the daring clothes, the magnetic appeal that has drawn a circle of admirers around her. If the room were a solar system, she would be the sun—and at the outer reaches, you notice, are several other women seated quietly in her shadow.

Why does this woman command all the attention? Psychologists, image experts, and dating advisers propose a host of explanations: It's her extraverted personality, her come-hither look, her approachable persona. But an evolutionary biologist observing the scene would offer a more surprising interpretation, one that may help explain barroom dynamics and much more: It's her "real" time of the month. The belle of the bar is likely reaching peak fertility, while her drabber companions are slogging through a non-fertile phase.

Not long ago, such an explanation would have been intellectual heresy. Sure, biologists could tell when chimpanzees were ready to mate: Once every 28 days, the genitalia of female chimps swell and turn a dramatic shade of pink. And estrus, as the state of sexual receptivity is known, is also readily apparent in less exotic animals, as anyone who's seen a house cat in heat can attest. Every female mammal on earth, it was believed, advertises her period of greatest fertility—except the female human. In woman, estrus was "lost" somewhere in the long meander of evolution. "That's the conventional, traditional view of human estrus," says Randy Thornhill, professor of biology at the University of New Mexico. "But it turns out to be wrong."

Over the past decade, evolutionary biologists and psychologists have uncovered abundant evidence that women do, in fact, provide clues to the timing of ovulation, the moment when an egg is released and ready to be fertilized. Though these changes are far subtler than those in other species, they have a powerful effect on women's perceptions, preferences, and behavior—and the reaction of others to her. Monthly shifts even affect *men's* feelings and actions. Indeed, the invisible but influential turns of the reproductive cycle shape the everyday behavior of us all. "Human ovulation is not an observable event, and men and women have no explicit awareness of it," says Martie Haselton, associate professor of communication studies and psychology at UCLA. "But the effects of the menstrual cycle on human behavior are surprisingly strong."

Take, for example, women's preferences in male partners. We may think that each woman has an unchanging "type"—but it turns out that women prefer quite different kinds of men depending on whether or not they are fertile. In the two days or so of the ovulatory phase—the time when women are most likely to become pregnant—they gravitate toward men with more "masculine" traits. That means a man who sports a leaner, V-shaped body, and a face with a squarer chin, straighter, heavier eyebrows, and thinner lips; one who speaks in a lower-pitched voice, and displays more aggressive, dominant behavior. When a woman is in the follicular or luteal phases—during which the uterus sheds its lining and then builds it up again, and in which she generally cannot become pregnant—she prefers men with softer features, less-defined bodies, higher voices, and a gentler manner.

So pronounced are these preferences that Thornhill and his University of New Mexico colleague Steven Gangestad have proposed that women actually have two sexualities: one when they're ovulating, and another during the rest of the month. These distinct modes emerge out of two competing reproductive goals. "Women want to get the highest-quality genes for their children," says Thornhill, and high genetic quality in a man is indicated by his degree of testosteronization—the extent to which the male hormone testosterone has affected his brain, his face, and the rest of his body.

Women actually have two sexualities: One when they're ovulating, and another during the rest of the month.

Once she is pregnant or in the non-fertile part of her cycle, however, a woman's aims do an abrupt about-face: She wants to secure the most generous and stable source of goods for herself and her offspring. Now the nice-guy provider starts to look appealing. "When women are in what we call the extended-sexuality phase, their preferences shift towards men who appear to have a willingness to share resources like food and protection with her and her children," says Thornhill.

The influence of the menstrual cycle on women is apparent not only in whom they desire but in how they act. Women who are in the ovulatory phase show more interest in erotic materials than women in the luteal or follicular phases; given a choice of movies to watch, they select ones with more romantic or sexual themes. They take more care with their appearance, and they choose more revealing clothes to wear. In 2004, a group of researchers from the University of Vienna digitally analyzed pictures of 351 women going out to Austrian nightclubs and collected a saliva sample from each. Women whose clothes were tight or showed a lot of skin had higher levels of estradiol, a female hormone that is elevated around the time of ovulation.

It even appears that ovulating women are more receptive to the advances of men—handsome French men at least. In a study led by psychologist Nicolas Guéguen of the University of South Brittany, 22 percent of women in their fertile phase accepted an attractive man's invitation for a date, while only 8 percent of women who were not ovulating said yes. Perhaps the fertile women were open to a stranger's overtures because they were feeling especially good about themselves; studies by Martie Haselton and others have found that women judge themselves as sexier and more attractive when they are in the ovulatory phase than at other times of the month.

And they may actually *be* more attractive. Women's faces and bodies undergo subtle changes over the course of the menstrual cycle, research reveals. On fertile days, their voices go up in pitch, their breasts become more symmetrical, and their waist-hip ratio is accentuated (the ratio of the circumference of a woman's waist to that of her hips is a marker of general health and fertility). Subjects shown pictures of the same woman taken over the course of a month pick the one from her fertile period as the most attractive, and men offered T-shirts worn by women in different phases say that the one worn during ovulation smells best.

Whether they're responding to biochemical cues like body odor, to changes in women's appearance, or to women's altered attitudes and behaviors, research shows that men act differently according to the menstrual phase of the women they encounter. A study by Thornhill and Gangestad reported that a man with an ovulating female partner is more likely to engage in mate-guarding behaviors, such as paying close attention to her whereabouts and calling her cell phone at random times to see what she's up to. He is also more agreeable in his interactions with her, and more likely to give her gifts.

One of the most arresting studies of male responses to female fertility cues was conducted by Geoffrey Miller, an associate professor of psychology at the University of New Mexico. Miller found that 18 "lap dancers"—strip club workers who perform provocative dances for male customers—who were menstruating earned an average of about $184 per

five-hour shift, while those who were ovulating earned about $354—almost twice as much money, offered by clients who were told nothing about the dancers' cycles.

Moreover, dancers taking birth control pills earned about $193 per shift—more than menstruating women, but much less than women in estrus—and their tips showed no variation across the month. "Hormonal contraception places the female body in a state of pseudo-pregnancy, and it seems that on some level the male customers recognized the women's biological status and responded to it in economic terms," says Miller. Other studies have demonstrated that the pill effectively eliminates the biological and psychological changes associated with estrus, with unexplored effects on women's long-term mate choices.

Modern contraception, then, maybe disrupting an adaptation forged over many thousands of years of evolution. But the precise nature of that adaptation remains to be figured out. There are three principal theories, the first of which is known as the "signaling hypothesis": With her tight clothes, alluring scent, and seductive waist-hip ratio, a woman in estrus is sending out a signal not unlike the chimp or the cat in heat. "Obviously, women who didn't attract mates and have sex when they were fertile were not going to leave behind any offspring at all," notes Kim Wallen, a professor of psychology and behavioral neuroendocrinology at Emory University.

Yet there's reason to think that matters are more complicated than that. Rather than a simple exchange of information between the sexes—the woman communicates that she's ready to mate, and the man obliges—something altogether more shrewd and devious seems to be afoot. According to this hypothesis, men and women are engaged in an eons-old co-evolutionary race, in which one sex makes a move and the other matches it.

By identifying a female's fertile phase, a male can maximize his efforts to impregnate her and to keep other males from doing the same. Women, meanwhile, are strongly motivated to conceal the timing of ovulation. If a man isn't sure when his partner is fertile, he can't restrict her movements or limit her interactions. Hidden ovulation also allows females to discreetly mate with different partners, since none of the potential fathers can be sure of the paternity of the offspring. Her efforts at subterfuge, however, are always incomplete. "It's difficult for women to fully conceal all signs of fertility—some of them inevitably leak out," says Martie Haselton. "We call this the 'leaky cues hypothesis.'"

In another spin of the evolutionary wheel, men have evolved to recognize the signs women let slip. "Human males can detect estrus—not as well as male wombats, but at rates reliably higher than chance," says Thornhill. Research published earlier this year by psychologists Saul Miller and Jon Maner of Florida State University reported that men's testosterone levels spiked after smelling a T-shirt worn by an ovulating woman.

A third hypothesis is trickiest of all. It proposes that the pattern of changes in women that accompany the menstrual cycle is itself a marker of youth and reproductive health (in addition to a sign of transitory fertility), so women have evolved to display cyclical changes, whether they are truly fertile or not.

The effects of the menstrual cycle aren't confined to dating and mating. Female gonadal hormones "not only influence

---

A Pregnant Pause

Forget Decorating the Nursery. Gestating a Fetus Brings out Far More Adaptive Concerns and Behaviors in Women.

If the phases of the menstrual cycle produce distinctive behaviors in women, so too do the nine months of pregnancy. During gestation, evolution's aim is to protect mother and fetus from disease, infection, and contamination. A pregnant woman is vulnerable to such dangers, especially during her first trimester, because her immune system is suppressed to prevent it from attacking the fetus as a foreign body.

Daniel Fessler, an anthropologist at the University of California, Los Angeles, has studied a suite of such protective behaviors that accompany pregnancy. Women in the critical first trimester report more intense feelings of disgust than do women who are farther along in their pregnancies. Such sensitivity likely "compensates" for women's increased vulnerability by prompting them to avoid potential sources of illness.

For the same reason, Fessler has found, women make different dietary choices when they are pregnant. The food cravings and aversions, odor sensitivity, and nausea that many women develop during pregnancy all help protect the fetus from dietary pathogens. Meat is a principal source of such dangerous organisms, Fessler notes, so it's no surprise that it's high on pregnant women's list of foods to avoid.

Women may even spurn meat during some phases of their menstrual cycle, leading Fessler to a bold theory: Our male ancestors ate more meat than their female counterparts, leading them to become our species' principal hunters, leading in turn to the gender-based division of labor that we still largely practice today.

There is evidence that pregnancy leads women to treat people, and not just nutrients, in particular ways. Benedict Jones, a professor of psychology at the University of Aberdeen in Scotland, showed pictures to 115 pregnant women and 857 nonpregnant controls. The women were asked to pick which of two faces they preferred in the photographs; one set had been digitally manipulated to look healthy, the other to look diseased. Women who were pregnant showed a stronger preference for the healthy-looking faces—evidence Jones argues, that pregnant women are unconsciously motivated to avoid people who may be carrying infectious diseases that could disrupt fetal development.

In our ancestral past, the individuals bearing illnesses to which we lack immunity were more likely to be strangers, people outside our clan or tribe. In a 2007 experiment, Fessler found that "ethnocentrism"—the tendency to prefer the members of one's own group—peaked among women in their first trimester of pregnancy. Shown an essay by an American praising the United States, and an essay critical of the U.S. written by a foreigner, women early in their pregnancies reported stronger pro-American feelings.

---

ovulation and reproductive behavior but also affect cognitive functions, affective state, vulnerability to drugs of abuse, and pain sensitivity," notes psychiatrist and neuroscientist Karen Berman of the National Institute of Mental Health. Women who take stimulants such as amphetamine and cocaine, for example, will be more strongly affected by the drugs if they're in the follicular (pre-ovulatory) phase of their menstrual cycle. Women tend to consume more calories, especially from sweets, when they're in the luteal phase. And women seem to take more risks, and experience more pleasure when those risks pay off, during fertile days of the month.

Female hormones affect cognitive functions, affective state, vulnerability to drugs of abuse, and pain sensitivity.

An unpublished study by economists Matthew Pearson and Burkhard Schipper found that in a series of sealed-bid auctions set up by the experimenters, women bid significantly higher amounts at times when they were more likely to conceive. Pearson and Schipper, both professors at the University of California, Davis, speculate that women are "predisposed by hormones to generally behave more riskily during the fertile phase of their menstrual cycle"—a tendency that originally functioned "to increase the probability of conception, quality

of offspring, and genetic variety," but which now extends into other domains of life.

Even as these monthly shifts affect women's everyday experience, they may also have larger consequences—for the conduct of scientific investigations, for example. For decades scientists have been puzzled over inconsistencies in the reports of research on gender differences. A review of experimental pain studies, for instance, found that women felt more intense pain, at lower thresholds, than men—but only about two-thirds of the time. Psychologists Jeffrey Sherman and Linda LeResche of the University of Washington suggest that this may be because experimenters were ignoring a crucial variable. "Few studies on sex differences before 1995 recorded the time in the menstrual cycle when experimental manipulations took place, or accounted for the variability associated with female reproductive hormones during the cycle," write Sherman and LeResche. More recent investigations have begun taking the menstrual cycle into account when evaluating women's perceptions and responses, and have found that women are more sensitive to pain during phases when estrogen levels are low.

The monthly revolutions of women's reproductive cycles may also help account for their heightened vulnerability to psychological disorders like depression and anxiety. Before puberty, psychiatric conditions are far more common in boys than in girls. But once the reproductive years begin, women become the more susceptible sex, and it's believed that sex hormones account for much of this difference. Estrogen and progesterone, which rise to their highest levels when women are ovulating, have anxiety-reducing effects, and the subsequent drop in the levels of these hormones may leave women more sensitive to stress than men. Although higher levels of estrogen and progesterone generally give reproductive-age women some protection against psychotic illnesses like schizophrenia, the monthly hormonal "withdrawal" they experience seems to make them more vulnerable to mood disorders such as anxiety and depression.

All this talk of shifting moods and monthly changes may well raise a concern: Will such research reinforce old stereotypes of women as hysterical, irrational, at the mercy of their hormones? Quite the opposite, says Geoffrey Miller. "The traditional and rather patronizing male view was that women are fickle, that their preferences are random and arbitrary," he says. "Now it turns out that what looked like fickleness is actually deeply adaptive, and is shared with the females of most animal species. There is a deep logic to the shifts in female desire."

This logic operates below our conscious awareness, of course: Many generations of humans have faithfully followed it without knowing a thing about evolutionary theory. But once we do learn about the effects of the menstrual cycle on our perceptions and behavior, we can put that knowledge to good use. Women can keep a journal of their fluctuating moods and desires over the course of a month, matching up the entries with their cycles to identify a pattern; according to Miller, many female evolutionary biologists keep such diaries.

Gordon Gallup, an evolutionary psychologist at SUNY Albany, suggests that women use knowledge of their monthly cycles to plan important events. "If you have a first date coming up, or even a job interview, try to time it to coincide with your most fertile period," he advises. "The initial impression you make may be affected by the stage of your menstrual cycle." By the same token, says Gallup, if you're in a line of work in which your income depends on snap evaluations by others—a waitress, say, or a lap dancer—taking birth control pills "is like shooting yourself in the foot," since you miss out on the bountiful tips garnered by women in estrus.

A young woman should try to time a first date or job interview to coincide with her most fertile phase.

Psychologist Kim Wallen notes that women can also use knowledge of their menstrual cycles to manage their sexuality. "Research shows that women are more likely to take social risks around the time of ovulation," he says. "Women who know that's the case can choose not to put themselves in risky situations, such as drinking too much at a bar or party, at that time of the month." And if a woman should feel attracted to a man who would make an inappropriate partner, says Wallen, she can restrain her impulse, knowing that soon enough her preferences will shift and her desire will wane. "The adolescent male doesn't

have that option," he points out. "If he lusts after someone today, he'll still be lusting after her next week and next month."

A familiarity with the changes associated with estrus can even help us make sense of our feelings about long-term romantic partners. Women who experience an attraction to men other than their husbands or boyfriends need not conclude that there's anything amiss in their relationships, says Martie Haselton. "If a woman understands the evolutionary underpinnings of these impulses, she can reassure herself that these feelings don't mean that she doesn't love her partner or isn't 'meant' to be with him," she says. "The goal she's trying to achieve— to have a stable, loving, monogamous relationship—is not the goal that evolution has built her to act upon."

Although we can consciously choose to resist evolution's dictates, says Haselton, "the fingerprints of evolution are all over the behavior we engage in today."

Critical Thinking

1. What evidence is there that a woman's reproductive cycle affects her preferences, perceptions of self, and behavior with respect to men?

2. In what ways do men respond to women's fertility cycles?

3. How and why does the author think that modern contraception disrupts an adaptation forged many thousands of years ago?

4. Be familiar with the three principle theories regarding ovulation: the "signaling hypothesis," the notion of "hidden ovulation," and the idea that the menstrual cycle is a marker of youth and reproductive health.

5. What evidence is there that women are more likely to take risks when ovulating? Why would this be so?

6. In what ways can an understanding of women's shifting moods during the menstrual cycle be used for their benefit?

Create Central

www.mhhe.com/createcentral

Internet References

Gender & History
    www.blackwellpublishing.com/journal.asp?ref=0953-5233&site=1
Sexuality Studies
    https://sxs.sfsu.edu/ https://sxs.sfsu.edu
Sexuality Studies.net
    http://sexualitystudies.net/programs
The Kinsey Institute
    www.kinseyinstitute.org/about

ANNIE MURPHY PAUL is the author of *Origins: How the Nine Months Before Birth Shape the Rest of Our Lives,* published in 2010.

Article   Prepared by: Elvio Angeloni

Powers of Two

Coupling up might have been the best move our ancestors ever made.

Blake Edgar

Learning Outcomes

After reading this article, you will be able to:

- Discuss the benefits of monogamy for humans.
- Discuss the various theories that have been proposed for the rise of monogamy in human evolution.

In Brief

Even in societies where polygamy is permitted, monogamy is by far the most common human mating arrangement. In this regard, we are unusual animals: fewer than 10 percent of mammals form exclusive sexual relationships.

How humans got this way has been the subject of scientific debate for decades, and it is still an open question. But new research is clarifying matters.

We now know that the first hominins, which emerged more than seven million years ago, might have been monogamous. Humans stayed (mostly) monogamous for good reason: it helped them evolve into the big-brained world conquerors they are today.

Mammals are not big on monogamy. In fewer than 10 percent of species is it common for two individuals to mate exclusively. The primate wing of the group is only slightly more prone to pairing off. Although 15 to 29 percent of primate species favor living together as couples, far fewer commit to monogamy as humans know it—an exclusive sexual partnership between two individuals.

Humans obviously have an imperfect track record. People have affairs, get divorced and, in some cultures, marry multiple mates. In fact, polygamy appears in most of the world's societies. Yet even where polygamy is permitted, it is the minority arrangement. Most human societies are organized around the assumption that a large fraction of the population will pair off into enduring, sexually exclusive couples. And monogamy seems to have done our species good. "Pair bonds," as scientists call monogamous relationships, were a crucial adaptation that arose in an archaic forebear that became central to human social systems and our evolutionary success. "We have a very big advantage over many other species by having pair bonds," says University of Montreal anthropologist Bernard Chapais.

The monogamous couple also forms the basis for something uniquely human—the vast, complex social networks in which we live. Other primate young establish kinship links only through their mother; humans trace kinship from both parents, broadening each generation's family ties. Among humans, social networks extend to include other families and even unrelated groups in widening ripples of relationships. In Chapais's view, such group ties, along with monogamy, constitute "two of the most consequential features of human society."

Scientists have struggled for decades to understand the origins and implications of human monogamy. Basic questions such as when we started to pair up for life, why it was advantageous and how coupling might have spurred our success as a species remain unresolved and contentious, but new research has brought us closer to solving the mystery.

The Origins of Coupling

It is entirely possible that our most distant ancestors were monogamous. Fossil evidence, says anthropologist C. Owen Lovejoy of Kent State University, suggests that monogamy predates even *Ardipithecus ramidus,* the species best known from a 4.4-million-year-old partial female skeleton, nicknamed "Ardi," discovered in the Middle Awash region of Ethiopia. In Lovejoy's hypothesis, soon after the split from the last common ancestor between the great ape and human evolutionary branches more than seven million years ago, our predecessors adopted a transformative trio of behaviors: carrying food in arms freed by bipedal posture, forming pair bonds and concealing external signals of female ovulation. Evolving together, these innovations gave hominins, the tribe that emerged when early humans diverged from chimpanzees, a reproductive edge over apes.

According to this hypothesis, an ancestral polygamous mating system was replaced by pair bonding when lower-ranked hominin males diverted energy from fighting one another toward finding food to bring females as an incentive to mate. Females preferred reliable providers to aggressive competitors and bonded with the better foragers. Eventually females lost the skin swelling or other signs of sexual receptivity that would have attracted different males while their partners were off gathering food.

For evidence, Lovejoy points to *Ar. ramidus's* teeth. Compared with living and fossil apes, *Ar. ramidus* shows a stark reduction in the differences between male and female canine-tooth size. Evolution has honed the dagger-like canines of many male primates into formidable weapons used to fight for access to mates. Not so for early hominins. Picture the canines in a male gorilla's gaping jaws; now peer inside your own mouth. Humans of both sexes have small, stubby canines—an unthreatening trait unique to hominins, including the earliest *Ardipithecus* specimens.

A rough correlation also exists between mating behavior in primates and sexual dimorphism—that is, differences in body mass and size between males and females of the same species. The more dimorphic a primate species is, the more likely it is that males fight over females. At one extreme, polygamous gorilla males grow to be more than twice as massive as females. At the opposite extreme, both male and female gibbons, which are mainly monogamous, are nearly equal in mass. Humans lie closer to gibbons on the dimorphism spectrum: human males can be up to 20 percent more massive than females.

There is only so much we can make of the fossil record, though. Paleoanthropologist J. Michael Plavcan of the University of Arkansas urges caution in making the leap from fossilized bones to social behavior in hominins. Consider *Australopithecus afarensis*, the species to which "Lucy" belonged, which lived between 3.9 million and 3 million years ago. Like *Ardipithecus*, *A. afarensis* had small canines, but its skeleton displays a level of dimorphism between that of modern chimpanzees and gorillas. "You have [a level of] body-size dimorphism suggesting that [*A. afarensis*] males were competing for females and [a] loss of canine dimorphism that suggests they weren't," Plavcan says. "It's a puzzle."

Many anthropologists also dispute Lovejoy's conclusion that monogamy nurtured by males providing food for their mates and offspring has been a hominin strategy for millions of years. Last year in the journal *Evolutionary Anthropology,* Chapais argued that the unique features of human family and social structure (monogamy, kinship ties through both parents and expanding social circles) emerged in a stepwise sequence.

Before the first step, Chapais said, both male and female hominins were, like chimpanzees, promiscuous with partners. Then came a transition to polygamy, which is found in gorillas. But keeping many mates is hard work. It involves a lot of fighting other males and guarding females. Monogamy might have emerged as the best way to reduce the effort of polygamy.

Chapais declines to speculate about when this shift happened and what species were involved. But other researchers are homing in on the period between 2 million and 1.5 million years ago, after the origin of our genus *Homo* and coincident with physical changes that show up in *Homo erectus,* most likely the first hominin species to successfully migrate beyond Africa. *H. erectus* possessed a much larger body, proportioned more like that of a modern human, than its predecessors. Roughly twice the size of Lucy's species, *H. erectus* also seems to be less sexually dimorphic than australopithecines and the earliest members of *Homo*. Limited fossil evidence suggests that *H. erectus* females started to approach the physical stature of males and to have a similar degree of dimorphism as in modern humans, which together could suggest that *H. erectus* had a less competitive way of life than its ancestors. Because primates with similar body sizes tend to be monogamous, this change could signal a shift toward more exclusive mating behavior.

A Strategic Partnership

If scientists cannot agree on when humans became monogamous, we can hardly expect them to agree on why it happened. In 2013, two independent research teams published separate statistical studies of existing literature to determine which behaviors could have been drivers of monogamy. Both studies aimed to determine the best explanation for monogamy from three persistent hypotheses, generally known as female spacing, infanticide avoidance and male parental care.

The female-spacing hypothesis posits that monogamy arises after females begin to establish larger territories to gain more access to limited food resources and, in the process, put more distance between one another. With females farther apart, males have a harder time finding and keeping multiple mates. Settling down with a single partner makes life easier, reducing a male's risk of being injured while patrolling his territory and enabling him to ensure that his mate's offspring are his own.

Zoologists Dieter Lukas and Tim Clutton-Brock, both at the University of Cambridge, found evidence for this idea in a statistical analysis of 2,545 species of mammals. They described their findings in a paper published in *Science*. The data indicated to them that mammals started out solitary, but then one species or another switched to monogamy 61 different times during their evolutionary history. Monogamy most frequently emerged in carnivores and primates, suggesting that species will tend toward mating in pairs when its females require a rich but rare diet (such as protein-rich carcasses or ripe fruits) that can usually be obtained only by searching a large area. Their findings provided the strongest statistical support for the conclusion that increasingly scattered, solitary females drove males to solicit single partners.

Lukas acknowledges that although the hypothesis may work for nonhumans, it might not be so apt for humans: it is difficult to reconcile the inherent sociality of humans with a hypothesis that depends on a low density of available females. It may be that our ancestors were too social for females to have been scattered across the savanna like other mammals. But the theory could potentially hold for humans if monogamy arose in hominins before our tendency to dwell in groups did.

The second leading hypothesis holds that monogamy originated from the threat of lethal violence toward offspring. If a rival male challenged or supplanted a dominant male in a community, the usurper could kill infants that he had not sired. Mothers would stop lactating and start ovulating again, giving the marauding male a chance to spread his genes. To prevent infanticide, a female would select a male ally who could defend her and her baby.

Anthropologist Kit Opie of University College London cites evidence for the infanticide-avoidance hypothesis in a study published in the *Proceedings of the National Academy of Sciences USA*. Opie and his colleagues ran computer simulations of primate evolutionary history for 230 primate species; they then applied what is called a Bayesian statistical analysis to determine which of the three prominent hypotheses for the origin of monogamy had the highest probability of being correct. They identified a significant correlation between monogamy in primates and each of the three hypothetical triggers, but only an increase in the threat of infanticide consistently preceded the appearance of monogamy in multiple primate lineages.

The biology and behavior of modern primates add some plausibility to the conclusion that infanticide is a spur to monogamy. Primates are uniquely at risk for infanticide: they have big brains that need time to develop, which leaves babies dependent and vulnerable for long periods after birth. And the killing of babies has been observed in more than 50 primate species; it typically involves a male from outside a group attacking an unweaned infant in a bid for dominance or access to females. But there are limits to the evidence: nearly all these species have either promiscuous or polygamous mating systems, so the distribution of infanticide in living primates does not fit the prediction that monogamy should evolve when infanticide is a big threat.

The third hypothesis for why monogamy evolved highlights a male pulling his weight with parental duties. When a baby becomes too costly in terms of calories and energy for a mother to raise on her own, the father who stays with the family and provides food or other forms of care increases his offspring's chances of survival and encourages closer ties with the mother A related idea, proposed by anthropologist Lee Gettler of the University of Notre Dame, holds that the mere carrying of offspring by fathers fosters monogamy. Mothers have to meet the considerable nutritional demands of nursing infants. Yet for primates and human hunter-gatherers, hauling an infant, especially without the benefit of a sling or other restraint, required an expense of energy comparable to breast-feeding. Carrying by males could have freed females to fulfill their own energetic needs by foraging.

South America's Azara's owl monkey may offer some insight into how paternal care would reinforce monogamy. These monkeys live in small family groups, with an adult male-and-female pair and an infant, plus a juvenile or two. A mother monkey carries a newborn on her thigh just after birth. But the baby's father assumes most of the carrying and caretaking—grooming, playing and feeding—from the time the baby is two weeks old. The adult partners literally stay in touch with frequent tail contact, and the male's mere proximity to both the female and his young may promote deeper emotional ties.

Indeed, a study published in March in the *Proceedings of the Royal Society B* presented genetic evidence that Azara's owl monkey pairs remain monogamous—the first genetic confirmation for any nonhuman primate. DNA collected from several study groups revealed that all the females and all but one of the males in 17 pairs were the most likely parents of 35 offspring. "They go all the way and commit to a monogamous relationship in genetic terms," says anthropologist Eduardo Fernandez-Duque, now at Yale University and a co-author of the study. Mating bonds between Azara's owl monkeys last an average of nine years, and monkeys that stay with the same partner achieve greater reproductive success—the end game of evolution under any mating system.

What do the two recent statistical studies have to say about the paternal care hypothesis? Both concluded that paternal care seemed the least likely among the competing hypotheses to trigger monogamous mating—but, Lukas says, "paternal care may still explain why a species stays monogamous."

It Takes a Village

A Monogamous set of parents is not enough to raise an ape as smart and social as a human, says anthropologist Sarah Hrdy of the University of California, Davis. A human baby consumes some 13 million calories on its long journey from birth to maturity, a heavy burden for a mother to bear even with a mate helping. This demand might explain why in many societies, human mothers rely on "alloparents" (such as the kin of either parent or other group members) to help provide food and child care. "Human mothers are willing to let others hold their babies right from birth," Hrdy notes. "That's amazing, and it's remarkably unapelike." No ape engages in anything like alloparenting.

Hrdy maintains that cooperative breeding, a social system in which alloparents help care for young, evolved among our ancient ancestors starting with *H. erectus* nearly two million years ago. This species had a much larger body and brain than its ancestors; by one estimate, it took 40 percent more metabolic energy to run an *H. erectus* body relative to previous hominins. If *H. erectus* started down a humanlike path of delayed development and prolonged dependency, cooperative alloparents might have been required to support the energetic demands of raising bigger-brained babies.

Without cooperative breeding, conclude Karin Isler and Carel van Schaik, both at the University of Zurich, early *Homo* would not have broken through the hypothetical "gray ceiling" that constrains an ape's brain to a maximum volume of about 700 cm³. To pay the energetic cost of having an enlarged brain, an animal must reduce its rate of birth or its rate of growth, or both. But humans have achieved shorter weaning periods and greater reproductive success than a creature with a brain volume ranging from 1,100 to 1,700 cm³ should have been able to. Isler and van Schaik attribute this success to alloparenting, which enabled *H. erectus* to have offspring more frequently while providing those offspring enough energy to grow a large brain.

It was cooperation, then, whether in the form of monogamous pairs, nuclear families or tribes, that enabled humans to succeed when all our fossil ancestors and cousins went extinct. In fact, cooperation may be the greatest skill we have acquired during the past two million years—one that enabled our young genus to survive through periods of environmental change and stress and one that may well determine our geologically young species' future.

Critical Thinking

1. Discuss the relationship between mating behavior and sexual dimorphism in primate species.

2. What have been the various theories proposed for the rise of monogamy among humans and what has been the evidence for them?

3. What is "cooperative breeding" and why does it seem to have been important in human evolution?

More to Explore

Reexamining Human Origins in Light of Ardipithecus ramidus. C. Owen Lovejoy in Science, Vol. 326, pages 74,74e1–74.e8; October 2, 2009.

Monogamy, Strongly Bonded Groups, and the Evolution of Human Social Structure. Bernard Chapais in Evolutionary Anthropology, Vol. 22, No. 2, pages 52–65; March/April 2013.

The Evolution of Social Monogamy in Mammals. D. Lukas and T. H. Clutton-Brock in Science, Vol. 341, pages 526–530; August 2, 2013.

Male Infanticide Leads to Social Monogamy in Primates. Christopher Opie et al. in Proceedings of the National Academy of Sciences USA, Vol. 110, No. 33, pages 13,328–13, 332; August 13, 2013.

From our Archives

Evolution of Human Walking. C. Owen Lovejoy; November 1988.
scientificamerican.com/magazine/sa

Internet References

Electronic Zoo/NetVet-Primate Page
http://netvet.wustl.edu/primates.htm
Journal of Mammology
http://www.bioone.org/doi/abs/10.1644/06-MAMM-A-417.1Evolutionary Demography Group
National Primate Research Center
http://pin.primate.wisc.edu/factsheets

BLAKE EDGAR is co-author of From Lucy to Language and other books and a contributing editor at Archaeology Magazine. He is a senior acquisitions editor at the University of California Press.

Article   Prepared by: Elvio Angeloni, *Pasadena City College*

When Do Girls Rule the Womb?

JENNIFER ABBASI

Learning Outcomes

After reading this article, you will be able to:

- Discuss the ways in which a sex ratio imbalance within populations might lead to reproductive success.

- Describe "integrated evolutionary social demography."

A s a demographer, Shige Song was trained to focus on the social forces that change the proportion of males and females in a population. His studies of sex ratio in China, India, and South Korea, where the birth of boys has significantly outpaced girls over the past few decades, had focused exclusively on the effect of cultural preferences for sons. Demographic studies since the 1980s have suggested son preference and sex-selective abortions of girls were the main causes of the skewed sex ratio in these countries.

What demographers have not been able to explain is why trends in sex ratio at birth also exist in societies that don't value sons more than daughters. In the second half of the 1900s, more girls were born than usual in North America and most of Europe, while boy births significantly outpaced girls in Ireland, France, Italy, and Spain. "It became clear to me that the standard social science model may not be adequate to explain sex ratio," Song says. His controversial new theory has less to do with social forces among people, and more to do with simple biology.

Enter Adaptations

While demographers were struggling to understand sex ratio anomalies in the context of culture, evolutionary biologists had largely embraced an idea put forth in 1973 by biologist Robert Trivers and mathematician Dan Willard. The Harvard-based pair theorized that as the physical condition of a female declines—if she's nutritionally deprived, for example—she'll tend to produce a lower ratio of male to female offspring. Evidence of the theory came from red deer and humans; in both species, adverse conditions in the mother's environment during pregnancy are correlated with a shift toward female births.

Although natural selection ideally favors a 50/50, or .500, sex ratio in a population, mammals typically produce slightly more males than females. Because sex ratio is biased toward males, the figure is expressed by dividing male births by total births. It's estimated that women give birth to 3 percent more boys, for a standard .515 sex ratio (with 48.5 percent female births). When fewer boys and more girls are born than that, it's described as a sex ratio decline.

Evolutionary biologists say male mortality, which is overall higher than that of females, explains the male bias in sex ratio: A slightly skewed sex ratio at birth that favors males ensures that there are roughly an equal number of males and females of reproductive age. (Theoretically, a .500 sex ratio at birth may be possible if the gender difference in mortality is eliminated.)

But under certain conditions, biologists say, an imbalance favoring female births can improve the reproductive success of an individual organism. Trivers and Willard argued that the strongest and most dominant males of a species were far more likely to leave offspring than weaker males, while virtually all females would reproduce. According to this so-called adaptive sex ratio adjustment hypothesis, healthy mothers were better off producing sons, who would likely be fit and go on to reproduce, whereas mothers in less prime condition would benefit more from daughters, who would reproduce regardless of their low health status. The strategy allowed a mother to "maximize her eventual reproductive success," the two wrote in their seminal paper.

Just how adaptive sex selection may occur is unknown, but there's evidence that poor maternal nutrition disproportionately affects male offspring. Plentiful food sources are consistently linked with a male-biased sex ratio in nonhuman mammals, and a 2008 study found that British women with the best nutrition during conception were significantly more likely to give birth to boys than women with the poorest diet. (The researchers found no socioeconomic link to fetal gender.)

Glucose levels, which may drop in women who don't get enough to eat, could have something to do with it, says Elissa Cameron, an evolutionary biologist at the University of Tasmania. In 2008 she showed that in the pre-embryonic stage of development, males have lower survival rates than females when glucose levels are low, causing more females to be born. Trivers believes sex selection may happen even earlier, at the time of conception.

Famine as Experiment

While working as a social demographer at the Chinese Academy of Social Sciences in 2008, Song became interested in the sex ratio decline that came out of the devastating Great Chinese Famine in the mid-twentieth century. Scholars had noticed a drop in male births during the 1960s, but they attributed it to data error "because they focused exclusively on the search for social explanations, and there were none," says Song, like a cultural son preference. He saw the famine as a natural experiment for the adaptive sex ratio adjustment hypothesis.

In a paper published recently in the journal *Proceedings of the Royal Society B* (Biological Sciences) that looked at demographic data from more than 310,000 Chinese women, Song demonstrated a dramatic sex ratio decrease more than a year after the two-year famine began and lasting about two years after it ended, followed by an equally significant bounce back to pre-famine proportions.

Trivers says the findings are consistent with previous studies of post-communist Poland and historical Portugal in which poor economic conditions, and in turn poor nutrition, predicted the birth of more girls. "Evolutionary theories provide a simple and elegant framework to explain and even predict such changes," says Song, who is now a sociologist at Queens College of the City University of New York.

To that end, Song wants to reexamine sex ratio phenomena through a new framework he calls "integrated evolutionary social demography." This type of cross-disciplinary model might help explain, for example, why the sex ratio returned to normal levels around 2007 in South Korea, despite enduring cultural son preference there. And the sex ratio decline in the West, where the proportion of boys and girls moves closer to 1-to-1, might be explained by improved life expectancies reducing the gender difference in mortality in some regions, Song says.

But there's still a long way to go before demographers embrace evolutionary theory. A panel of sociologists at the National Science Foundation recently turned down three of Song's funding proposals; one reviewer even used the term "grade school reasoning" to describe the logic behind the adaptive sex ratio hypothesis. "The only way to make this change happen is to bring more funding, federal and private, into the field," Song says—a grim solution in today's economic climate. "As an individual researcher, the only thing I can do is to try to publish."

Critical Thinking

1. Explain why the standard social science model is not adequate for understanding sex ratios in some societies.

2. What sex ratio does natural selection seem to favor and what constitutes a "decline"? How do evolutionary biologists explain the favored ratio?

3. Discuss the "sex ratio adjustment hypothesis" and how and why it might work. What do glucose levels have to do with it?

4. How did the Great Chinese Famine and the decline of economic conditions in post-communist Poland and historical Portugal seem to support the sex ratio adjustment hypothesis?

5. Describe "integrated evolutionary social demography."

Create Central

www.mhhe.com/createcentral

Internet References

Evolutionary Demography Group
    http://blogs.lshtm.ac.uk/evolutionarydemography/
Evolutionary Demography Society
    http://www.sdu.dk/en/om_sdu/institutter_centre/maxo/evodemos

---

Jennifer Abbasi is a Portland-based science writer and a frequent contributor to *Discover*.

Jennifer Abassi, "When Do Girls Rule the Womb?" From *Discover Magazine*, November 2013. Reprinted by permission of the author.

Unit 4

UNIT

Prepared by: Elvio Angeloni, *Pasadena City College*

The Fossil Evidence

A primary focal point of this book, as well as of the whole of physical anthropology, is the search for, and the interpretation of, fossil evidence for hominid (meaning human or humanlike) evolution. Paleoanthropologists carry out this task by conducting painstaking excavations and detailed analyses that serve as a basis for understanding our past. Every fragment found is cherished like a ray of light that may help to illuminate the path taken by our ancestors in the process of becoming "us." At least, that is what we would like to believe. In reality, each discovery leads to further mystery, and for every fossil-hunting paleoanthropologist who thinks his or her find supports a particular theory, there are many others anxious to express their disagreement. How wonderful it would be, we sometimes think, in moments of frustration over inconclusive data, if the fossils would just speak for themselves, and every primordial piece of humanity were to carry with it a self-evident explanation for its place in the evolutionary story. Paleoanthropology would then be more of a quantitative, mechanical problem of amassing enough material to reconstruct our ancestral development than a qualitative problem of interpreting what it all means. It would certainly be a simpler process, but would it be as interesting?

Most scientists tolerate, welcome, or even (dare it be said?) thrive on controversy, recognizing that diversity of opinion refreshes the mind, rouses students, and captures the imagination of the general public. After all, where would paleoanthropology be without the gadflies, the near-mythic heroes, and, lest we forget, the research funds they generate? Consider, for example, the issue of the differing roles played by males and females in the transition to humanity and all that it implies with regard to bipedalism, tool-making, and the origin of the family. Did bipedalism evolve in the grasslands or in the forests of equaltorial Africa? Did bipedalism develop as a means of gathering fruits and vegetables or pursuing prey? Should the primary theme of human evolution be summed up as "man the hunter" and "woman the gatherer"? Indeed, for early hominid evolution, how about "man the hunted"?

Not all the research and theoretical speculations taking place in the field of paleoanthropology are controversial. Most students of human evolution, in fact, go about their work quietly and methodically, each year finding more hominid fossil sites and increasing our understanding of the general environmental circumstances in which our human predecessors lived. The hypotheses formed from this systematic and thought-provoking work have had the cumulative effect of enriching our understanding of the details of human evolution.

As we mull over the controversies, we should not take them as reflecting an inherent weakness of the field of paleoanthropology, but rather as reflective of its strength: the ability and willingness to scrutinize, question, and reflect (endlessly) on every bit of evidence.

Contrary to the way that the proponents of creationism or "intelligent design theory" would have it, an admission of doubt is not an expression of ignorance but simply a frank recognition of the imperfect state of our knowledge. If we are to increase our understanding of ourselves, we must maintain an atmosphere of free inquiry without preconceived notions and unquestioning commitment to a particular point of view.

To paraphrase anthropologist Ashley Montagu, "while creationism embraces certainty without proof, science embraces proof without certainty."

Article   Prepared by Elvio Angeloni, Pasadena City College

Our True Dawn

CATHERINE BRAHIC

Learning Outcomes

After reading this article, you will be able to:

- Discuss the paleontological and the genetic evidence for when our ancestors split from the apes.

- Draw the early hominid family tree.

Line them up in your head. Generation after generation of your ancestors, reaching back in time through civilisations, ice ages, an epic migration out of Africa, to the very origin of our species. And on the other side, take a chimp and line up its ancestors. How far back do you have to go, how many generations have to pass, before the two lines meet?

This is one of the biggest and hardest questions in human evolution. We know that at some point we shared a common ancestor with chimps, but exactly when—and what that ancestor was like—have been maddeningly hard to pin down. Palaeontologists have searched for fossil remains, and geneticists have rummaged through the historical documents that are human and chimp DNA. Both made discoveries, but they did not see eye to eye.

No more. New estimates for when our lineage and chimps went their separate ways suggest that some of our established ideas are staggeringly wrong. If correct, they demand a rewrite of human prehistory, starting from the very beginning.

When was that beginning? The obvious first place to look for answers is in the fossil record. But fossil humans—or more strictly hominins, the group that includes us and all our extinct relatives from after the split—are notoriously thin on the ground and difficult to interpret.

Geneticists have more to work with. DNA contains telltale traces of events in a species's past, including information about common ancestry and speciation. In theory, calculating the timing of a speciation event should be straightforward. As two species diverge from a common ancestor their DNA becomes increasingly different, largely due to the accumulation of random mutations. The amount of genetic difference between two related species is therefore proportional to the length of time since they diverged. To estimate when the human-chimp split occurred, geneticists can simply count the differences in matching stretches of chimp and human DNA and divide it by the rate at which mutations accumulate. This is known as the molecular clock method.

But there's a catch. To arrive at the answer you have to know how fast the mutations arise. And that leads you back to square one: you first need to know how long ago we split from chimpanzees.

To get around this catch-22, geneticists turned to orangutans. Fossils suggest that they split from our lineage between 10 and 20 million years ago. Using this fudge, geneticists arrived at a mutation rate of about 75 mutations per genome per generation. In other words, offspring of humans and chimps each have 75 new mutations that they did not inherit from their parents.

Fossils or DNA

This number rests on several big assumptions, not least that the orang-utan fossil record is a reliable witness—which most agree it is not. Even so, it led to a guess that human ancestors split from chimpanzees between 4 and 6 million years ago.

When fossil-hunters hear this number, they cry foul. The lower end of the estimate is particularly hard to swallow. Australopithecus afarensis—an early hominin from east Africa— already has distinctly human characteristics yet dates back at least 3.85 million years. Its canines were small, for instance. And it walked upright.

Both of these traits are considered hominin, meaning they evolved in our lineage after the split and did not appear on the chimp side. And yet it is hard to see how they could have evolved so quickly, in perhaps as little as 150,000 years after the split.

"Geneticists ignored the palaeontologists completely," says Owen Lovejoy of Kent State University in Ohio. "We would get estimates around 4 million years, and yet there are unmistakable and highly evolved hominins that go back almost 4 million years. To claim a 4 million year divergence date is just silly."

Even a 5- to 6-million-year split was met with scepticism. That's largely because of three recently discovered fossils from Africa dating from around the same period. All three predate Australopithecus, but still bear unmistakable marks of humanity. Though the interpretation of the remains is controversial, many regard them as being post-split.

Simply put, the palaeontologists were sure there was little chance that the DNA results were accurate. Humanity, they affirmed, had to be older than the geneticists claimed.

History looks set to prove them right. In the past three years, researchers studying human populations have for the first time been able to observe mutations almost as they happen. And that makes all the difference. Instead of relying on an estimate based on rare fossils, we can now watch the molecular clock ticking in real time. "Until we were able to compare genomes of children with their parents, we could not estimate the mutation rate in humans," says Aylwyn Scally of the Wellcome Trust Sanger Institute in Cambridge, UK.

In September, Augustine Kong of Decode Genetics in Reykjavik, Iceland, and colleagues published one such groundbreaking study. After scanning the genomes of 78 children and their parents to count the number of new mutations in each child's genome, they found that every child carries an average of 36 new mutations (Nature, vol 488, p 471). Crucially, that is half what was previously assumed, meaning the molecular clock ticks more slowly than we thought—pushing the human-chimp split further back in time.

How far back exactly? Earlier this year, Kevin Langergraber at Boston University and his colleagues solved another piece of the puzzle. Mutation rates in studies like Kong's are measured per generation. To convert this into an estimate of when our ancestors split from chimps, you need to know how long a generation is—in other words, the average age at reproduction. We have a good handle on this for humans, but not in other primates. For chimps, estimates ranged from 15 to 25 years.

Using data from 226 offspring born in eight wild chimp populations, Langergraber found that, on average, chimps reproduce when they are 24-and-a-half (PNAS, vol 109, p 15716). Based on the new numbers, his team estimated the human lineage went its separate way at least 7 million years ago, and possibly as far back as 13 million years ago.

"It's clear that if this is right, most textbooks dealing with the history of our species will have to be rewritten," says Klaus Zuberbühler at the University of St Andrews, UK, who helped collate data for the study. "The significance can hardly be underestimated."

John Hawks of the University of Wisconsin-Madison agrees. "I think that this will affect pretty much every event in human evolution, from the initial divergence of our lineage to the dispersal out of Africa."

Perhaps the most significant implication is in the search for the earliest members of the human tribe. For now Australopithecus is the oldest accepted hominin, but an earlier split brings other species into the frame.

Golden Age

The late 1990s and early 2000s was a golden age of discovery for palaeoanthropologists. In the space of a decade, the remains of three potential new hominins were discovered in the deserts of east and central Africa. The most complete was Ardipithecus ramidus, a 4.4-million-year-old skeleton from Afar, Ethiopia, nicknamed Ardi. This was later joined by Sahelanthropus tchadensis, 6 to 7 million years old, and Orrorin tugenensis, about 6 million years old.

Ardipithecus is by far the best known of the three. Roughly the size of a chimp, the skeleton includes human-like teeth, a small skull and the lower limbs of an animal that could walk upright (though it also had an opposable big toe for clasping branches). A possible relative—Ardipithecus kadabba—has also been identified from teeth and a few bone fragments, pushing back the origin of the genus to around 5.8 million years ago.

Sahelanthropus is known from a single skull from Chad, nicknamed Toumai. Like Ardipithecus, its teeth are small and human-like, and the middle of its face is short—another human trait. The shape of the hole where the spine would have inserted at the base of the skull hints that it could walk on two legs, although this is hotly debated.

Orrorin, meanwhile, is known only from a handful of teeth plus some leg and finger bones, which suggest it also walked upright but still climbed trees.

All together the bones would barely fill two shoeboxes, but they made a big noise. It was generally thought that when we finally managed to dig up the earliest hominins, we would find something that looked like a chimp. And yet Ardi, Toumai and Orrorin had distinctly human characteristics. "They upset the received wisdom," says Tim White of the University of California, Berkeley, who led the Ardi discovery.

Some were quick to claim them as human ancestors. But the old molecular clock said otherwise: they were too early. And so they were dismissed as side-branches on the family tree, dead-end experiments in evolution with little or no relevance to the main event.

Now, with the new molecular clock estimates, they are being welcomed back into the fold. "The argument that they are too early has evaporated," says White, who thinks all three are members of the same genus.

The timing certainly looks right. "If you look at the consensus of recent mutation-rate measurements, Sahelanthropus is just about on the boundary," says Scally, who recently published a review of the revisions and their consequences for evolution (Nature Review Genetics, vol 13, p 745). "Whether it's a human, a proto-human, or in a period when humans and chimpanzees are gradually separating, I don't think anyone can say. But from a genetic perspective, I certainly don't think you can rule it out, which people used to do."

The anatomy makes sense too, says White. "It seems to those of us who study these fossils that the way you get from the last common ancestor to Australopithecus is via something like Ardi. It had already evolved in the direction of Australopithecus. In other words, it's post-split."

"Does Ardi represent a species that is on the direct line?" he continues. "We don't know because we don't have enough fossils from other places yet. But we can't rule it out."

Another possibility that cannot be ruled out is that the split is even further back in time. The slow accumulation of mutations means that new estimates of the mutation rate still have big margins for error. In general, geneticists and palaeoanthropologists seem comfortable with a revised figure of 7 to 8 million years. Some, however, go further.

"For me, a 13-million-year-old split could be right on the button," says Lovejoy. "If you go back 10 to 15 million years, the planet was covered in apes, many beginning to show the kinds of anatomical adaptations that you see in modern humans."

Lovejoy is out on his own, though. A week after Kong and colleagues published their new estimate, another team—including many of the same researchers—published another.

They analysed DNA from more than 85,000 Icelanders, focusing on short stretches of DNA called microsatellites. According to co-author David Reich of Harvard University these are a more reliable record of mutations.

The rate they found was not quite as slow as Kong's. As a result, their estimate of the timing of the split is a more constrained 7.5 million years (Nature Genetics, vol 44, p 1161).

There are a few other loose ends to tidy up. Another problem with Kong's estimate, says Reich, is that if you use it to date the split between orang-utans and African apes—humans, chimps and gorillas—you get something in the range of 30 million years, wildly inconsistent with the maximum 20 million years suggested by the fossil record.

In an attempt to reconcile the two, Scally has proposed that as our ancestors evolved from small primates into large apes, the number of mutations they accumulated with each passing generation decreased. This is in keeping with what is seen in other mammals. "It is observed quite widely, including in primates, that species with larger body size tend to have longer generation times," says Scally. Longer generations mean slower mutation rates.

This would be plausible, says Reich, if it weren't that for it to be right, mutation rates in our ancestors and in orang-utans would have had to have dropped at exactly the same time. "I find such an extreme event hard to believe," he says. Despite that, Reich says, "Scally's hypothesis is probably the best one out there."

Quibbles aside, it now seems certain that our lineage is considerably older than we once thought. And that has consequences for the rest of human prehistory. The molecular clock has been used to date a number of key events, not least when our ancestors left Africa. That has been estimated by looking at genetic differences between the Yoruba people of Nigeria and Europeans and Asians.

Early genetic estimates suggested this happened 50,000 years ago. So when fossil remains in Israel and archaeological sites in India were found to be around 100,000 years old, there was some explaining to do. The Israeli bones were dismissed as the remains of an early, dead-end excursion, and the

Indian sites as an error, pure and simple. The new molecular clock resolves the discrepancy, pushing the departure back to between 90,000 and 130,000 years ago.

It does something similar for the split between us and Neanderthals. Bones found in a cave in Atapuerca, Spain, and attributed to the probable ancestor of Neanderthals, Homo heidelbergensis, date to between 400,000 and 600,000 years ago. But this created a problem as the molecular clock suggested H. heidelbergensis appeared after that. But the new estimates mean it is in fact around 500,000 years old.

Other key events await revision. But the main finding is clear. The human lineage is significantly older, and our closest living relatives more distant, than we once thought. We are used to thinking of ourselves as separate and distinct from the rest of the animal kingdom. We just got a bit more separate, and a bit more distinct.

Critical Thinking

1. How do the methods used by paleontologists and geneticists differ with respect to determining when our ancestors split from the apes?
2. What is the one "catch" with respect to the geneticists' method and how did they try to get around it? Why did the fossil hunters cry "foul"?
3. Why was even a 5- to 6-million-year split met with skepticism?
4. Why does history look set to prove the fossil hunters right?
5. How have Ardi, Toumai, and Orrorin "upset the received wisdom"?
6. What does the slow accumulation of mutations mean with respect to margin of error for mutation rates?
7. How does the DNA study of Icelanders affect the estimate of the hominin split with apes? What does Scally propose in order to account for a slower mutation rate than indicated by the Icelander study? What does Reich see as the problem here?
8. How does the new molecular clock correspond with fossil remains in Israel and India? How about with the split with Neanderthals?

Create Central

www.mhhe.com/createcentral

Internet References

Fossil Hominids FAQ
www.talkorigins.org/faqs/homs
Institute of Human Origins
http://iho.asu.edu/node/27

Article   Prepared by: Elvio Angeloni

Welcome to the Family

The latest molecular analyses and fossil finds suggest that the story of human evolution is far more complex—and more interesting—than anyone imagined.

BERNARD WOOD

Learning Outcomes

After reading this article, you will be able to:

- Understand and appreciate the diversity of lineages during hominin evolution.

- Explain why we should expect a great deal of diversity in hominin evolution.

S
o what do you think?" said Lee Berger. He had just opened the lids of two big wooden boxes, each containing the carefully laid out fossilized bones of a humanlike skeleton from Malapa, South Africa. These two individuals, who had drawn their last breath two million years ago, had created quite a stir. Most fossils are "isolated" finds—a jawbone here, a foot bone there. Scientists then have to figure out whether the pieces belong to the same individual. Think of walking down the highway and finding parts of cars—a broken fender here, part of a transmission there. Do they belong to the same model, or even make, of car? Or might they not have come from a car at all but from a pickup?

In contrast, the skeletons from Malapa, though not complete, are intact enough to reduce the possibility of random commingling. Like "Lucy" (unearthed in Ethiopia in 1974) and the "Turkana Boy" (found in Kenya in 1984), they have so much more to say than individual fossils. But they had made the headlines not because they are complete and so well preserved but because Berger, a paleoanthropologist at the University of the Witwatersrand, Johannesburg, had suggested that the individuals were part of a population that was directly ancestral to our own genus, *Homo*.

We all have ancestors. I still have an aged living parent. I had the good fortune to have known all four of my grandparents, and I can even dimly remember three of my great-grandparents. But I also have close relatives who are not ancestors. Not many—my father and I were both only children—but I did have a couple of uncles and aunts. They are an essential part of the family tree of their descendants, but in terms of my family tree they are the equivalent of "optional extras" on an automobile. So Berger wanted me to stop admiring the details of the teeth and jaws and tell him if I thought the Malapa skeletons were the evolutionary equivalent of my parents and grandparents or of my uncles and aunts. In other words, did they belong to a population that was a direct ancestor or just a close relative of modern humans?

When I first started studying human fossils in East Africa nearly 50 years ago, the conventional wisdom was that almost all our extinct close relatives were direct ancestors, and as you went further and further back into the past each was less humanlike and more apelike. But we now know from genetic studies and from fossil evidence of the Neandertals and the so-called Hobbit of Flores, Indonesia (*Homo floresiensis*), that our direct ancestors shared the planet over the past few hundred thousand years with several of our close relatives. Furthermore, other fossil discoveries make it clear that much earlier in our prehistory (four million to one million years ago) there were also periods when our ancestors and several close relatives walked the earth at the same time. The presence of multiple evolutionary branches at any one time makes it much more difficult to identify direct ancestors of modern humans than paleontologists anticipated even 20 years ago. Yet the challenge also means that the story of human evolution is far more intricate and fascinating than most of us realized.

A Single Branch or Several?

At the time I entered the field in 1968, Charles Darwin's conception of the Tree of Life held firm sway. He argued that the living world is linked in the same way that the branches of a tree are connected. In Darwin's Tree of Life, all the species alive today sit on the outer surface of the tree, and all the species that are no longer living are located closer to the trunk. Just as each individual modern human must have ancestors, so does each species alive today. In theory, then, the only branches, or lineages, that must be in the Tree of Life are the ones that lead from a living species down into the depths of the tree, and the only extinct species that have to be within the Tree of Life are the ones situated on those connecting branches; any others represent evolutionary dead ends.

In the case of modern humans and the living apes, this rule means the only branches and species that need to be in our particular part of the tree are the ones that link us to the common ancestor we share with chimpanzees and bonobos—a creature now thought on the basis of molecular evidence to have lived between about eight million and five million years ago.

In the 1960s the outermost branch of the Tree of Life leading to modern humans looked pretty straightforward. At its base was *Australopithecus,* the ape-man that paleoanthropologists had been recovering in southern Africa since the mid-1920s. *Australopithecus,* the thinking went, was replaced by the taller, larger-brained *Homo erectus* from Asia, which spread to Europe and evolved into the Neandertals, which in turn evolved into *Homo sapiens* (aka modern humans). All these were interpreted as direct ancestors of modern humans—the equivalent of my parents, grandparents and great-grandparents. Only one type of hominin (modern humans and any extinct relatives that are more closely related to humans than to chimpanzees or bonobos), called the robust australopiths because of their large jaws and chewing teeth, were surmised to be on a short twig of the human branch and thus the equivalent of my uncle and aunt.

This thinking changed when Louis and Mary Leakey's discoveries of hominins at Olduvai Gorge in Tanzania shifted the focus of research into early hominins that lived more than one million years ago from southern to East Africa. The focus changed not only because the trickle of fossil discoveries in East Africa in the early 1960s turned into a torrent but also because the context of the fossil evidence in East Africa—particularly with respect to its dating—was very different from that in southern Africa.

In the south, the hominin fossils were—and still are—mostly found in caves that form in rocks made of dolomite (a magnesium-rich carbonate). Although researchers occasionally find a well-preserved skeleton of an individual (such as those from Malapa), most of the early hominin fossils found in these caves were leftovers from the meals of leopards and other predators. These unconsumed bones and teeth were washed into the cave along with soil from the surface. Once inside the cave, the soil and bones formed what are called talus cones. These are untidy versions of the neat cones of sand in the bottom of an old-fashioned egg timer, and the layers, or strata, in the cave do not always follow the general rule that the older layers are at the bottom and the youngest at the top. As if this was not frustrating enough, researchers were until recently at a loss to know how to date the sediments in the caves, and in the early 1960s all investigators could do was fit the hominin finds in a very rough-and-ready time sequence based on the types of fossil animals found in the caves.

In contrast, hominin fossil evidence from East Africa comes from sites close to the Eastern Rift Valley, which slices through this part of Africa from the Red Sea in the north to the shores of Lake Malawi and beyond in the south. Instead of being found in caves, the hominin fossils from East Africa are found in sediments laid down around lakes or along riverbanks. Many of these rock layers preserve the direction of the earth's magnetic field at the time they were laid down, and because they are open-air sites the strata incorporate ash expelled from the many volcanoes generated in and around the Eastern Rift Valley by the movement of tectonic plates. These features mean that at each site researchers have ways of establishing the age of the strata independent of the fossils they contain. In addition, because the layers of volcanic ash function like a series of date-stamped blankets thrown over the region, they allow researchers to correlate fossils deposited thousands of miles apart.

Many of the richest East African hominin fossil sites, such as those in the Omo-Turkana basin and farther north along the Awash River, contain strata that represent millions of years of time. Thus, it is possible to give minimum "start" and "finish" dates for each particular group of fossil hominins. This specificity makes it clear that even within East Africa—let alone between East and southern Africa—there were many times in the past one million to four million years when more than one—and in some periods, several—hominins lived contemporaneously. For example, across a million years (from roughly 2.3 million to 1.4 million years ago), two very different kinds of hominins—*Paranthropus boisei* and *Homo habilis*—lived in the same region of East Africa. They were so different that a prehistoric safari guide would have made the point that their skulls and teeth are almost never confused, no matter how fragmentary the fossil evidence. It is also clear that the hominins at the sites in East Africa are different from the ones found in southern Africa—but more on that later.

Finding evidence of *P. boisei* and *H. habilis* in the strata that record thousands of years does not necessarily mean the two hominins had to take turns at the same water hole. But it does mean that one, or perhaps both, of these hominins was not ancestral to modern humans. Although evidence from much later in human evolution is consistent with a small amount of interbreeding between Neandertals and modern humans, in my view the much greater physical differences between *P. boisei* and *H. habilis* indicate that interbreeding was much less likely. And even if it did occur, it did little to blur the substantial differences between these two species. In other words, the image of a single, simple branch no longer seems apt for representing humans a couple of million years ago. Our early ancestry looks more like a bundle of twigs—one might even think it looks like a tangled bush.

There is also evidence of multiple lineages in our more recent past. For example, Neandertals have been recognized as a separate species for more than 150 years, and as time goes by researchers discover more and more ways in which they differ from modern humans. We also know that a third hominin, namely *H. erectus,* probably survived much later than was originally thought and that *H. floresiensis,* although it may have been confined to the island of Flores, is almost certainly a fourth hominin that lived on the planet within the past 100,000 years. Evidence of a distinctive fifth hominin, the Denisovans, has come from ancient DNA extracted from a 40,000-year-old finger bone. And evidence has emerged for at least one more "ghost lineage" in the DNA of living modern humans from 100,000 years ago. Thus, our recent evolutionary history is much "bushier" than people thought even 10 years ago.

Perhaps the discovery of bushiness in our evolution should not have been surprising. Contemporary existence of multiple related species seems to have been the rule in the past for many groups of mammals, so why should hominins have been any different? Still, critics of the bushy family tree have charged that paleoanthropologists have been overzealous in identifying new species from their finds—presumably out of a desire for fame and further research funding.

My prejudice, on the other hand, is that we are most likely dealing with a real phenomenon. First, there are sound, logical reasons to suspect that the fossil record always underestimates the number of species. Second, we know from living animals that many uncontested species are difficult to distinguish using the bones and teeth—the so-called hard tissues, which is all that survives into the fossil record. Furthermore, most of the mammal species that were living between three million and one million years ago have no direct living descendants. Therefore, the existence of several contemporary early hominins with no direct living descendants is not "odd" after all.

If it is true that hominins had rich diversity in their past, it behooves biologists to uncover the evolutionary pressures that triggered it. Climate is one of the obvious candidates. Climates and thus habitats change over time—they show trends, and they oscillate within those trends. By and large over the period we are considering, there is a trend toward cooler and drier conditions, but within that trend the climate oscillates at predictable

intervals, so at times it will be hotter and wetter, and at other times it will be cooler and drier. The type of posture, diet and locomotion that worked at one time may not be so successful at another. Another pressure favoring hominin diversity may have been competition among hominins; if two hominins shared a habitat, even in a very general sense, they would have tended to force each other into different survival strategies. This phenomenon, called character displacement, may explain how *H. habilis* and *P. boisei* came to have such different teeth and jaws—with one group favoring tough, fibrous foods such as grasses and the other leaning toward a diet that included softer, but harder to find, fruits plus the occasional meal of meat or bone marrow. Moreover, as hominins evolved different cultures, their different worldviews and practices could have militated against species merging as the result of interbreeding.

In addition to anatomical differences, researchers can now analyze fossils on a molecular level. Yet when it comes to early hominins—for whom we do not yet have genetic evidence—distinguishing the equivalent of my parents, grandparents, and great-grandparents from the equivalent of my uncles and aunts remains challenging. Just because two fossils have similarly shaped jaws or teeth does not mean they share a recent evolutionary history. These overlaps can occur because similar ecological challenges prompt similar morphological solutions. By way of illustration, consider an ax design that works as well to cut down gum trees in Australia as it does to fell spruce in northern Europe; Australians and Europeans could well have hit on the same design without one group having introduced it to the other. We also know that morphology is not infinitely evolvable—for any type of animal or plant, there are a finite number of anatomical or physiological solutions to the same ecological challenge. Thus, the discovery of a shared feature in fossils from two species does not necessarily mean that they are direct taxonomic buddies; they could merely be close relatives that have converged on the same physical solution to a similar ecological challenge.

So what does the future hold for identifying our direct ancestors? I am willing to go a step further than supporting the view that many hominin species roamed the planet simultaneously. I predict that the increased hominin diversity that has been identified in the past four million years will be shown to extend back even further. I think this in part because researchers have not been looking as long or as hard for hominins that lived in even earlier times. Consequently, they have explored fewer sites from before four million years than after. Admittedly, the work is hard. Hominins are among the scarcest mammals in the fossil record. You have to sort through a lot of pig and antelope fossils before you can expect to find the occasional hominin. But if we make a concerted effort to find them, they will surely turn up.

Another reason to predict that more early hominin species remain to be discovered: the fossil records of the more common mammals have nearly as many lineages before three million years as they do after that time. Why would we not expect hominins to show the same pattern? Finally, existing early hominin sites cover no more than 3 percent of the land–mass of Africa, probably less. It is unlikely that such a small geographical sample has managed to capture evidence of all the early hominin species that ever lived on that continent.

And yet each new discovery from before four million years most likely will bring even less certainty. The closer you get to the split between the human and the chimpanzee-plus-bonobo lineages, the more difficult it will be to tell a direct human ancestor from a close relative. It will also be harder to be sure that any new species is a hominin rather than an ancestor of chimpanzees and bonobos or even a species belonging to a lineage that has no living representative. If paleoanthropology is challenging and difficult now—and I remain to be convinced that the Malapa skeletons were direct human ancestors—it is only going to get more so in the future. But it is these challenges that make the field so fascinating.

Critical Thinking

1. Discuss the evidence for multiple lineages among hominins of the past.

2. Why should it not be surprising that multiple lineages have existed during the evolution of homins?

3. Discuss the possible causes for hominin diversity in the past.

Internet References

Evolutionary Demography Group
http://blogs.lshtm.ac.uk/evolutionarydemography/
Evolutionary Demography Society
http://www.sdu.dk/en/om_sdu/institutter_centre/maxo/evodemos

More to Explore

Fossils Raise Questions about Human Ancestiy. Ewen Callaway in Nature. Published online September 8, 2011.

Human Evolution: Fifty Years after Homo habilis. Bernard Wood in Nature, Vol. 508, pages 31–33; April 3, 2014.

What Does It Mean to Be Human? Smithsonian Institution's Human Origins Initiative: http://humanorigins.si.edu

From our Archives

Shattered Ancestry. Katherine Harmon; February 2013.

Becoming Human: Our Past, Present and Future. Editors of **Scientific American; Scientific American** eBooks, September 23, 2013.

Fossil Hominids FAQ
www.talkorigins.org/faqs/homs
Institute of Human Origins
http://iho.asu.edu/node/27
Long Foreground: Human Prehistory
www.public.wsu.edu/gened/learn-modules/top_longfor/timeline/00. . .

BERNARD WOOD is a medically trained paleoanthropologist at George Washington University. His interest in human evolution research began in 1968, when as a medical student, he joined Richard Leakey's expedition to northern Kenya.

Article Prepared by: Elvio Angeloni, *Pasadena City College*

The First Cookout

Kate Wong

Learning Outcomes

After reading this article, you will be able to:

- Discuss Richard Wrangham's theory as to how cooking food made us human.
- Discuss the implications of Richard Wrangham's theory for how we should eat today and why.

With our supersized brains and shrunken teeth and guts, we humans are bizarre primates. Richard Wrangham of Harvard University has long argued that these and other peculiar traits of our kind arose as humans turned to cooking to improve food quality—making it softer and easier to digest and thus a richer source of energy. Humans, unlike any other animal, cannot survive on raw food in the wild, he observes. "We need to have our food cooked."

Based on the anatomy of our fossil forebears, Wrangham thinks that *Homo erectus* had mastered cooking with fire by 1.8 million years ago. Critics have countered that he lacks evidence to support the claim that cooking enhances digestibility and that the oldest known traces of fire are nowhere near as old as his hypothesis predicts. New findings, Wrangham says, lend support to his ideas.

Scientific American: How did you come up with the cooking hypothesis?

Wrangham: I think of two strands. One is that I was trying to figure out what was responsible for the evolution of the human body form, and I was sensitive to the fact that humans everywhere use fire. I started thinking about how long ago you would have to go back before humans did not use fire. And that suggested to me the hypothesis that they always used it because they would not have survived without it. Humans as a genus [*Homo*] are committed to sleeping on

the ground. I do not want to sleep on the ground in Africa without fire to keep the wild animals at bay.

The other strand is that I've studied chimpanzees and their feeding behavior for many years. I've eaten everything that I can get ahold of that chimpanzees eat. And I have been very much aware of the deeply unsatisfying nature of those foods because they are often quite fibrous, relatively dry, and contain little sugar, and they are often strong-tasting—in other words, really nasty. So here we are, two very closely related species with completely different dietary habits. It was an obvious hypothesis that cooking does something special for the food we find in nature. But I was astonished to discover that there was no systematic evidence showing what cooking does to the net energetic gain that we get from our foods.

For the past 14 years I've been focused on that question because to make a satisfactory claim about humans being adapted to cooked food, we have to produce some real evidence about what cooking does to food. Experiments conducted by Rachel N. Carmody of Harvard University have now given us the evidence: if we cook, we get more energy from our food.

Other researchers hold that increased access to meat allowed the teeth and gut to shrink. Why do you think cooking better explains these changes?

It's quite clear that humans began eating meat from large animals by 2.5 million years ago and have left a steady record of cut marks on bones since then. The cooking hypothesis does not deny the importance of meat eating. But there is a core difficulty with attributing changes in digestive anatomy to this shift.

Selection pressure on digestive anatomy is strongest when food is scarce. Under such conditions, animals have very little fat on them, and fat-poor meat is a very poor food because if you have more than about 30 percent protein in your diet, then your ability to get rid of ammonia fast enough is overwhelmed. Nowadays in surveys of hunters and gatherers, what you find is that during periods of food scarcity, there is always a substantial inclusion of plants. Very often it's tubers. To eat those raw, you would have to have the digestive apparatus to handle tough, fibrous, low-carbohydrate plant foods—that is, large teeth and a big gut.

So your idea is that by cooking those plant foods, our ancestors could evolve a smaller gut and teeth—and avoid overdosing on lean meat. Let's turn now to what happened when food was not so scarce and animals were good to eat. You have argued that cooking may have helped early humans eat more meat by freeing them up to hunt. What is your logic?

A primate the size of an early human would be expected to spend about half of its day chewing, as chimpanzees do. Modern humans spend less than an hour a day, whether you're American or living in various subsistence societies around the world. So you've got four or five hours a day freed by the fact that you're eating relatively soft food. In hunter-gatherer life, men tend to spend this time hunting.

That observation raises the question of how much hunting was possible until our ancestors were able to reduce the amount of time they chewed. Chimpanzees like to eat meat, but their average hunt is just 20 minutes, after which they go back to eating fruit. Hunting is risky. If you fail, then you need to be able to eat your ordinary food. If you hunt too long without success, you won't have enough time to process your usual, lower-quality fare. It seems to me that it was only after cooking enabled individuals to save time on chewing that they could increase the amount of time spent on an activity that, for all its potential benefits, might not yield any food.

You have also suggested that cooking allowed the brain to expand. How would cooking do that?

With regard to the brain, fossils indicate a fairly steady increase in cranial capacity, starting shortly before two million years ago. There are lots of ideas about why selection favored larger brains, but the question of how our ancestors could afford them has been a puzzle. The problem is that brains use a disproportionate amount of energy and can never be turned off.

I have extended the idea put forward by Leslie C. Aiello, now at the Wenner-Gren Foundation in New York City, and Peter Wheeler of Liverpool John Moores University in England that after cooking became obligatory, the increase in food quality contributed to reduced gut size. Their newly small guts were energetically cheaper, allowing calories to be diverted to the brain.

In 2012, Karina Fonseca-Azevedo and Suzana Herculano-Houzel of the Federal University of Rio de Janeiro added a new wrinkle. Their calculations showed that on a raw diet, the number of calories needed to support a human-sized brain would require too many hours eating every day. They argued that cooking allowed our ancestors the extra energy needed to support more neurons, allowing the increase in brain size.

Cooking is not the only way to make food easier to digest. How does it compare with other methods?

Simply reducing the size of food particles and the structural integrity of food—through pounding, for example—makes it easier to digest. Carmody did a study that looked at tubers and meat as representative types of food that hunter-gatherers eat and asked how well mice fared when eating each of these foods, either raw versus cooked or whole versus pounded. She very carefully controlled the amount of food that the mice received, along with the amount of energy they expended moving around, and assessed their net energetic gain through looking at body-mass changes. She found that pounding had relatively little effect, whereas cooking led to significant increases in body weight whether the food was tubers or meat.

This is incredibly exciting because, amazingly, this is the first study that has ever been done to show that animals get more net energy out of their food when it is cooked than when it's raw. Second, it showed that even if pounding has some positive effects on energy gain, cooking has much bigger effects. [Editors' note: Wrangham was a co-author on the study, published in 2011.]

Is there any genetic evidence to support the cooking hypothesis?

There is essentially nothing published yet. But we're very aware that a really interesting question is going to be whether or not we can detect, in the human genome, evidence of selection for genes related to utilizing cooked food. They might be concerned with metabolism. They might be concerned with the immune system. They might be concerned somehow with responses to Maillard compounds, which are somewhat dangerous compounds produced by cooking. This is going to be a very exciting area in the future.

A central objection to the cooking hypothesis has been that there is no archaeological evidence of controlled fire as far back as the hypothesis predicts. Currently the oldest traces come from one-million-year-old deposits in Wonderwerk Cave in South Africa. But you have recently identified an independent line of evidence that humans tamed fire earlier than the archaeological record suggests. How does that work support your thinking?

Chimpanzees love honey, yet they eat very little of it because they get chased away by bees. African hunters and gatherers, in contrast, eat somewhere between 100 and 1,000 times as much honey as chimpanzees do because they use fire. Smoke interferes with the olfactory system of the bees, and under those conditions, the bees do not attack. The question is: How long have humans been using smoke to get honey? That's where the honeyguide comes in. The greater honeyguide is an African species of bird that is adapted to guiding humans to honey. The bird is attracted to human activity—sounds of chopping, whistling, shouting, banging, and, nowadays, motor vehicles. On finding people, the bird starts fluttering in front of them and then leads them off with a special call and waits for them to follow. Honeyguides can lead humans a kilometer or more to a tree that has honey in it. The human then uses smoke to disarm the bees and opens the hive up with an ax to extract the honey inside. The bird gains access to the hive's wax, which it eats.

It used to be thought that the bird's guiding behavior [which is innate, not learned] originated in partnership with the honey badger and that humans moved in on this arrangement later. But in the past 30 years, it has become very clear that honey badgers are rarely, if ever, led to honey by honeyguides. If there's no living species other than humans that has this symbiotic relationship with the bird, could there have been some extinct species of something that favored the honeyguide showing this behavior? Well, obviously, the most reasonable candidates are the extinct ancestors of humans. The argument points very strongly to our ancestors having used fire long enough for natural selection to enable this relationship to develop.

Claire Spottiswoode of the University of Cambridge discovered that there are two kinds of greater honeyguide females: those that lay their eggs in ground nests and those that lay in tree nests. Then she found that the two types of behavior are associated with different lineages of mitochondrial DNA [DNA that is found in the energy-producing components of cells and passed down from mother to offspring]. Based on a fairly conservative assessment of the rate of mutation, Spottiswoode and her colleagues determined that the two lineages had been separated for about three million years, [providing a minimum estimate for the age of the greater honeyguide species]. That doesn't necessarily mean that the guiding habit, which depends on humans using fire, is that old—it could be more recent—but at least it tells you that the species is old enough to allow for much evolutionary change.

If cooking was a driving force in human evolution, does this conclusion have implications for how people should eat today?

It does remind us that eating raw food is a very different proposition from eating cooked food. Because we don't think about the consequences of processing our food, we are getting a misunderstanding of the net energy gain from eating. One of the ways in which this can be quite serious is if people who are dedicated to a raw-food diet don't understand the consequences for their children. If you just say, "Well, animals eat their food raw, and humans are animals, then it should be fine for us to eat our food raw," and you bring your children up this way, you're putting them at very severe risk. We are a different species from every other. It's fine to eat raw food if you want to lose weight. But if you want to gain weight, as with a child or an adult who's too thin, then you don't want to eat a raw diet.

Critical Thinking

1. How and why does Richard Wrangham think that cooking food made us into the humans we have become?

2. How does Wrangham answer his critics?

3. How did cooking enable humans to hunt for meat?

4. How did cooking food allow for brain expansion?

5. How does cooking food compare with other methods of making food more digestible?

6. Why is the bird, the honeyguide, a clue to when humans began using fire?

7. What are the implications of Wrangham's theory for how people should eat today and why?

Create Central

www.mhhe.com/createcentral

Internet References

Human Prehistory
http://users.hol.gr/~dilos/prehis.htm

Max Planck Institute for Evolutionary Anthropology
www.eva.mpg.de/english/index.htm

The Paleolithic Diet Page
www.paleodiet.com

KATE WONG is a senior editor at *Scientific American*.

Article   Prepared by Elvio Angeloni, *Pasadena City College*

Rethinking Neanderthals

Research suggests the so-called brutes fashioned tools, buried their dead, maybe cared for the sick and even conversed. But why, if they were so smart, did they disappear?

JOE ALPER

Learning Outcomes

After reading this article, you will be able to:

- Discuss the successful adaptation of the Neanderthals with respect to anatomy, technology, and sociality.

B runo Maureille unlocks the gate in a chain-link fence, and we walk into the fossil bed past a pile of limestone rubble, the detritus of an earlier dig. We're 280 miles southwest of Paris, in rolling farm country dotted with long-haired cattle and etched by meandering streams. Maureille, an anthropologist at the University of Bordeaux, oversees the excavation of this storied site called Los Pradelles, where for three decades researchers have been uncovering, fleck by fleck, the remains of humanity's most notorious relatives, the Neanderthals.

We clamber 15 feet down a steep embankment into a swimming pool-size pit. Two hollows in the surrounding limestone indicate where shelters once stood. I'm just marveling at the idea that Neanderthals lived here about 50,000 years ago when Maureille, inspecting a long ledge that a student has been painstakingly chipping away, interrupts my reverie and calls me over. He points to a whitish object resembling a snapped pencil that's embedded in the ledge. "Butchered reindeer bone," he says. "And here's a tool, probably used to cut meat from one of these bones." The tool, or lithic, is shaped like a hand-size D.

All around the pit, I now see, are other lithics and fossilized bones. The place, Maureille says, was probably a butchery where Neanderthals in small numbers processed the results of what appear to have been very successful hunts. That finding alone is significant, because for a long time paleoanthropologists have viewed Neanderthals as too dull and too clumsy to use efficient tools, never mind organize a hunt and divvy, up the game. Fact is, this site, along with others across Europe and in Asia, is helping overturn the familiar conception of Neanderthals as dumb brutes. Recent studies suggest they were imaginative enough to carve artful objects and perhaps clever enough to invent a language.

Neanderthals, traditionally designated *Homo sapiens neanderthalensis,* were not only "human" but also, it turns out, more "modern" than scientists previously allowed. "In the minds of the European anthropologists who first studied them, Neanderthals were the embodiment of primitive humans, sub-humans if you will," says Fred H. Smith, a physical anthropologist at Loyola University in Chicago who has been studying Neanderthal DNA. "They were believed to be scavengers who made primitive tools and were incapable of language or symbolic thought." Now, he says, researchers believe that Neanderthals "were highly intelligent, able to adapt to a wide variety of ecological zones, and capable of developing highly functional tools to help them do so. They were quite accomplished."

Contrary to the view that Neanderthals were evolutionary failures—they died out about 28,000 years ago—they actually had quite a run. "If you take success to mean the ability to survive in hostile, changing environments, then Neanderthals were a great success," says archaeologist John Shea of the State University of New York at Stony Brook. "They lived 250,000 years or more in the harshest climates experienced by primates, not just humans." In contrast, we modern humans have only been around for 100,000 years or so and moved into colder, temperate regions only in the past 40,000 years.

Though the fossil evidence is not definitive, Neanderthals appear to have descended from an earlier human species, *Homo erectus,* between 500,000 to 300,000 years ago. Neanderthals shared many features with their ancestors—a prominent brow, weak chin, sloping skull and large nose—but were as big-brained as the anatomically modern humans that later colonized Europe, *Homo sapiens.* At the same time, Neanderthals were stocky, a build that would have conserved heat efficiently. From musculature marks on Neanderthal fossils and the heft of arm and leg bones, researchers conclude they were also incredibly strong. Yet their hands were remarkably like those of modern humans; a study published this past March in *Nature* shows that Neanderthals, contrary to previous thinking, could touch index finger and thumb, which would have given them considerable dexterity.

Neanderthal fossils suggest that they must have endured a lot of pain. "When you look at adult Neanderthal fossils, particularly the bones of the arms and skull, you see [evidence of] fractures," says Erik Trinkaus, an anthropologist at Washington University in St. Louis. "I've yet to see an adult Neanderthal skeleton that doesn't have at least one fracture, and in adults in their 30s, it's common to see multiple healed fractures." (That they suffered so many broken bones suggests they hunted large animals up close, probably stabbing prey with heavy spears—a risky tactic.) In addition, fossil evidence indicates that Neanderthals suffered from a wide range of ailments, including pneumonia and malnourishment. Still, they persevered, in some cases living to the ripe old age of 45 or so.

Perhaps surprisingly, Neanderthals must also have been caring: to survive disabling injury or illness requires the help of fellow clan members, paleoanthropologists say. A telling example came from an Iraqi cave known as Shanidar, 250 miles north of Baghdad, near the border with Turkey and Iran. There, archaeologist Ralph Solecki discovered nine nearly complete Neanderthal skeletons in the late 1950s. One belonged to a 40- to 45-year-old male with several major fractures. A blow to the left side of his head had crushed an eye socket and almost certainly blinded him. The bones of his right shoulder and upper arm appeared shriveled, most likely the result of a trauma that led to the amputation of his right forearm. His right foot and lower right leg had also been broken while he was alive. Abnormal wear in his right knee, ankle and foot shows that he suffered from injury-induced arthritis that would have made walking painful, if not impossible. Researchers don't know how he was injured but believe that he could not have survived long without a hand from his fellow man.

"This was really the first demonstration that Neanderthals behaved in what we think of as a fundamentally human way," says Trinkaus, who in the 1970s helped reconstruct and catalog the Shanidar fossil collection in Baghdad. (One of the skeletons is held by the Smithsonian Institution's National Museum of Natural History.) "The result was that those of us studying Neanderthals started thinking about these people in terms of their behavior and not just their anatomy."

Neanderthals inhabited a vast area roughly from present-day England east to Uzbekistan and south nearly to the Red Sea. Their time spanned periods in which glaciers advanced and retreated again and again, but the Neanderthals adjusted. When the glaciers moved in and edible plants became scarcer, they relied more heavily on large, hoofed animals for food, hunting the reindeer and wild horses that grazed the steppes and tundra.

Paleoanthropologists have no idea how many Neanderthals existed (crude estimates are in the many thousands), but archaeologists have found more fossils from Neanderthals than from any extinct human species. The first Neanderthal fossil was uncovered in Belgium in 1830, though nobody accurately identified it for more than a century. In 1848, the Forbes Quarry in Gibraltar yielded one of the most complete Neanderthal skulls ever found, but it, too, went unidentified, for 15 years. The name Neanderthal arose after quarrymen in Germany's Neander Valley found a cranium and several long bones in 1856; they gave the specimens to a local naturalist, Johann Karl Fuhlrott, who soon recognized them as the legacy of a previously unknown type of human. Over the years, France, the Iberian Peninsula, southern Italy and the Levant have yielded abundances of Neanderthal remains, and those finds are being supplemented by newly opened excavations in Ukraine and Georgia. "It seems that everywhere we look, we're finding Neanderthal remains," says Loyola's Smith. "It's an exciting time to be studying Neanderthals."

Clues to some Neanderthal ways of life come from chemical analyses of fossilized bones, which confirm that Neanderthals were meat eaters. Microscopic studies hint at cannibalism; fossilized deer and Neanderthal bones found at the same site bear identical scrape marks, as though the same tool removed the muscle from both animals.

There are hints of cannibalism: deer and Neanderthal bones at the same site bear identical scrape marks.

The arrangement of fossilized Neanderthal skeletons in the ground demonstrates to many archaeologists that Neanderthals buried their dead. "They might not have done so with elaborate ritual, since there has never been solid evidence that they included symbolic objects in graves, but it is clear that they did not just dump their dead with the rest of the trash to be picked over by hyenas and other scavengers," says archaeologist Francesco d'Errico of the University of Bordeaux.

Paleoanthropologists generally agree that Neanderthals lived in groups of 10 to 15, counting children. That assessment is based on a few lines of evidence, including the limited remains at burial sites and the modest size of rock shelters. Also, Neanderthals were top predators, and some top predators, such as lions and wolves, live in small groups.

Steven Kuhn, an archaeologist at the University of Arizona, says experts "can infer quite a bit about who Neanderthal was by studying tools in conjunction with the other artifacts they left behind." For instance, recovered stone tools are typically fashioned from nearby sources of flint or quartz, indicating to some researchers that a Neanderthal group did not necessarily range far.

The typical Neanderthal tool kit contained a variety of implements, including large spear points and knives that would have been hafted, or set in wooden handles. Other tools were suitable for cutting meat, cracking open bones (to get at fat-rich marrow) or scraping hides (useful for clothing, blankets or shelter). Yet other stone tools were used for woodworking;

among the very few wooden artifacts associated with Neanderthal sites are objects that resemble spears, plates and pegs.

I get a feel for Neanderthal handiwork in Maureille's office, where plastic milk crates are stacked three high in front of his desk. They're stuffed with plastic bags full of olive and tan flints from Les Pradelles. With his encouragement, I take a palm-size, D-shaped flint out of a bag. Its surface is scarred as though by chipping, and the flat side has a thin edge. I readily imagine I could scrape a hide with it or whittle a stick. The piece, Maureille says, is about 60,000 years old. "As you can see from the number of lithics we've found," he adds, referring to the crates piling up in his office, "Neanderthals were prolific and accomplished toolmakers."

Among the new approaches to Neanderthal study is what might be called paleo-mimicry, in which researchers themselves fashion tools to test their ideas. "What we do is make our own tools out of flint, use them as a Neanderthal might have, and then look at the fine detail of the cutting edges with a high-powered microscope," explains Michael Bisson, chairman of anthropology at McGill University in Montreal. "A tool used to work wood will have one kind of wear pattern that differs from that seen when a tool is used to cut meat from a bone, and we can see those different patterns on the implements recovered from Neanderthal sites." Similarly, tools used to scrape hide show few microscopic scars, their edges having been smoothed by repeated rubbing against skin, just as stropping a straight razor will hone its edge. As Kuhn, who has also tried to duplicate Neanderthal handicraft, says: "There is no evidence of really fine, precise work, but they were skilled in what they did."

Based on the consistent form and quality of the tools found at sites across Europe and western Asia, it appears likely that Neanderthal was able to pass along his toolmaking techniques to others. "Each Neanderthal or Neanderthal group did not have to reinvent the wheel when it came to their technologies," says Bisson.

The kinds of tools that Neanderthals began making about 200,000 years ago are known as Mousterian, after the site in France where thousands of artifacts were first found. Neanderthals struck off pieces from a rock "core" to make an implement, but the "flaking" process was not random; they evidently examined a core much as a diamond cutter analyzes a rough gemstone today, trying to strike just the spot that would yield "flakes," for knives or spear points, requiring little sharpening or shaping.

Around 40,000 years ago, Neanderthals innovated again. In what passes for the blink of an eye in paleoanthropology, some Neanderthals were suddenly making long, thin stone blades and hafting more tools. Excavations in southwest France and northern Spain have uncovered Neanderthal tools betraying a more refined technique involving, Kuhn speculates, the use of soft hammers made of antler or bone.

What happened? According to the conventional wisdom, there was a culture clash. In the early 20th century, when researchers first discovered those "improved" lithics—called

Châtelperronian and Uluzzian, depending on where they were found—they saw the relics as evidence that modern humans, Homo sapiens or Cro-Magnon, had arrived in Neanderthal territory. That's because the tools resembled those unequivocally associated with anatomically modern humans, who began colonizing western Europe 38,000 years ago. And early efforts to assign a date to those Neanderthal lithics yielded time frames consistent with the arrival of modern humans.

But more recent discoveries and studies, including tests that showed the lithics to be older than previously believed, have prompted d'Errico and others to argue that Neanderthals advanced on their own. "They could respond to some change in their environment that required them to improve their technology," he says. "They could behave like modern humans."

Meanwhile, these "late" Neanderthals also discovered ornamentation, says d'Errico and his archaeologist colleague João Zilhão of the University of Lisbon. Their evidence includes items made of bone, ivory and animal teeth marked with grooves and perforations. The researchers and others have also found dozens of pieces of sharpened manganese dioxide—black crayons, essentially—that Neanderthals probably used to color animal skins or even their own. In his office at the University of Bordeaux, d'Errico hands me a chunk of manganese dioxide. It feels silky, like soapstone. "Toward the end of their time on earth," he says, "Neanderthals were using technology as advanced as that of contemporary anatomically modern humans and were using symbolism in much the same way."

Generally, anthropologists and archaeologists today proffer two scenarios for how Neanderthals became increasingly resourceful in the days before they vanished. On the one hand, it may be that Neanderthals picked up a few new technologies from invading humans in an effort to copy their cousins. On the other, Neanderthals learned to innovate in parallel with anatomically modern human beings, our ancestors.

Most researchers agree that Neanderthals were skilled hunters and craftsmen who made tools, used fire, buried their dead (at least on occasion), cared for their sick and injured and even had a few symbolic notions. Likewise, most researchers believe that Neanderthals probably had some facility for language, at least as we usually think of it. It's not far-fetched to think that language skills developed when Neanderthal groups mingled and exchanged mates; such interactions may have been necessary for survival, some researchers speculate, because Neanderthal groups were too small to sustain the species. "You need to have a breeding population of at least 250 adults, so some kind of exchange had to take place," says archaeologist Ofer Bar-Yosef of Harvard University. "We see this type of behavior in all hunter-gatherer cultures, which is essentially what Neanderthals had."

But if Neanderthals were so smart, why did they go extinct? "That's a question we'll never really have an answer to," says Clive Finlayson, who runs the Gibraltar Museum, "though it doesn't stop any of us from putting forth some pretty elaborate scenarios." Many researchers are loath even to speculate on the cause of Neanderthals' demise, but Finlayson suggests that a combination of climate change and the cumulative effect of repeated population busts eventually did them in. "I think it's the culmination of 100,000 years of climate hitting Neanderthals hard, their population diving during the cold years, rebounding some during warm years, then diving further when it got cold again," Finlayson says.

As Neanderthals retreated into present-day southern Spain and parts of Croatia toward the end of their time, modern human beings were right on their heels. Some researchers, like Smith, believe that Neanderthals and Cro-Magnon humans probably mated, if only in limited numbers. The question of whether Neanderthals and modern humans bred might be resolved within a decade by scientists studying DNA samples from Neanderthal and Cro-Magnon fossils.

As Neanderthals retreated, modern humans were right on their heels. The two may have mated—or tried to.

But others argue that any encounter was likely to be hostile. "Brotherly love is not the way I'd describe any interaction between different groups of humans," Shea says. In fact, he speculates that modern humans were superior warriors and wiped out the Neanderthals. "Modern humans are very competitive and really good at using projectile weapons to kill from a distance," he says, adding they also probably worked together better in large groups, providing a battlefield edge.

In the end, Neanderthals, though handy, big-brained, brawny and persistent, went the way of every human species but one. "There have been a great many experiments at being human preceding us and none of them made it, so we should not think poorly of Neanderthal just because they went extinct," says Rick Potts, head of the Smithsonian's Human Origins Program. "Given that Neanderthal possessed the very traits that we think guarantee our success should make us pause about our place here on earth."

Critical Thinking

1. Discuss the general ways in which Neanderthals should be considered successful—and not failures.
2. What features did they share with their ancestors, *Homo erectus*? With anatomically modern humans?

3. Why were they stocky in build? What indications are there that they were incredibly strong? In what way were their hands like those of modern humans?
4. What indications are there that they must have endured a lot of pain?
5. Why can we conclude that they were very caring?
6. How did the Neanderthals adjust when the glaciers moved in?
7. Why is there a "hint" of cannibalism? That they buried their dead?
8. Why do we think that they lived in groups of about 10 to 15? That each group did not range far?
9. What kinds of tools did the Neanderthals have?
10. What is "paleo-mimcry" and how has it helped us to understand Neanderthal tool-making?
11. How do we know that they were able to pass along tool-making techniques?
12. In what sense was the Mousterian flaking process not random?
13. In what ways did the Neanderthals innovate again around 40,000 years ago?
14. What two scenarios are preferred to explain Neanderthals' increasing resourcefulness? What do most researchers agree upon about Neanderthals?
15. Why is it not far-fetched to think that they had language?
16. Discuss the differing points of view as to what may have happened to the Neanderthals.
17. Why should we not think poorly of them just because they went extinct? What should make us pause about our place on earth?

Create Central

www.mhhe.com/createcentral

Internet References

Fossil Hominids FAQ
www.talkorigins.org/faqs/homs
Long Foreground: Human Prehistory
www.public.wsu.edu/gened/learn-modules/top_longfor/timeline/00...
Max Planck Institute for Evolutionary Biology
www.staff.eva.mpg.de/~paabo

JOE ALPER, a freelance writer in Louisville, Colorado, is a frequent contributor to *Science* magazine. This is his first article for *Smithsonian*.

Alper, Joe. From *Smithsonian*, June 2003, pp. 83–87. Copyright © 2003 by Joe Alper. Reprinted by permission of the author.

Article   Prepared by: Elvio Angeloni

Neandertal Minds

KATE WONG

Learning Outcomes

After reading this article, you will be able to:

- Discuss the anatomical evidence that relates to similarities and differences between Neandertals and modern homo sapiens.
- Evaluate the archeological evidence that seems to show that Neandertals thought much like we do.

On a clear day in Gibraltar, looking out of Gorham's Cave, you can see the rugged northern coast of Morocco looming purple above the turquoise sea. Inside the cave, quiet prevails, save for the lapping of waves against its rocky beach. But offshore, the strait separating this southernmost tip of the Iberian Peninsula from the African continent bustles with activity. Fishing vessels troll the waters for tuna and marlin, cruise ships carry tourists gawking at Gibraltar's hulking limestone massif, and tankers ferry crude oil from the Mediterranean to points west. With its swift, nutrient-rich currents, mild climate and gateway location, the area has attracted humans for millennia.

One impressive group dwelled in the region for tens of thousands of years, weathering several ice ages here. During such times lower sea levels exposed a vast coastal plain in front of the cave, land that supported a variety of animals and plants. These individuals cleverly exploited the local bounty. They hunted large animals such as ibex and seals and small ones such as rabbits and pigeons; they fished for bream and gathered mussels and limpets from the distant shore; they harvested pine nuts from the surrounding evergreens. Sometimes they took ravens and eagles for their plumage to bedeck themselves with the beautiful black flight feathers. And they engraved their cave floor with symbols whose meaning has since been lost to time.

In all these ways, these people behaved just like our own *Homo sapiens* ancestors, who arose in Africa with the same anatomy we have today and later colonized every corner of the globe. But they were not these anatomically modern humans. They were Neandertals, our stocky, heavy-browed cousins, known to have lived in Eurasia between 350,000 and 39,000 years ago—those same Neandertals whose name has come to be synonymous in pop culture with idiocy and brutishness.

The scientific basis for that popular pejorative view has deep roots. Back in the early 1900s the discovery of the first largely complete Neandertal skeleton, from the site of La Chapelle-aux-Saints in France, gave rise to the group's image problem: deformities now known to reflect the old age of the individual were seen as signs of degeneracy and subhumanness.

Since then, the pendulum of paleoanthropological opinion has swung repeatedly between researchers who see Neandertals as cognitively inferior to *H. sapiens* and those who see them as our mental equals. Now a rash of new discoveries is fanning the debate. Some fossil and ancient DNA analyses seem to suggest that Neandertal brains were indeed different—and less capable—than those of *H. sapiens*. Yet mounting archaeological evidence indicates that Neandertals behaved in many of the same ways that their anatomically modern contemporaries did.

As scientists advance into the Neandertal mind, the mystery of why our closest relatives went extinct after reigning for hundreds of thousands of years is deepening. The race is on to solve this extinction riddle: such insight will help reveal what it was that distinguished our kind from the rest of the human family—and set anatomically modern humans on the path to becoming the enormously successful species we are today.

Bony Inklings

Paleoanthropologists have long sought clues to Neandertal cognition in the fossilized skulls they left behind. By studying casts of the interior of the braincase, researchers can reconstruct the external form of an extinct human's brain, which reveals the overall size as well as the shape of certain of its regions. But those analyses have failed to turn up much in the way of clear-cut differences between Neandertal brains and those of *H. sapiens*. (Some experts think Neandertals were just another population of *H. sapiens*. This article treats the two groups as different human species, albeit very closely related ones.) Neandertal brains were a little flatter than ours, but they were just as big—indeed, in many cases they were larger, explains paleoneurologist Ralph Holloway of Columbia University. And their frontal lobes—which govern problem solving, among other tasks—were almost identical to those of *H. sapiens*, judging from the impression they left on the inside of the braincase. That impression does not reveal the internal extent or structure of those key brain regions, however. "Endocasts are the most direct evidence of brain evolution, but they are extremely limited in terms of giving you solid information about behavior," Holloway admits.

In a widely publicized study published in 2013, Eiluned Pearce of the University of Oxford and her colleagues purportedly got around some of the limitations of endocasts and provided a way of estimating the size of internal brain areas. The team used eye-socket size as a proxy for the size of the visual cortex, which is the brain region that processes visual signals. They found that the Neandertal skulls they measured had significantly larger eye sockets than modern humans have—the better for coping with the lower light levels available in their high-latitude homes, according to one theory—and thus larger visual cortices. With more real estate dedicated to processing visual information, Neandertals would have had less neural tissue left over for other brain regions, including the ones that help us maintain extensive social networks, which can buffer against hard times, the researchers argued.

Holloway is not convinced. His own endocast work indicates that there is no way to delineate and measure the visual cortex. And Neandertal faces are larger than those of anatomically modern humans, which might explain their larger eye sockets. Moreover, people today are hugely variable in the proportion of visual cortex they have relative to other brain regions, he observes, and this anatomical variability does not appear to correspond to differences in behavior.

Other fossil analyses have yielded similarly equivocal signals about the Neandertal mind. Studies of limb asymmetry and wear marks on tools as well as on the teeth (from using them to grasp items such as animal hides during processing) indicate that Neandertals were as right-handed as we moderns are. A strong tendency toward favoring the right hand is one of the traits that distinguishes *H. sapiens* from chimpanzees and corresponds to asymmetries in the brain that are believed to be related to language—a key component of modern human behavior. Yet studies of skull shape in Neandertal specimens representing a range of developmental stages indicate that the Neandertals attained their large brain size through a different developmental pathway than that of *H. sapiens*. Although

Neandertal brains started off growing like modern brains in the womb, they diverged from the modern growth pattern after birth, during a critical window for cognitive development.

Those developmental differences may have deep evolutionary roots. An analysis of some 17 skulls dated to 430,000 years ago from the fossil site of Sima de los Huesos, in the Atapuerca Mountains in northern Spain, has shown that members of the population there, believed to have been Neandertal precursors, had smaller brains than later members of the lineage. The finding suggests that Neandertals did not inherit their large brain size from the last common ancestor of Neandertals and modern humans; instead the two species underwent a parallel brain expansion later in their evolution. Although Neandertal brains ended up approximately as large as ours, their independent evolution would have left plenty of opportunities for the emergence of brain differences apart from size, such as those affecting connectivity.

Genetic Hints

Glimpses of some of those differences have come from DNA analyses. Since the publication of a draft of the Neandertal genome in 2010, geneticists have been mining ancient DNA to see how Neandertals and *H. sapiens* compare. Intriguingly, the Neandertals turn out to have carried a very similar variant we have of a gene called FOXP2 that is thought to play a role in speech and language in humans. But other parts of the Neandertal genome appear to contrast with ours in significant ways. For one thing, Neandertals seem to have carried different versions of other genes involved in language, including CNTNAP2. Further, of the 87 genes in modern humans that differ significantly from their counterparts in Neandertals and another archaic hominin group, the Denisovans, several are involved in brain development and function.

Differences in the genetic codes of Neandertals and modern humans are not the whole story, however. The switching on and off of genes could have distinguished moderns from Neandertals, too, so that the groups differed in how robustly and under what circumstances they produced the substances encoded by their genes. Indeed, FOXP2 itself appears to have been expressed differently in Neandertals than in *H. sapiens*, even though the protein it made was the same. Scientists have begun studying gene regulation in Neandertals and other extinct humans by examining the patterns of chemical tags known as methyl groups in ancient genomes. These tags are known to influence gene activity.

But whether or not differences in DNA sequences and gene activity translate to differences in cognition is the big question.

To that end, intriguing clues have emerged from studies of people today who carry a small percentage of Neandertal DNA as a result of long-ago interbreeding between Neandertals and *H. sapiens*.

Geneticist John Blangero of the Texas Biomedical Research Institute runs a long-term study of extended families in San Antonio aimed at finding genes involved in complex diseases such as diabetes. In recent years he and his colleagues had begun looking at brain structure and function in the study participants. A biological anthropologist by training, Blangero started at one point to wonder how he could use living humans to answer such questions as what cognitive abilities Neandertals had.

A plan began to take shape. Over the course of their disease research, Blangero and his team had obtained whole-genome sequences and MRI scans of the brains of hundreds of patients. And they had developed a statistical method to gauge the effects of certain disease-linked gene variants on observable traits. Blangero realized that with the aid of their statistical tool, they could use the Neandertal genomes and his group's genetic and MRI data from living people to estimate the effects of the full complement of Neandertal genetic variants—the so-called polygeno-type—on traits related to cognition.

Their results suggest that several key brain regions were smaller in Neandertals than in modern humans, including the gray matter surface area (which helps to process information in the brain), Broca's area (which seems to be involved in language) and the amygdala (which controls emotions and motivation). The findings also indicate that Neandertals would have had less white matter, translating to reduced brain connectivity. And other traits would have compromised their ability to learn and remember words. "Neandertals were almost certainly less cognitively adept," asserts Blangero, who presented his preliminary findings at the annual meeting of the American Association of Physical Anthropologists in Calgary last April. "I'm willing to bet on that one."

Of course, without living Neandertals around today, Blangero cannot conduct cognitive assessments that would confirm or refute his inference. But there is, in theory, another way to put his hunch to the test. It would be possible, using existing technology, to study Neandertal brain cell function by genetically modifying modern human cells to have Neandertal DNA sequences, programming them to become neurons and observing the Neandertalized cells in petri dishes. Scientists could then examine the abilities of the neurons to conduct electrical impulses, to migrate to different brain regions and to produce projections (neurites) that aid in cell communication, for instance. Blangero notes that although there are ethical issues to consider where the creation of Neandertal cells is concerned, such work might actually help researchers identify genes involved in modern human brain disorders if the genetic changes compromise neuron function. Such findings could, in turn, lead to the discovery of new drug targets.

Not everyone is ready to draw conclusions about the Neandertal mind from DNA. John Hawks of the University of Wisconsin-Madison observes that Neandertals may have carried gene variants that affected their brain function but that have no counterparts in people today for comparison. He notes that if one were to predict Neandertal skin color based on the genes they share with modern humans, one would surmise that they had dark skin. Yet scientists now know Neandertals had some genes no longer in circulation that probably lightened their skin. But a bigger problem with attempting to suss out how Neandertal brains worked from their genes, Hawks says, is that for the most part researchers do not know how genes affect thought in our own kind. "We know next to nothing about Neandertal cognition from genetics because we know next to nothing about [modern] human cognition from genetics," he asserts.

Archaeological Insights

Given the limitations of the fossil anatomy and the fact that ancient DNA research is still in its infancy, many researchers say the clearest window on the Neandertal mind is the cultural record these extinct humans left behind. For a long time, that record did not paint a particularly flattering picture of our vanished cousins. Early modern Europeans left behind elegant art, complex tools and remainders of meals attesting to an ability to exploit a wide variety of animals and plants that enabled them to adapt to new environments and shifting climate. Neandertals, in contrast, seemed to lack art and other symbolic remains; their tools were comparatively simple; and they appeared to have had a foraging strategy narrowly focused on large game. Stuck in their ways, the thinking went, the Neandertals simply could not adapt to deteriorating climate conditions and competition from the invading moderns.

In the 1990s, however, archaeologists began to find evidence contradicting that scenario—namely, a handful of decorative items and advanced tools attributed to Neandertals. Ever since, researchers have been at loggerheads over whether these items are Neandertal inventions as claimed; doubt has arisen because the items date to the end of the Neandertal dynasty, by which time *H. sapiens* was in the area, too. (Anatomically modern humans appear to have reached Europe by around 44,000 to 41,500 years ago, hundreds of thousands of years after Neandertals settled there.) Some skeptics think that *H. sapiens* made the sophisticated artifacts, which later got mixed in with the Neandertal remains. Alternatively, they offer, Neandertals may have copied the ingenious moderns or stolen their goods.

But that position is becoming harder to uphold in the face of a raft of discoveries over the past few years that evince Neandertal savvy prior to the spread of anatomically modern humans throughout Europe. "There's been a real sea change. Every month brings something new and surprising that Neandertals did," observes David Frayer of the University of Kansas. "And the new evidence is always that they were more sophisticated, not hicks."

Some of the most surprising discoveries reveal aesthetics and abstract thought in Neandertal cultures that predated the arrival of *H. sapiens*. These finds include the engraving and signs of feather use from Gorham's Cave. In fact, artifacts of this nature have turned up at archaeological sites across Europe. At the Grotta di Fumane in Italy's Veneto region, archaeologists found signs of feather use and a fossil snail shell collected from at least 100 kilometers away that had been stained red, suspended on a string and worn as a pendant at least 47,600 years ago. Cueva de los Aviones and Cueva Antón in southeastern Spain have also yielded seashells bearing traces of pigment. Some seem to have served as cups for mixing and holding red, yellow and sparkly black pigments that may have been cosmetics; others bear holes indicating that they were worn as jewelry. The modified shells date to as many as 50,000 years ago.

Other Neandertal leavings indicate that their yen for decorating reaches back further still. Sites in France and Italy document a tradition of harvesting eagle talons that spans from 90,000 to 40,000 years ago. Cut marks on the bones show that the Neandertals focused their efforts on obtaining the claws, not the flesh. This finding led investigators to conclude that the Neandertals exploited the eagles for symbolic reasons—probably to adorn themselves with the impressive talons—rather than dietary ones.

Even older hints of Neandertal aesthetics come from the site of Maastricht-Belvedere in the Netherlands, where archaeologists have found small splatters of red ochre, or iron oxide, in deposits dating to between 250,000 and 200,000 years ago at minimum. The scarlet pigment had been finely ground and mixed into a liquid that then dripped onto the ground. Researchers cannot know for sure what those Neandertals were doing with the red liquid, but painting is one obvious possibility. Indeed, when red ochre turns up at early modern human sites, investigators assume that it was used for decorative purposes.

In addition to rendering a far more resplendent portrait of our much maligned cousins, these new discoveries provide crucial insights into the Neandertal mind. Archaeologists have long considered art, including body decoration, to be a key indicator of modern cognitive abilities because it means that the makers had the capacity to conceive of something in the abstract and to convey that information in symbols. Symbolic thinking underpins our ability to communicate via language—one of the defining traits of modern humans and one that is seen as critical to our success as a species. If Neandertals thought symbolically, as they appear to have done, then they probably had language, too. In fact, abstract thought may have dawned in the human lineage even before the last common ancestor of Neandertals and *H. sapiens:* in December researchers unveiled a mussel shell from Indonesia that they contend was engraved with a geometric pattern by a more primitive ancestor, *Homo erectus,* around 500,000 years ago.

Symbolic thought is not the only component of behavior believed to have helped *H. sapiens* get ahead, however. The manufacture of tools with specialized uses is another element, one that Neandertals appear to have mastered as well. In 2013, Marie Soressi of Leiden University in the Netherlands and her collaborators announced their discovery of bone tools known as lissoirs—implements that leather workers today use to render animal hides more pliable, lustrous and impermeable to the elements—at two Neandertal sites in the Dordogne region of France dating to between 53,000 and 41,000 years ago. Judging from the wear marks on the artifacts, Neandertals used them for the same purpose. The Neandertals made the lissoirs from deer ribs, shaping the end of the bone that attaches to the sternum to form a rounded tip. To wield the tool, they pressed the tip into a dry hide at an angle and pushed it across the surface repeatedly, smoothing and softening the skin.

Fresh evidence of Neandertal ingenuity has also come from the site of Abri du Maras in southern France, which sheltered Neandertals around 90,000 years ago. Microscopic analyses of stone tools from the site, conducted by Bruce Hardy of Kenyon College and his colleagues, revealed traces of all manner of activities once thought to be beyond the ken of the species. For instance, the team found remnants of twisted plant fibers that would have been used for making string or cords, which then could have been fashioned into nets, traps and bags. Traces of wood turned up as well, suggesting that the Neandertals crafted tools from that material.

Residue analysis additionally gives the lie to the notion that Neandertals were perilously picky eaters. Studies of the chemical makeup of their teeth, along with analyses of animal remains from Neandertal sites, have suggested that Neandertals relied heavily on large, dangerous prey such as mammoth and bison rather than an array of animals depending on availability, as anatomically modern humans did. The Abri du Maras Neandertals apparently exploited a veritable menagerie of creatures, including small, fast animals such as rabbits and fish—all species previously thought to be out of reach for Neandertals, with their low-tech gear.

Some scholars have argued that an ability to live partly on plant foods gave *H. sapiens* an edge over Neandertals, allowing them to reap more sustenance from the same area of land. (Subsisting on plants is trickier for humans than for other primates because our big brains demand a lot of calories, and yet our small guts are poorly suited to digesting large quantities of raw roughage—a combination that requires intimate knowledge of plant foods and how to prepare them.) But the Abri du Maras Neandertals gathered edible plants, including parsnip and burdock, as well as edible mushrooms. And they were not alone.

According to studies led by Amanda Henry of the Max Planck Institute for Evolutionary Anthropology in Leipzig, Germany, Neandertals across a broad swath of Eurasia—from

More to Explore

Brain Development after Birth Differs between Neanderthals and Modern Humans. Phillip Gunz et al. in Current Biology, Vol. 20, No. 21, pages R921–R922; November 9, 2010.

Impossible Neanderthals? Making String, Throwing Projectiles and Catching Small Game during Marine Isotope Stage 4 (Abri du Maras, France). Bruce L. Hardy et al. in Quaternary Science Reviews, Vol. 82, pages 23–40; December 15, 2013.

A Rock Engraving Made by Neanderthals in Gibraltar. Joaquín Rodríguez-Vidal et al. in Proceedings of the National Academy of the Sciences USA, Vol. 111, No. 37, pages 13,301–13,306; September 16, 2014.

From our Archives

Twilight of the Neandertals, Kate Wong; August 2009. scientificamerican.com/magazine/sa

Neandertal Legacy

Analysis of DNA recovered from several Neandertal fossils has revealed that Neandertals interbred with Homo sapiens after our species left Africa. Neandertal DNA lives on in many people today as a result of this long-ago mixing.

1.5%–2.1% of non-African, modern human DNA comes from Neandertals

Any given individual possesses only a small amount of Neandertal DNA. But not everyone carries the same bits. In fact, patching together Neandertal DNA pieces from a large sample of modern humans, scientists could reconstruct 35 to 70 percent of the Neandertal genome.

35%–70% of Neandertal genome persists in the gene pool of people today

FINDINGS

The Homo sapiens Effect

Neandertals ruled Eurasia for hundreds of thousands of years until anatomically modern H. sapiens from Africa invaded their turf. Then the Neandertals faded away. Some experts have proposed that Neandertals lost out to the moderns because they lacked the language and social skills, technological ingenuity and foraging savvy that the newcomers had. Any hints of Neandertal sophistication from late Neandertal archaeological sites were chalked up to the influence of H. sapiens. Recent efforts to pinpoint the timing of Neandertal extinction, by redating a number of sites in Europe, indicate that Neandertals overlapped with H. sapiens for thousands of years in some places—ample time for Neandertals to have learned the ways of the interlopers.

Yet over the past few years a flurry of discoveries attesting to Neandertal sophistication—from symbolic items and advanced tools to a wide variety of food remnants—have emerged from sites that clearly predate the arrival of H. sapiens. The question that scientists now face is whether the new arrivals were just better at these things or whether some other factor drove the Neandertals' demise.

Neandertal range

Early Homo sapiens range

Representative sites of Neandertal finds indicative of advanced behavior

250,000–45,000 Years Ago

Largest extent of Neandertal range and sites with signs of sophisticated behavior that may predate the arrival of anatomically modern humans.

THE NETHERLANDS

Liquid pigment

1 Maastricht-Belvedere 250,000–200,000 years ago

FRANCE

String, array of plant and animal remains, and possible projectile weapons

2 Abri du Maras 90,000

Eagle talons

3 Combe Grenal 90,000

4 Les Fieux 60,000–40,000

Burial

5 La Chapelle-aux-Saints 60,000

Leather-burnishing tools

6 Pech-de-l'Azé 53,400–49,400

7 Abri Peyrony 47,700–41,000

SPAIN

Pigment-stained marine shells

8 Cueva de los Aviones 50,000

ITALY

Painted shell and feather extraction

9 Grotta di Fumane 47,600

45,000–39,000 Years Ago

Neandertals and modern humans overlapped for as many as 5,400 years in some regions, which means that some later Neandertal cultural remains may be the product of modern human influence.

FRANCE

Ornaments, advanced bone and stone tools	Pigment-stained marine shells
10 Arcy-sur-Cure 44,500–40,000 11 Saint Césaire 42,000–40,500 12 La Quina 43,300–41,600 SPAIN	13 Cueva Antón 43,500–37,400 GIBRALTAR Rock engraving, feather extraction 14 Gorham's Cave More than 39,000

Iraq to Belgium—ate a variety of plants. Examining the tartar in Neandertal teeth and residues on stone tools, she determined that Neandertals consumed species closely related to modern wheat and barley, cooking them to make them palatable. She also found bits of starch from tubers and telltale components of date palms. The similarities to findings from early modern human sites were striking. "Any way we broke up the data, there were no significant differences between the groups," Henry remarks. "The evidence we have now does not suggest that the earliest modern humans in Eurasia were better at accessing plant foods."

A Long Farewell

If Neandertals actually behaved in ways once thought to distinguish anatomically modern humans and fuel their rise to world domination, that likeness makes their decline and eventual extinction all the more puzzling. Why did they die out while *H. sapiens* survived? One theory is that moderns had a bigger tool kit that may have boosted their foraging returns. Modern humans evolved in Africa, where their population size was larger than that of Neandertals, Henry explains. With more mouths to feed, preferred resources such as easy game would have declined, and the moderns would have had to develop new tools to obtain other kinds of food. When they brought this cutting-edge technology with them out of Africa and into Eurasia, they were able to exploit that environment more effectively than the resident Neandertals could. In other words, moderns honed their survival skills under more competitive circumstances than Neandertals had faced and thus entered Neandertal territory with an advantage over the incumbents.

Not only did the large population size of *H. sapiens* spur innovation, but it helped to keep new traditions alive rather than letting them fizzle out with the last member of a small, isolated group. The bigger, more connected membership of *H. sapiens* "increasingly provided a more efficient ratchet effect to maintain and build on knowledge compared with earlier humans, including the Neandertals," offers Chris Stringer of the Natural History Museum in London. Still, the arrival of moderns did not spell instant doom for Neandertals. The latest attempt to track their decline, carried out by Thomas Higham of Oxford and his colleagues, applied improved dating methods to pinpoint the ages of dozens of Neandertal and early modern European sites from Spain to Russia. The results indicate that the two groups shared the continent for some 2,600 to 5,400 years before the Neandertals finally disappeared, around 39,000 years ago.

That lengthy overlap would have left plenty of time for mating between the two factions. DNA analyses have found that people today who live outside Africa carry an average of least 1.5 to 2.1 percent Neandertal DNA—a legacy from dalliances between Neandertals and anatomically modern humans tens of thousands of years ago, after the latter group began spreading out of Africa.

Maybe, some experts offer, mixing between the smaller Neandertal population and the larger modern one led to the Neandertal's eventual demise by swamping their gene pool. "There were never very many of them, there were people coming in from other areas and mixing with them, and they faded out," Frayer surmises. "The history of all living forms is that they go extinct," he adds. "That's not necessarily a sign that they were stupid, or culturally incapable, or adaptively incapable. It's just what happens."

Critical Thinking

1. In what ways did Neandertals behave just like our own *Homo sapiens* ancestors during the Paleolithic period?

2. What does the archaeological and anatomical evidence indicate with respect to the possibility that Neandertals were capable of aesthetics, abstract thought, and language?

Internet References

Fossil Hominids FAQ
www.talkorigins.org/faqs/homs

Human Origins Institute
http://humanorigins.si.edu/

Max Planck Institute for Evolutionary Biology
http://wwwstaff.eva.mpg.de/~paabo/

KATE WONG is a senior editor at *Scientific American*.

Article   Prepared by: Elvio Angeloni, *Pasadena City College*

Human Hybrids

MICHAEL F. HAMMER

Learning Outcomes

After reading this article, you will be able to:

- Discuss the ways in which DNA technology has clarified the debate between the various models for human origins.

- Discuss the evidence for positive selection of archaic genes in modern populations.

It is hard to imagine today, but for most of humankind's evolutionary history, multiple humanlike species shared the earth. As recently as 40,000 years ago, *Homo sapiens* lived alongside several kindred forms, including the *Neandertals* and tiny *Homo floresiensis*. For decades scientists have debated exactly how *H. sapiens* originated and came to be the last human species standing. Thanks in large part to genetic studies in the 1980s, one theory emerged as the clear front runner. In this view, anatomically modern humans arose in Africa and spread out across the rest of the Old World, completely replacing the existing archaic groups. Exactly how this novel form became the last human species on the earth is mysterious. Perhaps the invaders killed off the natives they encountered, or outcompeted the strangers on their own turf, or simply reproduced at a higher rate. However it happened, the newcomers seemed to have eliminated their competitors without interbreeding with them.

This recent African replacement model, as it is known, has essentially served as the modern human origins paradigm for the past 25 years. Yet mounting evidence indicates that it is wrong. Recent advances in DNA sequencing technology have enabled researchers to dramatically scale-up data collection from living people and from extinct species. Analyses of these data with increasingly sophisticated computational tools indicate that the story of our family history is not as simple as most experts thought. It turns out that people today carry DNA inherited from *Neandertals* and other archaic humans, revealing that early *H. sapiens* mated with these other species and produced fertile offspring who were able to hand this genetic legacy down through thousands of generations. In addition to upsetting the conventional wisdom about our origins, the discoveries are driving new inquiries into how extensive the interbreeding was, which geographical areas it occurred in and whether modern humans show signs of benefiting from any of the genetic contributions from our prehistoric cousins.

Mysterious Origins

To fully appreciate the effect of these recent genetic findings on scientists' understanding of human evolution, we must look back to the 1980s, when the debate over the rise of *H. sapiens* was heating up. Examining the fossil data, paleoanthropologists agreed that an earlier member of our genus, *Homo erectus*, arose in Africa some two million years ago and began spreading out of that continent and into other regions of the Old World shortly thereafter. Yet they disagreed over how the ancestors of *H. sapiens* transitioned from that archaic form to our modern one, with its rounded braincase and delicately built skeleton—features that appear in the fossil record at around 195,000 years ago.

Proponents of the so called multiregional evolution model, developed by Milford H. Wolpoff of the University of Michigan and his colleagues, argued that the transformation occurred gradually among archaic populations wherever they lived throughout Africa, Eurasia, and Oceania because of a combination of migration and mating that allowed beneficial modern traits to spread among all these populations. In this scenario, although all modern humans shared particular physical features by the end of this transition, some regionally distinctive features inherited from archaic ancestors persisted, perhaps because these traits helped populations to adapt to their local environments. A variant of multiregional evolution put forward by Fred Smith, now at Illinois State University, called the Assimilation model, acknowledges a greater contribution of modern traits by populations from Africa.

In contrast, champions of the replacement model (also known as the Out of Africa model, among other names), including Christopher Stringer of the Natural History Museum in London, contended that anatomically modern humans arose as a distinct species in a single place—sub-Saharan Africa—and went on to completely replace all archaic humans everywhere without interbreeding with them. A looser version of this theory—the Hybridization model proposed by Günter Bräuer of the University of Hamburg in Germany—allows for the occasional production of hybrids between these modern humans and the archaic groups they met up with as they pushed into new lands.

With only the fossil evidence to go on, the debate seemed locked in a stalemate. Genetics changed that situation. With the advent of DNA technology, scientists developed methods for piecing together the past by analyzing genetic variation in contemporary human populations and using it to reconstruct evolutionary trees for individual genes. By studying a gene tree, researchers could infer when and where the last common ancestor of all the variants of a given gene existed, thus yielding insights into the population of origin for the ancestral sequence.

In a landmark study published in 1987, Allan C. Wilson of the University of California, Berkeley, and his colleagues reported that the evolutionary tree for the DNA found in mitochondria—the energy-producing components of cells—traced back to a female ancestor who lived in an African population around 200,000 years ago. (Mitochondrial DNA, or mtDNA, is passed down from mother to child and treated as a single gene in ancestry studies.) These findings fit the expectations of the replacement model, as did subsequent studies of small sections of nuclear DNA, including the paternally inherited Y chromosome.

Further genetic support for the replacement model came a decade later, when Svante Pääbo, now at the Max Planck Institute for Evolutionary Anthropology in Leipzig, Germany, and his colleagues succeeded in extracting and analyzing a fragment of mtDNA from Neandertal bones. The study found that the Neandertal mtDNA sequences were distinct from those of contemporary humans and that there was no sign of interbreeding between them—a result that subsequent studies of mtDNA from additional Neandertal specimens confirmed.

To many researchers, these ancient mtDNA findings put the nail in the coffin of the multiregional evolution and assimilation models. Others, however, maintained that their reasoning suffered from a fundamental problem. The absence of a signal for interbreeding in any single independent region of the genome, such as in mtDNA, does not necessarily mean that other regions of the genome also lack signs of interbreeding. Further, any particular region of the genome that is tested could lack signs of interbreeding even if interbreeding did occur because DNA

from other species (introgressed DNA) that provided no survival advantage to *H. sapiens* would tend to disappear from the gene pool over time by chance.

The best way to approach the question of whether *H. sapiens* interbred with archaic species, such as the *Neandertals,* is thus to compare many regions of their genomes or, ideally, their entire genomes. Yet even before such data became available for archaic humans, some early genetic studies of modern human DNA bucked the majority trend and found data contrary to the replacement model. One clear example came from a 2005 study led by Daniel Garrigan, then a postdoctoral researcher in my laboratory. Garrigan looked at DNA sequences from a nonfunctional region of the X chromosome known as RRM2P4. Analyses of its reconstructed tree pointed to an origin for the sequence, not in Africa but in East Asia around 1.5 million years ago, implying that the DNA came from an archaic Asian species that intermixed with the *H. sapiens* originally from Africa. Similarly, that same year our lab discovered variation in another nonfunctional region of the X chromosome, Xp21.1, with a gene tree showing two divergent branches that had probably been evolving in complete isolation from one another for around a million years. One of these branches was presumably introduced into anatomically modern populations by an archaic African species. The RRM2P4 and Xp21.1 evidence thus hinted that anatomically modern humans mated with archaic humans from Asia and Africa, respectively, rather than simply replacing them without interbreeding.

Our Archaic DNA

More recently, advances in sequencing technology have enabled scientists to quickly sequence entire nuclear genomes—including those of extinct humans, such as *Neandertals.* In 2010, Pääbo's group reported that it had reconstructed the better part of a *Neandertal* genome, based on DNA from several *Neandertal* fossils from Croatia. Contrary to the team's expectations, the work revealed that *Neandertals* made a small but significant contribution to the modern human gene pool: non-Africans today exhibit a 1 to 4 percent *Neandertal* contribution to their genomes on average. To explain this result, the researchers proposed that interbreeding between *Neandertals* and the ancestors of all non-Africans probably occurred during the limited period when these two groups overlapped in the Middle East, perhaps 80,000 to 50,000 years ago.

Hot on the heels of the *Neandertal* genome announcement, Pääbo's team revealed an even more startling discovery. The researchers had obtained an mtDNA sequence from a piece of an approximately 40,000-year-old finger bone found in Denisova Cave in the Altai Mountains in Siberia. Although researchers could not determine from the anatomy of the bone what species it represented, the genome sequence showed that this individual belonged to a population that was slightly more closely related to *Neandertals* than it or *Neandertals* were to our species. Further, after comparing the Denisovan sequence with its counterpart in modern populations, the team found a significant amount of DNA from a Denisovan-like population—a contribution of 1 to 6 percent—in Melanesians, Aboriginal Australians, Polynesians, and some related groups in the western Pacific but not in Africans or Eurasians.

To explain this increasingly complex pattern of DNA sharing, the researchers proposed that interbreeding with various archaic forms had occurred at two different times: first, when anatomically modern humans initially migrated out of Africa and mated with *Neandertals* and, later, when the descendants of these initial migrants made their way to Southeast Asia and encountered Denisovan-like humans. The doubly mixed ancestors of present-day groups such as Melanesians then reached Oceania around 45,000 years ago, and a second wave of anatomically modern humans migrated to East Asia without interbreeding with Denisovan-like ancestors.

Although discussion of interbreeding in human evolution typically focuses on mating between anatomically modern humans and *Neandertals* in Europe or other archaic forms in Asia, the greatest opportunity for interspecies coupling would have been in Africa, where anatomically modern humans and various archaic forms coexisted for much longer than they did anywhere else. Unfortunately, the tropical environments of the African rain forest do not favor the preservation of DNA in ancient remains. Without an African ancient DNA sequence to reference, geneticists are currently limited to scouring the genomes of modern-day Africans for signs of archaic admixture.

To that end, my team at the University of Arizona, in collaboration with Jeffrey D. Wall of the University of California, San Francisco, gathered sequence data from 61 regions of the genome in a sample of three sub-Saharan African populations. Using computer-based simulations to test various evolutionary scenarios, we concluded in a 2011 report that these populations received a 2 percent contribution of genetic material from an extinct human population. This group would have split off from the ancestors of anatomically modern humans some 700,000 years ago and interbred with moderns around 35,000 years ago in Central Africa.

Another genetic hint of archaic admixture in Africa has come from a study of an unusual Y chromosome sequence obtained from an African-American man living in South Carolina whose DNA was submitted to a direct-to-consumer genetic testing company for analysis. His particular variant had never been seen before. Comparing his Y sequence against those of other humans, as well as chimpanzees, my team determined

that his sequence represents a previously unknown Y chromosome lineage that branched off the Y chromosome tree more than 300,000 years ago. We then searched a database of nearly 6,000 African Y chromosomes and identified 11 matches—all of which came from men who lived in a very small area of western Cameroon. The finding, published in March in the *American Journal of Human Genetics*, indicates that the last common ancestor of all modern Y chromosome variants is 70 percent older than previously thought. The presence of this very ancient lineage in contemporary people is a possible sign of interbreeding between *H. sapiens* and an unknown archaic species in western Central Africa.

Recently, the fossil record, too, has yielded support for the possibility of interbreeding within Africa. Just after the publication of our results in 2011, a group of paleontologists working at the Iwo Eleru site in Nigeria reanalyzed remains that exhibit cranial features intermediate between those of archaic and modern humans and determined that they date to just 13,000 years ago—long after anatomically modern *H. sapiens* had debuted. These results, along with similar findings from the Ishango site in the Democratic Republic of the Congo, suggest that the evolution of anatomical modernity in Africa may have been more complicated than any of the leading models for modern human origins have envisioned. Either archaic humans lived alongside modern ones in the recent past, or populations with both modern and archaic features interbred over millennia.

Beneficial Contributions?

Although the analyses of *Neandertal* and Denisovan DNA provide increasing evidence that archaic humans contributed to our genetic heritage, many aspects of this interbreeding remain unresolved. Current estimates of the percentage of our genome that was contributed by *Neandertals* and Denisovan-like humans are based on a method that does not provide much information about how and when mixing occurred. To learn more, researchers need to improve their understanding of exactly which stretches of the genome came from archaic humans and which archaic species contributed what. During his dissertation work in my lab, Fernando L. Mendez took steps toward doing exactly that. He found strong evidence that some contemporary non-Africans carry a stretch of chromosome 12 containing the gene STAT2 (which is involved in the body's first line of defense against viral pathogens) that came from *Neandertals*.

Detailed studies of DNA regions inherited from archaic ancestors will also help tackle the question of whether acquiring these genetic variants conferred an adaptive advantage to early *H. sapiens*. Indeed, STAT2 provides a fascinating example of an apparently advantageous archaic variant entering the modern human gene pool. Approximately 10 percent of people from Eurasia and Oceania carry the *Neandertal*-like variant of STAT2. Interestingly, it occurs at a roughly 10-fold higher frequency in Melanesia than in East Asia. Analysis suggests that this DNA segment rose to high frequency through positive natural selection (that is, because it aided reproductive success or survival) rather than merely by chance, implying that it benefited the anatomically modern populations of Melanesia.

Similarly, a *Neandertal*-like section of the so-called human leukocyte antigen (HLA) region of the genome appears to have risen to relatively high frequency in Eurasian populations as a result of positive natural selection related to its role in fighting pathogens. Perhaps we should not be surprised to find archaic contributions containing genes that function to increase immunity. It is easy to imagine that the acquisition of a gene variant that is adapted to fending off pathogens in non-African environments would immediately benefit human ancestors as they expanded from Africa into new habitats.

In light of the accumulating evidence for interbreeding between anatomically modern *H. sapiens* and archaic humans both inside Africa and beyond its confines, the replacement model is no longer tenable. Modern and archaic species of *Homo* were able to produce viable hybrid offspring. Thus, archaic forms could go extinct while still leaving behind their genetic footprints in the modern human genome. That said, the genomes of people today seem to derive mostly from African ancestors—contributions from archaic Eurasians are smaller than either the multiregional evolution or assimilation models predict.

A number of researchers now favor Bräuer's hybridization model, which holds that mating between *H. sapiens* and archaic species was limited to a few isolated instances. I agree that such interbreeding appears to have been rare after modern humans began spreading out of Africa, but I think there is more to the story than that. Given the complexity of the African fossil record, which indicates that a variety of transitional human groups, with a mosaic of archaic and modern features, lived over an extensive geographic area from Morocco to South Africa between roughly 200,000 and 35,000 years ago, I favor a model that involves interspecies mating during the archaic-to-modern transition. Sometimes called African multiregional evolution, this scenario allows for the possibility that some of the traits that make us anatomically modern were inherited from transitional forms before they went extinct. To my mind, African multiregional evolution, in combination with Bräuer's hybridization model, best explains genetic and fossil data to date.

Before scientists can assess this model for modern human origins fully, we will need to better understand which genes code for anatomically modern traits and decipher their evolutionary history. Further analysis of both archaic and modern genomes should aid researchers in pinpointing when and where mixing occurred—and whether the archaic genes that entered the modern human gene pool benefited the populations that acquired them. This information will help us evaluate the hypothesis that interbreeding with archaic populations that were well adapted to their local environments lent traits to *H. sapiens* that spurred its rise to global preeminence. The sharing of genes through occasional interspecies mating is one way that evolutionary novelties arise in many species of animals and plants, so it should not be surprising if the same process occurred in our own past.

Many loose ends remain. Yet one thing is clear: the roots of modern humans trace back to not just a single ancestral population in Africa but to populations throughout the Old World. Although archaic humans have often been seen as rivals of modern humans, scientists now must seriously consider the possibility that they were the secret of *H. sapiens*' success.

Critical Thinking

1. Compare and contrast the African replacement model for modern human origins with the multiregional evolution model, the assimilation model, and the hybridization model.

2. Discuss the ways in which DNA technology originally supported the replacement model and the "fundamental problem" with it cited by some researchers.

3. How have more recent DNA studies indicated some interbreeding between anatomically modern humans and archaic humans?

4. How has the fossil evidence yielded support for the possibility of interbreeding within Africa?

5. What evidence is there for positive selection of archaic genes in modern populations?

6. What does the DNA evidence seem to be saying about the various models, according to the author?

Create Central

www.mhhe.com/createcentral

Internet References

Human Prehistory
http://users.hol.gr/~dilos/prehis.htm
Max Planck Institute for Evolutionary Anthropology
www.eva.mpg.de/english/index.htm

MICHAEL F. HAMMER is a population geneticist at the University of Arizona. He studies patterns of genetic variation in modern-day populations to gain insights into the evolutionary origins of *Homo sapiens*.

Unit 5

UNIT

Prepared by: Elvio Angeloni, *Pasadena City College*

Late Hominid Evolution

The most important aspect of human evolution is also the most difficult to decipher from the fossil evidence: our development as sentient, social beings, capable of communicating by means of language.

We detect hints of incipient humanity in the form of crudely chipped tools, the telltale signs of a home base, or the artistic achievements of ornaments and cave art. Yet none of these indicators of a distinctly hominid way of life can provide us with the nuances of the everyday lives of these creatures, their social relations, or their supernatural beliefs, if any. Most of what remains is the rubble of bones and stones from which we interpret what we can of their lifestyle, thought processes, and ability to communicate.

It is understandable, then, that some questions regarding our most recent ancestors have yet to be fully answered. Did we derive entirely from people who represented a second wave of migration out of Africa and who replaced the archaic members of species (i.e. the remnants of a much earlier migration) according to the "replacement hypothesis"? Or did our modern *Homo sapiens* ancestors mate with archaic sapiens, as proposed in the "multiregional theory"? Recent evidence seems to say the answer is not as clear-cut as either side of the controversy would have it—that there was certainly some replacement and that there was also some degree of admixture. Did modern *Homo sapiens* truly usher in an "Upper Paleolithic Revolution," involving art, mortuary rituals, personal adornments, and more complex food-getting technologies and strategies? Or did such innovations come about on a piecemeal basis, scattered in time and place depending upon the needs of the people, including the archaic members of our species? Evidence suggests the latter.

Beyond the anatomical and technological adaptations, questions have arisen as to how our hominid forebears organized themselves socially and whether modern-day human behavior is inherited as a legacy of our evolutionary past or is a learned product of contemporary circumstances. Attempts to address these questions have given rise to the technique referred to as the "ethnographic analogy." This is a method whereby anthropologists use "ethnographies," or field studies, of modern-day hunters and gatherers whose lives we take to be the best approximations we have to what life might have been like for our ancestors. Granted, these contemporary foragers have been living under conditions of environmental and social change just as industrial peoples have. Nevertheless, it seems that, at least in some aspects of their lives, they have not changed as much as we have. So, if we are to make any enlightened assessments of prehistoric behavior patterns, we are better off looking at them than at ourselves.

As if to show that controversial interpretations of the evidence are not limited to the earlier hominid period, we can also see how long-held beliefs about recent human evolution are being shattered. Hominid migrations are being revised by new evidence coming from newly discovered fossils, artifacts, and even DNA.

For some scientists, these recent revelations fit quite comfortably with previously held positions; for others it seems that reputations, as well as theories, are at stake. How it all shakes out may cause some temporary discomfort for some, but in the long run, a better understanding of our evolutionary past will benefit all of us.

Article   Prepared by: Elvio Angeloni, *Pasadena City College*

The Story in the Stones

DAVID ROBSON

Learning Outcomes

After reading this article, you will be able to:

- Discuss the evidence for when our ancestors became uniquely human.

- Discuss the relationship between toolmaking, language, and cognitive skills in general in the development of our species.

- Explain how "working memory" fostered creativity and innovation in humans.

Sparks fly as stone meets stone and shards of rock ricochet off the furniture around me. Each strike makes me flinch, but Bruce Bradley is the picture of cool concentration as he chips away at his axe head. It is, after all, a skill he has been honing since before he can remember. "I was a natural born flint-knapper. Laugh at that if you want, but I've got video to prove it." As a baby, he says, he was often seen banging two rocks together in his parents' garden. Then, when his family moved to Arizona, he developed his talents by copying the Native American arrowheads scattered across the desert.

Decades later, Bradley makes stone tools spanning the breadth of human history. His workshop at the University of Exeter, UK, is full of this handiwork. Piles of rocks line the walls, and to one side a deerskin with a dark stain hangs on a wooden frame. It was butchered using some of his team's handmade tools, he tells me. "We've got a freezer out there full of dead parts—you could eat them if you wanted."

My interests lie elsewhere. The stone tools on the table in front of me are not just useful, they tell the story of our journey from simple ape to thinking human. Previous attempts to trace the history of the mind have relied on speculation as much as hard evidence but, over the past three years, Bradley's Learning to be Human project has taken a more precise approach to

looking inside the heads of the people who made these tools. Combining findings about stone-tool construction with neuroscience, psychology and archaeology, we can now estimate the origins of distinctly human mental abilities, such as when we first began to order our thoughts and actions, when our visual imagination blossomed, when we started to think about the past and future, and when we first played make-believe. There are even hints about the emergence of our capacity for patience, shame and suspicion—and the nature of our ancestors' dreams.

People have long sought a "secret ingredient" unique to human intelligence that could explain our extraordinary cognitive abilities. Most recently, the spotlight has fallen on size—the idea that a big brain is the key. However, it is becoming increasingly clear that there is no secret ingredient. Instead, our peculiar way of thinking results from a reorganisation of the different brain regions, as much as from their expansion (see "Size Isn't Everything"). What's more, this began long before we diverged from chimps, around six million years ago. Indeed, comparable but more modest changes can be seen in many of our nearest relatives. "In a way we're just an extreme great ape," says Jeroen Smaers at Stony Brook University, New York, who last year compared the brain evolution of 17 species of primates.

So what accelerated this evolution in our ancestral line beyond what was happening in other apes—and how did this give rise to new ways of thinking? Only by re-examining the archaeological record can we map out that path. And that's why I am in Bradley's workshop.

He pauses in his work to show me three stone tools. The first and crudest of them is a jagged rock that signals perhaps the first landmark moment in that journey. Aside from walking on two legs, our earlier ancestors were distinctly ape-like, and like chimps and other primates, they probably had limited tool use, picking pebbles off the ground to crush nuts. But things changed about 2.6 million years ago, with *Australopithecus garhi*. Rather than just using nature as they found it around them, they began to modify it, wielding one stone to chip the end off another and using the resulting sharp edge to butcher meat.

The idea of using one tool to create a more useful implement is itself a conceptual leap. But just as important is Bradley's discovery that it takes a dexterity and motor control not seen in other apes to create the jagged Oldowan-style tool in front of me. This includes coordinating your limbs so that one hand is doing a different job from the other. "You need one hand for support, one for striking," says Nada Khreisheh, Bradley's colleague—movements that chimps struggle to master even with training. If such bodily control seems like more of a hop than a leap, consider all the new opportunities it opened up—including the creation of better tools—that would reward increased intelligence, accelerating our evolution compared with the other apes. "I'm willing to bet there would be no consciousness on this planet if we didn't have flakable rocks," says Bradley.

Even with that trigger, our ancestors were slow to progress. Things didn't begin to take off until *Homo erectus,* about a million years later. *H. erectus* is significant for many reasons. As well as having broadly similar bodies to modern humans, they lived in bigger social groups than their predecessors. Successful communal living requires cooperation and the ability to detect and punish cheats who try to get something for nothing. According to Eva Jablonka at Tel Aviv University in Israel, those challenges may have spurred the evolution of complex emotions such as shame and embarrassment, which would help individuals toe the party line. "We became emotionally modern before we became cognitively modern," she says. But what really marks out the thinking of *H. erectus* is encapsulated in the second tool of the three in front of me, an exquisite leaf-shaped object known as an Acheulean hand axe.

Better by Design

We do not know what inspired this revolutionary design—it may even have come in a dream. The first attempts, which date from around 1.5 million years ago, were fairly crude, but over the following one million years Acheulean axes became thinner and more symmetrical as they began to embody a more systematic style of working. Bradley's demonstrations show that to achieve the more sophisticated designs, you need to prepare the surface of the rock—working away smaller chips to create an angle before striking off the larger, flatter flakes. "They take a lot more planning and understanding of force," he says as he chips away at his own rock. Breaking down a goal into a series of smaller actions in this way shows the beginnings of hierarchical thinking. Chunking and sequencing our actions seems so central to the way we operate today whether we are making a cup of tea or running a bath—that it's almost impossible to

imagine our minds working in any other way. But the refined Acheulean axes offer some of the first signs that our ancestors were beginning to develop the ability to organise their thoughts in these more complicated ways.

This innovation in axe design has been linked to another milestone in human cognition: language. It is such a complex system, dependent on many different thought processes, that its origins are sometimes described as evolution's biggest mystery, but there is some evidence suggesting that tool making could have been a catalyst. Bradley's collaborator, Dietrich Stout at Emory University in Atlanta, Georgia, points out that articulate vocalization requires precise movement of the lips and tongue. Chimps and other primates are unable to achieve these, but in our ancestors tool-making drove, the development of the brain areas involved in motor control that could later be co-opted for speech. Stout also notes that the sequential thinking needed to create the leaf-shaped hand axes is similar to the thinking that allows us to understand and construct sentences.

To test the theory, Stout used brain scans to try to pick apart the cognitive skills used in each type of tool making. As predicted, they show that people making replicas of the Oldowan tools have greatest activity in areas associated with the motor control needed to speak, while brain activity in those making the Late Acheulean tools shows an overlap with that normally associated with linguistic grammar. That includes the inferior frontal gyrus along the bottom of the frontal lobe—an area that expanded rapidly in the human line compared with other apes.

Language is, arguably, our only unique feature, and its emergence set us on a road that led away from every other animal. Unfortunately, this turning point in our journey is virtually invisible in the archaeological record: Bradley can show me no tools that definitively signify the first words. But there are hints that our ancestors had begun speaking by the time of *Homo heidelbergensis,* thought to have evolved from *H. erectus* at least 600,000 years ago.

Homo heidelbergensis was certainly more human in other respects. Its brain, at about 1200 cubic centimetres, was just a shade smaller than ours, providing a cognitive power that is evident in the variety of tools it used, including refined hand axes, cleavers, and spearheads. To envisage an amorphous lump of rock transformed into these different shapes and styles would have required good spatial cognition, perhaps signalling the birth of the visual imagination. *H. heidelbergensis* also revisited certain places again and again, sometimes scattering hand axes across the ground. Some read this apparently inexplicable waste of good handiwork as an early attempt to signpost sites of significance. That is skirting close to the mindset needed for symbolism. Crucially, *H. heidelbergensis* also possessed refinements in its vocal anatomy. For instance, traces in bones indicate that they had more nerves linking the brain and tongue than their predecessors, and their voice boxes seem to lack a balloon-like appendage that constrains vocalizations in other apes. Both of these changes would be needed to produce eloquent sounds.

Whenever it emerged, language brought a whole new set of mental challenges. "When I tell you a story, I can frighten you very easily," says Jablonka. "And you have to control this fear." It's easy to take that ability for granted, but chimps fail to make a good distinction between symbols and real things—they go wild when they see a picture of a banana, for instance. In a similar way, our ancestors may have struggled at first to understand the mental images conjured up by language. To deal with their immediate visceral reactions, Jablonka says, they must have developed greater control over their emotions—and they would have learned to be more sceptical and suspicious of others in the process. They also needed a better verbal memory, so that they could remember what others had told them, to differentiate it from what happened in their own lives. Out of that emerged the ability "to tell my own story, the autobiography", she says. If Jablonka is right, language contributed to our sense of self.

Beautifully Crafted

Our ancestors were probably still navigating these difficulties as the human mind approached the last stretch of its journey. To demonstrate this final mental leap, Bradley draws my attention to the third object on the table in front of us. The beautiful Levallois tool is carved from shiny black stone. With dimples lining its edge, it looks a little like an oyster shell. Bradley tells me the tool is little more use for cutting and scraping meat than the cruder hand-axes—its value was probably aesthetic, rather than practical. To make it, a base stone had to be fashioned into a circle before the "lid" was removed with one strike. That craftsmanship takes great skill and patience, as Bradley and Khreisheh's modern apprentices discovered. "People like making hand axes," says Khreisheh, "but they hate making Levallois tools." Since the process comprises many different stages, and the apprentices often need specific instruction, the mind that originally created this tool was probably capable of advanced hierarchical thinking and complex communication for tuition. These intricate objects first appear at least 300,000 years ago, but although they are found among the remains of our own species, they are most commonly associated with the Neanderthals.

Levallois tools provide some of the best evidence that Neanderthals shared much of the cognitive toolkit possessed by humans living at the same time. And herein lies the mystery. "Whatever the Neanderthals' cognitive leap was, it stopped; it didn't continue," says Bradley. So why did we develop more ambitious inventions and rich artistic cultures, while they hit a dead end? Answer that question, and you get a glimpse of the final stage in the evolution of the human mind.

Some think the solution is child's play literally. Since our ancestors first diverged from the other primates, childhood has continued to get longer, giving the brain more time to develop outside the womb. From the remains of bones and teeth, it seems that early human children took longer to develop than Neanderthal ones. Child psychologist Alison Gopnik at the University of California, Berkeley, argues that the extra time spent playing may have helped them develop "counter-factual thinking"—the ability to consider how things might be, not just how they are. That allowed them to imagine the environment in more creative ways, giving them greater control over their surroundings, she says. As a result, they could do things that might not have occurred to earlier humans, like inventing new tools and building shelters.

Frederick Coolidge and Thomas Wynn at the University of Colorado in Colorado Springs see a more dramatic trigger. They argue that our last cognitive leap was down to a chance mutation that increased our ability to hold several ideas in mind and manipulate them. Even in modern humans, this "working memory" is limited to about seven items. However, a small increase would have had huge consequences. An improved ability to remember what had just been said would have increased the sophistication of conversation, allowing more complex grammar with many different clauses. That means you can think and plan more hypothetically, using "what if" and "if, then" statements, for instance.

Working memory is also associated with creativity and innovation because it allows you to mentally explore different solutions to a problem. Wynn and Coolidge also point to research suggesting that enhanced working memory could have improved our long-term memory and future planning because it provides a bigger mental "blackboard" on which we can assemble the details of our past experiences and draw on them to work out the best way to proceed with the task ahead.

A Recipe for Success

This hypothesis has been strengthened in recent years by a wave of circumstantial evidence. For example, Lyn Wadley at the University of the Witwatersrand in Johannesburg, South Africa, has looked at the steps involved in making glues used to stick spearheads to poles. Earlier humans had simple adhesives such as plant gum, but she has found that in Sibudu cave, South Africa, about 70,000 years ago, they began to cook up the tree sap with red ochre and beeswax to produce a superior glue that doesn't break on impact or dissolve in water.

When Wadley tried to replicate the complex recipes, she found that she had to pay attention to many different factors, including the temperature of the fire, the moisture, and different proportions of ingredients depending on the quality of the tree gum. "It took a lot of coordination to ensure success," she says. That's only possible with an enhanced working memory to keep all the different elements in mind at once.

Further clues come from the food these people ate. Around this time, early modern humans began to hunt small game, such as small deer species and rodents. Former army survival expert Klint Janulis, now at the University of Oxford, tried the methods they used and found he needed to place 10 to 15 traps to capture enough food to make it worthwhile. "Within a couple of hours you can set enough traps to feed yourself, and maybe another person, for a day," he says. But that requires forethought, and keeping track of their locations needs just the kind of advanced cognition that Wynn and Coolidge suggest.

The timing of these advances at 70,000 years ago is particularly significant because they come just after the eruption of the Toba supervolcano in Indonesia, which plunged the world into a mini ice age and caused a human population crash in Africa. Any beneficial mutations within the small remaining population could spread quickly, leaving a permanent mark on their descendants. "All extant humans are ancestors of those 2000 or so humans," says Coolidge. If he and Wynn are right, then the explosion at Toba marked the beginning of the home stretch to modern thinking. Armed with this slightly superior thinking, we left Africa and took over the globe, while the Neanderthals and our other evolutionary cousins became extinct.

Of course, our journey isn't over and it is tempting to speculate how the human mind will evolve in the future. Wynn wonders if we will see further changes in working memory. "It's variable within populations," he says. "We suspect it may still be under evolutionary change." And it is possible that advances in technology could substantially change the mental challenges we face, just as stone tools did in the past. Claims that the internet is making us stupid have so far proven to be unfounded but the way we interact with one another is certainly changing and so are the mental skills associated with success.

Bradley is more interested in the past than the future. The air is now thick with flint dust as he hands me the finished axe. There are still many questions left to answer, he says, as we try to fill in the gaps between the known landmarks of cognitive evolution. "From our point of view it's just scratching the surface of what could be done." But he has already achieved one of his goals—he wanted to teach a new generation of flint-knappers the skills he has been refining since childhood.

There's also a chance that his handiwork will find a place next to the artifacts he so admires. The Smithsonian Institution in Washington DC, he says, is interested in collecting his life's work to demonstrate the progression of a modern day flint-knapper. "My body could even be a permanent exhibit there too, when I shift off this mortal coil," he jokes. It would be a fitting place of rest for the "natural born knapper" who has spent his life trying to understand how we learned to be human.

Sweet Dreams

Until about two million years ago, human ancestors probably settled for the night in trees. Some psychologists have proposed that the sensation of falling that we sometimes feel when we drop off is a remnant of an early warning system that stopped us descending so deeply into sleep that we ended up on the forest floor. Dozing on branches is likely to have ended with *Homo erectus*. "At 6 feet and 140 pounds, it was way too tall and heavy," says Frederick Coolidge at the University of Colorado in Colorado Springs. Instead, *H. erectus* slept on the ground, and this, Coolidge suggests, resulted in a great leap in cognition.

A more peaceful night's slumbers, without the constant risk of falling from a branch, would have allowed *H. erectus* to spend longer in rapid-eye-movement sleep and slow wave sleep, says Coolidge. These stages are known to be crucial for the consolidation of memories and associative thinking and that's not all. "It probably allowed many more creative dreams," he says. These could have had an impact on waking life.

Coolidge even speculates that the idea of the leaf-shaped Acheulean hand axe—a complex tool that signals a new way of thinking—might have come to a *H. erectus* knapper in one of those dreams.

Size Isn't Everything

Human intelligence has more to do with the organization of brain regions than it does with overall size. Tools may have played a key role in shaping parts of this complex organ.

Prefrontal Cortex

Self-control, introspection, social cognition

Lots of signal-transmitting "white matter" reflects this area's role in combining data from the senses and the rest of the brain. That could help with precise tool-making actions and with the insight needed for complex social relationships.

Frontostriatal System

Incremental learning of skills

As our ancestors evolved, there was a rapid increase in the size of this area relative to other brain regions. This would have improved their capacity for learning, allowing for the production of more complex tools.

Cerebellum

Sequential thinking

High connectivity between here and the frontal motor areas enables fine control of movement. This area may have grown as the tool-making and language skills of our ancestors developed.

2.6 Million Years Ago

Oldowan Tools Australopithecus garhi

* Dexterity * Motor control * Modification of nature

1.6 Million Years Ago

Acheulean Tools Homo erectus

* Hierarchical thinking * Planning * Complex emotions

600,000 Years Ago

Axes, Cleavers, Spears Homo heidelbergensis

* Language * Sense of self * Visual imagination * Emotional control * Symbolism

200,000 Years Ago

Homo sapiens

* Awareness of past and future * Creativity * Hypothetical thinking * Improved memory

300,000 Years Ago

Levallois Tools Neanderthals

* Advanced hierarchical thinking * Tuition * Patience

Critical Thinking

1. Discuss the various lines of evidence that indicate when and how our ancestors became uniquely human.

2. Discuss the stone tools that serve as landmarks in our ancestors' journey to become human and the specific cognitive skills enabled by such tools.

3. How are various language skills associated with the development of tools during human evolutionary development?

4. How might children play a role in "counter-factual thinking" and why would this be important?

5. How would the improvement of "working memory" foster creativity and innovation?

Create Central

www.mhhe.com/createcentral

Internet References

Human Prehistory

http://users.hol.gr/~dilos/prehis.htm

Max Planck Institute for Evolutionary Anthropology

www.eva.mpg.de/english/index.htm

DAVID ROBSON is a features editor at *New Scientist*.

Article Prepared by: Elvio Angeloni, *Pasadena City College*

King of Beasts

LARS WERDELIN

Learning Outcomes

After reading this article, you will be able to:

- Describe and explain the effect of hominin evolution on the composition of eastern and southern African carnivore communities around 2 million years ago.
- Discuss the effects of climate change on hominin evolution and the composition of carnivore communities in eastern and southern Africa around 2 million years ago.

Sunrise on the Serengeti, and life on the savanna is in full swing. Zebras and wildebeests graze the dewy grass; elephants and giraffes munch on acacia leaves; and lions and hyenas survey the scene, looking for their next meal. To visit this place is, in some ways, to see the world as it looked to our ancestors millions of years ago, long before humans began to wreak havoc on the planet—or so the conventional wisdom goes. Indeed, much of eastern Africa is often thought of as a pristine ecosystem, largely unchanged by our kind in the more than 2 million years since our genus, *Homo,* arose.

But new research paints a rather different picture of this supposedly unaltered place. In my studies of the fossil record of African carnivores, I have found that lions, hyenas, and other large-bodied carnivores that roam eastern Africa today represent only a small fraction of the diversity this group once had. Intriguingly, the decline of these carnivores began around the same time that early *Homo* started eating more meat, thus entering into competition with the carnivores. The timing of events hints that early humans are to blame for the extinction of these beasts—starting more than 2 million years ago, long before *Homo sapiens* came on the scene.

The rise of this new meat eater—and the loss of the big carnivores—would have triggered large-scale changes farther down the food chain, affecting the prey animals and even the plants those creatures ate. Thus, if my hypothesis is correct, our forebears began radically transforming ecosystems far earlier than previously thought, at a time when ancestral population sizes were quite small. *Homo,* it seems, has been a force of nature from the outset.

Vanished Carnivores

Fossil carnivores—which is to say, members of the Carnivora order of mammals—have captivated me ever since I first read about them in the books of Finnish paleontologist Björn Kurtén as a teenager. Back then, I just thought they were cool, and I knew that they played an essential role as regulators of herbivore populations, which would explode without these predators to keep them in check. Only after I began studying carnivore fossils professionally, however, did I come to appreciate how their relationship with humans has evolved over millions of years.

For two decades I have studied thousands of carnivore fossils from eastern and southern Africa, trying to get a handle on how the modern carnivore community evolved over the past 7 million years. I have conducted much of this research in collaboration with Margaret E. Lewis of Richard Stockton College, who is an expert on carnivore bones from the neck backward, whereas I specialize in their teeth and skulls. Our work has yielded a much higher resolution view than was previously available of how many kinds of carnivores there were in Africa at different times during this interval, which also spans the entire known history of human evolution. As we amassed more and more data, we gained a much clearer picture of the species that thrived and failed over time, and we began to realize that the decline of the large carnivores (those weighing 21.5 kilograms or more) coincided with a shift among human ancestors from a mostly vegetarian diet to one that relied more heavily on animal foods. To our great surprise, it looked as though our early ancestors might have been at fault for the loss of these species.

Snapshots of a few key fossil sites provide a sense of the transformation the African carnivore community underwent. The carnivores from the early part of this 7-million-year interval were nothing like the ones found today. Fossils dating to between 7.5 million and 5 million years ago from the site of Lothagam on the western shore of Lake Turkana in northern Kenya reveal sabertooth cats, strange long-legged hyenas, giant bear dogs (neither bears nor dogs but members of an extinct family of carnivores, the Amphicyonidae), and a leopard-size member of the mustelid family to which badgers belong. Smaller carnivores related to today's civets and mongooses also prowled there.

By 4 million years ago a familiar face had joined the carnivore cast. At the nearby site of Kanapoi, sabertooths and other now extinct lineages were still present, but the most common carnivore there was a hyena species ancestral to the brown hyena found in southern Africa today. Fast-forward another few hundred thousand years, and the carnivore community is even more recognizable. The 4.4-million-to 3.6-million-year-old site of Laetoli in the Serengeti of Tanzania, famed for its fossilized trail of footprints belonging to hominins (members of the human family), has remains of modern-looking cats along with the sabertooths. Early spotted hyenas, several dog species, a giant civet, and a variety of smaller carnivores lived there, too. At Hadar in Ethiopia, the final resting place of the 3.2-million-year-old Lucy skeleton, sabertooths, hyenas and dogs abound, along with giant otters that have no modern counterpart.

These and other sites in the time range of 4 million to 2.5 million years ago all tell the same story. Each has a slightly different mix of carnivore species, depending on the environmental setting, but all have the same general kinds of carnivores. For example, all the sites have hyenas, but they differ in the species of hyena that lived there. And more important, none indicates that these animals were any worse off as a result of the presence of hominins.

After peaking around 3.5 million years ago, the number of large carnivore species declined gradually over the next million and a half years or so, mostly because the rate at which new species originated slowed down while the extinction rate held steady. Still, on the whole, the big carnivores reigned supreme during this time; our small, slow, defenseless ancestors were merely food. But the tide was about to turn.

The record after 2 million years ago shows unmistakable changes in the composition of carnivore communities. With extinction rates increasing and origination rates remaining low, the number of large species began to nosedive, particularly after 1.5 million years ago. Not only did individual species die out, but entire groups of species, such as the sabertooth cats, disappeared. As these beasts of yore declined, modern species—including the lions, leopards, and jackals that inhabit Africa today—came to account for an ever increasing proportion of carnivore communities. By around 300,000 years ago the archaic carnivore lineages had all been winnowed out in eastern Africa and the modern carnivore community was in place.

A Wolf in Sheep's Clothing

The general pattern Lewis and I observed in our data fit with our intuitive understanding of the evolutionary history of African carnivores in that it confirmed that there were more kinds of large carnivores in the past than there are today. What we had not anticipated was the steep downturn after 1.5 million years ago. It was this timing that hinted our *Homo* ancestors might be at fault.

For the first few million years of human evolution, hominins were relatively small-brained, chimpanzee-size creatures that subsisted primarily on plant foods. But by 1.5 million years ago a new kind of hominin was on the scene—one that was bigger, smarter and armed with stone tools. This was *Homo erectus* (sometimes called *Homo ergaster*), the first member of the human family to really look like us—and the first to start eating much in the way of meat. Perhaps, Lewis and I reasoned, competition with this human predator, which was incorporating increasing amounts of animal protein from large herbivores into its diet, could explain the carnivore decline.

That explanation seemed promising, but the timing of the events nagged at me. If competition with *H. erectus* was to blame, then the steep decline in eastern Africa's large carnivore species should have started well before 1.5 million years ago because *H. erectus* had emerged by nearly 1.9 million years ago. Species numbers are a blunt instrument at best for tracking the progress of an entire order of mammals over time because a reduction in numbers of one of its group can be masked by an increase in another. If two sabertooth species go extinct but are replaced by lions and leopards, the numbers will remain the same, but the community will have undergone a major change because lions and leopards can take a broader range of prey than sabertooths could.

It occurred to me that I could get a better sense of what had befallen the large carnivores if I understood not just how many species there were at any given time but how diverse their ecological roles were. Carnivores vary a lot in how they make a living. The cats, for example, are highly adapted to eating meat and thus qualify as hypercarnivores. But other carnivores are omnivorous—dogs, for example, will eat a wide variety of food in addition to meat. Still others, such as raccoons, are hypocarnivores, eating very little meat and subsisting mainly on fruits and vegetables.

I decided to build on work the of my former postdoctoral student Gina D. Wesley-Hunt, now at Montgomery College, who had investigated the evolution of North American carnivores over the past 60 million years. As part of her study, Wesley-Hunt identified a set of traits related to the function of the jaws and teeth of carnivores. By studying these traits, she could quantify just how different species in a single carnivore community were from one another in terms of the kinds of foods they ate and hence their ecological roles. Using the fossil-coding scheme she developed to identify the function of the jaws and teeth (that is, the eating preferences they had evolved for), I coded 78 carnivore species—29 large and 49 small—from the African fossil record of the past 3.5 million years. I then analyzed the data, looking at how the number of different kinds of carnivores with different ecological roles living within the same community changed over time.

To visualize the diversity of form and inferred eating preferences in these fossil carnivores, I plugged the data from the coding scheme into a statistical analysis, thereby creating a two-dimensional plot that I call the morphospace. This morphospace represents the diversity of form (and inferred function) that exists within a group of related organisms, in this case the carnivores that lived in Africa over the past 3.5 million years. Plotting separate morphospaces for carnivores from distinct time intervals and comparing them offers a sense of how carnivore anatomy and eating habits shifted over time.

The results proved startling. As Lewis and I reported in March in *PLOS ONE*, it turns out that large carnivores that live in eastern Africa today occupy only a small fraction (less than 1.5 percent) of the morphospace of the carnivores in the 3.5-million-to three-million-year interval, when species diversity was at its highest. The group has lost nearly 99 percent of its so-called functional richness, which is to say today's carnivores fill far fewer kinds of ecological roles than their predecessors did. Moreover, the measured decrease in this functional richness began in the interval between two million and 1.5 million years ago, which means that the process must have started before that time—bringing the onset of this major decline in line with the origin of *H. erectus*. Although our work focused on carnivores from eastern Africa, modern large carnivores are basically the same across the continent. Thus, it is likely that the loss of functional richness we found in this region is representative of what happened to all of Africa's large carnivores.

Human activity is not the only possible cause of this loss of Africa's carnivores. Climate change has been implicated in many faunal changes in Africa over the course of the past few million years, and at first glance comparisons of climate and species numbers imply it is a front-runner in this case as well. Studies of modern carnivore species, however, suggest that the influence of climate on the functional richness of modern carnivore communities is slight. In general, carnivores are insensitive to climate and related environmental change, unlike mammalian herbivores, which are dependent on the distribution of plant food, which in turn is largely determined by climate. Furthermore, if climate change was the culprit, then the smaller carnivores should have declined, too—but they did not. Both the species richness and functional richness of the small carnivores have held up over most of the past 3.5 million years and may even have increased.

Nevertheless, to determine whether human activity was responsible for the decline of these carnivores, it would help to know how important meat was to early *Homo*. Archaeologists have long debated this question. Some think meat and hunting were critically important; others hold that meat was a marginal component of the diet at best, with the hominins merely scavenging a few scraps that carnivores rejected. But they generally agree that *Homo* did begin to obtain more protein from animals, perhaps including fish and shellfish, between 2 million and 1.5 million years ago in the Early Pleistocene period.

Anthropologist Henry Bunn of the University of Wisconsin–Madison envisions the transition to a meatier diet unfolding in three steps, the timings of which dovetail nicely with the idea that competition with early hominins drove many big carnivores to extinction. First, hominins occasionally butchered bones using primitive stone tools or naturally flaked blades. At this stage, which Bunn puts at around 2.6 million to 2.5 million years ago, based on the available archaeological evidence, they had only a slight ability to obtain meat. The second stage involved more habitual butchery, along with the skills to break bones to get at the marrow inside and to transport meat-rich parts of carcasses to a home base or similar. Bunn estimates that hominins reached this stage around 2.3 million to 1.9 million years ago and that by this point they could obtain meat on a regular basis through scavenging and possibly making their own kills. In the third stage, hominins butchered animal remains extensively and had access to intact carcasses because they were better at appropriating carnivore kills or possibly because they were routinely hunting the animals themselves. Bunn dates this last stage to between 1.8 million and 1.6 million years ago.

Thus, although they lacked the lethal teeth and claws and the sheer physical strength of the sabertooth cats and other large carnivores, hominins were able to level the playing field through their rapidly evolving intelligence and social cooperation—there is strength in numbers even if brawn is lacking. And in lean times, hominins would have had a distinct advantage over carnivores, especially hypercarnivores such as the sabertooths, because, being omnivorous, they had a much larger array of foods they could fall back on when their top choices were unavailable. During the worst times of the year, then, the hominin competitive edge would have been the greatest. (That the remaining large carnivores are all hypercarnivores reflects the fact that there were many more kinds of hypercarnivores to start with than omnivores or hypocarnivores.)

Food for Thought

Like any nascent hypothesis, this one comes with a series of problems that need resolution. The most significant of these issues concerns the timing of the events described here, both in terms of when the carnivores began going downhill and when humans started to pose a competitive threat to them. We need a clearer picture of what happened and when to draw firm conclusions about cause and effect. In addition, scientists do not know whether hominins were sufficiently numerous and competitive to cause such massive change to the carnivore community.

Pinpointing when the carnivore decline began requires either the discovery of additional fossils from the 2.5-million-to 2-million-year time interval or more refined techniques for analyzing the fossils we already have. I am currently working on developing such techniques. What I can definitely say at this point is that the onset of change in the carnivores had occurred by 1.8 million years ago and that the most refined analysis at present suggests that it occurred shortly before 2 million years ago. Whether this can be accurately matched up with events in hominin evolution, however, is not yet clear. Although Bunn's timetable is fully compatible with the scenario I have presented, it has not gone unchallenged. Other scholars suspect the first two stages occurred considerably later than he proposes.

Resolution of the issue of hominin numbers and competitive ability may never come. These aspects of early hominins are currently mostly a matter of opinion. Undoubtedly, population density was low, but how low is unknown. It may be possible to generate a series of simulations of both factors to see whether the hypothesis is viable given reasonable values for either or both. But hard evidence of how many hominins were around and how successful they were in getting hold of prey that would have otherwise ended up in a sabertooth's belly may always elude science's grasp. The absence of these data does not demonstrate that my hypothesis is false, however.

I hope that researchers skeptical of my hypothesis will come up with some ingenious ways of testing it. To that end, another aspect of this idea bears mention. Attempts to explain ecosystem change typically provide a bottom-up perspective, looking at how climate factors affect plants and how changes in those organisms affect the rest of the food chain up to the top predators. My hypothesis about eastern Africa's large carnivores provides a top-down view, considering how change in the top predators could affect the primary producers at the bottom of the food chain, such as grasses and trees.

The reintroduction of wolves to Yellowstone National Park and their effect on the herbivores living there, and by extension on the vegetation of the park, provide a stunning example of the impact of change among top predators. As the wolves became more plentiful, the elk they preyed on diminished in numbers. This in turn led to less feeding pressure on the plants and to lusher vegetation in those places where the herbivores were previously particularly common [see "Lessons from the Wolf," by Jim Robbins; *SCIENTIFIC AMERICAN*, June 2004].

The entry of early *Homo* into the carnivore niche in Africa could have triggered an even more dramatic cascade of ecological disruption than the one that occurred at Yellowstone. Whereas wolves were once a natural part of the Yellowstone ecosystem, meaning that the other species there retained at least some adaptations to their presence, early *Homo* had no such precedent. One would expect the introduction of such a new predator to have even greater consequences for the ecosystem than the reintroduction of one that had been there originally. Perhaps, then, the smoking gun in the case of the disappearing carnivores will turn up not among the remains of our hominin ancestors or the large carnivores themselves but among the remnants of herbivores and plants whose world was upended when *Homo* developed a taste for meat.

Critical Thinking

1. Contrast the composition of carnivore communities in eastern and southern Africa before and after 2 million years ago.

2. Discuss the changes in hominin evolution during this time and what happened particularly after 1.5 million years ago.

3. Discuss the concept of morphospace and how it helps us understand how the appearance of *Homo erectus* had an effect on the carnivore community.

4. Discuss the author's conclusions about whether or not climate change had an effect on the changes in the carnivore community.

5. Discuss the hominin transition to a meatier diet as suggested by Henry Bunn and how hominins achieved such a competitive edge over carnivores.

6. Discuss the problems with the author's hypothesis and how they might be resolved.

Create Central

www.mhhe.com/createcentral

Internet References

Institute of Human Origins
  http://iho.asu.edu/node/27
Long Foreground: Human Prehistory
  www.wsu.edu/gened/learn-modules/top_longfor/lfopen-index.html

---

LARS WERDELIN is a senior curator of fossil vertebrates at the Swedish Museum of Natural History in Stockholm. His research focuses on African carnivores and the relation between their evolution and that of humans.

Article   Prepared by Elvio Angeloni, *Pasadena City College*

The Birth of Childhood

Unlike other apes, humans depend on their parents for a long period after weaning. But when—and why—did our long childhood evolve?

ANN GIBBONS

Learning Outcomes

After reading this article, you will be able to:

- Explain why humans have such an extended period of childhood.
- Discuss the fossil evidence extension of childhood in the human evolutionary line.

Mel was just 3.5 years old when his mother died of pneumonia in 1987 in Tanzania. He had still been nursing and had no siblings, so his prospects were grim. He begged weakly for meat, and although adults gave him scraps, only a 12-year-old named Spindle shared his food regularly, protected him, and let him sleep with him at night. When Spindle took off for a month, another adolescent, Pax, came to Mel's rescue, giving him fruit and a place to sleep until Spindle returned. Mel survived to age 10.

Fortunately for Mel, he was an orphan chimpanzee living in the Gombe Stream National Park rather than a small child living in the slums of a big city. With only sporadic care from older children, a 3-year-old human orphan would not have survived.

Mel's story illustrates the uniqueness of one facet of human life: Unlike our close cousins the chimpanzees, we have a prolonged period of development after weaning, when children depend on their parents to feed them, until at least age 6 or 7. Street children from Kathmandu to Rio de Janeiro do not survive on their own unless they are at least 6. "There's no society where children can feed themselves after weaning," says anthropologist Kristen Hawkes of the University of Utah in Salt Lake City. By contrast, "chimpanzees don't have childhoods. They are independent soon after weaning," says anthropologist Barry Bogin of Loughborough University in Leicestershire, U.K.

Humans are also the only animals that stretch out the teenage years, having a final growth spurt and delaying reproduction until about 6 years after puberty. On average, women's first babies arrive at age 19, with a worldwide peak of first babies at

age 22.5. This lengthy period of development—comprised of infancy, juvenile years, and adolescence—is a hallmark of the human condition; researchers have known since the 1930s that we take twice as long as chimpanzees to reach adulthood. Even though we are only a bit bigger than chimpanzees, we mature and reproduce a decade later and live 2 to 3 decades longer, says Bogin.

Given that we are unique among mammals, researchers have been probing how this pattern of growth evolved. They have long scrutinized the few, fragile skulls and skeletons of ancient children and have now developed an arsenal of tools to better gauge how childhood has changed over the past 3 million years. Researchers are scanning skulls and teeth of every known juvenile with electron microscopes, micro-computed tomography scans, or powerful synchrotron x-rays and applying state-of-the-art methods to create three-dimensional virtual reconstructions of the skulls of infants and the pelvises of mothers. They're analyzing life histories in traditional cultures to help understand the advantages of the human condition. In addition, some new fossils are appearing. . . . Researchers report the first nearly complete pelvis of a female *Homo erectus,* which offers clues to the prenatal growth of this key human species.

All of this is creating some surprises. One direct human ancestor, whose skeleton looks much like our own, turns out to have grown up much faster than we do. The life histories of our closest evolutionary cousins, the Neandertals, remain controversial, but some researchers suspect that they may have had the longest childhoods of all. The new lines of evidence are helping researchers close in on the time when childhood began to lengthen. "Evidence suggests that much of what makes our life history unique took shape during the evolution of the genus *Homo* and not before," says anthropologist Holly Smith of the University of Michigan, Ann Arbor.

Live Fast, Die Young

Back in 1925, Australian anatomist Raymond Dart announced the discovery of that rarest of rare specimens, the skull of an early hominin child. Dart estimated that the australopithecine

Childhood Stages

	Age at Weaning (Years)	Age at Eruption of First Molar (Years)	Female Age at First Breeding (Years) (Estimated by 3rd Molar Eruption in Fossils)	Average Maximum Life Span (Years)
Chimpanzees, *Pan troglodytes*	4.0	4.0	11.5	45
Lucy, *Australopithecus afarensis*	4.0?	4.0?	11.5	45
Homo erectus	?	4.5	14.5 (est.)	60? (est.)
Modern humans, *Homo sapiens*	2.5	6.0	19.3	70

Milestones. Key events show that modern humans live slower and die later than our ancestors did.

he called the Taung baby had been about 6 years old when it died about 2 million years ago, because its first permanent molar had erupted. As modern parents know, the first of the baby teeth fall out and the first permanent molars appear at about age 6. Dart assumed that early hominins—the group made up of humans and our ancestors but not other apes—matured on much the same schedule as we do, an assumption held for 60 years. Growing up slowly was seen as a defining character of the human lineage.

Then in 1984, anatomists Christopher Dean and Timothy Bromage tested a new method to calculate the chronological ages of fossil children in a lab at University College London (UCL). Just as botanists add up tree rings to calculate the age of a tree, they counted microscopic lines on the surface of teeth that are laid down weekly as humans grow. The pair counted the lines on teeth of australopithecine children about as mature as the Taung child and were confounded: These hominin children were only about 3.5 years old rather than 6. They seemed to be closer to the chimpanzee pattern, in which the first permanent molar erupts at about age 3.5. "We concluded that [the australopithecines] were more like living great apes in their pace of development than modern humans," says Dean.

Their report in *Nature* in 1985 shook the field and focused researchers on the key questions of when and why our ancestors adopted the risky strategy of delaying reproduction. Many other slow-growing, large-bodied animals, such as rhinos, elephants, and chimpanzees, are now threatened with extinction, in part because they delay reproduction so long that their offspring risk dying before they replace themselves. Humans are the latest to begin reproducing, yet we seem immune from those risks, given that there are 6.6 billion of us on the planet. "When did we escape those constraints? When did we extend our childhood?" asks biological anthropologist Steven Leigh of the University of Illinois, Urbana-Champaign.

The Taung baby and the other australopithecine children, including the relatively recent discovery of a stunning fossil of a 3-year-old *Australopithecus afarensis* girl from Dikika, Ethiopia, show that it happened after the australopithecines. So researchers have zeroed in on early *Homo*, which appeared in Africa about 2 million years ago.

Unfortunately, there are only a few jaw bits of early *Homo* infants and young children to nail down their ages. Most of what we know comes from a single skeleton, a *H. erectus* boy

who died about 1.6 million years ago near Lake Turkana, Kenya. *H. erectus* was among the first human ancestors to share many key elements of the modern human body plan, with a brain considerably larger than that of earlier hominins. And unlike the petite australopithecines, this Turkana youth was big: He weighed 50 kilograms, stood 163 centimeters tall, and looked like he was 13 years old, based on modern human standards. Yet two independent tooth studies suggested ages from 8 or 9 to 10.5 years old.

Now a fresh look at the skeleton concludes that, despite the boy's size, he was closer to 8 years old when he died. Dean and Smith make this case in a paper in press in an edited volume, *The First Humans: Origin of the Genus* Homo. The skeleton and tooth microstructure of the boy and new data on other members of his species suggest that he attained more of his adult height and mass earlier than modern human children do. Today, "you won't find an 8-year-old boy with body weight, height, and skeletal age that are so much older," says Dean.

He and Smith concluded that the boy did not experience a "long, slow period of growth" after he was weaned but grew up earlier, more like a chimpanzee. They estimate the species' age at first reproduction at about 14.5, based on the eruption of its third molar, which in both humans and chimpanzees erupts at about the age they first reproduce. This 8-year-old Turkana Boy was probably more independent than a 13-year-old modern human, the researchers say, suggesting that *H. erectus* families were quite different from ours and did not stay together as long.

The new, remarkably complete female pelvis, however, suggests that life history changes had begun in *H. erectus*. Researchers led by Sileshi Semaw of the Stone Age Institute at Indiana University, Bloomington, found the pelvis in the badlands of Gona, Ethiopia. They present a chain of inference that leads from pelvis, to brain size, to life history strategy.

They assume that the nearly complete pelvis belongs to *H. erectus*, because other *H. erectus* fossils were found nearby and because it resembles fragmentary pelvises for the species. Lead author Scott Simpson of Case Western Reserve University in Cleveland, Ohio, paints a vivid picture of a short female with wide hips and an "obstetrically capacious" pelvic opening that could have birthed babies with brain sizes of up to 315 milliliters. That's 30% to 50% of the adult brain size for this species and larger than previously predicted based on a reconstruction of the Turkana Boy's incomplete pelvis. However, the new estimate does match with newborn brain size predicted by the size of adult brains in *H. erectus*, says Jeremy DeSilva of Worcester State College in Massachusetts, who made such calculations online in September in the *Journal of Human Evolution.*

The wide pelvis suggests *H. erectus* got a head start on its brain development, putting on extra gray matter in utero rather than later in childhood. That's similar to living people, whose brains grow rapidly before birth, says Simpson. But if *H. erectus*'s fetal growth approached that of modern humans, it built proportionally more of its brain before birth, because its brain never became as massive as our own.

Thus, *H. erectus* grew its brain before birth like a modern human, while during childhood it grew up faster like an ape. With a brain developing early, *H. erectus* toddlers may have spent less time as helpless children than modern humans do, says paleoanthropologist Alan Walker of Pennsylvania State University in State College. This suggests *H. erectus* children were neither chimplike nor humanlike but perhaps somewhere in between: "Early *H. erectus* possessed a life history unlike any species living today," write Dean and Smith. "If you look at its morphology, it fits in our genus, *Homo*," says Smith. "But in terms of life history, they fit with australopithecines."

Live Slow, Die Old?

If *H. erectus* was just beginning to slow down its life history, when did humans take the last steps, to our current late-maturing life plan? Three juvenile fossil members of *H. antecessor,* who died 800,000 years ago in Atapuerca, Spain, offer tantalizing clues. An initial study in 1999, based on rough estimates of tooth eruption, found that this species matured like a modern human, says José María Bermúdez de Castro of the Museo Nacional de Ciencias Naturales in Madrid. Detailed studies of tooth microstructure are eagerly awaited to confirm this.

In the meantime, another recent study has shown that childhood was fully extended by the time the first members of our species, *H. sapiens,* appeared in northern Africa about 200,000 years ago. In 2007, researchers examined the daily, internal tooth lines of a *H. sapiens* child who lived 160,000 years ago in Jebel Irhoud, Morocco. They used x-rays from a powerful particle accelerator in Grenoble, France (*Science,* 7 December 2007, p. 1546), to study the teeth without destroying them and found that the 8-year-old Jebel Irhoud child had grown as slowly as a modern 8-year-old, according to Harvard University paleoanthropologist Tanya Smith, who coled the study.

That analysis narrowed the window of time when humans evolved the last extension of our childhood to between 800,000 years ago and 200,000 years ago. To constrain it still further, Tanya Smith and her colleagues recently trained their x-ray vision on our closest relatives: the extinct Neandertals, who shared their last ancestor with us about 500,000 years ago. First, the researchers sliced a molar of a Belgian Neandertal that was at the same stage of dental development as the 8-year-old Jebel Irhoud child and counted its internal growth lines. They found that it had reached the same dental milestones more rapidly and proposed that Neandertals grew up faster than we

do. That suggests that a fully extended childhood evolved only in our species, in the past 200,000 years.

But Tanya Smith's results conflict with earlier studies by Dean and colleagues who also sliced Neandertal teeth and found that they had formed slowly, like those of modern humans. The case is not closed: Smith and paleontologist Paul Tafforeau of the European Synchrotron Radiation Facility in Grenoble, France, spent weeks last year imaging juvenile Neandertals and early members of *H. sapiens,* and they expect to publish within a year.

Meanwhile, new data with implications for Neandertal growth rates are coming in from other sources. The brain sizes of a Neandertal newborn and two infants show that they were at the upper end of the size range for modern humans, suggesting that their brains grew faster than ours after birth, according to virtual reconstructions by Christoph Zollikofer and anthropologist Marcia Ponce de León of the University of Zurich (*Science,* 12 September, p. 1429).

Those rapidly growing brains don't necessarily imply a rapid life history, warn Zollikofer and Ponce de León. They argue that because Neandertals' brains were more massive, they did not complete brain growth earlier than modern humans even though they grew at a faster rate. "They have to get those bigger brains somehow," says Holly Smith. For now, Neandertals' life history remains controversial.

Why Wait?

If childhood began to change in *H. erectus* and continued to get longer in our own species and possibly Neandertals, then the next question is why. What advantage did our ancestors gain from delaying reproduction so long? Many researchers agree that childhood allows us to learn from others, in order to improve our survival skills and prepare us to be better parents. Historically, researchers have also argued that humans need a long childhood to allow enough time for our larger brain to mature.

But in fact, a big brain doesn't directly cause the extension of childhood, because the brain is built relatively early. "Everyone speaks about slow human development, but the human brain develops very fast," says Zollikofer. It doubles in size in the first year of life and achieves 95% of its adult size by the age of 5 (although white matter grows at least to age 18). "We get our brains done; then, we sit around for much longer than other species before we reproduce," says Leigh. "It's almost like humans are building the outside, getting the scaffolding of the house up early, and then filling in after that."

However, there's a less direct connection between brains and life history: Big brains are so metabolically expensive that primates must postpone the age of reproduction in order to build them, according to a paper last year in the *Journal of Human Evolution* (*Science,* 15 June 2007, p. 1560). "The high metabolic costs of rapid brain growth require delayed maturation so that mothers can bear the metabolic burdens associated with high brain growth," says Leigh. "Fast brain growth tells us that maturation is late."

That's why Ponce de León and Zollikofer think that the Neandertals' rapid brain growth implies late, rather than early, maturation: Neandertal mothers must have been large and strong—and by implication, relatively old—to support infants with such big, fast-growing brains. Indeed, say the Zurich pair, Neandertals may have had even longer childhoods than we do now. Childhood, like brain size, may have reached its zenith in Neandertals and early *H. sapiens*. As our brains got smaller over the past 50,000 years, we might have begun reproducing slightly earlier than Neandertals.

To explore such questions, recent interdisciplinary studies are teasing out the reproductive advantages of waiting to become parents. Many analyses cite an influential life history model by evolutionary biologist Eric Charnov of the University of New Mexico, Albuquerque. The model shows that it pays to have babies early if parents face a high risk of death. Conversely, mammals that face a lower risk of dying benefit if they wait to reproduce, because older mothers can grow bigger, stronger bodies that grow bigger babies, who are more likely to survive. "The driving force of a prolonged life history schedule is almost certainly a reduction in mortality rates that allows growth and life span to extend and allows for reproduction to extend further into adulthood in a more spread-out manner," says Dean.

Researchers such as Loughborough's Bogin have applied Charnov's model to modern humans, proposing that delaying reproduction creates higher quality human mothers. Indeed, humans start having babies 8 years later than chimpanzees, and both species stop by about age 45 to 50. But once human mothers begin, they more than make up for their delayed start, pushing out babies on average 3.4 years apart in traditional forager societies without birth control, compared with 5.9 years for wild chimpanzees, says Bogin. This rapid-fire reproduction produces more babies for human hunter-gatherers, who have peak fertility rates of 0.31 babies per given year compared with 0.22 for chimpanzees. And human mothers who start even later than age 19 have more surviving babies. For example, in the 1950s, the Anabaptist Hutterites of North America, who eschewed birth control, had their first babies on average at age 22 and then bore children every 2 years. They produced an amazing nine children per mother, says Bogin, who has studied the group.

Such fecundity, however, requires a village or at least an extended family with fathers and grandmothers around to help provision and care for the young. That's something that other primates cannot provide consistently, if at all, says Hawkes (*Science,* 25 April 1997, p. 535). She proposed that grandmothers' provisioning allows mothers to wean early and have babies more closely together, a vivid example of the way humans use social connections to overcome biological constraints—and allow mothers to have more babies than they could raise on their own. "Late maturation works well for humans because culture lets us escape the constraints other primates have," says Leigh.

The key is to find out when our ancestors were weaned, says Holly Smith. Younger weaning implies that mothers had enough social support to feed weaned children and space babies more closely. "Weaning tells us when *Homo* species start stacking their young," says Smith. Indeed, Dean and Louise Humphrey of the Natural History Museum in London are testing a method that detects the chemical signature of weaning in human teeth. Humans may be slow starters, but our social safety net has allowed us to stack our babies closely together—and so win the reproductive sweepstakes, leaving chimpanzees, and the extinct Neandertals, far behind.

Critical Thinking

1. How does the case of Mel illustrate the contrast between chimpanzee and human childhood?

2. How do humans contrast with chimpanzees in terms of maturation and reproduction?

3. How were Dean and Bromage able to recalculate the age of the Taung child? What key questions did this cause researchers to focus upon?

4. What can be said about the Turkana boy and why? What is the estimate of this species' first reproduction? How would *H. erectus* families been different from ours?

5. What does the wide *H. erectus* pelvis suggest about its brain development and its life history?

6. What is the evidence as to when our ancestors took the last steps to our current late-maturing life plan?

7. Why does similar evidence for Neanderthals continue to be ambiguous?

8. What are the possible advantages to a long childhood? Why is the idea of allowing for brain growth not a likely explanation?

9. What is the advantage to postponing the age of reproduction?

10. Under what circumstance does it pay to have babies early? What is the benefit of having babies later? How do humans compare favorably with chimpanzees in this regard? Why does such fecundity require a village?

11. What would the time of weaning tell us about our ancestors?

Create Central

www.mhhe.com/createcentral

Internet References

Humanorigins.si.edu

http://humanorigins.si.edu/research

This website deals with evidence for the evolution of human characteristics.

American Anthropological Association Children and Childhood Interest Group

http://aaacig.usu.edu

Gibbons, Ann. From *Science Magazine,* November 2008, pp. 1040–1043. Copyright © 2008 by American Association for the Advancement of Science. Reprinted by permission via Rightslink. www.sciencemag.org

Article

Prepared by Elvio Angeloni, *Pasadena City College*

The Evolution of Grandparents

Senior citizens may have been the secret of our species' success.

Rachel Caspari

Learning Outcomes

After reading this article, you will be able to:

- Discuss the evidence for increased longevity in the human evolutionary line.
- Discuss the importance of longevity with respect to the human lifespan.

During the summer of 1963, when I was six years old, my family traveled from our home in Philadelphia to Los Angeles to visit my maternal relatives. I already knew my grandmother well: she helped my mother care for my twin brothers, who were only 18 months my junior, and me. When she was not with us, my grandmother lived with her mother, whom I met that summer for the first time. I come from a long-lived family. My grandmother was born in 1895, and her mother in the 1860s; both lived almost 100 years. We stayed with the two matriarchs for several weeks. Through their stories, I learned about my roots and where I belonged in a social network spanning four generations. Their reminiscences personally connected me to life at the end of the Civil War and the Reconstruction era and to the challenges my ancestors faced and the ways they persevered.

My story is not unique. Elders play critical roles in human societies around the globe, conveying wisdom and providing social and economic support for the families of their children and larger kin groups. In our modern era, people routinely live long enough to become grandparents. But this was not always the case. When did grandparents become prevalent, and how did their ubiquity affect human evolution?

Research my colleagues and I have been conducting indicates that grandparent-aged individuals became common relatively recently in human prehistory and that this change came at about the same time as cultural shifts toward distinctly modern behaviors—including a dependence on sophisticated symbol-based communication of the kind that underpins art and language. These findings suggest that living to an older age had profound effects on the population sizes, social interactions and genetics of early modern human groups and may explain why they were more successful than archaic humans, such as the Neandertals.

Live Fast, Die Young

The first step in figuring out when grandparents became a fixture in society is assessing the typical age breakdown of past populations—what percent were children, adults of childbearing age and parents of those younger adults? Reconstructing the demography of ancient populations is tricky business, however. For one thing, whole populations are never preserved in the fossil record. Rather paleontologists tend to recover fragments of individuals. For another, early humans did not necessarily mature at the same rate as modern humans. In fact, maturation rates differ even among contemporary human populations. But a handful of sites have yielded high enough numbers of human fossils in the same layers of sediment that scientists can confidently assess the age at death of the remains—which is key to understanding the makeup of a prehistoric group.

A rock-shelter located in the town of Krapina in Croatia, about 40 kilometers northwest of the city of Zagreb, is one such site. More than a century ago Croatian paleontologist Dragutin Gorjanović-Kramberger excavated and described the fragmentary remains of perhaps as many as 70 Neandertal individuals there, most of which came from a layer dated to about 130,000 years ago. The large number of fossils found close to one another, the apparently rapid accumulation of the sediments at the site and the fact that some of the remains share distinctive, genetically determined features all indicate that the Krapina bones approximate the remains of a single population of Neandertals. As often happens in the fossil record, the best-preserved remains at Krapina are teeth because the high mineral content of teeth protects them from degradation. Fortunately, teeth are also one of the best skeletal elements for determining age at death, which is achieved by analyzing surface wear and age-related changes in their internal structure.

In 1979, before I began my research into the evolution of grandparents, Milford H. Wolpoff of the University of Michigan at Ann Arbor published a paper, based on dental remains, that assessed how old the Krapina Neandertals were when they died. Molar teeth erupt sequentially. Using one of the fastest eruption schedules observed in modern-day humans as a guide, Wolpoff estimated that the first, second and third molars of Neandertals erupted at ages that rounded to six, 12 and 15, respectively. Wear from chewing accumulates at a steady pace over an individual's lifetime, so when the second molar emerges, the first already has six years of wear on it, and when the third emerges, the second has three years of wear on it.

Working backward, one can infer, for instance, that a first molar with 15 years of wear on it belonged to a 21-year-old Neandertal, a second molar with 15 years of wear on it belonged to a 27-year-old and a third molar with 15 years of wear on it belonged to a 30-year-old. (These estimates have an uncertainty of plus or minus one year.) This wear-based seriation method for determining age at death, adapted from a technique developed by dental researcher A.E.W. Miles in 1963, works best on samples with large numbers of juveniles, which Krapina has in abundance. The method loses accuracy when applied to the teeth of elderly individuals, whose tooth crowns can be too worn to evaluate reliably and in some cases may even be totally eroded.

Wolpoff's work indicated that the Krapina Neandertals died young. In 2005, a few years after I began researching the evolution of longevity, I decided to take another look at this sample using a novel approach. I wanted to make sure that we were not missing older individuals as a result of the inherent limitations of wear-based seriation. Working with Jakov Radovčić of the Croatian Natural History Museum in Zagreb, Steven A. Goldstein, Jeffrey A. Meganck and Dana L. Begun, all at Michigan, and undergraduate students from Central Michigan University, I developed a new nondestructive method—using high-resolution three-dimensional microcomputed tomography (μCT)—to reassess how old the Krapina individuals were when they died. Specifically, we looked at the degree of development of a type of tissue within the tooth called secondary dentin; the volume of secondary dentin increases with age and provides a way to assess how old an individual was at death when the tooth crown is too worn to be a good indicator.

Our initial findings, supplemented with scans provided by the Max Planck Institute for Evolutionary Anthropology in Leipzig, corroborated Wolpoff's results and validated the wear-based seriation method: the Krapina Neandertals had remarkably high mortality rates; no one survived past age 30. (This is not to say that Neandertals across the board never lived beyond 30. A few individuals from sites other than Krapina were around 40 when they died.)

By today's standards, the Krapina death pattern is unimaginable. After all, for most people age 30 is the prime of life. And hunter-gatherers lived beyond 30 in the recent past. Yet the Krapina Neandertals are not unique among early humans. The few other human fossil localities with large numbers of individuals preserved, such as the approximately 600,000-year-old Sima de los Huesos site in Atapuerca, Spain, show similar patterns. The Sima de los Huesos people had very high levels of juvenile and young adult mortality, with no one surviving past 35 and very few living even that long. It is possible that catastrophic events or the particular conditions under which the remains became fossilized somehow selected against the preservation of older individuals at these sites. But the broad surveys of the human fossil record—including the material from these unusually rich sites and other sites containing fewer individuals—that my colleagues and I have conducted indicate that dying young was the rule, not the exception. To paraphrase words attributed to British philosopher Thomas Hobbes, prehistoric life really was nasty, brutish and short.

Rise of the Grandparents

This new μCT approach has the potential to provide a high-resolution picture of the ages of older individuals in other fossil human populations. But a few years ago, before we hit on this technique, Sang-Hee Lee of the University of California, Riverside, and I were ready to start looking for evidence of changes in longevity over the course of human evolution. We turned to the best approach available at the time: wear-based seriation.

We faced a daunting challenge, though. Most human fossils do not come from sites, such as Krapina, that preserve so many individuals that the remains can be considered reflective of their larger populations. And the smaller the number of contemporaneous individuals found at a site, the more difficult it is to reliably estimate how old members were when they died because of the statistical uncertainties associated with small samples.

But we realized that we could get at the question of when grandparents started becoming common in another way. Instead of asking how long individuals lived, we asked how many of them lived to be old. That is, rather than focusing on absolute ages, we calculated relative ages and asked what proportion of adults survived to the age at which one could first become a grandparent. Our objective was to evaluate changes over evolutionary time in the ratio of older to younger adults—the so-called OY ratio. Among primates, including humans up until very recently, the third molar erupts at about the same time that an individual becomes an adult and reaches reproductive age. Based on data from Neandertals and contemporary hunter-gatherer populations, we inferred that fossil humans got their third molars and had their first child at around age 15. And we considered double that age to mark the beginning of grandparenthood—just as some women today can potentially give birth at age 15 and those women can become grandmothers when their own children reach age 15 and reproduce.

For our purposes, then, any archaic individual judged to be 30 years old or more qualified as an older adult—one old enough to have become a grandparent. But the beauty of the OY ratio approach is that regardless of whether maturation occurred at 10, 15 or 20 years, the number of older and younger individuals in a sample would be unaffected because the start of older adulthood would change accordingly. And because we were only looking to place the fossils in these two broad categories, we could include large numbers of smaller fossil samples in our analysis without worrying about uncertainties in absolute ages.

We calculated the OY ratios for four large aggregates of fossil samples totaling 768 individuals spanning a period of three million years. One aggregate comprised later australopithecines—those primitive relatives of "Lucy," who lived in East Africa and South Africa from three million to 1.5 million years ago. Another aggregate consisted of early members of our genus, *Homo*, from around the globe who lived between two million and 500,000 years ago. The third group was the European Neandertals from 130,000 to 30,000 years ago. And the last consisted of modern Europeans from the early Upper Paleolithic period, who lived between about 30,000 and 20,000 years ago and left behind sophisticated cultural remains.

Although we expected to find increases in longevity over time, we were unprepared for how striking our results would turn out to be. We observed a small trend of increased longevity over time among all samples, but the difference between earlier humans and the modern humans of the Upper Paleolithic was a dramatic fivefold increase in the OY ratio. Thus, for every 10 young adult Neandertals who died between the ages of 15 and 30, there were only four older adults who survived past age 30; in contrast, for every 10 young adults in the European Upper Paleolithic death distribution, there were 20 potential grandparents. Wondering whether the higher numbers of burials at Upper Paleolithic sites might account for the high number of older adults in that sample, we re-analyzed our Upper Paleolithic sample, using only those remains that had not been buried. But we got similar results. The conclusion was inescapable: adult survivorship soared very late in human evolution.

Biology or Culture?

Now that Lee and I had established that the number of potential grandparents surged at some point in the evolution of anatomically modern humans, we had another question on our hands: What was it that brought about this change? There were two possibilities. Either longevity was one of the constellations of genetically controlled traits that biologically distinguished anatomically modern humans from their predecessors, or it did not come along with the emergence of modern anatomy and was instead the result of a later shift in behavior. Anatomically modern humans did not burst onto the evolutionary scene making the art and advanced weaponry that define Upper Paleolithic culture. They originated long before those Upper Paleolithic Europeans, more than 100,000 years ago, and for most of that time they and their anatomically archaic contemporaries the Neandertals used the same, simpler Middle Paleolithic technology. (Members of both groups appear to have dabbled in making art and sophisticated weapons before the Upper Paleolithic, but these traditions were ephemeral compared with the ubiquitous and enduring ones that characterize that later period.) Although our study indicated that a large increase in grandparents was unique to anatomically modern humans, it alone could not distinguish between the biological explanation and the cultural one, because the modern humans we looked at were both anatomically and behaviorally modern. Could we trace longevity back to earlier anatomically modern humans who were not yet behaviorally modern?

To address this question, Lee and I analyzed Middle Paleolithic humans from sites in western Asia dating to between about 110,000 and 40,000 years ago. Our sample included both Neandertals and modern humans, all associated with the same comparatively simple artifacts. This approach allowed us to compare the OY ratios of two biologically distinct groups (many scholars consider them to be separate species) who lived in the same region and had the same cultural complexity. We found that the Neandertals and modern humans from western Asia had statistically identical OY ratios, ruling out the possibility that a biological shift accounted for the increase in adult survivorship seen in Upper Paleolithic Europeans. Both western Asian groups had roughly even proportions of older and younger adults, putting their OY ratios between those of the Neandertals and early modern humans from Europe.

Compared with European Neandertals, a much larger proportion of western Asian Neandertals (and modern humans) lived to be grandparents. This is not unexpected—the more temperate environment of western Asia would have been far easier to survive in than the harsh ecological conditions of Ice Age Europe. Yet if the more temperate environment of western Asia accounts for the elevated adult survivorship seen in the Middle Paleolithic populations there, the longevity of Upper Paleolithic Europeans is even more impressive. Despite living in much harsher conditions, the Upper Paleolithic Europeans had an OY ratio more than double that of the Middle Paleolithic modern humans.

Senior Moments

We do not know exactly what those Upper Paleolithic Europeans started doing culturally that allowed so many more of them to live to older age. But there can be no doubt that this increased adult survivorship itself had far-reaching effects. As Kristen Hawkes of the University of Utah, Hillard Kaplan of the University of New Mexico and others have shown in their studies of several modern-day hunter-gatherer groups, grandparents routinely contribute economic and social resources to their descendants, increasing both the number of offspring their children can have and the survivorship of their grandchildren. Grandparents also reinforce complex social connections—like my grandmother did in telling stories of ancestors that linked me to other relatives in my generation. Such information is the foundation on which human social organization is built.

Elders transmit other kinds of cultural knowledge, too—from environmental (what kinds of plants are poisonous or where to find water during times of drought, for example) to technological (how to weave a basket or knap a stone knife, perhaps). Studies led by Pontus Strimling of Stockholm University have shown that repetition is a critical factor in the transmission of the rules and traditions of one's culture. Multigenerational families have more members to hammer home important lessons. Thus, longevity presumably fostered the intergenerational accumulation and transfer of information that encouraged the formation of intricate kinship systems and other social networks that allow us to help and be helped when the going gets tough.

Increases in longevity would also have translated into increases in population size by adding an age group that was not there in the past and that was still fertile. And large populations are major drivers of new behaviors. In 2009 Adam Powell of University College London and his colleagues published a paper in *Science* showing that population density figures importantly in the maintenance of cultural complexity. They and many other researchers argue that larger populations promoted the development of extensive trade networks, complex systems of cooperation, and material expressions of individual and group identity (jewelry, body paint, and so on). Viewed in that light, the hallmark features of the Upper Paleolithic—the explosive increase in the use of symbols, for instance, or the incorporation of exotic materials in tool manufacture—look as though they might well have been consequences of swelling population size.

Growing population size would have affected our forebears another way, too: by accelerating the pace of evolution. As John Hawks of the University of Wisconsin-Madison has emphasized, more people mean more mutations and opportunities for advantageous mutations to sweep through populations as their members reproduce. This trend may have had an even more striking effect on recent humans than on Upper Paleolithic ones, compounding the dramatic population growth that accompanied the domestication of plants 10,000 years ago. In their 2009 book *The 10,000 Year Explosion,* Gregory Cochran and Henry Harpending, both at the University of Utah, describe multiple gene variants—from those influencing skin color to those that determine tolerance of cow milk—that arose and spread swiftly over the past 10,000 years, thanks to the ever larger numbers of breeding individuals.

The relation between adult survivorship and the emergence of sophisticated new cultural traditions, starting with those of the Upper Paleolithic, was almost certainly a positive feedback process. Initially a by-product of some sort of cultural change, longevity became a prerequisite for the unique and complex behaviors that signal modernity. These innovations in turn promoted the importance and survivorship of older adults, which led to the population expansions that had such profound cultural and genetic effects on our predecessors. Older and wiser, indeed.

Critical Thinking

1. What are the critical roles played by elders around the world?

2. When did grandparent-aged individuals become common in human prehistory? What do these findings suggest?

3. Why is reconstructing the demography of ancient populations a tricky business? Why were sites such as Krapina useful in this regard?

4. How was Wolpoff able to estimate the ages of death at Krapina?

5. Describe the high mortality rates among the Neandertals at Krapina. How does this compare to today's standards? What indications are there that dying young was the rule?

6. Why did the author use the OY (older to younger adults) ratio?

7. What four aggregates of fossil samples were used?

8. What were the results?

9. What were the two possible explanations for increased longevity? Why was it important to know if longevity could be traced back to the early anatomically modern humans?

10. What was found in comparing Middle Paleolithic Neandertals with modern humans in western Asia? What was the significance of this find? How did western Asian Neandertals compare to the European Neandertals?

11. Why was the longevity of the Upper Paleolithic Europeans impressive?

12. Discuss the far-reaching effects that increased adult survivorship must have had on humanity.

Create Central

www.mhhe.com/createcentral

Internet References

American Anthropological Association Children and Childhood Interest Group
  http://aaacig.usu.edus

Humanorigins.si.edu
  http://humanorigins.si.edu/research

Article   Prepared by Elvio Angeloni, *Pasadena City College*

A Bigger, Better Brain

Observations of chimpanzees and dolphins strengthen the notion that humanlike intelligence may not be uniquely human.

MADDALENA BEARZI AND CRAIG STANFORD

Learning Outcomes

After reading this article, you will be able to:

- Discuss and explain the similarities between the brains of chimpanzees and dolphins.

- Why is a big, sophisticated brain an advantage in life?

When the orange sun rises in the east of Gombe National Park in Tanzania, it takes time to cross the mountain ridge above and warm the forest below. There, a party of chimpanzees is waking up. One by one they roll over, look up at the morning sky and slowly revive themselves. Each sits sleepily on the branch supporting his or her nest, peeing quietly onto the ground many meters below. Every tree has an ape or two, and one towering Chrysophyllum tree holds several nests. In minutes, the silent band descends to sit like boulders on the hillside.

Then, as if on cue, one of the older males gets up and begins walking from the sleeping area, heading north. Several males follow, but two walk instead to the west toward a lake. A mother and her infant embark southward, alone. A couple of young males stay put; later they will travel to the east, up into the rugged hills. What started out at dawn as a nesting party of 26 chimpanzees fragments into at least five separate parties of one to eight chimpanzees each, all venturing into a day of multiple decisions and complicated social encounters.

At the opposite side of the world, dawn begins to light up the coast of the Yucatan Peninsula in Mexico. Like clockwork, a group of dolphins passes the fisherman's rickety wharf at this time. Gordo, a chubby male bottlenose with a clear, deep notch halfway down his dorsal fin, is the first to appear in the morning mist. He makes his way slowly westward along the shoreline; the rest of the gang, a football field behind, follows. As the sun brightens, one dark grey body after another passes the pier. They are 14: a female with her calf and 12 others. Twenty or so meters past the wharf, they cluster together next to a colorful string of moored pangas. Some dive, others mill about at the surface.

A few at a time, the dolphins explore the sandy bottom with no sign of hurry while another group of dolphins leisurely joins them from the opposite direction. They are now 23 with a couple of calves next to their mothers, all tightly grouped in a murky patch of water that likely hides a fishy meal. Suddenly, the circle unwinds in two lively threads: Five animals move steadily back toward the wharf in a monklike procession; the others disappear quickly to the west. The sun is already high on the horizon. What seemed for a moment to be a singular and cohesive group has reshuffled and divided, ready for the complex tasks and interactions that will make up their day.

Chimpanzees and dolphins look completely different. One resembles people, more or less. The other has the body of a cruise missile. One has hands that can skillfully manipulate a tool, delicately groom a partner or converse in sign language. The other has no hands at all. Chimpanzees swing through the trees of African forests. Dolphins dive deep in oceans. These mammals, about as closely related as mice and elephants, haven't had a common ancestor for nearly 100 million years. It takes dissection to see how their organs and limbs share common features.

One of us (Maddalena) is a marine mammalogist who has studied bottlenose and other dolphin species for nearly 20 years in Santa Monica Bay, near Los Angeles, and other parts of the world. The other (Craig) is a primatologist who has observed chimpanzees and gorillas in Africa for more than 15 years. As unlikely as it might seem, we find more parallel behavioral traits in these species than we do in more closely related animals. What's even more compelling is that many of these distinctive traits are also found in humans—an observation that may have implications for the origin of human intelligence.

Humanlike intelligence may not be a quality that could only have emerged from our own recent evolutionary lineage. Instead convergent evolution could have played a role. Evidence for this argument is not yet irrefutable but it is increasing. And it all starts with one unusual quality shared by humans, chimpanzees and dolphins: the large size of their brains. The various dolphin species, the four great apes and Homo sapiens possess brains that are the cognitive crowning glory of Earth's millions of species.

A Rare Intelligence

Of all the species on our planet, only a handful has possessed a high degree of intellect: apes and humans (including many extinct forms of both), dolphins, whales, and some others, such as elephants. The brains of an ape and a dolphin differ in their external morphology and neuroanatomical organization, in particular their cortical cytoarchitecture, which in dolphins has less cellular differentiation. Despite these differences, primate (including human) and dolphin brains share important similarities. For one, the brains of dolphins and apes increased in size and complexity over their evolutionary history. Both possess a high encephalization quotient (EQ) due to their unusually large brain-to-body-size ratios. EQ is the ratio of an animal's actual brain size to its expected brain size based on measurements of other animals its size. In both dolphins and apes, the neocortex is also more elaborately developed compared to that of other animals. Also distinctive is the neocortical gyrification, or folding of the cerebral cortex—which in dolphins surpasses that of any primate—and the presence of spindleshaped neurons, called Von Economo neurons, which have been linked in people to social fluency and the ability to sense what others think. Only recently were those neurons found in bottlenose dolphins.

But why is a big, sophisticated brain an advantage in life? Dinosaurs had puny brains but flourished for hundreds of millions of years. Intelligence is an adaptation, but not necessarily the only or even the most effective one. What works best for a given organism depends on its environmental context. Some creatures have changed precious little over many millions of years. Other lineages, such as primates and cetaceans, have undergone dramatic changes and a mushrooming of brain size in just a few million years. Natural selection has acted to favor intelligence when it conferred survival and reproductive benefits and when it complemented traits that were genetically hard-wired.

Brain power has allowed dolphins and apes to possess communication and social skills so complex that we are only now beginning to understand how they work. Unlike most animals, apes and dolphins live in fluid societies and engage in relationships that require accurate memories of who is a friend and who owes whom a favor. The social alliances they become a part of can change as their needs change. Great apes possess an intellect often referred to as Machiavellian. They remember favors owed and debts incurred and they operate in a "service economy" of behavior exchange. Male chimpanzees form paramilitary patrol parties and hunting parties. They also shift alliances in accordance with their self-interest. They may work with one group to manipulate a female for sexual access and with another to overthrow an alpha male. We used to think that some of these alliances were based entirely on kinship. Anthony Goldberg and Richard Wrangham showed some years ago, however, that such coalitions are not necessarily based on genetic relatedness.

Some dolphins also form coalitions of males in order to sexually coerce females. As was very recently observed by David Lusseau of the University of Aberdeen in Scotland, these groupings can also cooperate to overthrow other male coalitions. The alliances allow for highly complex behavioral "agreements" between males of the same school who cooperate in pairs and triplets to sequester females likely to be in estrus. In other contexts, dolphins can also practice deceit and deception, practices that require a theory of mind—the ability to perceive mental states in oneself and in others. Stan Kuczaj of the University of Southern Mississippi and his colleagues observed intentional deception in Kelly, a female dolphin kept in captivity. Kelly had been trained—along with her tank-mates—to retrieve objects from the pool in exchange for fish. After all the other dolphins had finished with their retrieval chores and gone their own way, Kelly appeared at the surface with some objects of unknown origin in the hope of gaining more fish. After searching the pool, Kelly's trainer discovered a secret cache of "toys" that the dolphin had astutely concealed under a drain cover. Day after day, she had collected objects inadvertently dropped into the pool by tourists, to be used for barter with her trainers for fish. On closer observation, it also became clear that Kelly was extremely careful not to add or remove objects from her cache when other dolphins were present.

Great apes also seem to be skilled at deceiving one another. In Tanzania, one of us (Craig) once watched a low-ranking male chimpanzee named Beethoven use deception to mate with a female despite the presence of the alpha male called Wilkie. As a party of chimpanzees sat in a forest clearing, Beethoven made a charging display through the middle of the group, his hair standing on end and his arched posture indicating bravado. As a low-ranking male, this was taken by the alpha Wilkie as an act of insubordination. As Beethoven charged past Wilkie and into dense thickets, Wilkie pursued and launched into his own display, dragging branches, drumming tree trunks with his feet and generally trying to be maximally impressive. With Wilkie absorbed in his display of dominance, Beethoven furtively made his way back to the clearing and mated with an eagerly awaiting female.

Intelligence Opens the Toolbox

Our understanding of how chimpanzees and dolphins apply their intelligence to tool use is expanding as well. Jane Goodall and others showed decades ago that chimpanzees use sticks to harvest insects. A 2007 report by primatologist Jill Pruetz taught us more: She and her colleagues, working in Senegal, observed a chimpanzee use a stick it had peeled to a tapered end as a weapon to hunt another mammal, something once only seen in humans. The chimpanzee jabbed the stick into tree cavities until it found a bushbaby, a squirrel-sized primate, which the stick extracted. Although not exactly a spear, the stick was evidence that the chimpanzee had foreseen a problem in immobilizing and extracting its intended prey and had devised a solution.

Dolphins do not have hands to use tools, but wild Indian Ocean bottlenose dolphin females are the first "tool-using cetacean" ever documented. Marine biologist Rachel Smolker and colleagues in the early 1980s observed these animals carrying a large cone-shaped sponge on the tip of their elongated beaks, or rostra, like a mask. These "nose mittens" were used for protection against stinging organisms or sand abrasion, or to extract prey from the sea floor. In a 2005 publication, Michael Kriitzen of the University of Zurich and his colleagues, using mitochondrial DNA analyses, concluded that "sponging" was socially transmitted vertically within a single matrilineal group, from mother sponge-carriers to their female offspring.

Knowing how to use a tool is not the fundamental adaptation that a large brain provides. Instead, a large brain conveys the ability to learn and to imitate another's behavior to appropriate its benefits. Tools allow chimpanzees to harvest protein, fat and carbohydrates that would be otherwise unavailable. The added nutrition can help a gestating or lactating female through an otherwise lean time of year, and enhance her reproductive output over the course of her long life. The ability to respond to rapidly changing dynamics in the social group, such as when males form coalitions to control females, is not limited to higher primates and dolphins, but it certainly typifies many species among them. In each case, these skills require years of learning. But the payoff is a potential reproductive windfall.

For many years the study of chimpanzee technological culture consisted mostly of anecdotes, which are fascinating but not always convincing. But when chimpanzee researchers obtained enough long-term data that they were able to analyze cultural traditions from a range of field sites, they found unequivocal evidence for a systematic pattern of these traditions. Using tool use and other cultural data from the seven longest-running field studies in Africa, Andrew Whiten of the University of St. Andrews and his colleagues in 1999 found at least 39 behaviors that could be attributable to the influence of learned traditions. This number may seem rather limited compared with the myriad examples of such behavior in our species, where almost everything is learned at some level. But compared with other nonhuman animals, it is a long list. The logical conclusion here is that animals that live by their wits, as it were, tend to be like chimpanzees and us—big-brained and with a long period of growth and maturation during which key life skills can be acquired by watching one's elders and peers.

We can ask how and why certain cultural traditions, whether technological or social behavior, arise and spread. Biological evolution occurs primarily via natural selection and is preserved through the transfer of genetic material from one generation to the next. It is also an inefficient process, because of the time required for genes to pass to the next generation, and because each reproductive act requires (in all higher animals) the reshuffling of genes from mother and father. Cultural "evolution" does not require the massive shuffling of the genetic deck that can slow the rate of change to a glacial pace. If a cultural trait confers on its user higher odds of survival and enhanced reproduction, then it has a good chance of being passed on. Even though the tool-use innovation, for example, has no genetic basis, the tradition of its use, once established, should spread, to the reproductive benefit of the inventor. Thus an entirely nongenetic feature could have a long-term effect on the species. Only a few groups of animals on this planet exhibit cultural traits. Higher primates certainly are cultural animals. Cetaceans also exhibit elements of culture. A good example of social learning in dolphins is the vertical cultural transmission of foraging and feeding specializations and vocal dialects. John Ford, for instance, reported what he calls "interpod call mimicry" in the wild, showing that killer whales are capable of vocal learning.

Language Building Blocks

Scientists disagree about whether dolphins have language capabilities but evidence persists that they may, depending on how one defines it. In one of the best-known cases, Louis Herman and his colleagues at the Kewalo Basin Marine Mammal Lab in Honolulu in the 1980s devised two artificial languages to teach to bottlenose dolphins at their facility. Neither language approximated human conversation, but both were based on a set of grammatical rules. One was computer-generated and included high-pitched words. The other was a sign language conveyed by trainers' arm and hand signals.

In an underwater classroom, two animals, Ake and Phoenix, were taught a series of sentences, including some commands describing how to take a Frisbee through a particular hoop or to swim under another dolphin. The dolphins also displayed the ability to recognize meaningless phrases. When a trainer occasionally said something that didn't make sense in the created languages, for instance, Ake ignored the command.

Evidence that apes can acquire and use language, including sign language, has grown over decades. Perhaps the most persuasive evidence of language capability in nonhuman apes comes from primatologist Sue Savage-Rumbaugh, who for 30 years was affiliated with Georgia State University's Language Research Center. Kanzi, a male bonobo she worked with, learned to communicate by touching symbols on a lexicon board and understand some spoken English. Savage-Rumbaugh estimated he could produce 300 words himself and could understand more than 1,000 when spoken.

Work by Savage-Rumbaugh and many other researchers has conclusively settled at least two arguments over ape language. First, she demonstrated that apes understand and employ the concept of reference, using words as symbols to represent things in their environment. Second, they can spontaneously use and combine these words to make requests, give information and comment on the world around them. If there is a difference between what Kanzi comprehends and what a human toddler understands, scientists have not yet discovered it.

Evidence also exists that dolphins and chimpanzees can recognize themselves as individuals. Chimpanzees, gorillas, bonobos and orangutans not only recognize themselves in mirrors but also are able to understand that paint blotches they observe in mirrors during experiments were placed on their bodies. The same holds true for bottlenose dolphins. These experiments do not prove that the animals are self-aware in human terms. But they do provide evidence that these animals exhibit cognition, as does their behavior in the wild.

Large brains likely also help these animals succeed in foraging. Both chimpanzees and dolphins feed on widely scattered, temporarily available food. Many species of dolphins chase schools of fish; chimpanzees chase the fleeting appearances of ripe fruits in tree crowns. These two dietary specialties keep them moving all day long, in search of the next school, the next patch. Predicting where and when to search is one challenge. Chimpanzees have the spatial memory of forest rangers. They monitor particular fruit trees in the weeks leading up to the ripening of a crop and return to the right spot day after day until the bounty is gone. Dolphins have a taller order; they have to know where to locate rapidly moving fish schools without such obvious landmarks as trees, streams and mountains. For this they have sonar, a wonderfully evolved system that humans only relatively recently were able to replicate for their own uses. But in addition to their purely sensory adaptations, dolphins put their intelligence (and memory) to good use to find fish.

Chimpanzees mostly eat fruit but, like dolphins, they do hunt. And their hunting is social. They will attack groups of monkeys they encounter during their rambles in search of fruit in African forests. The chase, capture and kill are heart stopping, often gruesome, and always illustrative of the chimpanzees' social nature. To a lion, the zebra it is chasing may be only a meal, but to a chimpanzee the chance to kill and share prey is not only nutritional, but socially significant as well. The monkeys and pigs and antelopes the chimpanzees capture sometimes become pawns in the social dynamics of the group. Researchers in a range of studies across Africa have shown that males use meat to negotiate new alliances, rub salt in the wounds of old rivals and secure status that a chimpanzee without prey cannot. Adult and adolescent males do most of the hunting, making about 90 percent of the kills recorded at Gombe. Females also hunt but more often receive a share of meat from the male who either captured the meat or stole it from the captor. Although lone chimpanzees, both male and female, sometimes hunt by themselves, most hunts are social.

For many dolphin species, hunting is also a social affair. Dolphins are efficient predators who use both agility and braininess to achieve success. Killer whales, the largest dolphins, display one of the most cooperative hunting practices. Feeding at the top of the food chain, transient killer whales prey on small marine mammals such as seals lying on beaches or slabs of ice, and scientists have observed coordinated and intentional stranding by killer whales in the waters of Patagonia. On occasion, the killing of a pinniped represents a learning lesson for the calf, which will use the same technique throughout its life. In groups, they also attack whales much larger than themselves without any sign of fear or hesitation and with a high degree of predatory success.

Being such accomplished ocean hunters makes dolphins a valuable asset for other ocean dwellers in search of a meal. In the coastal waters of Los Angeles, one of us (Maddalena) frequently observes sea lions in proximity to dolphins during feeding and foraging activities. Two predatory species travel and feed together, with no evident hostility or competition. Sea lions capitalize on the superior food-finding ability of echolocating common dolphins to find their own prey. The diverse hunting strategies employed by dolphin and ape societies are an excellent gauge of their social complexity, and another example of how brain complexity, social complexity and ecological complexity are all linked.

Familiar Yet Threatened

These growing insights into the intelligence of great apes and dolphins are emerging as these animals become increasingly threatened worldwide. As we reach farther and farther into tropical forests in search of timber, farmland and spaces for human dwellings, we disrupt the apes' terrestrial habitat. The ongoing hunting of these animals is also taking a toll. And as we continue to use the oceans as our dumping ground, we threaten dolphins' habitat. The incidental catching of nontarget species in commercial fishing activity, known as bycatch, is just one of the major problems facing these animals today. Many conservationists believe that a century from now, great apes will survive only in a few carefully protected sanctuaries or in captivity. Dolphin populations are much less visible than those of great apes but the threats to them are also insidious. Today, several dolphin species are either critically endangered, endangered, threatened or of unknown status.

As scientists who have spent many years studying dolphins and apes in the wild, we believe that our research must incorporate respect and a sense of stewardship for the animals we study. We have both reached the same conclusion: Without conservation and protection of these species and the ecosystems in which they live, they will not survive to see the next century. Sadly, this projection comes just as we are beginning to better understand their complex abilities and social interactions.

Bibliography

Bearzi, M., and C. B. Stanford. 2008. *Beautiful Minds: The Parallel Lives of Great Apes and Dolphins*. Cambridge: Harvard University Press.

Butti, C, C. C. Sherwood, A. Y. Hakeem, J. M. Allman, and P. R. Hof. 2009. Total number and volume of Von Economo neurons in the cerebral cortex of cetaceans. *The Journal of Comparative Neurology, Research in Systems Neuroscience* 515:243–259.

Goldberg, T. L., and R. W. Wrangham. 1997. Genetic correlates of social behaviour in wild chimpanzees: Evidence from mitochondrial DNA. *Animal Behaviour* 54:559–570.

Kriitzen, M., J. Mann, M. R. Heithaus, R. C. Connor, L. Bejder, and W. B. Sherwin. 2005. Cultural transmission of tool use in bottlenose dolphins. Proceedings of the National Academy of Sciences of the U.S.A. 105:8939–8943.

Lusseau, D. 2007. Why are male social relationships complex in the Doubtful Sound bottlenose dolphin population? *PLoS ONE* 2(4):e348.

Marino, L. 2002. Convergence of complex cognitive abilities in cetaceans and primates. *Brain, Behavior and Evolution* 59:21–32.

Marino, L. 1996. What can dolphins tell us about primate evolution? *Evolutionary Anthropology* 5:73–110.

Marino, L. et al. 2007. Cetaceans have complex brains for complex cognition. *PLoS Biology* 139:966–972.

Pruetz, J. D., and P. Bertolani. 2007. Savanna chimpanzees, *Pan troglodytes verus,* hunt with tools. *Current Biology* 17:1–6.

Reiss, D., B. McCowan, and L. Marino. 1997. Communicative and other cognitive characteristics of bottlenose dolphins. *Trends in Cognitive Sciences* 1:123–156.

Reiss, D., and L. Marino. 2001. Mirror self-recognition in the bottlenose dolphin: A case of cognitive convergence. Proceedings of the National Academy of Sciences 98:5937–5942.

Smolker, R., A. Richards, R. Connor, J. Mann, and P. Berggren. 1997. Sponge carrying by dolphins (*Delphindea, Tursiops sp.*) A foraging specialization involving tool use? *Ethology* 103:454–465.

Stanford, C. 2007. *Apes of the Impenetrable Forest.* Upper Saddle River, NJ: Prentice Hall (Primate Field Studies Series).

Whiten, A., J. Goodall, W. C. McGrew, T. Nishida, V. Reynolds,
Y. Sugiyama, C. E. G. Tutin, R. W. Wrangham, and C. Boesch. 1999. Cultures in chimpanzees. *Nature* 399:682–685.

Critical Thinking

1. What are some of the important similarities shared by primate and dolphin brains?

2. Why is a big, sophisticated brain an advantage in the social lives of both dolphins and chimpanzees?

3. How do chimpanzees and dolphins each apply their intelligence to tool use?

4. What are the other, more fundamental advantages of having a large brain?

5. What have long-term studies revealed about tool use and how it is acquired?

6. Why is "cultural evolution" rather than natural selection a more effective way of transferring technological or social behavior?

7. How do the authors assess the language ability and cognition among chimpanzees and dolphins?

8. How have large brains helped both chimpanzees and dolphins in foraging for food?

Create Central

www.mhhe.com/createcentral

Internet References

Humanorigins.si.edu
http://humanorigins.si.edu/research

Journal of Human Evolution
www.journals.elsevier.com/journal-of-human-evolution

Society for Neuroscience
www.sfn.org/public-outreach/brainfacts-dot-org

MADDALENA BEARZI is president and cofounder of the Ocean Conservation Society and a nature and travel journalist. She received her PhD in biology at the University of California, Los Angeles, and has studied dolphins and whales in California and other parts of the world for more than 20 years. **CRAIG STANFORD** is a professor of anthropology and biological sciences at the University of Southern California and codirector of its Jane Goodall Research Center. He received his PhD in anthropology from the University of California, Berkeley, and has conducted field research on great apes in Africa for more than 15 years.

Article   Prepared by Elvio Angeloni, *Pasadena City College*

The Naked Truth

Recent findings lay bare the origins of human hairlessness—and hint that naked skin was a key factor in the emergence of other human traits.

Nina G. Jablonski

Learning Outcomes

After reading this article, you will be able to:

- Explain the importance of body hair for mammals in general.
- Explain why humans are the most hairless of the primates.

Among primates, humans are unique in having nearly naked skin. Every other member of our extended family has a dense covering of fur—from the short, black pelage of the howler monkey to the flowing copper coat of the orangutan—as do most other mammals. Yes, we humans have hair on our heads and elsewhere, but compared with our relatives, even the hairiest person is basically bare.

How did we come to be so denuded? Scholars have pondered this question for centuries. Finding answers has been difficult, however: most of the hallmark transitions in human evolution—such as the emergence of upright walking—are recorded directly in the fossils of our predecessors, but none of the known remains preserves impressions of human skin. In recent years, though, researchers have realized that the fossil record does contain indirect hints about our transformation from hirsute to hairless. Thanks to these clues and insights gleaned over the past decade from genomics and physiology,

I and others have pieced together a compelling account of why and when humans shed their fur. In addition to explaining a very peculiar quirk of our appearance, the scenario suggests that naked skin itself played a crucial role in the evolution of other characteristic human traits, including our large brain and dependence on language.

Hairy Situations

To understand why our ancestors lost their body hair, we must first consider why other species have coats in the first place. Hair is a type of body covering that is unique to mammals. Indeed, it is a defining characteristic of the class: all mammals possess at least some hair, and most of them have it in abundance. It provides insulation and protection against abrasion, moisture, damaging rays of sunlight, and potentially harmful

---

Key Concepts

- Humans are the only primate species that has mostly naked skin.
- Loss of fur was an adaptation to changing environmental conditions that forced our ancestors to travel longer distances for food and water.
- Analyses of fossils and genes hint at when this transformation occurred.
- The evolution of hairlessness helped to set the stage for the emergence of large brains and symbolic thought.

—The Editors

Benefits of Hairlessness
Furry Vs. Naked

Naked human skin is better at ridding the body of excess heat than is fur-covered skin. Mammals possess three types of glands for the purpose: apocrine, eccrine and sebaceous. In most mammals the outermost layer of the skin, known as the epidermis, contains an abundance of apocrine glands. These glands cluster around hair follicles and coat the fur in a lather of oily sweat. Evaporation of this sweat, which cools the animal by drawing heat away from the skin, occurs at the surface of the fur. But the more the animal perspires, the less effectively it eliminates heat because the fur becomes matted, hampering evaporation. In the human epidermis, in contrast, eccrine glands predominate. These glands reside close to the skin surface and discharge thin, watery sweat through tiny pores. In addition to evaporating directly from the skin surface, this eccrine sweat vaporizes more readily than apocrine sweat, thus permitting improved cooling.

parasites and microbes. It also works as camouflage to confuse predators, and its distinctive patterns allow members of the same species to recognize one another. Furthermore, mammals can use their fur in social displays to indicate aggression or agitation: when a dog "raises its hackles" by involuntarily elevating the hairs on its neck and back, it is sending a clear signal to challengers to stay away.

Yet even though fur serves these many important purposes, a number of mammal lineages have evolved hair that is so sparse and fine as to serve no function. Many of these creatures live underground or dwell exclusively in the water. In subterranean mammals, such as the naked mole rat, hairlessness evolved as a response to living in large underground colonies, where the benefits of hair are superfluous because the animals cannot see one another in the dark and because their social structure is such that they simply huddle together for warmth. In marine mammals that never venture ashore, such as whales, naked skin facilitates long-distance swimming and diving by reducing drag on the skin's surface. To compensate for the lack of external insulation, these animals have blubber under the skin. In contrast, semiaquatic mammals—otters, for example—have dense, waterproof fur that traps air to provide positive buoyancy, thus decreasing the effort needed to float. This fur also protects their skin on land.

The largest terrestrial mammals—namely, elephants, rhinoceroses and hippopotamuses—also evolved naked skin because they are at constant risk of overheating. The larger an animal is, the less surface area it has relative to overall body mass and the harder it is for the creature to rid its body of excess heat. (On the flip side, mice and other small animals, which have a high surface-to-volume ratio, often struggle to retain sufficient heat.) During the Pleistocene epoch, which spans the time between two million and 10,000 years ago, the mammoths and other relatives of modern elephants and rhinoceroses were "woolly" because they lived in cold environments, and external insulation helped them conserve body heat and lower their food intake. But all of today's megaherbivores live in sweltering conditions, where a fur coat would be deadly for beasts of such immense proportions.

Human hairlessness is not an evolutionary adaptation to living underground or in the water—the popular embrace of the so-called aquatic ape hypothesis notwithstanding [*see box on next page*]. Neither is it the result of large body size. But our bare skin is related to staying cool, as our superior sweating abilities suggest.

Sweating It Out

Keeping cool is a big problem for many mammals, not just the giant ones, especially when they live in hot places and generate abundant heat from prolonged walking or running. These animals must carefully regulate their core body temperature because their tissues and organs, specifically the brain, can become damaged by overheating.

Mammals employ a variety of tactics to avoid burning up: dogs pant, many cat species are most active during the cooler evening hours, and many antelopes can off-load heat from the blood in their arteries to blood in small veins that has been cooled by breathing through the nose. But for primates,

including humans, sweating is the primary strategy. Sweating cools the body through the production of liquid on the skin's surface that then evaporates, drawing heat energy away from the skin in the process. This whole-body cooling mechanism operates according to the same principle as an evaporative cooler (also known as a swamp cooler), and it is highly effective in preventing the dangerous overheating of the brain, as well as of other body parts.

Not all sweat is the same, however. Mammalian skin contains three types of glands—sebaceous, apocrine and eccrine—that together produce sweat. In most species, sebaceous and apocrine glands are the dominant sweat glands and are located near the base of hair follicles. Their secretions combine to coat hairs with an oily, sometimes foamy, mixture (think of the lather a racehorse generates when it runs). This type of sweat helps to cool the animal. But its ability to dissipate heat is limited. G. Edgar Folk, Jr., of the University of Iowa and his colleagues showed nearly two decades ago that the effectiveness of cooling diminishes as an animal's coat becomes wet and matted with this thick, oily sweat. The loss of efficiency arises because evaporation occurs at the surface of the fur, not at the surface of the skin itself, thus impeding the transfer of heat. Under conditions of duress, heat transfer is inefficient, requiring that the animal drink large amounts of water, which may not be readily available. Fur-covered mammals forced to exercise energetically or for prolonged periods in the heat of day will collapse from heat exhaustion.

Humans, in addition to lacking fur, possess an extraordinary number of eccrine glands—between two million and five million—that can produce up to 12 liters of thin, watery sweat a day. Eccrine glands do not cluster near hair follicles; instead they reside relatively close to the surface of the skin and discharge sweat through tiny pores. This combination of naked skin and watery sweat that sits directly atop it rather than collecting in the fur allows humans to eliminate excess heat very efficiently. In fact, according to a 2007 paper in *Sports Medicine* by Daniel E. Lieberman of Harvard University and Dennis M. Bramble of the University of Utah, our cooling system is so superior that in a marathon on a hot day, a human could outcompete a horse.

Showing Some Skin

Because humans are the only primates that lack coats and have an abundance of eccrine glands, something must have happened since our hominid lineage diverged from the line leading to our closest living relative, the chimpanzee, that favored the emergence of naked, sweaty skin. Perhaps not surprisingly, the transformation seems to have begun with climate change.

By using fossils of animals and plants to reconstruct ancient ecological conditions, scientists have determined that starting around three million years ago the earth entered into a phase of global cooling that had a drying effect in East and Central Africa, where human ancestors lived. With this decline in regular rainfall, the wooded environments favored by early hominids gave way to open savanna grasslands, and the foods that our ancestors the australopithecines subsisted on—fruits,

Alternative Ideas
Why the Aquatic Ape Theory Doesn't Hold Water

Among the many theories that attempt to explain the evolution of naked skin in humans, the aquatic ape theory (AAT)—which posits that humans went through an aquatic phase in their evolution—has attracted the most popular attention and support. First enunciated by English zoologist Sir Alister Hardy in a popular scientific article in 1960, the AAT later found a champion in writer Elaine Morgan, who continues to promote the theory in her lectures and writings. The problem is, the theory is demonstrably wrong.

The AAT holds that around five million to seven million years ago tectonic upheavals in the Rift Valley of East Africa cut early human ancestors off from their preferred tropical forest environments. As a result, they had to adapt to a semiaquatic life in marshes, along coasts and in floodplains, where they lived for about a million years. Evidence of this aquatic phase, Morgan argues, comes from several anatomical features humans share with aquatic and semiaquatic mammals but not with savanna mammals. These traits include our bare skin, a reduced number of apocrine glands, and fat deposits directly under the skin.

The AAT is untenable for three major reasons. First, aquatic mammals themselves differ considerably in the degree to which they exhibit Morgan's aquatic traits. Thus, there is no simple connection between, say, the amount of hair an animal has and the environment in which it lives. Second, the fossil record shows that watery habitats were thick with hungry crocodiles and aggressive hippopotamuses. Our small, defenseless ancestors would not have stood a chance in an encounter with such creatures. Third, the AAT is overly complex. It holds that our forebears shifted from a terrestrial way of life to a semiaquatic one and then returned to living on terra firma full-time. As John H. Langdon of the University of Indianapolis has argued, a more straightforward interpretation of the fossil record is that humans always lived on land, where the driving force behind the evolution of naked skin was climate change that favored savanna grasslands over woodlands. And from a scientific perspective, the simplest explanation is usually the correct one.

—N.J.

---

leaves, tubers and seeds—became scarcer, more patchily distributed and subject to seasonal availability, as did permanent sources or freshwater. In response to this dwindling of resources, our forebears would have had to abandon their relatively leisurely foraging habits for a much more consistently active way of life just to stay hydrated and obtain enough calories, traveling ever longer distances in search of water and edible plant foods.

It is around this time that hominids also began incorporating meat into their diet, is revealed by the appearance of stone tools and butchered animal bones in the archaeological record around 2.6 million years ago. Animal foods are considerably richer in calories than are plant foods, but they are rarer on the landscape. Carnivorous animals therefore, need to range farther and wider than their herbivorous counterparts to procure a sufficient amount of food. Prey animals are also moving targets, save for the occasional carcass, which means predators must expend that much more energy to obtain their meal. In the case of human hunters and scavengers, natural selection morphed the apelike proportions of the australopithecines, who still spent some time in the trees, into a long-legged body built for sustained striding and running. (This modern form also no doubt helped our ancestors avoid becoming dinner themselves when out in the open.)

But these elevated activity levels came at a price: a greatly increased risk of overheating. Beginning in the 1980s, Peter Wheeler of Liverpool John Moores University in England published a series of papers in which he simulated how hot ancestral humans would have become out on the savanna. Wheeler's work, together with research my colleagues and I published in 1994, shows that the increase in walking and running, during which muscle activity builds up heat internally, would have

required that hominids both enhance their eccrine sweating ability and lose their body hair to avoid overheating.

When did this metamorphosis occur? Although the human fossil record does not preserve skin, researchers do have a rough idea of when our forebears began engaging in modern patterns of movement. Studies conducted independently by Lieberman and Christopher Ruff of Johns Hopkins University have shown that by about 1.6 million years ago an early member of our genus called *Homo ergaster* had evolved essentially modern body proportions, which would have permitted prolonged walking and running. Moreover, details of the joint surfaces of the ankle, knee and hip make clear that these hominids actually exerted themselves in this way. Thus,

When Nakedness Evolved
Ancestors on the Move

Although the fossil record does not preserve any direct evidence of ancient human skin, scientists can estimate when nakedness evolved based on other fossil clues. Protohumans such as the australopithecines probably led relatively sedentary lives, as today's apes do, because they lived in or near wooded environments rich in plant foods and freshwater. But as woodlands shrank and grasslands expanded, later ancestors, such as *Homo ergaster*, had to travel ever farther in search of sustenance—including meat. This species, which arose by 1.6 million years ago, was probably the first to possess naked skin and eccrine sweat, which would have offset the body heat generated by such elevated activity levels.

Beating the Heat

Naked skin is not the only adaptation humans evolved to maintain a healthy body temperature in the sweltering tropics where our ancestors lived. They also developed longer limbs, increasing their surface-to-volume ratio, which in turn facilitated the loss of excess heat. That trend seems to be continuing even today. The best evidence of this sustained adaptation comes from populations in East Africa, such as the Dinka of southern Sudan. It is surely no coincidence that these people, who live in one of the hottest places on earth, also have extremely long limbs.

Why do modern humans exhibit such a wide range of limb proportions? As our forebears migrated out of tropical Africa into cooler parts of the world, the selection pressures changed, allowing for a variety of body shapes to evolve.

Of Lice and Men

In recent years researchers have looked to lice for clues to why humans lost their body hair. In 2003 Mark Pagel of the University of Reading in England and Walter Bodmer of John Radcliffe Hospital in Oxford proposed that humans shed their fur to rid their bodies of disease-spreading lice and other fur-dwelling parasites and to advertise the health of their skin. Other investigators have studied head and body lice for insight into how long after becoming bare-skinned our ancestors began to cover up with clothing.

Although body lice feed on blood, they live on clothing. Thus, the origin of body lice provides a minimum estimate for the dawn of hominid garb. By comparing gene sequences of organisms, investigators can learn roughly when the species arose. Such analyses in lice indicate that whereas head lice have plagued humans from the start, body lice evolved much later. The timing of their appearance hints that humans went naked for more than a million years before getting dressed.

according to the fossil evidence, the transition to naked skin and an eccrine-based sweating system must have been well under way by 1.6 million years ago to offset the greater heat loads that accompanied our predecessors' newly strenuous way of life.

Another clue to when hominids evolved naked skin has come from investigations into the genetics of skin color. In an ingenious study published in 2004, Alan R. Rogers of the University of Utah and his colleagues examined sequences of the human *MC1R* gene, which is among the genes responsible for producing skin pigmentation. The team showed that a specific gene variant always found in Africans with dark pigmentation originated as many as 1.2 million years ago. Early human ancestors are believed to have had pinkish skin covered with black fur, much as chimpanzees do, so the evolution of permanently dark skin was presumably a requisite evolutionary follow-up to the loss of our sun-shielding body hair. Rogers's estimate thus provides a minimum age for the dawn of nakedness.

Skin Deep

Less certain than why and when we became naked is how hominids evolved bare flesh. The genetic evidence for the evolution of nakedness has been difficult to locate because many genes contribute to the appearance and function of our skin. Nevertheless, hints have emerged from large-scale comparisons of the sequences of DNA "code letters," or nucleotides, in the entire genomes of different organisms. Comparison of the human and chimp genomes reveals that one of the most significant differences between chimp DNA and our own lies in the genes that code for proteins that control properties of the skin. The human versions of some of those genes encode proteins that help to make our skin particularly waterproof and scuff-resistant—critical properties, given the absence of protective fur. This finding implies that the advent of those gene variants contributed to the origin of nakedness by mitigating its consequences.

The outstanding barrier capabilities of our skin arise from the structure and makeup of its outermost layer, the stratum corneum (SC) of the epidermis. The SC has what has been described as a bricks-and-mortar composition. In this arrangement, multiple layers of flattened dead cells called corneocytes, which contain the protein keratin and other substances, are the bricks; ultrathin layers of lipids surrounding each of the corneocytes make up the mortar.

Most of the genes that direct the development of the SC are ancient, and their sequences are highly conserved among vertebrates. That the genes undergirding the human SC are so distinctive signifies, therefore, that the advent of those genes was important to survival. These genes encode the production of a unique combination of proteins that occur only in the epidermis, including novel types of keratin and involucrin. A number of laboratories are currently attempting to unravel the precise mechanisms responsible for regulating the manufacture of these proteins.

Other researchers are looking at the evolution of keratins in body hair, with the aim of determining the mechanisms responsible for the sparseness and fineness of body hair on the surface of human skin. To that end, Roland Moll of Philipps University in Marburg, Germany, and his colleagues have shown that the keratins present in human body hair are extremely fragile, which is why these hairs break so easily compared with those of other animals. This finding, detailed in a paper Moll published in 2008, suggests that human hair keratins were not as important to survival as the hair keratins of other primates were over the course of evolution and thus became weak.

Another question geneticists are eager to answer is how human skin came to contain such an abundance of eccrine glands. Almost certainly this accumulation occurred through changes in the genes that determine the fate of epidermal stem cells, which are unspecialized, in the embryo. Early in development, groups of epidermal stem cells in specific locations interact with cells of the underlying dermis, and genetically driven chemical signals within these niches direct the differentiation of the stem cells into hair follicles, eccrine glands, apocrine glands, sebaceous glands or plain epidermis. Many research groups are now investigating how epidermal stem cell niches are established and maintained, and this work should clarify what directs the fate of embryonic epidermal cells and how more of these cells become eccrine sweat glands in humans.

Not Entirely Nude

However it was that we became naked apes, evolution did leave a few body parts covered. Any explanation of why humans lost their fur therefore must also account for why we retain it in some places. Hair in the armpits and groin probably serves both to propagate pheromones (chemicals that serve to elicit a behavioral response from other individuals) and to help keep these areas lubricated during locomotion. As for hair on the head, it was most likely retained to help shield against excess heat on the top of the head. That notion may sound paradoxical, but having dense hair on the head creates a barrier layer of air between the sweating scalp and the hot surface of the hair. Thus, on a hot, sunny day the hair absorbs the heat while the barrier layer of air remains cooler, allowing sweat on the scalp to evaporate into that layer of air. Tightly curled hair provides the optimum head covering in this regard, because it increases the thickness of the space between the surface of the hair and the scalp, allowing air to blow through. Much remains to be discovered about the evolution of human head hair, but it is possible that tightly curled hair was the original condition in modern humans and that other hair types evolved as humans dispersed out of tropical Africa.

With regard to our body hair, the question is why it is so variable. There are many populations whose members have hardly any body hair at all and some populations of hirsute folks. Those with the least body hair tend to live in the tropics, whereas those with the most tend to live outside the tropics. Yet the hair on these nontropical people provides no warmth to speak of. These differences in hairiness clearly stem to some extent from testosterone, because males in all populations have more body hair than females do. A number of theories aimed at explaining this imbalance attribute it to sexual selection. For example, one posits that females prefer males with fuller beards and thicker body hair because these traits occur in tandem with virility and strength. Another proposes that males have evolved a preference for females with more juvenile features. These are interesting hypotheses, but no one has actually tested them in a modern human population; thus, we do not know, for instance, whether hairy men are in fact more vigorous or fecund than their sleeker counterparts. In the absence of any empirical evidence, it is still anybody's guess why human body hair varies the way it does.

Naked Ambitions

Going furless was not merely a means to an end; it had profound consequences for subsequent phases of human evolution. The loss of most of our body hair and the gain of the ability to dissipate excess body heat through eccrine sweating helped to make possible the dramatic enlargement of our most temperature-sensitive organ, the brain. Whereas the australopithecines had a brain that was, on average, 400 cubic centimeters—roughly the size of a chimp's brain—*H. ergaster* had a brain twice that large. And within a million years the human brain swelled another 400 cubic centimeters, reaching its modern size. No doubt other factors influenced the expansion of our gray matter—the adoption of a sufficiently caloric diet to fuel this energetically demanding tissue, for example. But shedding our body hair was surely a critical step in becoming brainy.

> **Going furless was not merely a means to an end; it had profound consequences for subsequent phases of human evolution.**

Our hairlessness also had social repercussions. Although we can technically raise and lower our hackles when the small muscles at the base of our hair follicles contract and relax, our body hairs are so thin and wispy that we do not put on much of a show compared with the displays of our cats and dogs or of our chimpanzee cousins. Neither do we have the built-in advertising—or camouflage—offered by zebra stripes, leopard spots, and the like. Indeed, one might even speculate that universal human traits such as social blushing and complex facial expressions evolved to compensate for our lost ability to communicate through our fur. Likewise, body paint, cosmetics, tattoos and other types of skin decoration are found in various combinations in all cultures, because they convey group membership, status and other vital social information formerly encoded by fur. We also employ body postures and gestures to broadcast our emotional states and intentions. And we use language to speak our mind in detail. Viewed this way, naked skin did not just cool us down—it made us human.

More to Explore

Skin Deep. Nina G. Jablonski and George Chaplin in *Scientific American,* vol. 287, no. 4, pages 74–81; October 2002.

Genetic Variation at the MC1R Locus and the Time since Loss of Human Body Hair. Alan R. Rogers, D. Iltis and S. Wooding in *Current Anthropology,* vol. 45, no. 1, pages 105–108; February 2004.

Initial Sequence of the Chimpanzee Genome and Comparison with the Human Genome. Chimpanzee Sequencing and Analysis Consortium in *Nature,* vol. 437, pages 69–87; September 1, 2005.

Skin: A Natural History. Nina G. Jablonski. University of California Press, 2006.

The Evolution of Marathon Running: Capabilities in Humans. Daniel E. Lieberman and Dennis M. Bramble in *Sports Medicine,* vol. 37, nos. 4–5, pages 288–290; 2007.

Critical Thinking

1. What benefits does body hair provide for various mammals?

2. Why have some mammal lineages evolved hair so sparse and fine as to serve no function?

3. What is human bare skin related to, according to the author?

4. Why is keeping cool important for some mammals?

5. In contrast to other mammals, what is the primary strategy for keeping cool among primates?

6. How is the human system of cooling more effective than that of other mammals?

7. How does the evolution of the human cooling system relate to changes in environment, food accessibility, and the availability of water? How did the switch to meat-eating result in a long-legged body built for sustained striding and running?

8. At what price did this elevated activity come? What was required, according to Peter Wheeler?

9. When was the transition to naked skin and an eccrine-based sweating system well under way, according to the fossil evidence?

10. Why did evolution leave a few body parts covered?

11. Why is tightly curled hair thought to be the original condition in modern humans?

12. How has going furless had profound effects upon making us human?

Create Central

www.mhhe.com/createcentral

Internet References

Ethnic and Racial Studies
www.tandfonline.com/rers

Journal of Human Evolution
www.journals.elsevier.com/journal-of-human-evolution

Nina G. Jablonski is head of the anthropology department at Pennsylvania State University. Her research focuses on the natural history of human skin, the origin of bipedalism, the evolution and biogeography of Old World monkeys, and the paleoecology of mammals that lived during the past two million years. She has conducted fieldwork in China, Kenya and Nepal. This is her second article for *Scientific American*. The first, co-authored with George Chaplin and published in October 2002, described the evolution of human skin color.

Article   Prepared by: Elvio Angeloni, *Pasadena City College*

Long Live the Humans

HEATHER PRINGLE

Learning Outcomes

After reading this article, you will be able to:

- Discuss the evidence contradicting the notion that human longevity is due to recent advent of vaccines, antibiotics, and other medical advances.

- Discuss the ways in which natural selection has resulted in our species' ability to fight off bacteria, viruses, and other microbes since the evolutionary split with chimpanzees.

On a Sunday morning in a decaying and dangerous inner-city barrio in Lima, Peru, an unmarked white van carrying nearly a dozen bodies rumbles to a stop on the grounds of the National Institute of Neurological Sciences. Seated in a small waiting area to the rear of the building, a throng of well-dressed researchers and government officials watches intently. As the driver clambers out, an assistant hustles off in search of a hospital gurney. Within minutes, two men wheel the first body into the institute's imaging unit.

Onlooker Caleb Finch, a biologist at the University of Southern California, has been waiting for this moment for months. Tall, gaunt and graying, with a Father Time–style beard, the 74-year-old scientist has devoted his career to the study of human aging. Our kind is remarkably long-lived compared with other primates. Our nearest surviving relatives, the chimpanzees, have a life expectancy at birth of about 13 years. In contrast, babies born in the U.S. in 2009 possessed a life expectancy at birth of 78.5 years. Finch has come to Lima to find out why—by peering into the distant past. The cadavers in the van belong to men, women, and children who perished along this stretch of coastal desert as much as 1,800 years ago, long before the Spanish conquest. Cocooned in dusty textiles and interred in arid desert tombs, their naturally mummified bodies preserve critical new clues to the mystery of human longevity.

As envoys from an era long before modern health care, they will offer case studies of aging in the past. Finch walks over to the van, grinning as he surveys the cargo. "That's a pack of mummies," he says.

Most researchers chalk up our supersized life span to the advent of vaccines, antibiotics, and other medical advances, the development of efficient urban sanitation systems, and the availability of fresh, nutritious vegetables and fruit year-round. Indeed, much demographic evidence shows that these factors greatly extended human life over the past 200 years. But critical as they were to extending human life, they are only part of the longevity puzzle, Finch warrants. Marshaling data from fields as diverse as physical anthropology, primatology, genetics, and medicine, he now proposes a controversial new hypothesis: that the trend toward slower aging and longer lives began much, much earlier, as our human ancestors evolved an increasingly powerful defense system to fight off the many pathogens and irritants in ancient environments. If Finch is right, future research on the complex links among infection, host defense and the chronic diseases of the elderly may revolutionize scientists' understanding of aging and how to cope with the challenges it brings.

And Many More

Hints that modern health practices might not be solely responsible for our long life span have come from studies of contemporary hunter-gatherer groups. In 1985, Nicholas Blurton-Jones, a biological anthropologist at the University of California, Los Angeles, set off by Land Rover across the trackless bush in Tanzania's Lake Eyasi basin. With field assistant Gudo Mahiya, Blurton-Jones traveled to the isolated camps of the Hadza, hunter-gatherers who lived much as their ancestors had, hunting baboons and wildebeest, digging starchy tubers and collecting honey during the rainy season from hives of the African honeybee. Journeying from one camp to another, the two researchers collected basic demographic data, checking each Hadza household and recording the names and ages of the inhabitants. Then the pair updated this census information six times in the 15 years that followed, noting down the names of all who had died and the causes of their death. In addition, Blurton-Jones obtained some earlier census data on the Hadza from two other researchers.

The Hadza lived—as ancient humans and chimpanzees did—in a natural environment teeming with pathogens and parasites. They lacked running water and sewage systems, defecating in a zone 20 to 40 meters away from their camps, and they rarely sought out medical care. Yet as Blurton-Jones and Mahiya discovered, the Hadza enjoyed much longer lives than chimpanzees did. Indeed, the Hadza had a life expectancy at birth of 32.7 years. And if they reached adulthood, they could expect to live 40 more years, nearly three times longer than a chimpanzee reaching adulthood. Some Hadza elders survived into their 80s. Clearly, their relatively long lives owed little to medical and technological advances.

Moreover, the Hadza were not alone. In 2007, two anthropologists, Michael Gurven of U.C. Santa Barbara and Hillard Kaplan of the University of New Mexico analyzed data from all five modern hunter-gatherer societies that researchers had studied demographically. Infections counted for 72 percent of the deaths, and each group revealed a very similar J-shaped mortality curve—with child mortality as high as 30 percent, low death rates in early adulthood and exponentially rising mortality after the age of 40. Then Gurven and Kaplan compared these curves with those of both wild and captive chimpanzees: the simians experienced the sharp uptick of adult mortality at least 10 years earlier than human hunter-gatherers. "It appears that chimpanzees age much faster than humans," concluded Gurven and Kaplan in their paper detailing the findings, "and die earlier, even in protected environments."

Yet when, exactly, did humans begin living longer? To obtain clues, anthropologists Rachel Caspari of Central Michigan University and Sang-Hee Lee of U.C. Riverside examined the remains of 768 individuals from four ancestral human groups spanning millions of years. By assessing the degree of dental wear, which accumulates at a constant pace from chewing, they estimated the ratio of young adults around 15 years of age to older adults around age 30 (old enough to be a grandparent) in each of the four groups. Their studies revealed that living to 30 and beyond became common only recently in our prehistoric past. Among the australopithecines, which emerged in Africa around 4.4 million years ago, most individuals died before their 30th birthday. Moreover, the ratio of thirtysomethings to 15-year-olds was just 0.12. In contrast, *Homo sapiens* who roamed Europe between 44,000 and 10,000 years ago often lived to 30 or more, achieving a ratio of 2.08 [see "The

Evolution of Grandparents," by Rachel Caspari; *SCIENTIFIC AMERICAN,* August 2011].

Calculating the life expectancy of early *H. sapiens* populations is challenging, however: detailed demographic data, such as that supplied by both census records and death registrations, are lacking for much of our long past. So Finch and his colleague Eileen Crimmins, a gerontologist at the University of Southern California, analyzed the earliest, virtually complete statistical set of that nature available—data first gathered in Sweden in 1751, decades before the advent of modern medicine and hygiene. The study revealed that mid-18th-century Swedes had a life expectancy at birth of 35. But those who survived bacterial infections and contagious diseases such as smallpox during childhood and reached the age of 20 could reasonably look forward to another 40 years.

To Finch, these findings raised a major question. The 18th century Swedes lived cheek by jowl in large, permanent villages, towns and cities, where they were exposed to serious health risks unknown to small communities of mobile chimpanzees. So why did the Swedes live longer? The answer, it turns out, may lie in the meaty diets of their early human ancestors and the evolution of genes that protected them from the many hazards of carnivory.

Meat-eating Genes

Chimpanzees spend most of their waking hours in a sweet pursuit: foraging for figs and other ripe fruits. In search of fructose-rich fare, they range over large territories, only occasionally using the same night nest twice in a row. They are skilled at hunting small mammals such as the red colobus monkey, but they do not deliberately set out searching for these prey. Nor do they consume large quantities of meat. Primatologists studying wild chimpanzees in Tanzania have calculated that meat makes up 5 percent or less of the simians' annual diet there, whereas research in Uganda shows that animal fat constitutes only 2.5 percent of their yearly fare by dry weight.

In all likelihood, Finch says, the earliest members of the human family consumed a similar plant-based diet. Yet sometime between 3.4 million and 2.5 million years ago, our ancestors incorporated a major new source of animal protein. As sites in Ethiopia show, they began butchering the remains of large, hoofed mammals such as antelopes with simple stone tools, smashing the bones to get at the fat-rich marrow, slicing off strips of meat, and leaving behind telltale cut marks on femurs and ribs. And by 1.8 million years ago, if not earlier, humans began actively hunting large game and bringing entire carcasses back to camp. The new abundance of calories and protein most likely helped to fuel brain growth but also increased exposure to infections. Finch suggests that this risk favored the rise and spread of adaptations that allowed our predecessors to survive attacks by pathogens and thus live longer.

The trend toward increasing carnivory would have exposed our ancestors to pathogens in several ways. Early humans who scavenged the carcasses of dead animals, and who dined on raw meat and viscera, boosted their chances of ingesting infectious pathogens. Moreover, as humans took up hunting large animals, they faced greater risks of lacerations and fractured bones when closing in on their prey: such injuries could lead to deadly infections. Even cookery, which may have emerged as early as one million years ago, if not earlier, posed perils. Inhaling wood smoke daily exposes humans to high levels of endotoxins and soot particles. Roasting and charring meat improves both the taste and digestibility but creates chemical modifications known as advanced glycation end products, which contribute to serious diseases such as diabetes. Our ancestors' later embrace of agriculture and animal husbandry, which began some 11,500 years ago, added new dangers. The daily proximity of humans to domesticated goats, sheep, pigs, cattle and chickens, for example, elevated the risk of contracting bacterial and viral infections from animals. Moreover, as families settled permanently in villages, sewage from humans and livestock contaminated local water supplies. Pathogenic bacteria thrived.

Even so, humans exposed to such health risks in 1751 in Sweden lived longer than their simian relatives. To tease out clues to this longevity, Finch began studying the scientific literature on chimpanzee and human genomes. Previously published studies by others showed that the two genomes were around 99 percent identical. But in the uniquely human 1 percent, evolutionary biologist Hernán Dopazo, then at the Prince Felipe Research Center in Valencia, Spain, and his colleagues discerned a disproportionately high number of genes that had undergone positive selection and that played key roles in host defense and immunity—specifically in a part of the defense system known as the inflammatory response. Positive selection favors genes that hone our ability to survive and reproduce, which allows them to become more frequent in populations over time, a process that leaves a distinctive "signature" in the DNA sequence. Dopazo's findings added new weight to an idea growing in Finch's mind. He wondered if natural selection had endowed ancient humans with a souped-up system for fighting off the microbial threats and warding off other health hazards posed by increased meat consumption, thereby extending our life span.

In the war against bacteria, viruses and other microbes that seek to invade our tissues, the human host defense system brandishes two powerful weapons: the innate immune system and the adaptive immune system. The innate system is the first responder. It mobilizes immediately at the scene of an attack or injury to eliminate pathogens and heal damaged tissue, and it

essentially responds in the same way to all threats. The adaptive system, in contrast, kicks into gear more slowly, customizing its response to particular pathogens. In doing so, it creates an immunological memory that confers lifelong protection against the invader.

The inflammatory response is part of the innate immune system. It goes to work when tissues suffer damage from microbes, traumatic wounds, injuries, or toxins, and, as Finch points out, physicians have long recognized its hallmarks. Some 2,000 years ago Aulus Cornelius Celsus, a Roman medical author, described four cardinal signs of inflammation—heat, redness, swelling, and pain. The heat, Finch explains, comes from mitochondria, the power plants of our cells, which begin releasing energy as heat. It acts as a form of sterilization "because many bacteria are unable to grow when the temperature rises above 40 degrees Celsius," he adds. The swelling, on the other hand, results as damaged cells release chemicals that prompt blood cells to leak fluids into nearby tissues, thereby isolating the injured area from contact with healthy tissues.

Finch began examining the human-specific changes in genes related to host defense. He was quickly struck by the changes that had affected the apolipoprotein E (APOE) gene. This important gene strongly influences the transport and metabolism of lipids, the development of the brain and the workings of the immune system. It has three primary, uniquely human variants (alleles), of which APOE e4 and APOE e3 are the most prevalent.

APOE e4's DNA sequences closely resemble those in chimpanzee APOE, strongly suggesting that it is the ancestral human variant that emerged near the beginning of the *Homo* genus more than two million years ago and thus may have had the earliest effect on our longevity. Differing in several critical amino acids from the chimp version, APOE e4 vigorously ramps up the acute phase of inflammation. It boosts the production of proteins such as interleukin-6, which helps to increase body temperature, and tumor necrosis factor—alpha, which induces fever and inhibits viruses from replicating. Equipped with this supercharged defense system, children in ancient human families had a better chance of fighting off harmful microbes that they unwittingly ingested in food and encountered in their surroundings. "When humans left the canopy and went out onto the savanna," Finch notes, "they had a much higher exposure to infectious stimuli. The savanna is knee-deep in herbivore dung, and humans were out there in bare feet."

Moreover, early humans who carried APOE e4 most likely profited in another key way. This variant facilitates both the intestinal absorption of lipids and the efficient storage of fat in body tissue. During times when game was scarce and hunting poor, early APOE e4 carriers could draw on this banked fat, upping the odds of their survival.

Even today children who carry APOE e4 enjoy an advantage over those who do not. In one study of youngsters from impoverished families living in a Brazilian shantytown, APOE e4 carriers succumbed to fewer bouts of diarrheal disease brought on by *Escherichia coli* or *Giardia* infections than noncarriers did. And they scored higher on cognitive tests, most likely as a result of their greater absorption of cholesterol—a dietary requirement for neurons to develop in the brain. "So this would have been adaptive, we think," Finch remarks.

A Deferred Cost

All told, APOE e4 seems to be a key part of the puzzle of human longevity. Ironically, now that we live longer, this gene variant appears to double-cross us later in life. Its debilitating effects became apparent only as our human ancestors increasingly survived to middle age and beyond. In Lima, Finch and an international team of cardiologists, radiologists, biologists, and anthropologists are now searching for traces of these afflictions in the preserved cardiovascular tissues of ancient adult mummies.

Inside the crowded imaging unit in Lima, Finch hovers over a technician's computer. It has been a long, trying morning. Several of the mummy bundles transported to the unit are too large to fit into the CT scanner. Others, when scanned, reveal little more than skeletal remains, raising doubts that the preservation of human tissue in the bundles will be adequate for the study.

But no one is giving up. On the screen is a crisp, three-dimensional CT scan of a bundle just wheeled in from the van. Hunching forward, cardiologists Gregory Thomas of Long Beach Memorial Medical Center in California and Randall C. Thompson of the University of Missouri School of Medicine—Kansas City scrutinize an anatomical landscape rendered strangely foreign by centuries of decay and desiccation. As the technician scrolls up and down the image, the two cardiologists gradually pick out preserved soft tissue and the snaking trails of major arteries. The relief in the room is palpable. Then, unable to resist, the two cardiologists take a quick preliminary look along the arteries for small, dense, white patches—calcified plaque that signals an advanced stage of atherosclerosis, or hardening of the arteries, the leading cause of fatal heart attacks and strokes. The individual has clearly calcified arteries.

Cardiologists have traditionally regarded atherosclerosis as a disease of modern civilization. Contemporary behaviors such as smoking cigarettes, eschewing exercise, dining on high-calorie diets and packing on the pounds are all known to increase the risk of hardened arteries. Moreover, several recent studies point to an emerging atherosclerosis epidemic in the developing world, as societies there grow more affluent and increasingly embrace a modern, Western lifestyle. Yet, in 2010, Thomas

and a group of his colleagues decided to test the idea that atherosclerosis is a disease of modern, affluent life by taking CT scans of ancient human mummies and examining their arteries.

The team started in Egypt, with 52 mummies dating between 3,500 and 2,000 years ago. Biological anthropologist Muhammad Al-Tohamy Soliman of the National Research Center in Giza estimated the age at death for each individual, based on an examination of dental and skeletal development. Then the medical team pored over the scans. Discussing the images during weekly Skype calls, they identified cardiovascular tissue in nearly 85 percent of the mummies. To their surprise, 45 percent of these had definite or probable atherosclerosis—clear evidence that one ancient population suffered from the disease. "We were [also] a bit surprised by just how much atherosclerosis we found in ancient Egyptians who were young," recalls team member James Sutherland, a radiologist at the South Coast Radiologic Medical Group in Laguna Hills, Calif. "The average age of death was around 40."

When their paper came out in the *Journal of the American College of Cardiology* in the spring of 2011, Finch contacted the team immediately, proposing a new explanation for the high levels of atherosclerosis detected in the study. The ancient Egyptians, Finch noted, were no strangers to pestilence and infection. Previous studies showed that many ancient Egyptians were exposed to a wide range of infectious diseases, including malaria, tuberculosis, and schistosomiasis (an ailment caused by tiny parasitic worms found in contaminated water). APOE e4 carriers, with their enhanced immune systems, tended to survive many childhood infections. But they experienced decades' worth of chronic high levels of inflammation in the pathogen-rich environment—levels that are now linked to several deadly diseases of old age, including atherosclerosis and Alzheimer's. Indeed, the arterial plaques that characterize atherosclerosis seem to accumulate during inflammation and wound healing in the vascular wall. "And while it might be pushing it to say the senile plaques of Alzheimer's are some form of scab, like the plaques on artery vessels, they have many of the same components," Finch suggests.

Thomas and his colleagues asked Finch to join their team. Together they decided to gather more data, examining the cardiovascular tissues of ancient mummies from a wide range of cultures. The Egyptians in their first study likely came from affluent upper classes that could afford mummification: such individuals may have exercised rarely and dined frequently on high-calorie foods. So the team expanded the study to other, very different cultures. They examined existing CT scans of ancestral Puebloan mummies from Utah and century-old Unangan mummies from Alaska. In addition, they analyzed the scans they had taken of pre-Hispanic mummies from coastal Peru. Those individuals dated to as early as 1500 B.C.

This past March the team published its findings in the *Lancet*. Among the 137 examined mummies, 34 percent had probable or definite atherosclerosis. Significantly, the scans revealed the disease in all four ancient populations, including the hunting-and-gathering Unangan people, who ate a largely marine diet. The findings clearly challenged the idea that atherosclerosis was a modern disease and pointed to another explanation. "The high level of chronic infection and inflammation in pre-modern conditions might have promoted the inflammatory aspects of atherosclerosis," the team wrote.

Perhaps, Finch says, the ancient gene variant that ramped up our inflammatory response and boosted the chances of our survival to the age of reproduction—APOE e4—came with a steep, deferred cost: heart attacks, strokes, Alzheimer's, and other chronic diseases of aging. In fact, APOE e4 appears to be a classic case of something biologists call antagonistic pleiotropy, in which a gene has a strong positive effect on the young and an adverse impact on the old. "I think these are very intriguing ideas," says Steven Austad, a biologist and gerontologist at the University of Texas Health Science Center at San Antonio. "And what evidence we have supports them."

Refining Immune Response

Research also points to other gene variants that contributed to our longevity. At roughly the same time that *H. sapiens* emerged in Africa some 200,000 years ago, a second major APOE variant emerged. This allele, known as APOE e3, enhanced health among adults in the 40- to 70-year-old range and helped to slow the aging process, and today it has a prevalence of between 60 and 90 percent in human populations. As Finch points out, APOE e3 carriers produce a less vigorous inflammatory response than those with the ancestral variant. Moreover, they appear better adapted to meat- and fat-rich diets. Generally speaking, they have lower blood cholesterol and are less prone to the diseases that strip the old of their vitality: coronary heart disease, cognitive decline, and Alzheimer's. Indeed, carriers of the more recent variant enjoy life expectancies as much as six years longer than their APOE e4 neighbors. "APOE e3," Finch notes, "may have been a factor in the evolution of long life spans."

APOE is not the only gene linked to the evolution of human longevity, however. At U.C. San Diego, Ajit Varki, a professor of medicine, and his colleagues are investigating several other genes that may have undergone changes that boosted our chances of survival and extended our lives. Varki's research focuses on the SIGLEC genes that play key roles related to host defense. These genes express proteins that straddle our cell membranes and act a little like sentries. Their function "is to recognize friends, not foes," Varki explains. It is no easy matter. To fool these sentries, infectious pathogens evolve camouflage consisting of proteins that mimic those borne by "friends."

In 2012, Varki and his team published a study in the *Proceedings of the National Academy of Sciences USA* that identified two key changes in these genes that dated to at least 200,000 to 100,000 years ago and that honed our ability to fight off pathogens. One change produced a new human variant of the ancestral primate gene SIGLEC 17. This variant, however, was nonfunctional. A second event deleted the ancestral gene SIGLEC 13 entirely. To better understand these changes, Varki and his colleagues experimentally resurrected the proteins once expressed by SIGLEC 13 and 17. Both ancestral proteins, they discovered, had been "hacked" by pathogens responsible for two life-threatening infections in babies: group B *Streptococcus* and *E. coli* K1. So as natural selection began weeding out these compromised genes from our genome, the odds of survival rose in human infants.

Such findings add new fuel to the hypothesis that pumped-up immune systems played an important role in lengthening human lives. "Our immune systems went through a lot of changes," Varki says. And as geneticists and biologists continue to investigate the uniquely human part of our genome, many are starting to look for other gene variants and genetic events that contributed to our long lives today.

Yet already the findings are giving some researchers pause for thought. Public health messages have long warned that lifestyle choices such as couch-potato evenings and calorie-rich diets are largely to blame for the high incidence of atherosclerosis, heart attacks, and strokes. But the new research—particularly the studies on ancient mummies—suggests that the picture may not be quite so simple. Our DNA and an overcharged immune system may well contribute to the development of such diseases. "So maybe we have a little less control over atherosclerosis than we thought," muses cardiologist Thompson. "Maybe our mental framework should be shifted." And perhaps, he adds, researchers should be looking for undiscovered risk factors.

The new findings are also raising a fundamental question about human longevity. Can we, or should we, expect the trend toward longer lives to continue? Some scientists have predicted that babies born after 2000 in countries where life expectancy had already been high—including the U.S., Canada, the U.K. and Japan—will live to 100 years of age. Finch is quietly skeptical, however. The emerging trend toward obesity in many human populations and toward environmental deterioration brought about by climate change, he says, could well affect human longevity negatively and throw a major wrench into the works. "I think there is a reason to be cautious about that," Finch concludes. "But time will tell."

In Brief

Humans live far longer than other primates, a phenomenon that has traditionally been credited to modern medicine, food availability and sanitation systems.

But new research suggests that although these factors have extended human life span over the past 200 years, the trend actually began far earlier than that.

As human ancestors ate more meat, they evolved defenses against its attendant pathogens. These defenses contribute to longevity but foster disease later in life.

Critical Thinking

1. How long do chimpanzees live compared to Americans? To what have most researchers attributed our longevity? How do studies of contemporary hunter-gatherer groups contradict this view?

2. What does a study of ancestral remains spanning millions of years tell us about hominin longevity?

3. What can we learn from the 1751 Swedish data?

4. Discuss the health risks our ancestors assumed in becoming hunter-gatherers and, later, in taking on animal husbandry and agriculture.

5. Discuss the ways in which natural selection has resulted in our ability to fight off bacteria, viruses, and other microbes since the evolutionary split with chimpanzees.

6. How is it that the APOE e4 gene seems to have been selected as a way to boost our chances for survival to the age of reproduction and, yet, appears to "double-cross" us later in life?

Create Central

www.mhhe.com/createcentral

Internet References

Evolution and Medicine Network
http://evmedreview.com

The Paleolithic Diet Page
www.paleodiet.com

HEATHER PRINGLE is a Canadian science writer and a contributing correspondent for *Science*.

Article   Prepared by: Elvio Angeloni

Searching for the Human Age

Geologists mine for rock-solid evidence of the Anthropocene.

GAYATHRI VAIDYANATHAN

Learning Outcomes

After reading this article, you will be able to:

- Discuss the notion that we are living in the Anthropocene, or Human Age.

- Discuss the objections to the idea that we are living in the Anthropocene.

Gary Stinchcomb walks into a Paleo-Indian dig site shaded by a canopy of trees in Pennsylvania's Lehigh Gorge State Park. He weaves past holes dug by looters hunting for pieces of human prehistory: knives, scrapers, projectile points.

At a tarp sheltering a 6-foot-deep pit, he stops and climbs into the hole. On the bottom are large boulders left behind by glaciers some 12,000 years ago. It was around that time that Paleo-Indians arrived in this part of the Lehigh Valley.

Stinchcomb, a geologist at Murray State University in Kentucky, is there looking for traces of a more recent past. He is searching for evidence that Earth has entered the Anthropocene, a new epoch defined by the idea that humans have surpassed nature as the primary shapers of the planet.

Scientists are divided over whether to formally recognize the Anthropocene, or the Human Age, as a bona fide geologic time period. To establish a new epoch, geologists usually have to find clear evidence in the rock record of a massive, planet-altering shift. Human-caused change is undeniable, but have we truly become master engineers of the planet?

Stinchcomb believes he's found a way to resolve some of the debate. The clues for humanity's entrance into the Anthropocene, he says, lie in the traces we've left behind in layers of sediment and soil. What's needed is a concerted effort to plot these imprints and use them to show when the epoch of the past 11,500 years, the Holocene, could have yielded to the Anthropocene.

"I think there is a way we can go out and systematically map this stuff," he says. "You need to start building the evidence so everyone can go out and say, 'There it is; that is the Anthropocene boundary.'"

Digging through the Past

Rock and sedimentary layers hold the clues to understanding the major episodes in our planet's 4.6 billion-year history. Take the Mesozoic period, which ended with the massive crash of an asteroid or comet into the Yucatan Peninsula 66 million years ago that is thought to have killed off most dinosaurs. Geologists found the evidence for the Mesozoic's demise in a thin layer of iridium, a rare metal found on asteroids, isolated in the rock record at El Kef, Tunisia. The scientists who found it hammered a golden spike into a hillside to mark the boundary.

Proponents of the Anthropocene theory point out that few corners of the planet have escaped the mark of humanity. Factories, power plants and cars have spewed enough greenhouse gases to change the fundamental chemistry of the atmosphere. The gases trap heat, raising global temperatures. Bulldozers and excavators are now the globe's prime earth movers—more so than rivers, glaciers, wind and volcanoes combined. About one-third of the world's animals are threatened or endangered.

It may be enough to sift through human history, rather than dirt, to find "Year Zero"—the point when the world entered the Human Age. But Stinchcomb thinks that to really lock in the Anthropocene, old-fashioned geology, combined with a bit of archaeology, offers the best hope.

Inside the excavated pit in the Lehigh Valley, he studies the walls. They resemble a layered cake. Each time the river flooded, it threw up a fresh layer of sediment onto the banks. He points to the river's floods, captured in the strata. "The whole sequence is a series of ancient floods, some more extreme than others," Stinchcomb says. "They indirectly reflect what you have around you [at the time of the flood]—whether you've got vegetation cover and what type it is, for instance."

He picks up a trowel and scrapes sediment from a prominent layer near the top. The black contrasts sharply with the dull brown sediments of other floods. Stinchcomb and his colleagues have dated the carbon in the layer to the beginning of the Industrial Revolution in the 1820s. The source? Coal silt.

"It is one of the earliest spots in Pennsylvania where coal mining really took off," Stinchcomb says, pointing at a nearby mountain called Summit Hill. Miners there discovered the Mammoth coal bed in the 1700s and extracted it rapidly, floating the coal down the Lehigh River on flatboats. Some of the material spilled and settled on the riverbed. When the river flooded, it threw coal silt onto the banks.

The resulting coal layer is as clear a geologic mark as a volcanic eruption. Stinchcomb calls it an "anthropogenic event"—a geologic layer caused solely by humans.

If scientists can identify enough of these human-derived layers within the last 10,000 to 12,000 years and zero in on when the most significant ones occurred, that point in time would be a good candidate for the Anthropocene boundary, Stinchcomb says.

Evolution of a New Age

Nobel laureate Paul Crutzen first posed the idea of the Human Age at a geology conference in 2000. He put the birth date of the new epoch at the period after the Industrial Revolution, when humans were causing massive shifts in the biosphere, triggered by coal production. Scientists drilling ice cores out of Greenland have found lead from fly ash, a byproduct of coal combustion, dating back to the era.

Later, William Ruddiman, an emeritus paleo-climatologist at the University of Virginia, placed the origins of the Anthropocene at about 5,000 years ago, when farmers in Southeast Asia were learning to irrigate fields to grow rice. When plants died and decomposed, they released methane, a potent green house gas. Ruddiman theorized that early farmers had released enough methane to warm temperatures globally.

The idea gripped Stinchcomb, who has a background in both archaeology and geology. After seeing Ruddiman lecture on his theory, "I kept asking myself, if people could have altered the climate that early, what else have they done?" he recalls.

Yet another proposal for Year Zero came from a London-based group of scientists and geologists called the Anthropocene Working Group. They suggested the epoch began in the 1950s, when pollutants, plastic and—most notably—radioactive compounds from atomic explosions began accumulating in remote corners of the planet.

The debate over Year Zero intensified. In 2009, Stinchcomb decided to settle the debate the old-fashioned way—with a shovel and a trowel—and began exploring the pits in Lehigh Valley.

Three years later, at the annual meeting of the Geological Society of America, Stinchcomb presented his theory to a standing-room-only crowd: Scientists can map out anthropogenic events captured in sediments in the earth, he said. The events would need to have a clear anthropogenic origin, like the layer of coal in the Lehigh River Valley.

Mapping anthropogenic events from the beginning of the Holocene to today would create a timeline of human impacts on Earth. If anthropogenic events cluster around a particular time period, that would be a strong contender for Year Zero, Stinchcomb told the crowd.

'Ask Me in a Million Years'

Some geologists, however, think it is too early in our species history to declare human dominance over the Earth. University of Cambridge stratigrapher Philip Gibbard, an expert on the Quaternary period encompassing the past 2.6 million years, points out that a pandemic could decimate the population.

Cities would fall and buildings would crumble back into sediment, he says. The climate would reset after a few millennia. The rock record would contain evidence of civilization, but it would only be a brief spike, contained wholly within the Holocene.

To Gibbard, talk of a new Human Age is a bit premature. "Ask me in a million years," he says.

Stinchcomb gets Gibbard's point of view. After all, the layer of coal that Stinchcomb and his colleagues have excavated is very recent compared with the 4.6 billion-year history of the planet.

"I think we have impacted the planet to a degree that is widespread and measurable," he says. "[But] we are definitely not masters of this planet. We are still very much a species vulnerable to natural changes."

Stinchcomb wants to see more scientists map localized anthropogenic events to create a "basket" of markers. With enough evidence from around the world, the debate over the Human Age could finally be settled.

Back in the Lehigh Valley, Stinchcomb follows the river upstream. He comes across a pile of clamshells and broken wine bottles. He plunges a long rod with a scoop at the end, called a split-spoon, into the ground, and brings up red brick. There had been a home here, probably when a coal town thrived nearby. Today, some red dust and debris are all that's left. It was a minuscule moment in time, already taken over by the forest.

Critical Thinking

1. Why are scientists divided over the idea that we are living in the Anthropocene, or Human Age?
2. If there is such a thing, when did it begin and how can it be identified?

Internet References

Journal of Biodiversity & Endangered Species
http://esciencecentral.org/journals/biodiversity-endangered-species.php

NatureServe
http://www.natureserve.org/

Unit 6

UNIT

Prepared by: Elvio Angeloni, *Pasadena City College*

Human Diversity

The field of biological anthropology has come a long way since the days when one of its primary concerns was the classification of human beings according to racial type. Although human diversity is still a matter of major interest in terms of how and why we differ from one another, most anthropologists have concluded that human beings cannot be sorted into sharply distinct entities called "races." Without denying the fact of human variation throughout the world, the prevailing view today is that the differences between us exist along geographical gradients, as differences in degree, rather than in terms of the separate and discrete entities as were perceived in the past.

One of the old ways of looking at human "races" was that each such group was a subspecies of humans that, if left reproductively isolated long enough, would eventually evolve into separate species. While this concept of subspecies, or racial varieties within a species, would seem to apply to some living creatures (such as the dog and wolf or the horse and zebra) and might even be relevant to hominid diversification in the past, the current consensus is that it does not apply today, at least not within the human species.

A more recent attempt to salvage the idea of human races has been to perceive them not so much as reproductively isolated entities, but as many clusters of gene frequencies, separable only by the fact that the proportions of traits (such as skin color, hair form, etc.) differ in each artificially constructed group. Some scientists, such as those who work in the area of forensic physical anthropology, appreciate the practical value of this approach. In a similar manner, our ability to reconstruct human prehistory is dependent upon an understanding of human variation.

Lest anyone think that anthropologists are "in denial" regarding the existence of human races and are merely expressing an anthropological version of political correctness, it should be pointed out that serious, scholarly attempts to classify people in terms of precise, biological units have been going on now for 200 years, and, so far, nothing of scientific value has come of them.

Complicating the matter is the fact that there are actually two concepts of race: the strictly biological one, as described above, and the more popular cultural one, which has been around since time immemorial. These two perspectives have resulted not only in fuzzy thinking about racial biology, but they have led to confusion as to which traits are truly biological in origin and which ones are environmentally and socially influenced. This confusion has infected the way we think about people and, therefore, the way we treat each other in the social arena.

What we should recognize, claim most anthropologists, is that, despite the superficial physical and biological differences between us, when it comes to intelligence, all human beings are basically the same. The degrees of variation within our species may be accounted for by the subtle, and changing, selective forces experienced as one moves from one geographical area to another. However, no matter what the environmental pressures have been, the same intellectual demands have been made upon all of us. This is not to say, of course, that we do not vary from each other as individuals. Rather, what is being said is that when we look at these artificially created groups of people called "races," we find a varying range of intellectual skills within each group. Indeed, even when we look at traits other than intelligence, we find much greater variation within each group than we find between such groups.

It is time, therefore, to put the idea of human "races" to rest, at least as far as science is concerned. If such notions remain in the realm of social discourse, then so be it. That is where the problems associated with notions of race have to be resolved anyway. As one anthropologist, Jonathan Marks, has put it: "You may group humans into a small number of races if you want to, but you are denied biology as a support for it."

Article   Prepared by Elvio Angeloni, *Pasadena City College*

Skin Deep

Throughout the world, human skin color has evolved to be dark enough to prevent sunlight from destroying the nutrient folate but light enough to foster the production of vitamin D.

NINA G. JABLONSKI AND GEORGE CHAPLIN

Learning Outcomes

After reading this article, you will be able to:

- Discuss the general loss of body hair during human evolution.
- Explain why skin color varies among humans

Among primates, only humans have a mostly naked skin that comes in different colors. Geographers and anthropologists have long recognized that the distribution of skin colors among indigenous populations is not random: darker peoples tend to be found nearer the equator, lighter ones closer to the poles. For years, the prevailing theory has been that darker skins evolved to protect against skin cancer. But a series of discoveries has led us to construct a new framework for understanding the evolutionary basis of variations in human skin color. Recent epidemiological and physiological evidence suggests to us that the worldwide pattern of human skin color is the product of natural selection acting to regulate the effects of the sun's ultraviolet (UV) radiation on key nutrients crucial to reproductive success.

From Hirsute to Hairless

The evolution of skin pigmentation is linked with that of hairlessness, and to comprehend both these stories, we need to page back in human history. Human beings have been evolving as an independent lineage of apes since at least seven million years ago, when our immediate ancestors diverged from those of our closest relatives, chimpanzees. Because chimpanzees have changed less over time than humans have, they can provide an idea of what human anatomy and physiology must have been like. Chimpanzees' skin is light in color and is covered by hair over most of their bodies. Young animals have pink faces, hands, and feet and become freckled or dark in these areas only as they are exposed to sun with age. The earliest humans almost certainly had a light skin covered with hair. Presumably hair loss occurred first, then skin color changed. But that leads to the question, When did we lose our hair?

The skeletons of ancient humans—such as the well-known skeleton of Lucy, which dates to about 3.2 million years ago—give us a good idea of the build and the way of life of our ancestors. The daily activities of Lucy and other hominids that lived before about three million years ago appear to have been similar to those of primates living on the open savannas of Africa today. They probably spent much of their day foraging for food over three to four miles before retiring to the safety of trees to sleep.

By 1.6 million years ago, however, we see evidence that this pattern had begun to change dramatically. The famous skeleton of Turkana Boy—which belonged to the species *Homo ergaster*—is that of a long-legged, striding biped that probably walked long distances. These more active early humans faced the problem of staying cool and protecting their brains from overheating. Peter Wheeler of John Moores University in Liverpool, England, has shown that this was accomplished through an increase in the number of sweat glands on the surface of the body and a reduction in the covering of body hair. Once rid of most of their hair, early members of the genus *Homo* then encountered the challenge of protecting their skin from the damaging effects of sunlight, especially UV rays.

Built-In Sunscreen

In chimpanzees, the skin on the hairless parts of the body contains cells called melanocytes that are capable of synthesizing the dark-brown pigment melanin in response to exposure to UV radiation. When humans became mostly hairless, the ability of the skin to produce melanin assumed new importance. Melanin is nature's sunscreen: it is a large organic molecule that Overview/Skin Color Evolution serves the dual purpose of physically and chemically filtering the harmful effects of UV radiation; it absorbs UV rays, causing them to lose energy, and it neutralizes harmful chemicals called free radicals that form in the skin after damage by UV radiation.

Overview/Skin Color Evolution

- After losing their hair as an adaptation for keeping cool, early hominids gained pigmented skins. Scientists initially thought that such pigmentation arose to protect against skin-cancer-causing ultra-violet [UV] radiation.
- Skin cancers tend to arise after reproductive age, however. An alternative theory suggests that dark skin might have evolved primarily to protect against the breakdown of folate, a nutrient essential for fertility and for fetal development.
- Skin that is too dark blocks the sunlight necessary for catalyzing the production of vitamin D, which is crucial for maternal and fetal bones. Accordingly, humans have evolved to be light enough to make sufficient vitamin B yet dark enough to protect their stores of folate.
- As a result of recent human migrations, many people now live in areas that receive more [or less] UV radiation than is appropriate for their skin color.

Anthropologists and biologists have generally reasoned that high concentrations of melanin arose in the skin of peoples in tropical areas because it protected them against skin cancer. James E. Cleaver of the University of California at San Francisco, for instance, has shown that people with the disease xeroderma pigmentosum, in which melanocytes are destroyed by exposure to the sun, suffer from significantly higher than normal rates of squamous and basal cell carcinomas, which are usually easily treated. Malignant melanomas are more frequently fatal, but they are rare (representing 4 percent of skin cancer diagnoses) and tend to strike only light-skinned people. But all skin cancers typically arise later in life, in most cases after the first reproductive years, so they could not have exerted enough evolutionary pressure for skin protection alone to account for darker skin colors. Accordingly, we began to ask what role melanin might play in human evolution.

The Folate Connection

In 1991 one of US (Jablonski) ran across what turned out to be a critical paper published in 1978 by Richard F. Branda and John W. Eaton, now at the University of Vermont and the University of Louisville, respectively. These investigators showed that light-skinned people who had been exposed to simulated strong sunlight had abnormally low levels of the essential B vitamin folate in their blood. The scientists also observed that subjecting human blood serum to the same conditions resulted in a 50-percent loss of folate content within one hour.

The significance of these findings to reproduction—and hence evolution—became clear when we learned of research being conducted on a major class of birth defects by our colleagues at the University of Western Australia. There Fiona J. Stanley and Carol Bower had established by the late 1980s that

folate deficiency in pregnant women is related to an increased risk of neural tube defects such as spina bifida, in which the arches of the spinal vertebrae fail to close around the spinal cord. Many research groups throughout the world have since confirmed this correlation, and efforts to supplement foods with folate and to educate women about the importance of the nutrient have become widespread.

We discovered soon afterward that folate is important not only in preventing neural tube defects but also in a host of other processes. Because folate is essential for the synthesis of DNA in dividing cells, anything that involves rapid cell proliferation, such as spermatogenesis (the production of sperm cells), requires folate. Male rats and mice with chemically induced folate deficiency have impaired spermatogenesis and are infertile. Although no comparable studies of humans have been conducted, Wai Yee Wong and his colleagues at the University Medical Center of Nijmegen in the Netherlands have recently reported that folic acid treatment can boost the sperm counts of men with fertility problems.

Such observations led us to hypothesize that dark skin evolved to protect the body's folate stores from destruction. Our idea was supported by a report published in 1996 by Argentine pediatrician Pablo Lapunzina, who found that three young and otherwise healthy women whom he had attended gave birth to infants with neural tube defects after using sun beds to tan themselves in the early weeks of pregnancy. Our evidence about the breakdown of folate by UV radiation thus supplements what is already known about the harmful (skin-cancer-causing) effects of UV radiation on DNA.

Human Skin on the Move

The earliest members of *Homo sapiens*, or modern humans, evolved in Africa between 120,000 and 100,000 years ago and had darkly pigmented skin adapted to the conditions of UV radiation and heat that existed near the equator. As modern humans began to venture out of the tropics, however, they encountered environments in which they received significantly less UV radiation during the year. Under these conditions their high concentrations of natural sunscreen probably proved detrimental. Dark skin contains so much melanin that very little UV radiation, and specifically very little of the shorter-wavelength UVB radiation, can penetrate the skin. Although most of the effects of UVB are harmful, the rays perform one indispensable function: initiating the formation of vitamin D in the skin. Dark-skinned people living in the tropics generally receive sufficient UV radiation during the year for UVB to penetrate the skin and allow them to make vitamin D. Outside the tropics this is not the case. The solution, across evolutionary time, has been for migrants to northern latitudes to lose skin pigmentation.

The connection between the evolution of lightly pigmented skin and vitamin D synthesis was elaborated by W. Farnsworth Loomis of Brandeis University in 1967. He established the importance of vitamin D to reproductive success because of its role in enabling calcium absorption by the intestines, which in turn makes possible the normal development of the skeleton and the maintenance of a healthy immune system. Research led by

Michael Holick of the Boston University School of Medicine has, over the past 20 years, further cemented the significance of vitamin D in development and immunity. His team also showed that not all sunlight contains enough UVB to stimulate vitamin D production. In Boston, for instance, which is located at about 42 degrees north latitude, human skin cells begin to produce vitamin D only after mid-March. In the wintertime there isn't enough UVB to do the job. We realized that this was another piece of evidence essential to the skin color story.

During the course of our research in the early 1990s, we searched in vain to find sources of data on actual UV radiation levels at the earth's surface. We were rewarded in 1996, when we contacted Elizabeth Weatherhead of the Cooperative Institute for Research in Environmental Sciences at the University of Colorado at Boulder. She shared with us a database of measurements of UV radiation at the earth's surface taken by NASA's Total Ozone Mapping Spectrophotometer satellite between 1978 and 1993. We were then able to model the distribution of UV radiation on the earth and relate the satellite data to the amount of UVB necessary to produce vitamin D.

We found that the earth's surface could be divided into three vitamin D zones: one comprising the tropics, one the subtropics and temperate regions, and the last the circumpolar regions north and south of about 45 degrees latitude. In the first, the dosage of UVB throughout the year is high enough that humans have ample opportunity to synthesize vitamin D all year. In the second, at least one month during the year has insufficient UVB radiation, and in the third area not enough UVB arrives on average during the entire year to prompt vitamin D synthesis. This distribution could explain why indigenous peoples in the tropics generally have dark skin, whereas people in the subtropics and temperate regions are lighter-skinned but have the ability to tan, and those who live in regions near the poles tend to be very light skinned and burn easily.

One of the most interesting aspects of this investigation was the examination of groups that did not precisely fit the predicted skin-color pattern. An example is the Inuit people of Alaska and northern Canada. The Inuit exhibit skin color that is somewhat darker than would be predicted given the UV levels at their latitude. This is probably caused by two factors. The first is that they are relatively recent inhabitants of these climes, having migrated to North America only roughly 5,000 years ago. The second is that the traditional diet of the Inuit is extremely high in foods containing vitamin D, especially fish and marine mammals. This vitamin D-rich diet offsets the problem that they would otherwise have with vitamin D synthesis in their skin at northern latitudes and permits them to remain more darkly pigmented.

Our analysis of the potential to synthesize vitamin D allowed us to understand another trait related to human skin color: women in all populations are generally lighter-skinned than men. (Our data show that women tend to be between 3 and 4 percent lighter than men.) Scientists have often speculated on the reasons, and most have argued that the phenomenon stems from sexual selection—the preference of men for women of lighter color. We contend that although this is probably part of the story, it is not the original reason for the sexual difference. Females have

significantly greater needs for calcium throughout their reproductive lives, especially during pregnancy and lactation, and must be able to make the most of the calcium contained in food. We propose, therefore, that women tend to be lighter-skinned than men to allow slightly more UVB rays to penetrate their skin and thereby increase their ability to produce vitamin D. In areas of the world that receive a large amount of UV radiation, women are indeed at the knife's edge of natural selection, needing to maximize the photoprotective function of their skin on the one hand and the ability to synthesize vitamin D on the other.

Where Culture and Biology Meet

As modern humans moved throughout the Old World about 100,000 years ago, their skin adapted to the environmental conditions that prevailed in different regions. The skin color of the indigenous people of Africa has had the longest time to adapt because anatomically modern humans first evolved there. The skin-color changes that modern humans underwent as they moved from one continent to another—first Asia, then Austro-Melanesia, then Europe and, finally, the Americas—can be reconstructed to some extent. It is important to remember, however, that those humans had clothing and shelter to help protect them from the elements. In some places, they also had the ability to harvest foods that were extraordinarily rich in vitamin D, as in the case of the Inuit. These two factors had profound effects on the tempo and degree of skin-color evolution in human populations.

Africa is an environmentally heterogeneous continent. A number of the earliest movements of contemporary humans outside equatorial Africa were into southern Africa. The descendants of some of these early colonizers, the Khoisan (previously known as Hottentots), are still found in southern Africa and have significantly lighter skin than indigenous equatorial Africans do—a clear adaptation to the lower levels of UV radiation that prevail at the southern extremity of the continent.

Interestingly, however, human skin color in southern Africa is not uniform. Populations of Bantu-language speakers who live in southern Africa today are far darker than the Khoisan. We know from the history of this region that Bantu speakers migrated into this region recently—probably within the past 1,000 years—from parts of West Africa near the equator. The skin-color difference between the Khoisan and Bantu speakers such as the Zulu indicates that the length of time that a group has inhabited a particular region is important in understanding why they have the color they do.

Cultural behaviors have probably also strongly influenced the evolution of skin color in recent human history. This effect can be seen in the indigenous peoples who live on the eastern and western banks of the Red Sea. The tribes on the western side, which speak so-called Nilo-Hamitic languages, are thought to have inhabited this region for as long as 6,000 years. These individuals are distinguished by very darkly pigmented skin and long, thin bodies with long limbs, which are excellent biological adaptations for dissipating heat and intense UV radiation. In contrast, modern agricultural and pastoral groups on the eastern bank of the Red Sea, on the Arabian Peninsula, have lived there for only about 2,000 years. These earliest Arab people, of European origin, have adapted to very similar environmental conditions by almost exclusively cultural means—wearing heavy protective clothing and devising portable shade in the form of tents. (Without such clothing, one would have expected their skin to have begun to darken.) Generally speaking, the more recently a group has migrated into an area, the more extensive its cultural, as opposed to biological, adaptations to the area will be.

Perils of Recent Migrations

Despite great improvements in overall human health in the past century, some diseases have appeared or reemerged in populations that had previously been little affected by them. One of these is skin cancer, especially basal and squamous cell carcinomas, among light-skinned peoples. Another is rickets, brought about by severe vitamin D deficiency, in dark-skinned peoples. Why are we seeing these conditions?

As people move from an area with one pattern of UV radiation to another region, biological and cultural adaptations have not been able to keep pace. The light-skinned people of northern European origin who bask in the sun of Florida or northern Australia increasingly pay the price in the form of premature aging of the skin and skin cancers, not to mention the unknown cost in human life of folate depletion. Conversely, a number of dark-skinned people of southern Asian and African origin now living in the northern U.K., northern Europe or the northeastern U.S. suffer from a lack of UV radiation and vitamin D, an insidious problem that manifests itself in high rates of rickets and other diseases related to vitamin D deficiency.

The ability of skin color to adapt over long periods to the various environments to which humans have moved reflects the importance of skin color to our survival. But its unstable nature also makes it one of the least useful characteristics in determining the evolutionary relations between human groups. Early Western scientists used skin color improperly to delineate human races, but the beauty of science is that it can and does correct itself. Our current knowledge of the evolution of human skin indicates that variations in skin color, like most of our physical attributes, can be explained by adaptation to the environment through natural selection. We look ahead to the day when the vestiges of old scientific mistakes will be erased and replaced by a better understanding of human origins and diversity. Our variation in skin color should be celebrated as one of the most visible manifestations of our evolution as a species.

More to Explore

The Evolution of Human Skin Coloration. Nina G. Jablonski and George Chaplin in *Journal of Human Evolution,* vol. 39, no. 1, pages 57–106; July 1, 2000. An abstract of the article is available online at www.idealibrary.com/links/doi/10.1006/jhev.2000.0403.

Why Skin Comes in Colors. Blake Edgar in *California Wild,* vol. 53, no. 1, pages 6–7; Winter 2000. The article is also

available at www.calacademy.org/calwild/winter2000/html/horizons.html.

The Biology of Skin Color: Black and White. Gina Kirchweger in *Discover,* vol. 22, no. 2, pages 32–33; February 2001. The article is also available at www.discover.com/feb_01/featbiology.html.

Critical Thinking

1. Why did our ancestors lose most of their body hair? What was the resulting challenge?

2. What is the function of melanin?

3. What is the relationship between light skin, exposure to the sun, and skin cancer? Why is this insufficient to explain darker skin colors?

4. Discuss the evidence that relates skin color to folate deficiency.

5. How do the authors describe the earliest member of *Homo sapiens,* or modern humans in this context? Why would skin color become lighter as people moved out of the tropics? How is vitamin D production important to health?

6. Discuss the three vitamin D zones on the earth's surface and how they help to explain skin color variations.

7. Why don't the Inuit precisely fit the predicted skin color pattern?

8. Why do women tend to be lighter skinned than men?

9. What two factors have had profound effects on the tempo and degree of skin color evolution in human populations? Give some examples.

10. Discuss the "perils of recent migrations" and the examples cited.

11. Why is skin color unreliable as a means to delineate human races?

12. Why should we celebrate our variation in skin color?

Create Central

www.mhhe.com/createcentral

Internet References

Ethnic and Racial Studies
www.tandfonline.com/rers

Journal of Human Evolution
www.journals.elsevier.com/journal-of-human-evolution

NINA G. JABLONSKI and **GEORGE CHAPLIN** work at the California Academy of Sciences in San Francisco, where Jablonski is Irvine Chair and curator of anthropology and Chaplin is a research associate in the department of anthropology. Jablonski's research centers on the evolutionary adaptations of monkeys, apes and humans. She is particularly interested in how primates have responded to changes over time in the global environment. Chaplin is a private geographic information systems consultant who specializes in describing and analyzing geographic trends in biodiversity. In 2001 he was awarded the Student of the Year prize by the Association of Geographic Information in London for his master's thesis on the environmental correlates of skin color.

Jablonski, Nina G.; Chaplin, George. From *Scientific American*, October 2002, pp. 75–81. Copyright © 2002 by Scientific American, a division of Nature America, Inc. All rights reserved. Reprinted by permission.

Article   Prepared by Elvio Angeloni, *Pasadena City College*

How Real Is Race?
Using Anthropology to Make Sense of Human Diversity

Race is not a scientifically valid biological category, and yet it remains important as a socially constructed category. Once educators grasp this concept, they can use the suggestions and resources the authors offer here to help their students make sense of race.

Carol Mukhopadhyay and Rosemary C. Henze

Learning Outcomes

After reading this article, you will be able to:

- Discuss whether the human species can be subdivided into racial categories and support your position.

- Explain how and why the concept of race developed.

- Discuss both the positive and negative aspects of racial classification.

Surely we've all heard people say there is only one race—the human race. We've also heard and seen overwhelming evidence that would seem to contradict this view. After all, the U.S. Census divides us into groups based on race, and there are certainly observable physical differences among people—skin color, nose and eye shape, body type, hair color and texture, and so on. In the world of education, the message of racial differences as biological "facts" is reinforced when we are told that we should understand specific learning styles and behavior patterns of black, Asian, Native American, white, and Latino children and when books such as *The Bell Curve* make pseudoscientific claims about race and learning.[1]

How can educators make sense of these conflicting messages about race? And why should they bother? Whether we think of all human beings as one race, or as four or five distinct races, or as hundreds of races, does anything really change? If we accept that the concept of race is fundamentally flawed, does that mean that young African Americans are less likely to be followed by security guards in department stores? Are people going to stop thinking of Asians as the "model" minority? Will racism become a thing of the past?

Many educators understandably would like to have clear information to help them teach students about human biological

variability. While multicultural education materials are now widely available, they rarely address basic questions about why we look different from one another and what these biological differences do (and do not) mean. Multicultural education emphasizes respecting differences and finding ways to include all students, especially those who have been historically marginalized. Multicultural education has helped us to understand racism and has provided a rich body of literature on antiracist teaching strategies, and this has been all to the good. But it has not helped us understand the two concepts of race: the biological one and the social one.

In this article, we explain what anthropologists mean when they say that "races don't exist" (in other words, when they reject the concept of race as a scientifically valid biological category) and why they argue instead that "race" is a socially constructed category. We'll also discuss why this is such an important understanding and what it means for educators and students who face the social reality of race and racism every day. And finally, we'll offer some suggestions and resources for teachers who want to include teaching about race in their classes.

Why Race Isn't Biologically Real

For the past several decades, biological anthropologists have been arguing that races don't really exist, or, more precisely, that the concept of race has no validity as a biological category. What exactly does this mean?

First, anthropologists are unraveling a deeply embedded ideology, a long-standing European and American racial world view.[2] Historically, the idea of race emerged in Europe in the 17th and 18th centuries, coinciding with the growth of colonialism and the transatlantic slave trade. Attempts were made to classify humans into "natural," geographically distinct "races," hierarchically ordered by their closeness to God's original forms. Europeans were, not surprisingly, at the top, with the most perfect form represented by a female skull from the Caucasus Mountains, near the purported location of Noah's ark and the origin of humans. Hence the origins of the racial term "Caucasian" or "Caucasoid" for those of European ancestry.[3]

In the late 19th century, anthropologists sought to reconstruct human prehistory and trace the evolution of human cultural institutions. Physical and cultural evolution were seen as moving in tandem; "advances" in human mental capacity were thought to be responsible for human cultural inventions, such as marriage, family, law, and agriculture. If cultural "evolution" was propelled by biological evolution, according to this logic, the more "advanced" cultures must be more biologically and intellectually evolved. Physical indicators of evolutionary rank, such as skull size, were sought in order to classify and rank human groups along an evolutionary path from more "primitive" to more "advanced" races.

Nineteenth-century European scientists disagreed on when the "races" began. Theologians had long argued that there was "one human origin," Adam and Eve, and that certain races subsequently "degenerated" (predictably, the non-Europeans). Some evolutionary scientists, however, began to argue for multiple origins, with distinct races evolving in different places and times. By the beginning of the 20th century, European and American science viewed races as natural, long-standing divisions of the human species, evolving at different rates biologically and hence culturally. By such logic was racial inequality naturalized and legitimized.

When contemporary scientists, including anthropologists, assert that races are not scientifically valid, they are rejecting at least three fundamental premises of this old racial ideology: 1) the archaic subspecies concept, 2) the divisibility of contemporary humans into scientifically valid biological groupings, and 3) the link between racial traits and social, cultural, and political status.

1. *There were no distinct, archaic human subspecies.* The first premise anthropologists reject is that humans were originally divided, by nature or God, into a small set of biologically distinct, fixed species, subspecies, or races. Anthropologists now know conclusively, from fossil and DNA evidence, that contemporary humans are one variable species, with our roots in Africa, which moved out of Africa into a wide range of environments around the world, producing hundreds, perhaps thousands, of culturally and genetically distinct populations. Local populations, through natural selection as well as random genetic mutation, acquired some distinctive genetic traits, such as shovel-shaped incisor teeth, hairy ears, or red hair. Adaptation to human cultural inventions—such as agriculture, which creates concentrations of water that allow malaria-carrying mosquitoes to breed—also produced higher frequencies of sickle-cell genes (related to malaria resistance) in human populations in some parts of Africa, India, Arabia, and the Mediterranean.[4] At the same time, continuous migration and intermating between local populations prevented us from branching off into distinct subspecies or species and instead created a richer and more variable gene pool, producing new combinations and permutations of the human genome.

Human prehistory and history, then, are a continuing story of fusion and fission, of a myriad of populations, emerging and shifting over time and space, sometimes isolated temporarily, then fusing and producing new formations. There have been thousands and thousands of groups throughout human history, marrying in and, more often, out; they have disappeared and reemerged in new forms over time.

In short, there are no "basic" or "ancient" races; there are no stable, "natural," permanent, or even long-standing groupings called races. There have never have been any "pure" races. All human populations are historically specific mixtures of the human gene pool. This is human evolution, and we see these same processes at work in the 19th and 20th centuries and today. "Races" are ephemeral—here today, gone tomorrow.

2. *Contemporary humans are not divisible into biological races.* When anthropologists say races aren't biologically real, they also reject the idea that *modern* humans can be divided into scientifically valid, biologically distinct groupings or races. For races to be real as biological categories, the classification must be based on objective, consistent, and reliable biological criteria. The classification system must also have predictive value that will make it useful in research.

Scientists have demonstrated that both the concept of race and racial criteria are subjective, arbitrary, and inconsistently applied.[5] U.S. racial categories, such as the ones used in the Census, aren't valid in part because the biological attributes used to define races and create racial classifications rely on only a few visible, superficial, genetic traits—such as skin color and hair texture—and ignore the remaining preponderance of human variation. Alternative, equally visible racial classifications could be constructed using such criteria as hair color, eye color, height, weight, ear shape, or hairiness. However, there are less visible genetic traits that have far greater biological significance. For example, there are at least 13 genetic factors related to hemoglobin, the protein that helps carry oxygen to tissues, and there is also significant variation in the ABO, RH, and other blood systems. We could create racial classifications based on genetic factors that affect susceptibility to diabetes or to certain kinds of breast cancer or to the ability to digest milk. In sum, given the variety of possible biologically based traits for classifying human beings, the criteria used in U.S. racial categorizations are highly arbitrary and subjective. Our discussion here focuses on the U.S. concept of race. While racial concepts are no doubt similar in Canada and Europe, this is not true in other parts of the Americas.[6]

The number of potential biologically based racial groupings is enormous. Not only are there millions of genetic traits, but most genetic traits—even culturally salient but superficial traits such as skin color, hair texture, eye shape, and eye color—do not cluster together. Darker skin can cluster with straight hair as well as with very curly hair or with hairy or nonhairy bodies; paler skin can cluster with straight or curly hair or with black or blond hair or with lighter to darker eyes. Each trait could produce a different racial classification. For example, if one used height as a criterion rather than skin pigmentation, then the Northern Afghan population would be in the same racial category as the Swedes and the Tutsi of Rwanda. There are huge numbers of genetically influenced traits, visible and non-visible, which could be used to classify humans into biologically distinct groups. There is no "natural" classification—no co-occurring clusters of racial traits. There are just alternatives, with different implications and uses.

Racial classifications are also unscientific because they are unreliable and unstable over time. Individuals cannot reliably be "raced," partly because the criteria are so subjective and unscientific. Robert Hahn, a medical anthropologist, found that 37% of babies described as Native American on their birth certificates ended up in a different racial category on their death certificates.[7] Racial identifications by forensic anthropologists, long touted as accurate, have been shown to be disturbingly unreliable, even in relatively ethnically homogeneous areas, such as Missouri and Ohio.[8] Forensic evidence from such urban areas as San Jose, California, or New York City is even more problematic.

Racial categories used by the U.S. Census Bureau have changed over time. In 1900, races included "mulatto, quadroon, or octoroon" in addition to "black." Southern Europeans and Jews were deemed to be separate races before World War II. Asian Indians ("Hindus") were initially categorized as "Caucasoid"—except for voting rights. The number and definitions of races in the most recent U.S. Census reflect the instability—and hence unreliability—of the concept of race. And U.S. racial classifications simply don't work in much of the rest of the world. Brazil is a classic, often-studied example, but they also don't work in South Asia, an area that includes over one-fifth of the world's population.

Historical and contemporary European and American racial categories are huge, biologically diverse macro-categories. Members of the same racial group tend to be similar in a few genetic ways that are often biologically irrelevant. Moreover, the genetic variability found within each racial grouping is far greater than the genetic similarity. Africa, by itself, is home to distinct populations whose average height ranges from less than five feet (the Mbuti) to over six feet (the Tutsi). Estimates suggest that contemporary racial variation accounts for less than 7% of all human genetic variation.[9] U.S. races, then, are not biologically distinct or biologically meaningful, scientifically based groupings of the human species.

3. *Race as biology has no scientific value.* An additional critique of the concept of race is that racial categories, as defined biologically, are not very useful in understanding other phenomena, whether biological or cultural.

There is no substantial evidence that race, as a biological category, and "racial" characteristics, such as skin color, hair texture, and eye shape, are causally linked to behavior, to capacities, to individual and group accomplishments, to cultural institutions, or to propensities to engage in any specific activities. In the area of academic achievement, the focus on race as biology can lead researchers to ignore underlying nonbiological causal factors. One classic study found that controlling for socioeconomic and other environmental variables eliminated purported "racial" differences in I.Q. scores and academic achievement between African American, Mexican American, and European American students.[10]

Health professionals have also critiqued the concept of race. Alan Goodman and others have shown that race does not help physicians with diagnosis, prevention, or treatment of medical diseases.[11] Racial categories and a false ideology of race as "biology" encourage both doctors and their patients to view medical conditions as necessarily genetic, ignoring possible environmental sources. Hypertension, infant birthweights, osteoporosis, ovarian cysts—all traditionally viewed as "racial" (i.e., genetically based)—now seem to reflect environmental rather than racially linked genetic factors. The Centers for Disease Control concluded in 1993 that most associations between race and disease have no genetic or biological basis and that the concept of "race" is therefore not useful in public health.

As a result of recent evolution and constant interbreeding between groups of humans, two individuals from different "races" are just as likely to be more similar to one another genetically than two individuals from the same "race." This being so, race-as-biology has no predictive value.

If Not Race, Then What?

Classifications are usually created for some purpose. Alan Goodman and other biological anthropologists suggest that investigators focus on using traits relevant to the problem at hand. For example, if a particular blood factor puts an individual at risk for a disease, then classify individuals on that basis for that purpose.

Some suggest using the term "population" or "breeding population" to refer to the multitude of small, often geographically localized, groups that have developed high frequencies of one or more somewhat distinctive biological traits (e.g., shovel-shaped incisors) in response to biological, historical, and cultural factors. But others point out that there could be thousands of such groups, depending on the classifying criteria used, and that the groups would be merging and recombining over time and space. Moreover, the variability "captured" would reflect only a fraction of the variability in the human species.

Most anthropologists now use the concept of "clines" to help understand how genetic traits are distributed.[12] New data indicate that biological traits, such as blood type or skin color, are distributed in geographic gradations or "clines"; that is, the frequency of a trait varies continuously over a geographic area. For example, the genes for type B blood increase in frequency in an east-to-west direction (reflecting, in part, the travels of Genghis Khan and his army). In contrast, skin pigmentation grades from north to south, with increasing pigmentation as one gets closer to the equator. The frequency of the gene for sickle cell decreases from West Africa moving northeast.

Virtually all traits have distinct geographic distributions. Genes controlling skin color, body size and shape (head, limbs, lips, fingers, nose, ears), hairiness, and blood type are each distributed in different patterns over geographic space. Once again, for biological races to exist, these traits would have to co-vary, but they don't. Instead, biological traits produce a nearly infinite number of potential races. This is why anthropologists conclude that there are no scientifically distinguishable biological races—only thousands of clines!

So What Is Race Then?

We hope we have made the point that the concept of separate, biologically distinct human races is not scientifically defensible. Unfortunately, racial ideology, by focusing on a few physical attributes, traps us into a discourse about race as biology rather than race as a cultural construction. The concept of race is a cultural invention, a culturally and historically specific way of thinking about, categorizing, and treating human beings.[13] It is about social divisions within society, about social categories and identities, about power and privilege. It has been and remains a particular type of ideology for legitimizing social inequality between groups with different ancestries, national origins, and histories. Indeed, the concept of race is also a major system of social identity, affecting one's own self-perception and how one is perceived and treated by others.

But race does have a biological component, one that can trick us into thinking that races are scientifically valid, biological subdivisions of the human species. As noted earlier, geographically localized populations—as a result of adaptation, migration, and chance—tend to have some characteristic physical traits. While these may be traits that characterize an entire population, such as hairy ears, it is more accurate to talk about the relative frequency of a particular trait, such as blood type O, in one population as compared to another, or the relative amount of pigmentation of individuals in a population, relative to other populations. Some traits, such as skin color, reflect climatic conditions; others, such as eye color and shape, probably reflect random, historical processes and migration patterns. The U.S. was peopled by populations from geographically distinct regions of the world—voluntary immigrants, forced African slaves, and indigenous American groups. Therefore, dominant northwestern European ethnic groups, such as the English and Germans, were able to exploit certain visually salient biological traits, especially skin color, as markers of race.

The effectiveness of these physical traits as markers of one's race depended, of course, on their being preserved in future generations. So dominant cultural groups created elaborate social and physical barriers to mating, reproduction, and marriage that crossed racial lines. The most explicit were the so-called anti-miscegenation laws, which outlawed sex between members of different races, whether married or not. These laws were not declared unconstitutional by the U.S. Supreme Court until the 1967 case of *Loving v. Virginia.*[14] Another vehicle was the cultural definition of kinship, whereby children of interracial (often forced) matings acquired the racial status of their lower-ranking parent; this was the so-called one-drop rule or hypodescent. Especially during the time of slavery, the lower-ranking parent was generally the mother, and thus the long-standing European cultural tradition of affiliating socially "legitimate" children with the father's kinship group was effectively reversed.

In contrast, there have been fewer social or legal barriers in the U.S. to mating and marriage between Italians, British, Germans, Swedes, and others of European ancestry. Consequently, the physical and cultural characteristics of European regional populations are less evident in the U.S. With intermarriage, distinct European identities were submerged in the culturally relevant macroracial category of "white"—more accurately, European American.

Thus even the biological dimension of contemporary racial groupings is the result of sociocultural processes. That is, humans as cultural beings first gave social significance to some physical differences between groups and then tried to perpetuate these "racial markers" by preventing social and physical intercourse between members of the groups. Although the dominant racial ideology was about maintaining racial "purity," the issue was not about biology; it was about maintaining social, political, and economic privilege.[15]

Why Is This Understanding Important for Educators?

We hope we've convinced you that race isn't biologically "real" and that race in the U.S. and elsewhere is a historical, social, and cultural creation. But so what? What is the significance of this way of viewing race for teachers, students, and society?

1. *The potential for change.* First, it is important to understand that, while races are biological fictions, they are social realities. Race may not be "real" in a biological sense, but it surely is "real" socially, politically, economically, and psychologically. Race and racism profoundly structure who we are, how we are treated, how we treat others, and our access to resources and rights.

Perhaps the most important message educators can take from the foregoing discussion is that race, racial classifications, racial stratification, and other forms of racism, including racial ideology, rather than being part of our biology, are part of our culture. Like other cultural forms, both the concept of race and our racial classifications are part of a system we have created. This means that we have the ability to change the system, to transform it, and even to totally eradicate it. Educators, in their role as transmitters of official culture, are particularly well poised to be active change agents in such a transformation.

But how, you may well ask, can teachers or anybody else make people stop classifying by race? And are there any good reasons to do so? These familiar categories—black, white, Asian, Native American, and so on—seem so embedded in U.S. society. They seem so "natural." Of course, that's how culture works. It seems "natural" to think of chicken, but not rats, as food. But, as we have shown above, the labels and underlying constructs that we use to talk about human diversity are unstable, depending on particular social, political, and historical contexts. Individuals in positions of authority, of course, have the ability to change them institutionally. But ordinary people also have the ability to change how they classify and label people in their everyday lives.

Several questions arise at this point. Do we as educators consciously want to change our way of conceptualizing and discussing human biological variation? What makes the "race as biology" assumption so dangerous? Are we going to continue to classify people by race, even while recognizing that it is a social construct? What vested interests do people have in holding onto—or rejecting—racial categories? How can we become more sophisticated in our understanding of how systems of classification work while also becoming more critical of our own ways of classifying people? Are there alternative ways of thinking about, classifying, and labeling human beings that might be more empowering for students, teachers, and community members? By eliminating or changing labels, will we change the power structures that perpetuate privilege and entitlement? Moving beyond race as biology forces us to confront these and other issues.

2. *The dangers of using racial classifications.* Categories and classifications are not intrinsically good or bad. People have always grouped others in ways that were important within a given society. However, the myth of race as biology is dangerous because it conflates physical attributes, such as skin color, with unrelated qualities, such as intelligence. Racial labels delude people into thinking that race predicts such other outcomes and behaviors as achievement in sports, music, or school; rates of employment; pregnancies outside marriage; or drug use. Race was historically equated with intelligence and, on that basis, was used to justify slavery and educational discrimination; it later provided the rationale that supported the genocide of Jews, blacks, Gypsies, and other "inferior" races under Hitler. So using racial categories brings along this history, like unwanted baggage.

Macroracial categories are dangerous in that the categories oversimplify and mask complex human differences. Saying that someone is Asian tells us virtually nothing concrete, but it brings with it a host of stereotypes, such as "model minority," "quiet," "good at math," "inscrutable," and so on. Yet the Asian label includes a wide range of groups, such as Koreans, Filipinos, and Vietnamese, with distinct histories and languages. The same is true for "white," a term that homogenizes the multiple nationalities, languages, and cultures that constitute Europe. The label "African American" ignores the enormous linguistic, physical, and cultural diversity of the peoples of Africa. The term "black" conflates people of African descent who were brought to the U.S. as slaves with recent immigrants from Africa and the Caribbean. These macroracial labels oversimplify and reduce human diversity to four or five giant groups. Apart from being bad science, these categories don't predict anything helpful—yet they have acquired a life of their own.

Macroracial categories, such as those used in the U.S. Census and other institutional data-collection efforts, force people to use labels that may not represent their own self-identity or classifying system. They must either select an existing category or select "other"—by definition, a kind of nonidentity. The impossibility, until recently, of selecting more than one ethnic/racial category implicitly stigmatizes multiracial individuals. And the term "mixed" wrongly implies that there are such things as "pure" races, an ideology with no basis in science. The recent expansion of the number of U.S. Census categories still cannot accommodate the diversity of the U.S. population, which includes people whose ancestry ranges from Egypt, Brazil, Sri Lanka, Ghana, and the Dominican Republic to Iceland and Korea.

3. *How macroracial categories have served people in positive ways.* Having noted some negative aspects, it is equally important to discuss how macroracial categories also serve society. Recall that labels are not intrinsically "good" or "bad." It depends on what people do with them. During the 1960s, the U.S. civil rights movement helped bring about consciousness and pride in being African American. This consciousness—known by terms such as ethnic pride and black power—united people who had been the victims of racism and oppression. From that consciousness sprang such educational interventions as black and Chicano history classes, ethnic studies departments, Afrocentric schools, and other efforts to empower young people. The movement to engender pride in and knowledge of one's ancestry has had a powerful impact. Many individuals are deeply attached to these racial labels as part of a positive identity. As one community activist put it, "Why should I give up being a race? I like being a race."

Racial classification can also have positive impact by allowing educators to monitor how equitably our institutions are serving the public. Racial categories are used by schools to disaggregate data on student outcomes, including achievement, attendance, discipline, course placements, college attendance rates, and other areas of school and student performance. These data are then used to examine whether certain groups of students are disproportionately represented in any outcome areas. For example, a school might discover that the percentage of Latino students who receive some type of disciplinary intervention is higher than that for other school populations. The school can then consider what it can do to change this outcome. Teachers might ask, Is there something about the way Latino students are treated in the school that leads to higher disciplinary referral rates? What other factors might be involved?

The racial classifications that educators use to monitor student outcome data reflect our society's social construction of race. As such, the categories represent groups that have been historically disenfranchised, oppressed, or marginalized. Without data disaggregated by race, gender, and other categories, it would be difficult to identify problems stemming from race-based institutional and societal factors that privilege certain groups, such as the widespread U.S. practice of tracking by so-called ability. Without data broken out according to racial, gender, and ethnic categories, schools would not be able to assess the positive impact intervention programs have had on different groups of students.

4. *Shifting the conversation from biology to culture.* One function of the myth of race as biology has been to distract us from the underlying causes of social inequality in the United States. Dismantling the myth of race as biology means that we must now shift our focus to analyzing the social, economic, political, and historical conditions that breed and serve to perpetuate social inequality. For educators, this means helping students to recognize and understand socioeconomic stratification, who benefits and who is harmed by racial discrimination, and how we as individuals and institutional agents can act to dismantle ideologies, institutions, and practices that harm young people.

There is another, more profound implication of the impermanence of race. Culture, acting collectively, and humans, acting individually, can make races disappear. That is, we can mate and marry across populations, thus destroying the racial "markers" that have been used to facilitate categorization and differential treatment of people of different ancestry and social rank. An understanding of human biological variation reveals the positive, indeed essential, role that intermating and intermarriage have played in human evolution and human adaptation. Rather than "mongrelizing" a "pure species," mating between different populations enriches the genetic pool. It is society, rather than nature—and socially and economically stratified societies, for the most part—that restricts social and sexual intercourse and severely penalizes those who mate across racial and other socially created lines.

Suggestions and Resources for Educators

Anthropological knowledge about race informs us about what race is and is not, but it cannot guide educational decision making. The underlying goal of social justice can help educators in making policy decisions, such as whether to use racial and ethnic categories to monitor educational outcomes. As long as we continue to see racially based disparities in young peoples' school achievement, then we must monitor and investigate the social conditions that produce these disparities. We must be careful, however, to avoid "biologizing" the classification; that is, we must avoid assuming genetic explanations for racial differences in behaviors and educational outcomes or even diseases.

As we pursue a more socially just world, educators should also continue to support young people's quest for knowledge about the history and struggles of their own people, as well as those of other groups, so that students in the future will not be able to point to their textbooks and say, "My people are not included in the curriculum." In the process, we can encourage both curiosity about and respect for human diversity, and we can emphasize the importance that historical and social context plays in creating social inequality. We can also encourage comparative studies of racial and other forms of social stratification, further challenging the notion that there is a biological explanation for oppression and inequality. In short, students will understand that there is no biological explanation for a group's historical position as either oppressed—or oppressor. We can encourage these studies to point out variations and fine distinctions within human racial groupings.

In addition to viewing the treatment of race and racial categories through a social-justice lens, we would apply another criterion that we call "depth of knowledge." We believe that it is important to challenge and inspire young people by exposing them to the best of our current knowledge in the sciences, social sciences, and other disciplines. Until now, most students in our education system have not been exposed to systematic, scientifically based teaching about race and human biological variation. One reason is that many social studies teachers may think they lack sufficient background in genetics and human biology. At the same time, many biology teachers may feel uncomfortable teaching about race as a social construct. The null move for teachers seems to be to say that we should all be "color

blind." However, this does not help educate students about human diversity, both biological and social. In rare cases when students have the opportunity to engage in studies of race, ethnicity, culture, and ways to end racism, they are both interested and intellectually challenged.[16] One high school teacher who teaches students about race said he wants to dispel the notion that teaching about diversity is "touchy feely." "We don't just want to touch diversity; we want to approach it academically. . . . We feel we have a definite discipline."[17]

Rather than shield students and ourselves from current scientific knowledge about race, including its contradictions and controversies, we submit that educators should be providing opportunities for students to learn what anthropologists, geneticists, and other scientists, including social scientists, have to say about human biological variation and the issue of race. Particularly in middle schools, high schools, and beyond, students should be involved in inquiry projects and social action projects, in critical examination of the labels we currently use, and in analysis of the reasons for and against using them in particular contexts. Rather than tell students that they should or should not use racial labels (except for slurs), educators should be creating projects in which students explore together the range of possible ways of classifying people and the implications and political significance of alternative approaches in different contexts.

We would like to conclude by offering readers some ideas for student inquiry and by suggesting some resources that can serve to get teachers in all subject areas started on the quest to learn about human biological variation and ways to teach about it.

1. *Ideas for student inquiry.* Here are some examples of how teachers might engage students in critically examining the social, historical, and cultural construction of racial categories.

- Have students create and employ alternative "racial" classification schemes using as many observable and nonobservable physical differences as they can think of (e.g., foot size, height, ear shape, eyebrow shape, waist/shoulder ratio, hairiness). What do the groups look like? What does this tell us about macroracial classifications based on skin pigmentation and other surface features?
- Show students U.S. Census forms from 1870, 1950, and 2000, and ask them to place themselves in the most appropriate category.[18] Or show a photograph of a person of multiple ethnic ancestry and ask students to place this person in one of the categories from these three censuses. Ask them why they think the census form has changed over time and what that says about the meaning of "race."
- Ask immigrant students to investigate the racial/ethnic categories used in their country of origin and to reflect on how well they mesh with the U.S. categories. For example, have students from Mexico taken on an identity as Latino or Hispanic? And what does it mean for them to become part of a larger "macro" race in the U.S.?[19]
- Ask students how they feel when someone asks them to "represent their race." For example, how do students

who identify themselves as African Americans feel when someone asks, "How do African Americans feel about this issue?" or "What's the African American perspective on this?"

- Discuss "reverse discrimination." When did this term come into use and why? Who is being discriminated against when discrimination is reversed?
- Discuss "political correctness." Where did this term come from? Who uses it and for what purposes? And why did it emerge?

2. *Resources for teachers.* The following examples will give readers a place to start in compiling resources available for teaching about race.

- Two major anthropological associations have produced highly readable position statements on the topic of race and human biological variation. First, the American Anthropological Association website features both the AAA position and a summary of testimony given in conjunction with the debates on the 2000 census categories. Second, the official statement of the American Association of Physical Anthropologists has appeared in that organization's journal.[20]
- The American Anthropological Association is making a special effort to disseminate understandings about race and human variation to the broader public. *AnthroNotes,* designed for precollege teachers, is a superb resource that offers concrete approaches to teaching about race, human diversity, and human evolution. It is available at no charge from the Anthropology Outreach Office (anthroutreach@nmnh.si.edu). Several past issues of *AnthroNotes* treat race and ethnicity.[21] Anthropologists have produced materials for precollege teachers and teacher educators that deal with cultural diversity; some include strategies for teaching about culture and human diversity.[22] Others provide useful overviews of relevant topics.[23]
- The AAA is currently engaged in a public education initiative called Understanding Race and Human Variation, which will involve a traveling museum exhibit and a website. The Ford Foundation has contributed one million dollars to this project.
- In 1999, the AAA created a special commission called the Anthropology Education Commission (AEC) to "help achieve significant progress towards the integration of anthropological concepts, methods, and issues into pre-K through community college and adult education as a means of increasing public understanding of anthropology." The two teaching modules by Leonard Lieberman and by Lieberman and Patricia Rice, which we cited above, are available at no charge on the AEC website (www.aaanet.org/committees/commissions/aec). The AEC webpage contains extensive resources that teachers can use to teach anthropological concepts and methods, including some that address race.

Anthropologists recognize an obligation to disseminate their knowledge of human biological variation and the social construction of race to the wider public. We hope that this article and the resources we have provided will contribute to this effort.

Notes

1. Richard Herrnstein and Charles Murray, *The Bell Curve: Intelligence and Class Structure in American Life* (New York: Free Press, 1994).

2. Audrey Smedley, *Race in North America: Origin and Evolution of a Worldview* (Boulder, Colo.: Westview Press, 1998).

3. Jonathan Marks, *Human Biodiversity: Genes, Race, and History* (New York: Aldine de Gruyter, 1995).

4. Leonard Lieberman and Patricia Rice, "Races or Clines?," p. 7, available on the Anthropology Education Commission page of the American Anthropological Association website, www.aaanet.org/committees/commissions/aec—click on Teaching About Race.

5. George J. Armelagos and Alan H. Goodman, "Race, Racism, and Anthropology," in Alan H. Goodman and Thomas L. Leatherman, eds., *Building a New Biocultural Synthesis: Political-Economic Perspectives on Human Biology* (Ann Arbor: University of Michigan Press, 1998).

6. Jeffrey M. Fish, "Mixed Blood," in James Spradley and William McCurdy, eds., *Conformity and Conflict,* 11th ed. (New York: Allyn & Bacon, 2002), pp. 270–80.

7. Alan Goodman, "Bred in the Bone?," *Sciences,* vol. 37, no. 2, 1997, p. 24.

8. Ibid., p. 22.

9. Leonard Lieberman, "'Race' 1997 and 2001: A Race Odyssey," available on the Anthropology Education Commission page of the American Anthropological Association website, www.aaanet.org/committees/commissions/aec—click on Teaching About Race.

10. Jane Mercer, "Ethnic Differences in IQ Scores: What Do They Mean? (A Response to Lloyd Dunn)," *Hispanic Journal of Behavioral Sciences,* vol. 10, 1988, pp. 199–218.

11. Goodman, op. cit.

12. Lieberman and Rice, op. cit.

13. Carol Mukhopadhyay and Yolanda Moses, "Reestablishing 'Race' in Anthropological Discourse," *American Anthropologist,* vol. 99, 1997, pp. 517–33.

14. Janet Hyde and John DeLamater, *Understanding Human Sexuality,* 6th ed. (New York: McGraw-Hill, 1997).

15. Smedley, op. cit.

16. Karen Donaldson, *Through Students' Eyes: Combating Racism in United States Schools* (Westport, Conn.: Praeger, 1996); and Rosemary C. Henze, "Curricular Approaches to Developing Positive Interethnic Relations," *Journal of Negro Education,* vol. 68, 2001, pp. 529–49.

17. Henze, p. 539.

18. American Anthropological Association. (2002). Front End Evaluation of *Understanding Race and Human Variability.* Arlington, VA: American Anthropological Association.

19. Clara Rodriguez, *Changing Race: Latinos, the Census, and the History of Ethnicity in the United States* (New York: New York

University Press, 2000); and Gilberto Arriaza, "The School Yard as a Stage: Missing Culture Clues in Symbolic Fighting," *Multicultural Education Journal,* Spring 2003, in press.

20. American Anthropological Association, "AAA Statement on Race," www.aaanet.org/stmts/racepp.htm; and American Association of Physical Anthropologists, "AAPA Statement on Biological Aspects of Race," *American Journal of Physical Anthropology,* vol. 101, 1996, pp. 569–70.

21. Alison S. Brooks et al., "Race and Ethnicity in America," in Ruth O. Selig and Marilyn R. London, eds., *Anthropology Explored: The Best of Smithsonian AnthroNotes* (Washington, D.C.: Smithsonian Institution Press), pp. 315–26; E. L. Cerrini-Long, "Ethnicity in the U.S.A.: An Anthropological Model," *AnthroNotes,* vol. 15, no. 3, 1993; William L. Merrill, "Identity Transformation in Colonial Northern Mexico," *AnthroNotes,* vol. 19, no. 2, 1997, pp. 1–8; and Boyce Rensberger, "Forget the Old Labels: Here's a New Way to Look at Race," *AnthroNotes,* vol. 18, no. 1, 1996, pp. 1–7.

22. Hilda Hernandez and Carol C. Mukhopadhyay, *Integrating Multicultural Perspectives in Teacher Education: A Curriculum Resource Guide* (Chico: California State University, 1985); and Conrad P. Kottak, R. Furlow White, and Patricia Rice, eds. *The Teaching of Anthropology: Problems, Issues, and Decisions* (Mountain View, Calif.: Mayfield Publishing, 1996).

23. Faye Harrison, "The Persistent Power of 'Race' in the Cultural and Political Economy of Racism," *Annual Review of Anthropology,* vol. 24, 1995, pp. 47–74; and Ida Susser and Thomas Patterson, eds., *Cultural Diversity in the United States: A Critical Reader* (Malden, Mass.: Blackwell, 2001).

Critical Thinking

1. What physical characteristics do the authors list as being the basis for racial divisions?

2. What is the historical origin of the concept of race?

3. On what three bases do contemporary scientists criticize the traditional race concept? Explain each.

4. What are some of the "less visible genetic traits that have far greater biological significance"? How would racial classifications based on these look?

5. How have racial classifications used by the U.S. Census Bureau changed over time?

6. What does it mean to say that the genetic variation within each racial grouping is greater than the genetic similarity?

7. What evidence exists that race or racial characteristics are causally linked to behavior? What about the relationship between race and health? What were some of the traditional "racial" health problems? How are they now viewed?

8. What terms have anthropologists sought to replace "race" with? What is the meaning of each of these terms? Which term do the authors seem to prefer?

9. Why was the United States, in particular, a place where racial ideas found fertile ground? What are anti-miscegenation laws? What is "hypodescent" or the "one-drop rule"?

10. What do you think about the prospects for change? What has your experience of race been in your own educational background?

11. What are some of the dangers of racial classifications listed by the authors? What are some of the problems they mention with the terms "Asian," "African American," and "black"?

12. What are some of the positive ways "macroracial categories have served people"?

13. What is the point (as they advise) of "shifting the conversation from biology to culture"?

14. What do you think of the suggestions they make ("ideas for student inquiry") for teaching about the notion of race?

Create Central

www.mhhe.com/createcentral

Internet References

Human Genome Project Information
www.ornl.gov/TechResources/Human_Genome/home.html

OMIM Home Page-Online Mendelian Inheritance in Man
www.ncbi.nlm.nih.gov

CAROL MUKHOPADHYAY is a professor in the Department of Anthropology, San Josè State University, San Josè, Calif., where **ROSEMARY C. HENZE** is an associate professor in the Department of Linguistics and Language Development. They wish to thank Gilberto Arriaza, Paul Erickson, Alan Goodman, and Yolanda Moses for their comments on this article.

Mukhopadhyay, Carol;Henze, Rosemary C. From *Phi Delta Kappan,* May 2003. Copyright © 2003 by Phi Delta Kappan. Reprinted with permission of Phi Delta Kappa International. All rights reserved. www.pdkintl.org

Article

Prepared by Elvio Angeloni, *Pasadena City College*

The Tall and the Short of It

Barry Bogin

Learning Outcomes

After reading this article, you will be able to:

- Discuss "plasticity" and why it makes good evolutionary sense.

- Determine to what extent height is a barometer of the health of a society and explain why.

Baffled by your future prospects? As a biological anthropologist, I have just one word of advice for you: plasticity. *Plasticity* refers to the ability of many organisms, including humans, to alter themselves—their behavior or even their biology—in response to changes in the environment. We tend to think that our bodies get locked into their final form by our genes, but in fact we alter our bodies as the conditions surrounding us shift, particularly as we grow during childhood. Plasticity is as much a product of evolution's fine-tuning as any particular gene, and it makes just as much evolutionary good sense. Rather than being able to adapt to a single environment, we can, thanks to plasticity, change our bodies to cope with a wide range of environments. Combined with the genes we inherit from our parents, plasticity accounts for what we are and what we can become.

Anthropologists began to think about human plasticity around the turn of the century, but the concept was first clearly defined in 1969 by Gabriel Lasker, a biological anthropologist at Wayne State University in Detroit. At that time scientists tended to consider only those adaptations that were built into the genetic makeup of a person and passed on automatically to the next generation. A classic example of this is the ability of adults in some human societies to drink milk. As children, we all produce an enzyme called lactase, which we need to break down the sugar lactose in our mother's milk. In many of us, however, the lactase gene slows down dramatically as we approach adolescence—probably as the result of another gene that regulates its activity. When that regulating gene turns down the production of lactase, we can no longer digest milk.

Lactose intolerance—which causes intestinal gas and diarrhea—affects between 70 and 90 percent of African Americans, Native Americans, Asians, and people who come from around the Mediterranean. But others, such as people of central and western

European descent and the Fulani of West Africa, typically have no problem drinking milk as adults. That's because they are descended from societies with long histories of raising goats and cattle. Among these people there was a clear benefit to being able to drink milk, so natural selection gradually changed the regulation of their lactase gene, keeping it functioning throughout life.

That kind of adaptation takes many centuries to become established, but Lasker pointed out that there are two other kinds of adaptation in humans that need far less time to kick in. If people have to face a cold winter with little or no heat, for example, their metabolic rates rise over the course of a few weeks and they produce more body heat. When summer returns, the rates sink again.

Lasker's other mode of adaptation concerned the irreversible, lifelong modification of people as they develop—that is, their plasticity. Because we humans take so many years to grow to adulthood, and because we live in so many different environments, from forests to cities and from deserts to the Arctic, we are among the world's most variable species in our physical form and behavior. Indeed, we are one of the most plastic of all species.

In an age when DNA is king, it's worth considering why Americans are no longer the world's tallest people, and some Guatemalans no longer pygmies.

One of the most obvious manifestations of human malleability is our great range of height, and it is a subject I've made a special study of for the last 25 years. Consider these statistics: in 1850 Americans were the tallest people in the world, with American men averaging 5'6". Almost 150 years later, American men now average 5'8", but we have fallen in the standings and are now only the third tallest people in the world. In first place are the Dutch. Back in 1850 they averaged only 5'4"—the shortest men in Europe—but today they are a towering 5'10". (In these two groups, and just about everywhere else, women average about five inches less than men at all times.)

So what happened? Did all the short Dutch sail over to the United States? Did the Dutch back in Europe get an infusion of "tall genes"? Neither. In both America and the Netherlands life got better, but more so for the Dutch, and height increased as a result. We know this is true thanks in part to studies on how height is determined. It's the product of plasticity in our childhood and in our mothers' childhood as well. If a girl is undernourished and suffers poor health, the growth of her body, including her reproductive system, is usually reduced. With a shortage of raw materials, she can't build more cells to construct a bigger body; at the same time, she has to invest what materials she can get into repairing already existing cells and tissues from the damage caused by disease. Her shorter stature as an adult is the result of a compromise her body makes while growing up.

Such a woman can pass on her short stature to her child, but genes have nothing to do with it for either of them. If she becomes pregnant, her small reproductive system probably won't be able to supply a normal level of nutrients and oxygen to her fetus. This harsh environment reprograms the fetus to grow more slowly than it would if the woman was healthier, so she is more likely to give birth to a smaller baby. Low-birth-weight babies (weighing less than 5.5 pounds) tend to continue their prenatal program of slow growth through childhood. By the time they are teenagers, they are usually significantly shorter than people of normal birth weight. Some particularly striking evidence of this reprogramming comes from studies on monozygotic twins, which develop from a single fertilized egg cell and are therefore identical genetically. But in certain cases, monozygotic twins end up being nourished by unequal portions of the placenta. The twin with the smaller fraction of the placenta is often born with low birth weight, while the other one is normal. Follow-up studies show that this difference between the twins can last throughout their lives.

As such research suggests, we can use the average height of any group of people as a barometer of the health of their society. After the turn of the century both the United States and the Netherlands began to protect the health of their citizens by purifying drinking water, installing sewer systems, regulating the safety of food, and, most important, providing better health care and diets to children. The children responded to their changed environment by growing taller. But the differences in Dutch and American societies determined their differing heights today. The Dutch decided to provide public health benefits to all the public, including the poor. In the United States, meanwhile, improved health is enjoyed most by those who can afford it. The poor often lack adequate housing, sanitation, and health care. The difference in our two societies can be seen at birth: in 1990 only 4 percent of Dutch babies were born at low birth weight, compared with 7 percent in the United States. For white Americans the rate was 5.7 percent, and for black Americans the rate was a whopping 13.3 percent. The disparity between rich and poor in the United States carries through to adulthood: poor Americans are shorter than the better-off by about one inch. Thus, despite great affluence in the United States, our average height has fallen to third place.

People are often surprised when I tell them the Dutch are the tallest people in the world. Aren't they shrimps compared with the famously tall Tutsi (or "Watusi," as you probably first encountered them) of Central Africa? Actually, the supposed great height of the Tutsi is one of the most durable myths from the age of European exploration. Careful investigation reveals that today's Tutsi men average 5'7" and that they have maintained that average for more than 100 years. That means that back in the 1800s, when puny European men first met the Tutsi, the Europeans suffered strained necks from looking up all the time. The two-to-three-inch difference in average height back then could easily have turned into fantastic stories of African giants by European adventures and writers.

The Tutsi could be as tall or taller than the Dutch if equally good health care and diets were available in Rwanda and Burundi, where the Tutsi live. But poverty rules the lives of most African people, punctuated by warfare, which makes the conditions for growth during childhood even worse. And indeed, it turns out that the Tutsi and other Africans who migrate to Western Europe or North America at young ages end up taller than Africans remaining in Africa.

At the other end of the height spectrum, Pygmies tell a similar story. The shortest people in the world today are the Mbuti, the Efe, and other Pygmy peoples of Central Africa. Their average stature is almost 4'9" for adult men and 4'6" for women. Part of the reason Pygmies are short is indeed genetic: some evidently lack the genes for producing the growth-promoting hormones that course through other people's bodies, while others are genetically incapable of using these hormones to trigger the cascade of reactions that lead to growth. But another important reason for their small size is environmental. Pygmies living as hunter-gatherers in the forests of Central African countries appear to be undernourished, which further limits their growth. Pygmies who live on farms and ranches outside the forest are better fed than their hunter-gatherer relatives and are taller as well. Both genes and nutrition thus account for the size of Pygmies.

Peoples in other parts of the world have also been labeled pygmies, such as some groups in Southeast Asia and the Maya of Guatemala. Well-meaning explorers and scientists have often claimed that they are genetically short, but here we encounter another myth of height. A group of extremely short people in New Guinea, for example, turned out to eat a diet deficient in iodine and other essential nutrients. When they were supplied with cheap mineral and vitamin supplements, their supposedly genetic short stature vanished in their children, who grew to a more normal height.

Another way for these so-called pygmies to stop being pygmies is to immigrate to the United States. In my own research, I study the growth of two groups of Mayan children. One group lives in their homeland of Guatemala, and the other is a group of refugees living in the United States. The Maya in Guatemala live in the village of San Pedro, which has no safe source of drinking water. Most of the water is contaminated with fertilizers and pesticides used on nearby agricultural fields. Until recently, when a deep well was dug, the townspeople depended on an unreliable supply of water from rain-swollen streams. Most homes still lack running water and have only pit toilets. The parents of the Mayan children work mostly at clothing factories and are paid only a few dollars a day.

One way for the so-called pygmies of Guatemala to stop being pygmies is to immigrate to the United States.

I began working with the schoolchildren in this village in 1979, and my research shows that most of them eat only 80 percent of the food they need. Other research shows that almost 30 percent of the girls and 20 percent of the boys are deficient in iodine, that most of the children suffer from intestinal parasites, and that many have persistent ear and eye infections. As a consequence, their health is poor and their height reflects it: they average about three inches shorter than better-fed Guatemalan children.

The Mayan refugees I work with in the United States live in Los Angeles and in the rural agricultural community of Indiantown in central Florida. Although the adults work mostly in minimum-wage jobs, the children in these communities are generally better off than their counterparts in Guatemala. Most Maya arrived in the 1980s as refugees escaping a civil war as well as a political system that threatened them and their children. In the United States they found security and started new lives, and before long their children began growing faster and bigger. My data show that the average increase in height among the first generation of these immigrants was 2.2 inches, which means that these so-called pygmies have undergone one of the largest single-generation increases in height ever recorded. When people such as my own grandparents migrated from the poverty of rural life in Eastern Europe to the cities of the United States just after World War I, the increase in height of the next generation was only about one inch.

One reason for the rapid increase in stature is that in the United States the Maya have access to treated drinking water and to a reliable supply of food. Especially critical are school breakfast and lunch programs for children from low-income families, as well as public assistance programs such as the federal Woman, Infants, and Children (WIC) program and food stamps. That these programs improve health and growth is no secret. What is surprising is how fast they work. Mayan mothers in the United States tell me that even their babies are bigger and healthier than the babies they raised in Guatemala, and hospital statistics bear them out. These women must be enjoying a level of health so improved from that of their lives in Guatemala that their babies are growing faster in the womb. Of course, plasticity means that such changes are dependent on external conditions, and unfortunately the rising height—and health—of the Maya is in danger from political forces that are attempting to cut funding for food stamps and the WIC program. If that funding is cut, the negative impact on the lives of poor Americans,

including the Mayan refugees, will be as dramatic as were the former positive effects.

Height is only the most obvious example of plasticity's power; there are others to be found everywhere you look. The Andes-dwelling Quechua people of Peru are well-adapted to their high-altitude homes. Their large, barrel-shaped chests house big lungs that inspire huge amounts of air with each breath, and they manage to survive on the lower pressure of oxygen they breathe with an unusually high level of red blood cells. Yet these secrets of mountain living are not hereditary. Instead the bodies of young Quechua adapt as they grow in their particular environment, just as those of European children do when they live at high altitudes.

Plasticity may also have a hand in determining our risks for developing a number of diseases. For example, scientists have long been searching for a cause for Parkinson's disease. Because Parkinson's tends to run in families, it is natural to think there is a genetic cause. But while a genetic mutation linked to some types of Parkinson's disease was reported in mid-1997, the gene accounts for only a fraction of people with the disease. Many more people with Parkinson's do not have the gene, and not all people with the mutated gene develop the disease.

Ralph Garruto, a medical researcher and biological anthropologist at the National Institutes of Health, is investigating the role of the environment and human plasticity not only in Parkinson's but in Lou Gehrig's disease as well. Garruto and his team traveled to the islands of Guam and New Guinea, where rates of both diseases are 50 to 100 times higher than in the United States. Among the native Chamorro people of Guam these diseases kill one person out of every five over the age of 25. The scientists found that both diseases are linked to a shortage of calcium in the diet. This shortage sets off a cascade of events that result in the digestive system's absorbing too much of the aluminum present in the diet. The aluminum wreaks havoc on various parts of the body, including the brain, where it destroys neurons and eventually causes paralysis and death.

The most amazing discovery made by Garruto's team is that up to 70 percent of the people they studied in Guam had some brain damage, but only 20 percent progressed all the way to Parkinson's or Lou Gehrig's disease. Genes and plasticity seem to be working hand in hand to produce these lower-than-expected rates of disease. There is a certain amount of genetic variation in the ability that all people have in coping with calcium shortages—some can function better than others. But thanks to plasticity, it's also possible for people's bodies to gradually develop ways to protect themselves against aluminum poisoning. Some people develop biochemical barriers to the aluminum they eat, while others develop ways to prevent the aluminum from reaching the brain.

An appreciation of plasticity may temper some of our fears about these diseases and even offer some hope. For if Parkinson's and Lou Gehrig's diseases can be prevented among the Chamorro by plasticity, then maybe medical researchers can figure out a way to produce the same sort of plastic changes in you and me. Maybe Lou Gehrig's disease and Parkinson's disease—as well as many other, including some cancers—aren't our genetic doom but a product of our development, just like variations in human height. And maybe their danger will in time prove as illusory as the notion that the Tutsi are giants, or the Maya pygmies—or Americans still the tallest of the tall.

Critical Thinking

1. What is meant by "plasticity" and why does it make "evolutionary good sense"?

2. What is "lactose intolerance" and why is this not an example of plasticity?

3. What are two other kinds of adaptation, pointed out by Lasker, that are examples of plasticity?

4. Why are humans among the most variable of species?

5. How have Americans and the Dutch changed in height since 1850 and why?

6. What happens to humans from the fetus to adulthood in a harsh environment, and why?

7. What do studies of monozygotic twins tell us about "reprogramming"?

8. What similarities and differences occurred in the United States and the Netherlands with regard to health care, and what has been the result?

9. Explain the "durable myth" of the Tutsi.

10. What has happened to the Tutsi and other Africans who have migrated to Western Europe or North America?

11. How do various Pygmy groups tell a similar story?

12. How do the Mayans of Guatemala contrast with those in the United States and why?

13. What has been surprising with regard to US programs to improve health? What will happen if such funding is cut?

14. How do the Quechua illustrate plasticity and why?

15. What indications are there that Parkinson's and Lou Gherig's diseases exhibit plasticity?

Create Central

www.mhhe.com/createcentral

Internet References

American Society of Human Genetics
www.ashg.org

Ethnic and Racial Studies
www.tandfonline.com/rers

Journal of Human Evolution
www.journals.elsevier.com/journal-of-human-evolution

BARRY BOGIN is a professor of anthropology at the University of Michigan in Dearborn and the author of *Patterns of Human Growth*.

Bogin, Barry. From *Discover*, February 1998, pp. 40–44. Copyright © 1998 by Barry A. Bogin. Reprinted by permission of the author.

Article 36

Dead Men Do Tell Tales

The strange and fascinating cases of a forensic anthropologist.

WILLIAM R. MAPLES

"Empty vessel, garment cast,
We that wore you long shall last.
—Another night, another day."
So my bones within me say.

Therefore they shall do my will
To-day while I am master still,
And flesh and soul, now both are strong,
Shall hale the sullen slaves along,

Before this fire of sense decay,
This smoke of thought blow clean away,
And leave with ancient night alone
The stedfast and enduring bone.

—A. E. Housman,
The Immortal Part

As I write these lines, it is a windy, bright spring day in early March in Gainesville. The live oaks have cast their leaves, and the dogwoods and azaleas are beginning to bloom. Eager young students are bicycling across campus, browsing in Goering's bookstore, studying their textbooks on sunlit lawns near dormitories.

But I am not thinking of them. I am thinking of ghosts.

I am recalling five young students, four from the University of Florida, one from nearby Santa Fe Community College, who were tortured, mutilated and murdered with demonic cruelty in August 1990. In all, the five victims suffered sixty-one stab wounds, cuts or other disfigurements. One was beheaded, and her head was placed at eye level on a bookshelf near the door of her apartment. Four of the victims were female: Sonja Larson, eighteen, of Deerfield Beach; Christi Powell, seventeen, of Jacksonville; Christa Hoyt, eighteen, of Gainesville; and Tracy Paules, twenty-three, of Miami. One was male: Manny Taboada, twenty-three, of Miami. The horror these murders aroused at the time was so keen that thousands of students literally fled Gainesville, in fear of their lives.

Today, in early March, immured in a lamplit courtroom within the Alachua County Courthouse, a jury has finished staring at pictures of these five young people, taken after their bodies were

discovered. Black tape was placed over parts of the pictures considered so grisly they would have been prejudicial to the jury's reaching an impartial verdict. I can well understand these selective blackouts. In my long career I have seldom seen crime-scene photographs possessed of such sheer depravity.

In the same room with the jury, as they pondered these ghastly photographs, was the author of these terrors: the self-confessed murderer himself, Danny Harold Rolling, a drifter from Shreveport, Louisiana. Rolling claimed he was driven to kill because of abuse suffered as a child—it is a common excuse nowadays. He was arrested almost immediately on another charge after the quintuple murders (which were all committed within forty-eight hours), and only became a suspect in this case two months later, on November 2, 1990. As the prosecutor waved the horrible photographs before the jury, Rolling turned pale and appeared ill. "I've got to get out of here," he whispered at one point.

The jury was tasked with deciding his punishment: life in prison or death in the electric chair. It deliberated through one afternoon, into the evening, and reconvened the next morning, before reaching a verdict. The jury recommended death for Danny Rolling.

I remember how, in the years following his arrest, Rolling toyed with the investigators from prison, admitting nothing. He thought he had been too clever for the police. He thought he had removed all traces of his guilt from the crime scenes. He gathered up all but one piece of the duct tape he used to bind his victims. He washed two of their bodies with detergent after they were dead. He posed the bodies of the slaughtered young women in various lewd positions. Unfortunately for him, he left traces of his semen at the scene, and this identified him by means of DNA "fingerprinting."

Because of my background with weapons and wounds to bone, I was asked to be present at the autopsies, which were conducted by Dr. William Hamilton, the District 8 medical examiner. Hamilton is a quiet man of supreme competence. Unlike some of his brethren, he rigorously shuns the media limelight and works in silence. We have known each other for years, but from the first Hamilton struck me as remarkable and rare: a man who prefers to seek out the truth and to serve the people of his state with deeds of value, rather than chase the will-o'-the-wisp of fame. It is largely because of Hamilton's meticulous work that a close-meshed net of scientific evidence was drawn about Rolling. My own role in this case was minor. But I like to think that, wherever Rolling goes, I gave him one small nudge toward punishment and perdition.

My work centered around the murder weapon, and I was assisted by one of my best students, Dana Austin-Smith. Bones can reveal more about a murder weapon than skin and soft tissue, because they are not as elastic. Skin can stretch, distort, relax and finally deliquesce during decomposition. Bones, though more elastic than you might suppose, nevertheless can take and hold an impression from a murder weapon far longer, and far more accurately. By now I need not tell you that the pattern of the human skeleton is as familiar to me as the rooms of my house.

A large knife had been used in the murders. Its hilt left an imprint on one victim's back, and the point exited her chest on the opposite side, a distance of eight inches, during which the knife was fully sheathed, its entire length buried in the unfortunate girl's body. But allowing for compression of the rib cage from the force and fury of the blow, the blade length might have been somewhat shorter: say seven to eight inches, to be safe.

After preparing specimens of the damaged bones, I began to examine the knife marks under a low-power stereo-microscope. I found sharp cuts from the blade, marks both sharp and dull from the back of the blade, a point mark from the knife sunk in the body of a vertebra, and an array of bone wounds that gave me the width of the blade itself, from its cutting edge to its back.

I summarized the characteristics. Length: 7–8 inches. Width: 1.25–1.5 inches. A sharp, smooth, nonserrated cutting edge. A false edge resulting from the back of the blade being sharpened behind the tip. A certain shape of hilt where the blade joined the handle. A blade whose cross-section resembled an elongated pentagon. All in all, I concluded, this was a sturdy knife, like a military weapon. It was not a thin blade like a kitchen knife. This formidable weapon had cut through thick bone without any evidence of "blade chattering," a technical term describing the distinctive cutting pattern, which a thin blade makes when it jumps slightly from side to side during use.

On the afternoon of September 7, 1990, I was at the state attorney's office in Orlando on another case. I received a telephone call, asking me to join Dr. Hamilton and the leaders of the Gainesville Homicide Task Force for a meeting. It was a fast, hundred-mile drive for me, but I arrived around 4 P.M.

We were asked about the murder weapon. Could it have been an Air Force survival knife? I said no. That knife has a sawlike, ripping design on the back of the blade, which is only five inches long—far too short to match the weapon used in these murders. Then someone asked if it might be a Marine Corps utility knife, known as a Ka-Bar. I replied that it very well might.

After the meeting I pondered the question further. I knew the general shape of the Ka-Bar but wanted to be absolutely sure. That weekend I visited a knife shop in a nearby mall, where Ka-Bars were sold. I carefully examined one, measuring it with the one-meter tape measure I always carry with me. It fit exactly the dimensions of the wounds! The clerk regarded me with some curiosity. Why, he asked finally, was I making so many measurements? I made a vague reply, but as Margaret and I were walking back to the car, I told her what I thought. The weapon used in these ghastly murders had almost certainly been a Ka-Bar.

As I have said earlier, Rolling was in custody on an unrelated charge at this point. He had not yet been focused on as a suspect in the Gainesville murders. Over three years would pass before I learned that Rolling had indeed purchased a Ka-Bar at an Army-Navy store in Tallahassee on July 17, 1990, some weeks before the killings.

The police scanned many likely areas with metal detectors, but the actual murder weapon has not surfaced to this day. On the Thursday before Rolling was scheduled to go to trial, there was a crucial evidentiary hearing, one that changed the complexion of the case completely.

State Attorney Rod Smith won the court's approval to introduce into evidence a "replica weapon," a duplicate of the lost Ka-Bar we believed had been used to commit the crimes. Not only that: the *actual skeletal remains of the victims*, taken from their bodies during the autopsies, and bearing the atrocious nicks, slashes, scorings and gougings, which the knife had caused, and which had enabled me to measure its deadly dimensions with such exactitude, were going to be allowed into evidence as well. Thus, not only the blade, but the bones themselves would be placed before the jury's gaze.

"On the Thursday prior to the beginning of the trial," a court memorandum I have before me reads, "in closed discussions before the judge, part of the discussion was about the replica knife and the accurate work which Dr. Maples had done with the wounds. Also discussed were the skeletal remnants . . . "

The judge ruled that all these things would be allowed into evidence. The memorandum continues:

"It was obvious that Rolling didn't want to face the photographs, let alone the remnants . . . That was the evening the defense came to Mr. Smith and offered the first of a series of plea deals."

The murderer's resolve was crumbling in the face of these fearful resurrections. The knife he imagined was hidden forever was coming back to haunt him in court. The bones of his victims were ready to return from beyond death, to rise up and smite him. The trial would begin in ninety-six hours.

Rolling quailed. On February 15, 1994, as jury selection began in his trial, the accused man suddenly pleaded guilty to five counts of murder and three counts of rape.

"I've been running all my life," he declared. "And there are some things you can't run from anymore."

There began the punishment phase of the case, during which the jury had to decide whether Rolling deserved the death penalty or life in prison. Prosecutor Smith showed the jurors the replica knife, the twin of the Ka-Bar I had identified as the murder weapon. The bones were mercifully withheld from the jurors' sight. The dark blade danced back and forth before their eyes. Together with the hood Rolling wore, and the photographs of his victims, the knife must have made an overwhelming impression on the panel. Their verdict: Death. Rolling received five death sentences from Judge Stan Morris.

"Five years! You're going to go down in five years! You understand that? In less than five years!" screamed Mario Taboada, the brother of the slain Manuel Taboada. He was predicting that Rolling would exhaust all his appeals and be executed by 1999. The judge ordered Taboada ejected from the courtroom. Gradually the din subsided. One of the darkest chapters in Gainesville's history was closed.

All in all, the Rolling case was a significant victory for the science of forensic anthropology in Florida, one that saved the taxpayer the immense cost of a full-blown trial, and the victims' relatives the terrible pain of hearing in a public courtroom exactly how these innocent young people had died. It remains one of the most extraordinary cases in my experience, one that amply demonstrated the sheer power possessed by human bones: the power to bear witness to the truth beyond death; the power to avenge the innocent; the power to terrify the guilty.

ANNUAL EDITIONS

Today, at the side of 34th Street in Gainesville, near the crest of a hill, there is a brilliantly painted section of wall dedicated to student graffiti and free speech. Everyone in Gainesville knows it simply as "The Wall." It runs beneath a fence draped with kudzu vine at the boundary of the campus golf course, and its shape rather reminds you of a railroad cutting, revealing all sorts of multicolored minerals, some of them precious, some of them fool's gold.

Anyone is welcome to paint a message on this wall, which is by now a local landmark and a University of Florida tradition. Most of the messages are cheery, or silly, or affectionate, or whimsical. But amid the valentines, the happy birthday wishes and the pleas to save the rain forest is a single dark panel in the wall at the very top of the hill. It contains the names of the five murder victims, neatly lettered against a black background, accompanied by the single word: REMEMBER. If this panel fades or is accidentally defaced, someone always renews it and repaints the names. I pass it twice a day, and I do indeed remember.

I have purposely kept this account of the Gainesville murders for last, not because they struck so close to home—Rolling could have killed anywhere, in any town—but because I believe there is a moral to this melancholy tale. It is simply that the lamp of science, properly grasped and directed, can shine its rays into the very heart of darkness. It can seek out and snare the most artful evildoer in a bright, unequivocal beam of truth. It cannot raise the dead, but it can make them speak, accuse and identify the agent of death. With the capture and punishment of the criminal responsible, the families and relatives of those slain can win a small measure of peace amid their infinite sorrow. With each solved case, with every confession, we extend our knowledge of the criminal mind and its methods, and we render the threat of capture and punishment all the more real and credible.

Yet as I look back on my life, and ahead to the future, I am given pause by the vast amount of work that still needs to be done. Mine is a small field, and it is always going to be a small field; but there is no excuse for its being as small as it is today. Cases now throng in daily to the C. A. Pound Human Identification Laboratory, in such jostling multitudes that I cannot address them all and must focus only on the most serious ones. When the telephone rings, my heartbeat quickens. I know that it is most likely the police, and I know what they will say, for I have heard it hundreds of times now:

"Doc, we've got a problem . . . "

And the problem is always a body, or what is left of one. They tell me they've set up security around the remains. They tell me police officers are guarding and preserving the scene. They ask: can I come immediately? Because I no longer have an undergraduate class load, I am able to break free more often than not. If I am rescued by a murder from a dull and dismal faculty meeting, so much the better! In the case of the three shotgunned drug dealers found in a pit near La Belle, I enlisted the aid of an archaeologist colleague and we both managed to be in Fort Myers, 230 miles away, by dark. By 8 A.M. the next morning we were in the death pit, hard at work.

With crime moving to the forefront of the American domestic political agenda, it would appear likely that investigators such as myself can look forward to busy years and full employment. But against this must be weighed the fact that few universities are willing to underwrite programs like mine, which combine pure academic research with applications in the "real world," and the fact that few state law enforcement agencies have the money or

inclination to avail themselves of the services of a trained forensic anthropologist.

So we fall between two stools. We are regarded by our fellow academics almost as common laborers with dirty hands, who traffic in mundane, workaday police matters, instead of devoting ourselves to pure research. On the other hand the police tend to regard us as woolgatherers and cloud-dwellers from the ivory tower, with no experience of the dark side of life. When I am visiting a new law enforcement agency for the first time, I often assume the persona of the innocent, fuddy-duddy professor who has to have everything pointed out to him. This role-playing won't win me any Oscars, but it humors the police, does no harm and gets results far more quickly than would an attitude of haughty, know-it-all, intellectual arrogance.

Yet sometimes I am prey to doubts. Who will replace me, and others like me? Who will hire the students I train? I cannot say. The need is there. It cries out to heaven. As I compose these lines, there are forty-eight charred corpses left over from the fiery explosion at the Branch Davidian compound outside Waco, awaiting identification. My colleague, Clyde Snow, is in Chiapas, Mexico, looking at the bodies of slain Zapatista revolutionaries, to see if they were murdered by the Mexican army after they surrendered. Remains of MIAs from the Korean War are being returned to America, and their names are a riddle as yet unsolved. The mass graves in Bosnia shout to the skies for discovery and vengeance. Yet programs in forensic anthropology languish, and well-trained young scholars go begging for work.

In my lifetime I have seen programs rise and fall like shooting stars. Once upon a time, at the University of Kansas, three of the gods of forensic anthropology—Tom McKern, Ellis Kerley and Bill Bass—were all on the faculty *at the same time.* They attracted and taught scores of students, many of whom are among the leading people in our field today. Then, almost overnight, they were scattered to the four winds. Bass left one year, McKern and Kerley the next. The university hired a human geneticist, rather than anyone in bone. The same melancholy story is about to be repeated at the University of Arizona, where Walt Birkby has built up a fantastic program. Birkby's students are probably the best-trained of any in the United States. But Walt is retiring in a couple of years, and the university has already announced he will not be replaced. Therefore he has closed admission to his program. He takes no new students.

Bill Bass has just retired from Tennessee. The university is going to replace him with an assistant professor, but without Bill's active guidance that program will undoubtedly change. I will retire myself in a few years and, even though University of Florida President John Lombardi has worked miracles in other areas, I seriously doubt whether the C. A. Pound Human Identification Laboratory will survive my departure.

If these memoirs have demonstrated anything, I would hope that it is that forensic anthropology is a discipline useful to society. Had I the power to command it, I should decree that each state have at least one forensic anthropologist working in its crime laboratory. Climate and crime rates have to be taken into consideration of course. A forensic anthropologist would probably starve to death in a cold state like Maine or Minnesota—bodies last forever in those arctic regions! He might find little to do in a state like New Hampshire, where there are only a couple of dozen murders in a year. But here in the sunny, homicidal South there are plenty of bodies to go around, and plenty of bugs to feast on them. Decomposition is swift and sure, and nameless skeletons accumulate in thousands, each beseeching us silently for identification.

Larger states, such as Texas, California, New York, Florida and the like, could easily employ several scientists like me, and none would be idle, I assure you. I know from long experience that I can't begin to look at all the cases demanding my attention in the state of Florida. A handful of states, those having a single medical examiner with statewide responsibility, have appointed forensic anthropologists to that office, but they are few and far between. As our elected officials bay like bloodhounds over the crime issue, as our state budgets allocate large sums for prisons, police training and equipment, parole officers, boot camps for teenagers and heaven knows what else, they overlook utterly the need to fund research by universities to develop new scientific techniques necessary to apprehend criminals. The Forensic Sciences Foundation has started a small grant program to provide funds, largely supported by donations from members of the American Academy of Forensic Scientists. But none of us is a Croesus or a Rockefeller. Our little fund is growing painfully slowly. It can only provide a few modest grants each year.

Seldom does a week go by without my receiving a visit or a telephone call from some young person eager to go into forensic anthropology. Will I accept him or her as a student? Alas, I don't have the money to support large numbers of students, nor the space in which to teach and train them, nor the time to give them all the attention they deserve. Even if I were to take them in, where would they go when they left me, having won their doctorates? Where would they get jobs? No doubt a handful of them would, as I did, work their way into a university system and slowly establish a practice. Most wouldn't. That is the bitter truth.

The murder and suicide rate in the state of Florida could easily furnish cases for six full-time forensic anthropologists. In my daydreams I locate them on a mind-map of the state with stickpins: there would be one in the Panhandle, another in Gainesville, another in Orlando, one in southwest Florida and one, perhaps two, in Miami. Miami, as we all know, is a very special place: the deadliest city in the most crime-ridden state in the Union. Forensic anthropologists would find plenty to do there. They would be useful to state medical examiners in skeletonized cases, cases involving burn victims, decomposed bodies and the like. We could even help identify fresh bodies belonging to the nameless and the homeless, who are flocking to Florida—and to Florida's morgues—in ever increasing numbers nowadays. Some medical examiners' offices perform over three thousand autopsies each year.

I can't be everywhere. I have been under as many as four separate subpoenas, to testify in four separate cities, all on the same day. One prosecutor, jokingly I hope, actually threatened to throw me in jail if I did not testify for him, rather than in another case scheduled for that day! Ours is a very large state. If a decomposed body is found in the Florida Keys, there is no way I can be on the scene immediately. Sometimes the remains are shipped to me, if I cannot go to them. Federal Express won't transport human remains, including cremains, but the U. S. Post Office has no such qualms,

as long as the remains are identified as "evidence" or "specimens." But if we had a forensic anthropologist stationed in Miami, these cases could be attended to on the spot.

Such are the thoughts that sometimes visit me at night. But "sufficient unto the day is the evil thereof," as the Bible says. Whenever I am beset by doubts over the future of my discipline, or the career opportunities for my students, or the fate of my laboratory after I am gone, I look at the filing cabinets filled with case reports. Here at least is solid, measurable progress. Here I can claim to have made a difference.

In days when people knew more Latin than they do now, someone composed a deeply moving inscription that can still be read over the lintel of the New York City medical examiner's office:

Taceant Colloquia. Effugiat Risus. Hic Locus Est Ubi Mors Gaudet Succurrere Vitae.

[Let idle talk be silenced. Let laughter be banished. Here is the place where Death delights to succour Life.]

I have no room over my laboratory door lintel for an engraved inscription, but if I did I would choose the last words of the explorer, Robert Falcon Scott, who perished in the frozen wastes of Antarctica in 1912, of hunger and exposure, in a place that was only a few miles from food and safety. The last entry in his diary read:

Had we lived, I should have had a tale to tell of the hardihood, endurance and courage of my companions, that would have stirred the heart of every Englishman. These rough notes and our dead bodies must tell the tale.

That's how I feel about the skeletons here in my laboratory. They have tales to tell us, even though they are dead. It is up to me, the forensic anthropologist, to catch their mute cries and whispers, and to interpret them for the living, as long as I am able.

Critical Thinking

1. Why is it that bones can reveal more about a murder weapon than skin and soft tissue?

2. In what sense did the bones of the victims and the knife used to kill them come back to haunt Danny Harold Rolling at his murder trial?

3. Why does the author consider the Rolling case a "significant victory" for the science of forensic anthropology?

4. What is the "moral to this melancholy tale," according to the author?

5. Why is the field of forensic anthropology so small even though there is a great need?

6. How are forensic anthropologists regarded by their fellow academics? By the police?

7. To what doubts is the author sometimes prey to?

8. In what regions of the United States does the author see the greatest need and why?

Article   Prepared by: Elvio Angeloni

Evolution: Why Are Most of Us Right-Handed?

JASON G. GOLDMAN

Learning Outcomes

After reading this article, you will be able to:

- Discuss the evidence for why right-handedness may be deeply rooted in our evolutionary past.

- Discuss the relationship between language and right-handedness.

We humans don't typically agree on all that much, but there is at least one thing that an impressive amount of us accept: which hand is easiest to control. If you use one hand for writing, you probably use the same one for eating as well, and most of us—around 85 percent of our species—prefer our right hands. In fact, "there has never been any report of a human population in which left-handed individuals predominate", according to archaeologist Natalie Uomini at the University of Liverpool in the UK.

Lateralisation of limb use—that is, a bias towards one side or the other—usually begins in the brain. We know that some tasks are largely controlled by brain activity in the left hemisphere, while the right hemisphere governs other tasks. Confusingly, there is some crossing of nerves between the body and the brain, which means it's actually the left side of the brain that has more control over the right side of the body and vice versa. In other words, the brain's left hemisphere helps control the operation of the right hand, eye, leg and so on.

Some argue that this division of neurological labour has been a feature of animals for half a billion years. Perhaps it evolved because it is more efficient to allow the two hemispheres to carry out different computations at the same time. The left side of the brain, for instance, might have evolved to carry out routine operations—things like foraging for food—while the right

side was kept free to detect and react rapidly to unexpected challenges in the environment—an approaching predator, for instance. This can be seen in various fish, toads, and birds, which are all more likely to attack prey seen in the right eye.

So it is possible (though hard to prove) that as our hominin ancestors began walking on two legs rather than four, freeing up their hands to perform new tasks like making tools, they were predisposed to begin using those hands differently. Or, as cognitive scientist Stephanie Braccini and colleagues put it in a *Journal of Human Evolution* study, "a strengthening of individual asymmetry [may have] started as soon as early hominins assumed a habitual upright posture during tool use or foraging".

In support of the idea, Braccini and her colleagues' looked at handedness in chimpanzees, and found that when the apes stand on all fours, they displayed no real hand preferences. It was only when forced to assume an upright stance that a lateral preference emerged—although individual chimps in the study were equally likely to be left-handed as right-handed.

Evidently, then, something else was needed to push early humans from a lateral preference in general to the extremely high levels of right-handedness we see today.

We know roughly when that change occurred from experiments in which researchers made their own versions of ancient stone tools using either their left or right hands to chip—or knap—the tool into shape, before comparing them with the tools made by early hominins. Doing so suggests there is only limited evidence that hominin toolmakers working more than two million years ago were primarily right-handed.

However, stone tools that were made some 1.5 million years ago in Koobi Fora, Kenya, by two ancient human species—*Homo habilis* and *Homo erectus*—do show some evidence of species-wide right-handedness. And by the time a species called *Homo heidelbergensis* had appeared, perhaps around 600,000 years ago, there was a clear right-handed preference in prehistoric societies. Wear on the preserved teeth of *Homo heidelbergensis,* for instance, suggests that food was usually brought to the mouth with the right hand.

This tells us when that shift occurred, but not why. Some have argued that it all comes down to language. Just as most people are right-handed—a trait, remember, controlled by the left side of the brain—so do most people do the bulk of their linguistic processing in their brain's left hemisphere. Indeed, this left-brained specialization for language is even more common than right-handedness—which might suggest that as the left hemisphere evolved for language, the preference for the right hand may have intensified simply as a side effect. This is called the Homo loquens hypothesis: lateralisation in general was driven by the evolution of an upright, bipedal stance, while the rightward preference was driven, some time later, by the evolution of language.

Right-handedness, then, may simply be an accidental by-product of the way most of our brains are wired up. But proving the hypothesis is difficult, or even impossible, since it would ideally involve running neurological tests on our long-dead ancestors. The truth is we'll probably never quite know what the sequence of events was that led our species to lean so overwhelmingly on the right sides of our bodies and the left sides of our brains.

As for the left-handers out there? Take heart! According to a 1977 paper in the journal *Psychological Bulletin,* "there is remarkably little evidence for any association of left-handedness with deficit, as has often been suggested". In fact, some research shows that left-handed folks might even have an easier time recovering from brain damage. And their left hand seems to have the advantage of surprise in a fight, which means they can be *better at combat sports.* All of which suggests there are advantages to breaking from the norm.

Critical Thinking

1. Why has lateralization of brain function been a feature of animals for half a billion years?
2. What is the connection between lateralization of brain function and upright walking, tool-making, and language?
3. What might be the advantages of being left-handed for some humans?

Internet References

Flintnappng Magazine
http://flintknappingmagazine.blogspot.com/

Handedness Research Institute
http://handedness.org/

Goldman, Jason G. "Evolution: Why are most of us right-handed". From http://www.bbc.com/future/story/20141215-why-are-most-of-us-right-handed, December 16, 2014, *BBC.com Future,* BBC Worldwide Limited © 2014. Reprinted by permission.

Article   Prepared by: Elvio Angeloni

Still Evolving (After All These Years)

For 30,000 years our species has been changing remarkably quickly. And we're not done yet.

JOHN HAWKS

Learning Outcomes

After reading this article, you will be able to:

- Discuss the evidence for continuing human evolution since the transition from hunting and gathering to farming.

- Discuss the "shallowness" of races in terms of recent human evolution.

- Explain the relationship between population size and recent human evolution.

- Describe the ways in which today's scientist can watch human evolution in action.

Humans are willful creatures. No other species on the planet has gained so much mastery over its own fate. We have neutralized countless threats that once killed us in the millions: we have learned to protect ourselves from the elements and predators in the wild; we have developed cures and treatments for many deadly diseases; we have transformed the small gardens of our agrarian ancestors into the vast fields of industrial agriculture; and we have dramatically increased our chances of bearing healthy children despite all the usual difficulties.

Many people argue that our technological advancement—our ability to defy and control nature—has made humans exempt from natural selection and that human evolution has effectively ceased. There is no "survival of the fittest," the argument goes, if just about everyone survives into old age. This notion is more than just a stray thought in the public consciousness. Professional scientists such as Steven Jones of University College London and respected science communicators such as David Attenborough have also declared that human evolution is over.

But it is not. We have evolved in our recent past, and we will continue to do so as long as we are around. If we take the more than seven million years since humans split from our last common ancestor with chimpanzees and convert it to a 24-hour day, the past 30,000 years would take about a mere six minutes. Yet much has unfolded during this last chapter of our evolution: vast migrations into new environments, dramatic changes in diet and a more than 1,000-fold increase in global population. All those new people added many unique mutations to the total population. The result was a pulse of rapid natural selection. Human evolution is not stopping. If anything, it is accelerating.

An Anthropological Legacy

Skeletons of ancient people have long suggested that humans evolved certain traits swiftly and recently. About 11,000 years ago, as people started to transition from hunting and gathering to farming and cooking, human anatomy changed. Ten thousand years ago, for example, people's teeth averaged more than 10 percent larger in Europe, Asia and North Africa than today. When our ancestors started to eat softer cooked foods that required less chewing, their teeth and jaws shrank, bit by bit, each generation.

Although anthropologists have known about such traits for decades, only in the past 10 years has it become clear just how new they really are. Studies of human genomes have made the recent targets of selection highly visible to us. It turns out, for example, that descendants of farmers are much more likely to have a greater production of salivary amylase, a key enzyme that breaks down starches in food. Most people alive today have several copies of the gene that codes for amylase, AMY1. Modern hunter-gatherers—such as the Datooga in Tanzania—tend to have far fewer copies than people whose ancestors came from farming populations, whether they live in Africa, Asia or the Americas. Getting a jump on starch processing at the point of entry seems to have been an advantage for ancient farmers wherever they adopted starchy grains.

Another dietary adaptation is one of the best-studied examples of recent human evolution: lactose tolerance. Nearly everyone in the world is born with the ability to produce the enzyme lactase, which breaks down the milk sugar lactose and makes it easier to extract energy from milk—essential for the survival of a suckling child. Most people lose this ability by adulthood. At least five different times in our recent evolutionary past, as people started to discover dairy, a genetic mutation arose to lengthen the activity of the lactase gene. Three of the mutations originated in different parts of sub-Saharan Africa, where there is a long history of cattle herding. Another one of the five genetic tweaks is common in Arabia and seems to have sprung up in ancient populations of camel and goat herders.

The fifth and most common variant of the mutation that keeps the lactase gene turned on in adulthood is found today in human populations stretching from Ireland to India, with its highest frequencies across northern Europe. The mutation originated in a single individual 7,500 years ago (give or take a few thousand years). In 2011, scientists analyzed DNA recovered from Ötzi the Iceman, who was naturally mummified about 5,500 years ago in northern Italy. He did not have the lactose-tolerance mutation, a hint that it had not yet become common in this region thousands of years after its initial origin. In following years, researchers sequenced DNA extracted from the skeletons of farmers who lived in Europe more than 5,000 years ago. None carried the lactase mutation. Yet in the same region today, the lactase-persistence mutation occurs in hundreds of millions of people—more than 75 percent of the gene pool. This is not a paradox but the mathematical expectation of natural selection. A new mutation under selection grows exponentially, taking many generations to become common enough to notice in a population. But once it becomes common, its continued growth is very rapid and ultimately dominates.

The Shallowness of Races

What is perhaps most extraordinary about our recent evolution is how many common physical features are completely new to human anatomy. The thick, straight black hair shared by most East Asians, for example, arose only within the past 30,000 years, thanks to a mutation in a gene called EDAR, which is crucial for orchestrating the early development of skin, hair, teeth and nails. That genetic variant traveled with early colonizers of the Americas, all of whom share an evolutionary past with East Asians.

In fact, the overall evolutionary history of human skin, hair and eye pigmentation is surprisingly shallow. In the earliest stages of our evolution, all our ancestors had dark skin, hair and eyes. Since this initial state, dozens of genetic changes have lightened these features to some extent. A few of these changes are ancient variations present within Africa but more common elsewhere in the world. Most are new mutations that have emerged in one population or another: a change in a gene named TYRP1, for instance, that makes certain Solomon Islanders blond; the HERC2 mutation that results in blue eyes; changes to MC1R that causes red hairs to sprout instead of black ones; and a mutation in the SLC24A5 gene that lightens skin color and that is now found in up to 95 percent of Europeans. As in the case of lactase, ancient DNA is giving clear information about the antiquity of such mutations. Blue eyes seem to have appeared in people who lived more than 9,000 years ago, but the massive change to SLC24A5 is not found in the DNA of ancient skeletons from the same time period. Skin, hair, and eye color evolved with stunning speed.

Variations in pigmentation are some of the most obvious differences between the races and, in some ways, the easiest to study. Scientists have also investigated much odder and less evident features of human anatomy. Consider the variations of earwax. Most people in the world today have sticky earwax. In contrast, many East Asians have dry, flaky earwax that does not stick together. Anthropologists have known about this variation for more than 100 years, but geneticists did not uncover the cause until recently. Dry earwax results from a relatively new mutation to a gene called ABCC11. Only 30,000 to 20,000 years old, the mutation also affects the apocrine glands, which produce sweat. If you have stinky armpits and sticky earwax, chances are you have the original version of ABCC11. If you have dry earwax and a little less need for deodorant, you probably have the newer mutation.

A few thousand years before dry earwax first appeared among East Asians, another seemingly simple mutation started saving millions of Africans from a deadly disease. A gene called DARC produces a starchy molecule on the surface of red blood cells that mops up excess immune system molecules known as chemokines from the blood. About 45,000 years ago a mutation in DARC conferred remarkable resistance to *Plasmodium vivax*, one of the two most prevalent malaria parasites infecting humans today. The vivax parasites enter red blood cells through the DARC molecule encoded by the gene, so hindering the expression of DARC keeps the pathogens at bay. The absence of DARC also increased the amount of inflammation-causing chemokines circulating in the blood, which has in turn been linked to an increase in prostate cancer rates in African-American men. Yet on the whole, the mutation was so successful that 95 percent of people living below the Sahara now have it, whereas only 5 percent of Europeans and Asians do.

The Power of Random

We are used to thinking about evolution as a process of "good" genes replacing "bad" ones, but the most recent phase of human adaptation is a testament to the power of randomness in evolution. Beneficial mutations do not automatically persist. It all depends on timing and population size.

I first learned this lesson from the late anthropologist Frank Livingstone. The beginning of my training coincided with the end of his long career, during which he investigated the genetic basis for malaria resistance. More than 3,000 years ago in Africa and India, a mutation arose in the gene coding the oxygen-transporting blood cell molecule known as hemoglobin. When people inherited two copies of this mutation—dubbed hemoglobin S—they developed sickle cell anemia, a disease in which unusually shaped blood cells clog vessels. Red cells are normally supple and flexible enough to squeeze through tiny capillaries, but the mutant blood cells were rigid and pointed into the characteristic "sickle" shape. As it turns out, changing the shape of red blood cells also thwarted the ability of the malaria parasite to infect those cells.

Another mutation that interested Livingstone was hemoglobin E. Common in Southeast Asia today, hemoglobin E confers substantial malaria resistance without the severe side effects of hemoglobin S. "Hemoglobin E seems like it would be a lot better to have than hemoglobin S," I said in class one day. "Why didn't they get E in Africa?"

"It didn't happen there," Livingstone said.

His reply stunned me. I had supposed natural selection to be the most powerful force in evolution's arsenal. Humans had lived with deadly falciparum malaria for thousands of years in Africa. Surely natural selection would have weeded out less helpful mutations and hit on the most successful one.

Livingstone went on to show how the previous existence of hemoglobin S in a population made it harder for hemoglobin E to invade. Malaria rips through a population full of only normal hemoglobin carriers, and a new mutation that provides a slight advantage can quickly become more common. Yet a population already supplied with the protective hemoglobin S mutation will have a lower mortality risk. Sickle cell carriers still face formidable risks, but hemoglobin E is less of a relative advantage in a population that already has this imperfect form of malaria resistance. Perversely, what matters is not only the luck of having the mutation but also when the mutation happens. A partial adaptation with bad side effects can win, at least over the few thousand years humans have been adapting to malaria.

Ever since humans first began battling malaria, scores of different genetic changes emerged that increased immunity to the disease, different ones in different places. Each started as a serendipitous mutation that managed to persist in a local population despite being very rare at first. Any one of those mutations was, individually, unlikely to last long enough to become established, but the huge and rapidly increasing population size of our ancestors gave them many more rolls of the dice. As human populations have spread into new parts of the world and grown larger, they have rapidly adapted to their new homes precisely because those populations were so big.

Our Evolutionary Future

Human populations continue to evolve today. Unlike the distant past, where we must infer the action of selection from its long-term effects on genes, today scientists can watch human evolution in action, often by studying trends in health and reproduction. Even as medical technology, sanitation and vaccines have greatly extended life spans, birth rates in many populations still vacillate.

In sub-Saharan Africa, women who have a certain variant of a gene called FLT1 and who are pregnant in the malarial season are slightly more likely to bear children than are pregnant women who lack the variant, because the possessors have a lower risk that the placenta will be infected by malaria parasites. We do not yet understand how this gene reduces the risk of placental malaria, but the effect is profound and measurable.

Stephen Stearns of Yale University and his colleagues have examined years of records from long-term public health studies to see which traits may correlate with reproduction rates today. During the past 60 years, relatively short and heavy women in the U.S. who have low cholesterol counts had slightly more children on average than women who have the opposite traits. Why these traits have been related to family size is not yet clear.

New public health studies on the horizon, such as U.K. Bio-bank, will be tracking the genotypes and lifetime health of hundreds of thousands of people. Such studies are being undertaken because the interactions of genes are complicated, and we need to examine thousands of outcomes to understand which genetic changes underlie human health. Tracing the ancestry of human mutations gives us a tremendous power to observe evolution over hundreds of generations but can obscure the complex interactions of environment, survival, and fertility that unfolded in the past. We see the long-term winners, such as lactase persistence, but may miss the short-term dynamics. Human populations are about to become the most intensively observed long-term experiment in evolutionary biology.

What will the future of human evolution look like? Across the past few thousand years, human evolution has taken a distinctive path in different populations yet has maintained surprising commonality. New adaptive mutations may have elbowed their way into human populations, but they have not muscled out the old versions of genes. Instead the old, "ancestral" versions of genes mostly have remained with us. Meanwhile millions of people are moving between nations every year, leading to an unprecedented rate of genetic exchanges and mixture.

With such a high rate of genetic mixing, it may seem reasonable to expect that additive traits—for example, pigmentation, where many different genes have independent effects on skin color—will become ever more blended in future human populations. Could we be looking at a human future where we are a homogeneous slurry instead of a colorful stew of variability?

The answer is no. Many of the traits that differ between human populations are not additive. Even pigmentation is hardly so simple, as is readily seen in mixed populations in the U.S., Mexico, and Brazil. Instead of a featureless mass of café-au-lait-colored clones, we are already starting to see a glorious riot of variations—dark-skinned, freckled blondes, and striking combinations of green eyes and olive skin. Each of our descendants will be a living mosaic of human history.

More to Explore

Are Human Beings Still Evolving? It Would Seem That Evolution Is Impossible Now That the Ability to Reproduce Is Essentially Universally Available. Are We Nevertheless Changing as a Species? Meredith F. Small; Ask the Experts, ScientificAmerican.com, October 21, 1999.

African Adaptation to Digesting Milk Is "Strongest Signal of Selection Ever." Nikhil Swaminathan; ScientificAmerican.com, December 11, 2006.

Did Lactose Tolerance First Evolve in Central, Rather Than Northern Europe? Lynne Peeples; ScientificAmerican.com, August 28, 2009.

From our Archives

Evolution in the Future. Henry M. Lewis, Jr.; April 1941.

The Evolution of Man. Sherwood L. Washburn; September 1978.

The Future of Human Evolution. John Rennie; From the Editors, March 2001.
scientificamerican.com/magazine/sa

In Brief

Some scientists and science communicators have claimed that humans are no longer subject to natural selection and that human evolution has effectively ceased.

In fact, humans have evolved rapidly and remarkably in the past 30,000 years. Straight, black hair, blue eyes, and lactose tolerance are all examples of relatively recent traits.

Such rapid evolution has been possible for several reasons, including the switch from hunting and gathering to agrarian-based societies, which permitted human populations to grow much larger than before. The more people reproduce within a population, the higher the chance of new advantageous mutations.

Humans will undoubtedly continue to evolve into the future. Although it may seem that we are headed toward a cosmopolitan blend of human genes, future generations will likely be striking mosaics of our entire evolutionary past.

Many Commonplace Features of human biology are relatively new. Blue eyes, straight, thick black hair, the ability to digest milk in adulthood and some mutations that lightened skin all emerged in the past 30,000 years.

Findings
The Milk Mutation

Enjoying dairy in adulthood is a privilege that emerged relatively recently in our evolutionary history. We depend on the enzyme lactase to break down lactose, the sugar found in milk, but the human body usually stops producing lactase after adolescence. In fact, most of the world's adults are lactose-intolerant. Within the past 10,000 years, however, different populations of dairy farmers independently evolved genetic mutations that kept lactase active throughout life. Scientists have identified five such mutations, but there are likely several more. Collectively, all these adaptations explain the prevalence of lactose tolerance seen around the world today.

One of the so-called lactase-persistence mutations arose around 7,500 years ago among dairy farmers in a region between Central Europe and the northern Balkans. This is the most common lactase mutation in Europe today.

Three different lactase-persistence mutations originated in sub-Saharan Africa, the most common of which spread rapidly through the region in the past 7,000 years.

The world's first daily farmers lived in the Middle East and North Africa between 10,000 and 8,000 years ago. They primarily raised sheep, goats, and cattle, but at least one lactase-persistence mutation likely sprung up among camel herders.

Critical Thinking

1. What is the evidence for continuing human evolution since our ancestors transitioned from hunting and gathering to farming?

2. What are some of the more recent evolutionary adaptations made by humans and why?

3. What is the relationship between recent increases in human populations and evolutionary change?

4. How are scientists able to watch human evolution in action even today?

Internet References

American Journal of Physical Anthropology
http://onlinelibrary.wiley.com/journal/10.1002/(ISSN)1096-8644

Journal of Human Evolution
http://www.journals.elsevier.com/journal-of-human-evolution/

National Geographic Future of Food
natgeofood.com

The Paleolithic Diet Page
www.paleodiet.com

JOHN HAWKS is an anthropologist and an expert on human evolution at the University of Wisconsin-Madison.

Unit 7

UNIT

Prepared by: Elvio Angeloni, *Pasadena City College*

Living with the Past

Anthropology continues to evolve as a discipline, not only with respect to the tools and techniques of the trade, but also in the application of whatever knowledge we stand to gain about ourselves. Sometimes an awareness of our biological and behavioral past may help us to better understand the present. In the context of our bodily health, for instance, it may be instructive to know that some traditional hunters, such as the Inuit of the Arctic, would gorge themselves on fat, rarely saw a vegetable and, yet, were still healthier than we are today. When assessing the symptoms of disease, such as coughing or sneezing, should we interpret them as part of the aggressive strategies evolved by microbes to induce us to spread them to other human hosts or as part of our own evolved defense mechanisms to get rid of them? Finally, in the area of genetics, we find that, while there are many deleterious genes that get weeded out of the population by means of natural selection, there are other harmful ones, such as the genes for sickle cell anemia, cystic fibrosis, and iron deficiency anemia, that may actually have a good side to them and may therefore be perpetuated in the human species in spite of their downsides.

As we reflect upon where we have been and how we came to be as we are in the evolutionary sense, the inevitable question arises as to what will happen next. This is the most difficult issue of all, because our biological future depends so much on long-range environmental trends that no one seems to be able to predict. Take, for example, the sweeping effects of ecological change upon the viruses of the world, which in turn seem to be paving the way for new waves of human epidemics. There is no better example of this problem than the recent explosion of new diseases, such as the various strains of flu, Ebola, and HIV.

As we gain a better understanding of the processes of mutation and natural selection, and their relevance to human beings,

we might even gain some control over the evolutionary direction of our species. However, the issue of what is a beneficial application of scientific knowledge becomes a subject for debate. Who will have the final word as to how these technological breakthroughs are to be employed in the future? Even with the best of intentions, how can we be certain of the long-range consequences of our actions in such a complicated field?

Knowledge in itself, of course, is neutral—its potential for good or ill being determined by those who happen to be in the position to use it. Consider, for example, that some men may be dying from a genetically caused overabundance of iron in their blood systems in a trade-off that allows some women to absorb sufficient amounts of the element to guarantee their own survival. The question of whether we should eliminate such a gene that brings about this situation would seem to depend on which sex we decide should reap the benefit.

Much of what is being discussed here is known collectively as "Darwinian medicine," which is based upon the premise that an understanding of how we humans and the microbes that afflict us have evolved in relation to each other will help us to reduce disease and alleviate suffering. This perspective is even more important today, as we have come to live in ever more crowded conditions, thus making it easier for microbes to spread. At the same time, we must remain aware that someone, at some time, may actually use the same knowledge to increase rather than reduce the misery that exists in the world.

Since it has been our conscious decision making (and not the genetically predetermined behavior that characterizes some species) that has gotten us into this situation, then it is the conscious will of our generation and future generations that will get us out of it. But, can we wait much longer for humanity to collectively come to its senses? Or is it too late already?

Article   Prepared by: Elvio Angeloni, *Pasadena City College*

The Perfect Plague

The next killer germ could burst from the African rain forest—or from your family pet.

Jared Diamond and Nathan Wolfe

Learning Outcomes

After reading this article, you will be able to:

- Determine whether the concept of natural selection has any relevance to the treatment of disease and defend your answer.
- Describe the modern conditions for human pandemic diseases.

Shortly after one of us (Jared Diamond) boarded a flight from Hong Kong back to Los Angeles, the passenger in the next seat sneezed. She sneezed again—and again—and then she began coughing. Finally she gagged, pulled out the vomit bag from the seat back in front of her, threw up into the bag, stood up, squeezed past, and lurched to the toilet at the front of the plane. The woman was obviously miserable, but sympathy for her pain was not what I felt. Instead I was frightened and asked the flight attendant to move me to a seat as far from her as possible.

All I could think of was another sick person, a man from Guangdong province in southern China, who spent the night of February 21, 2003, at the Metropole Hotel in Hong Kong, an upscale establishment with a swimming pool, fitness center, restaurants, a bar, and all kinds of areas where visitors could socialize and connect. The man stayed a single night in room 911. Unfortunately for him and for many other people, he had picked up severe acute respiratory syndrome, or SARS—perhaps directly from an infected bat or from a small, arboreal mammal called a civet, common in one of Guangdong's famous "wet markets" that sell wild animals for food, or else from a person or chain of people ultimately infected from one of those animal sources.

In the course of his brief stay, the man initiated a SARS "super spreader" event that led to at least 16 more SARS cases among the hotel's guests and visitors and then to hundreds of other cases throughout Asia, Europe, and North America as those guests and visitors continued on their travels—just as my neighbor was now traveling to L.A. The infectiousness

of room 911's guest can be gauged from the fact that three months later, the carpet right outside the door and near the hotel elevator yielded genetic evidence of the SARS virus, presumably spewed out in his own sneezing, coughing, or vomiting.

I didn't end up with SARS, but my experience drives home the terrifying prospect of a novel, unstoppable infectious disease. Globalization, changing climate, and the threat of drug resistance have conspired to set the stage for that perfect microbial storm: a situation in which an emerging pathogen—another HIV or smallpox, perhaps—might burst on the scene and kill millions before we can respond.

Pathogen Paradox

To grasp the risk, we first must understand why *any* microbe would evolve to sicken or kill us. In evolutionary terms, how does destroying its host help a microbe to survive?

Think of your body as a potential "habitat" for tiny microbes, just as a forest provides a habitat for bigger creatures like birds and squirrels. The species living in the forests of our bodies include lice, worms, bacteria, viruses, and amoebas. Many of those denizens are benign and cause us no harm. But some microbes seem to go out of their way to make us sick—either mildly sick, as in the case of the common cold, or else sick to the point of killing us, as in the case of smallpox.

Killer microbes have long posed a paradox for evolutionary biologists. Why would a microbe evolve to devastate the very habitat on which it depends? By analogy, you might reason that there should be no squirrels that destroy the forest they live in, because such a species would quickly go extinct.

The answer stems from the fact that in order to survive over the long haul, any microbe restricted to humans must be able to spread from one victim to the next. There is a simple mathematical requirement here: On average, the germ must infect at least one new victim for every old one who either dies or recovers and purges himself of the microbe. If the average number of new victims per old drops to fewer than one, then the spread of the microbe is doomed.

A microbe can't walk or fly from one host to the next. Instead it must resort to a range of nefarious tricks. What from our point of view is simply a disease symptom can, from the bug's perspective, be an all-important means of enlisting our help to move around. Common microbe tricks are to make us cough or sneeze, suffer from diarrhea, or develop open sores on our skin. Respectively, these symptoms spread the microbe into our exhaled breath, into the local water supply via our feces, and onto the skin of those who touch us, explaining why a microbe might want to induce unpleasant symptoms in its victims.

Evolutionary biologists reason that keeping us alive and pumping out new microbes would be an excellent strategy for such a bug, which might therefore evolve to be less, not more, virulent over time. An example comes from the history of syphilis. When it first appeared in Europe in 1495, it caused severe and painful symptoms within a few months, but by 1546 it had begun evolving into the slowly progressing disease that we know today.

Yet if keeping us alive is strategically sound, why do some pathogens go so far as to actually kill us?

Sometimes a microbe's deadly rampage through a human population stems from an accident of nature. For instance, the microbe could be comfortably adapted to some animal host that it routinely inhabits without deadly consequences, but it could be maladapted to the human environment. The microbe may rarely infect people, but when it does, it may kill the human host, who becomes a literal dead end for the virus as well.

A microbe's deadly rampage through humans might stem from an accident of nature.

But what of those killer microbes that target humans, making us their primary host? Their survival strategy, evolutionary biologists now realize, differs from that of a disease like syphilis but works just as well. Take the cholera bacterium that gives us diarrhea or the smallpox virus that makes us develop skin sores; both of these can kill us in days to weeks. Such virulence may be evolutionary favored if, in the brief time between our becoming infected and dying, the fatal symptoms spread trillions of microbes to potential new victims. The fact that we may die is unfortunate for us but an acceptable cost for the microbe. In the world of evolution and natural selection, anything that the microbe does to us is fair—just as long as at least one new victim gets infected for each old one.

Hence the recipe for a killer disease is for the microbe to achieve a balance between two things: the probability of its killing us quickly once we become infected and its efficiency in leading our bodies to transmit the microbe to new victims.

Humanity's greatest predators can be seen only with the aid of a microscope. The virus responsible for AIDS; the SARS virus; *Vibrio cholerae* bacteria, responsible for cholera; and spores of anthrax.

Those two things are connected. The greater its efficiency in inducing lethal, bug-spreading syndromes (good for the microbe), the faster the microbe kills us (bad for the microbe). Following this logic, a pathogen may end up killing lots of people by one of two routes. In the style of HIV, it can keep the disease carrier alive for a long time, infecting new victims over the course of months or years. Or in the style of smallpox and cholera, it might kill quickly with explosive symptoms that can spread an infection to dozens of new victims within a day.

Searching for the Source

For epidemiologists hoping to stanch such outbreaks, tracking killer germs to the source is key. Do deadly pandemics arise spontaneously in human populations? Or are they "gifts" from other species, mutating and then crossing over to make us ill? Which ecosystems are spawning them, and can we catch them at the start, before they cause too much damage?

Some answers can be found in the history of yellow fever, a virus spread by mosquitoes. The cause of devastating human epidemics throughout history, yellow fever is still rife in tropical South America and Africa. Biologists now understand that yellow fever arose in tropical African monkeys, which, through the mosquito vector, infected (and continue to infect) tropical African people, some of whom unintentionally carried yellow fever with them on slave ships several hundred years ago to South America.

Mosquitoes bit the infected slaves and in turn carried the virus to South American monkeys. In due course, mosquitoes bit infected monkeys and transmitted yellow fever right back to the human population there.

In Venezuela today, the Ministry of Health keeps a lookout for the appearance of unusual numbers of dead wild monkeys, such as howler monkeys. Because the monkeys are so susceptible to yellow fever and can act as a reservoir from which the virus leaps to the human population, an explosion of monkey deaths serves as an advance warning system, signaling the need to vaccinate humans in the vicinity.

This pattern of cross-infection from animals to humans is par for the course in emerging infectious disease. In fact, the big killer diseases of history all came to us from microbes living in other species, overwhelmingly from other warm-blooded mammals and, to a lesser extent, from birds.

On reflection, this all makes sense. Each new animal host to which a microbe adapts represents a new habitat. It is easiest for a microbe to jump between closely related habitats, from an animal species with one sort of body chemistry to a closely related animal species with very similar body chemistry.

In the tropics, disease sources have included a host of wild animals, most notably the nonhuman primates. We can thank our primate cousins not just for yellow fever but also for HIV, dengue fever, hepatitis B, and vivax malaria. Other wild animal disease donors include rats, the source of the plague and typhus.

In temperate regions like the United States, meanwhile, ticks in suburban neighborhoods and domestic livestock living in proximity to humans have posed threats. Mammalian reservoirs like mice and chipmunks carry Lyme disease and tularemia; ticks transmit these diseases to humans. Cattle probably gave rise to the measles and tuberculosis. Smallpox is likely to have come from camels, biologists say, and flu from pigs and ducks.

The Next Wave

Today, with fewer people tending farms and more living in the suburbs, things have certainly changed. The principles of infectious disease are the same as they have always been, but modern conditions, including life in proximity to pets and mammal-filled woods, are exposing us to new pathogen reservoirs and new modes of transmitting disease.

One of us (Nathan Wolfe) has spent much of the last six years in the tropical African country of Cameroon, studying the kinds of interspecies jumps that such conditions might spawn. To examine the mechanisms, I worked with rural hunters who butchered wild animals for food. I collected blood samples from the hunters, from other people in their community, and from their animal prey. By testing all those samples, I identified microbes inhabiting the animal reservoirs and focused on those that showed up in the hunters' blood, making them candidates for firing up human disease.

> Three strains of influenza virus, including H5N1, better known as the avian flu virus. The influenza virus frequently mutates, creating new strains. This makes it difficult to produce vaccines and opens the door to another global influenza pandemic, such as the one that struck in 1918 and eventually killed more than 20 million people.

One evening I asked a group of hunters if they had ever cut themselves while butchering wild monkeys or apes. The response was incredulous laughter: "You don't know the answer to that?" Of course, they said. All of them had cut themselves once or more, thereby giving themselves ample opportunity to get infected from animal blood.

On reflection, I shouldn't have been surprised. I can't count all the times I have cut myself while chopping onions. The difference is that onions aren't closely related to us humans, and an onion virus has far less chance of taking hold in us than does a monkey virus.

The statistics are telling. Researchers like Mark Woolhouse, professor of infectious disease epidemiology at the University of Edinburgh in Scotland, have found at least 868 human pathogens that infect both animals and humans, although some are not as fearsome as they seem.

Overhyped microbes include anthrax (famous for the U.S. mail attacks in 2000), the Ebola and Marburg viruses (which can cause dramatic bleeding and high fever in their victims),

and the prion agent of mad cow disease (otherwise known as bovine spongiform encephalopathy, or BSE), which kills people by making their nervous systems degenerate. These bugs arouse terror because they kill so many of their victims. For example, in the 2000 Ebola outbreak, which struck the Gulu district of Uganda, 53 percent of the 425 people who contracted the disease died. The case fatality rate for BSE is 100 percent.

Although spectacularly lethal, these pathogens generally kill just a few hundred people at a time and then burn themselves out. They transmit from human to human too inefficiently to spread very widely; 100 percent of a small number of victims is still a small number of fatalities.

There are many reasons why an agent leaping from animals to humans might not affect more individuals. For example, humans do not normally bite, scratch, hunt, or eat each other. This surely contributes to the rarity or nonexistence of human-to-human transmission of rabies (acquired by the bite of an infected dog or bat); cat-scratch disease (which causes skin lesions and swollen lymph nodes); tularemia (a disease, often acquired when hunting and cutting up an infected rabbit, that can cause skin ulcers, swollen lymph nodes, and fever); and BSE (probably acquired by eating the nervous system tissue of infected cows).

Some outbreaks, once recognized, are relatively easy to control. Anthrax is treatable with antibiotics; after an initial malaria-like stage, the rapid onset and severity of Ebola and Marburg symptoms have made identification and containment straightforward.

In fact, within the last 40 years, only HIV (derived from chimpanzees) has taken off to cause a pandemic.

Back to the Future

If not anthrax or Ebola, which pathogens might spawn the next deadly pandemic in our midst?

New pandemics are most likely to be triggered by mutant strains of familiar microbe species, especially those that have caused plagues by churning out mutant strains in the past. For example, the highest known epidemic death toll in history was caused by a new strain of influenza virus that killed more than 20 million people in 1918 and 1919. Unfairly named Spanish influenza, it apparently emerged in Kansas during World War I, was carried by American troops to Europe, and then spread around the world in three waves before ebbing in outbreaks of declining virulence in the 1920s. Mutant strains of influenza or cholera remain prime candidates for another deadly outbreak. Both can persist in animal reservoirs or the environment, and both are adept at spawning new strains. Both pathogens also transmit efficiently, and it is possible that these two important diseases of the past could become important diseases of the future.

A future pandemic could also come from tuberculosis. New mutants have already arisen through the mechanism of drug resistance. And the disease lives on in the human population, especially among those with weakened immunity, including patients with HIV.

Also of concern are emerging sexually transmitted diseases, which, once introduced, may be difficult to control because it is hard to persuade humans to change sexual behavior or to abstain from sex. HIV offers a grim warning: Despite its huge global impact, the AIDS epidemic would have been far worse if the sexual transmissibility of HIV (which is actually rather modest) had equaled that of some other sexually transmitted agents, such as human papilloma virus (HPV). While the probability of HIV transmission varies with the stage of the disease and the type of sexual contact, it appears to pass from infected to uninfected individuals in less than 1 percent of acts of unprotected heterosexual intercourse, while the corresponding probability of HPV transmission is thought to be higher than 5 percent—probably much higher.

Similarly, it could be difficult to control emerging pathogens transmitted by pets, which increasingly include exotic species along with traditional domestic animals like dogs and cats. Already we are at risk of catching rabies from our dogs, toxoplasmosis and cat-scratch disease from our cats, and psittacosis from our parrots. Most people now accept the need to cull millions of farmyard animals in the face of epidemics like mad cow disease, but it is hard to imagine killing beloved puppies, bunnies, and kittens, even if those pets do turn out to offer a pathway for a dangerous new disease.

Have Plague, Will Travel

Once a killer disease has emerged, modern societies offer new ways for it to flourish and spread. Global travel, the close quarters of the urban environment, climate change, the evolution of drug-resistant microbes, and increasing numbers of the elderly or antibiotic-treated immunosuppressed could all aid the next great plague.

For example, rapid urbanization in Africa could transform yellow fever, Chikungunya fever (which causes severe joint pain and fever), and other rural African arboviruses (viruses, including yellow fever, spread by bloodsucking insects) into plagues of African cities, as has already happened with dengue hemorrhagic fever. One of us (Wolfe) theorizes that this might follow increasing demand in those cities for bush meat. Like urban people everywhere, urban Africans love to eat the foods enjoyed by their village-dwelling ancestors, and in tropical Africa this means bush meat. In that respect it's similar to the smoked fish and bagels that I eat in the United States, which give me some comforting memory of my Eastern European roots. But there's an important difference: The wild game that I see served in fancy restaurants in the capital of Cameroon is much more likely to transmit a dangerous virus to the person who hunted and butchered it, or to the cook who prepared it, or to the restaurant patron who ate the meat undercooked, than is my brunch of smoked fish and bagels.

By connecting distant places, meanwhile, globalization permits the long-distance transfer of microbes along with their insect vectors and their human victims, as evidenced not only by the spread of HIV around the world, but also by North American cases of cholera and SARS brought by infected passengers on jet flights from South America and Asia, respectively. Indeed, when a flight from Buenos Aires to Los Angeles stopped in Lima in 1992, it picked up some seafood infected with the cholera then making the rounds in Peru. As a result, dozens of passengers who arrived in Los Angeles, some of whom then changed planes and flew on to Nevada and even as far as Japan, found that they had contracted cholera. Within days that single airplane spread cholera 10,000 miles around the whole rim of the Pacific Basin.

The tuberculosis bacterium, *Mycobacterium tuberculosis*, has developed a resistance to antibiotics in many regions of the world, fueling a resurgence of this disease.

Consider as well those diseases thought of as "just" tropical because they are transmitted by tropical vectors: malaria transmitted by mosquitoes, sleeping sickness spread by tsetse flies, and Chagas' disease (associated with edema, fever, and heart disease) spread by kissing bugs. How will we feel about those tropical diseases if global warming enables their vectors to spread into temperate zones? While microbe and vector movement can be difficult to detect, modeling suggests that global warming will expand the reach of malaria to higher latitudes and into tropical mountain regions.

The transmission of emerging diseases has also been enhanced by a host of modern practices and technologies. The commercial bush meat trade has introduced retroviruses into human populations. Ecotourism has exposed first-world tourists to cutaneous leishmaniasis and other third-world diseases. Underequipped rural hospitals have facilitated Ebola virus outbreaks in Africa. Air conditioners and water circulation systems have spread Legionnaires' disease. Industrial food production was responsible in Europe for the spread of BSE. And intravenous drug use and blood transfusion have both spread HIV and hepatitis B and C.

We have the potential to avert the next HIV, saving millions of lives and billions of dollars.

All this shows that disease prevention and treatment need to be supplemented by a new effort: disease forecasting. This refers to the early detection of potential pandemics at a stage when we might still be able to localize them, before they have had the opportunity to infect a high percentage of the local population and thereby spread around the world, as happened with HIV. Already one of us (Wolfe) is working through a new initiative, the Global Viral Forecasting Initiative (GVFI), to do just that. GVFI works in countries throughout the world to monitor the entry and movement of new agents before they become pandemics. By studying emerging agents at the interface between humans and animals, GVFI hopes to stop new epidemics before they explode. Monitoring for the emergence of both new sexually transmitted diseases and pet-associated diseases would be good investments.

The predictions here are admittedly educated guesses—but they are educated by some of the best science available. The time to act is now. If we don't, then we will continue to be like the cardiologists of the 1950s, waiting for their patients' heart attacks and doing little to prevent them. If we do act, we have the potential to avert the next HIV, saving millions of lives and billions of dollars. The choice seems obvious.

Critical Thinking

1. How did the author's (Jared Diamond) airline experience illustrate the possible spread of a novel, unstoppable infectious disease?

2. What must a microbe be able to do to survive if it kills its host?

3. What are some of the "microbe tricks" designed to allow it to spread from one victim to the next?

4. Under what circumstance would keeping us alive be an excellent strategy?

5. When would virulence be evolutionarily favored?

6. In what sense does a recipe for a killer disease involve a balance between two things?

7. By what two routes may a pathogen end up killing lots of people?

8. Discuss the cross-infection from animals to humans as the explanation for the big killer disease of history and why this could easily happen.

9. What are the modern conditions exposing us to new pathogen reservoirs?

10. What is a principle way in which African hunters become exposed to infectious microbes?

11. Where are new pandemics likely to come from and why?

12. How have modern societies offered new ways for killer disease to flourish and spread?

13. What is "disease forecasting" and why is it important?

Create Central

www.mhhe.com/createcentral

Internet References

Evolution and Medicine Network
http://evmedreview.com

The Evolution & Medicine Review
http://evmedreview.com

Article

Prepared by: Elvio Angeloni, *Pasadena City College*

The Inuit Paradox

How can people who gorge on fat and rarely see a vegetable be healthier than we are?

PATRICIA GADSBY

Learning Outcomes

After reading this article, you will be able to:

- Describe some healthful habits we can learn by studying hunter-gatherers.

- Identify the traditional Inuit (Eskimo) practices that are important for their survival in the circumstances they live in and contrast them with the values professed by the society you live in.

P atricia Cochran, an Inupiat from Northwestern Alaska, is talking about the native foods of her childhood: "We pretty much had a subsistence way of life. Our food supply was right outside our front door. We did our hunting and foraging on the Seward Peninsula and along the Bering Sea."

"Our meat was seal and walrus, marine mammals that live in cold water and have lots of fat. We used seal oil for our cooking and as a dipping sauce for food. We had moose, caribou, and reindeer. We hunted ducks, geese, and little land birds like quail, called ptarmigan. We caught crab and lots of fish—salmon, whitefish, tomcod, pike, and char. Our fish were cooked, dried, smoked, or frozen. We ate frozen raw whitefish, sliced thin. The elders liked stinkfish, fish buried in seal bags or cans in the tundra and left to ferment. And fermented seal flipper, they liked that too."

Cochran's family also received shipments of whale meat from kin living farther north, near Barrow. Beluga was one she liked; raw muktuk, which is whale skin with its underlying blubber, she definitely did not. "To me it has a chew-on-a-tire consistency," she says, "but to many people it's a mainstay." In the short subarctic summers, the family searched for roots and greens and, best of all from a child's point of view, wild blueberries, crowberries, or salmonberries, which her aunts would mix with whipped fat to make a special treat called *akutuq*—in colloquial English, Eskimo ice cream.

Now Cochran directs the Alaska Native Science Commission, which promotes research on native cultures and the health

and environmental issues that affect them. She sits at her keyboard in Anchorage, a bustling city offering fare from Taco Bell to French cuisine. But at home Cochran keeps a freezer filled with fish, seal, walrus, reindeer, and whale meat, sent by her family up north, and she and her husband fish and go berry picking—"sometimes a challenge in Anchorage," she adds, laughing. "I eat fifty-fifty," she explains, half traditional, half regular American.

No one, not even residents of the northernmost villages on Earth, eats an entirely traditional northern diet anymore. Even the groups we came to know as Eskimo—which include the Inupiat and the Yupiks of Alaska, the Canadian Inuit and Inuvialuit, Inuit Greenlanders, and the Siberian Yupiks—have probably seen more changes in their diet in a lifetime than their ancestors did over thousands of years. The closer people live to towns and the more access they have to stores and cash-paying jobs, the more likely they are to have westernized their eating. And with westernization, at least on the North American continent, comes processed foods and cheap carbohydrates—Crisco, Tang, soda, cookies, chips, pizza, fries. "The young and urbanized," says Harriet Kuhnlein, director of the Centre for Indigenous Peoples' Nutrition and Environment at McGill University in Montreal, "are increasingly into fast food." So much so that type 2 diabetes, obesity, and other diseases of Western civilization are becoming causes for concern there too.

Today, when diet books top the best-seller list and nobody seems sure of what to eat to stay healthy, it's surprising to learn how well the Eskimo did on a high-protein, high-fat diet. Shaped by glacial temperatures, stark landscapes, and protracted winters, the traditional Eskimo diet had little in the way of plant food, no agricultural or dairy products, and was unusually low in carbohydrates. Mostly people subsisted on what they hunted and fished. Inland dwellers took advantage of caribou feeding on tundra mosses, lichens, and plants too tough for humans to stomach (though predigested vegetation in the animals' paunches became dinner as well). Coastal people exploited the sea. The main nutritional challenge was avoiding starvation in late winter if primary meat sources became too scarce or lean.

These foods hardly make up the "balanced" diet most of us grew up with, and they look nothing like the mix of grains, fruits, vegetables, meat, eggs, and dairy we're accustomed to seeing in conventional food pyramid diagrams. How could such a diet possibly be adequate? How did people get along on little else but fat and animal protein?

The diet of the far north shows that there are no essential foods—only essential nutrients.

What the diet of the Far North illustrates, says Harold Draper, a biochemist and expert in Eskimo nutrition, is that there are no essential foods—only essential nutrients. And humans can get those nutrients from diverse and eye-opening sources.

One might, for instance, imagine gross vitamin deficiencies arising from a diet with scarcely any fruits and vegetables. What furnishes vitamin A, vital for eyes and bones? We derive much of ours from colorful plant foods, constructing it from pigmented plant precursors called carotenoids (as in carrots). But vitamin A, which is oil soluble, is also plentiful in the oils of cold-water fishes and sea mammals, as well as in the animals' livers, where fat is processed. These dietary staples also provide vitamin D, another oil-soluble vitamin needed for bones. Those of us living in temperate and tropical climates, on the other hand, usually make vitamin D indirectly by exposing skin to strong sun—hardly an option in the Arctic winter—and by consuming fortified cow's milk, to which the indigenous northern groups had little access until recent decades and often don't tolerate all that well.

As for vitamin C, the source in the Eskimo diet was long a mystery. Most animals can synthesize their own vitamin C, or ascorbic acid, in their livers, but humans are among the exceptions, along with other primates and oddballs like guinea pigs and bats. If we don't ingest enough of it, we fall apart from scurvy, a gruesome connective-tissue disease. In the United States today we can get ample supplies from orange juice, citrus fruits, and fresh vegetables. But vitamin C oxidizes with time; getting enough from a ship's provisions was tricky for early 18th- and 19th-century voyagers to the polar regions. Scurvy—joint pain, rotting gums, leaky blood vessels, physical and mental degeneration—plagued European and U.S. expeditions even in the 20th century. However, Arctic peoples living on fresh fish and meat were free of the disease.

Impressed, the explorer Vilhjalmur Stefansson adopted an Eskimo-style diet for five years during the two Arctic expeditions he led between 1908 and 1918. "The thing to do is to find your antiscorbutics where you are," he wrote. "Pick them up as you go." In 1928, to convince skeptics, he and a young colleague spent a year on an Americanized version of the diet under medical supervision at Bellevue Hospital in New York City. The pair ate steaks, chops, organ meats like brain and liver,

poultry, fish, and fat with gusto. "If you have some fresh meat in your diet every day and don't overcook it," Stefansson declared triumphantly, "there will be enough C from that source alone to prevent scurvy."

In fact, all it takes to ward off scurvy is a daily dose of 10 milligrams, says Karen Fediuk, a consulting dietitian and former graduate student of Harriet Kuhnlein's who did her master's thesis on vitamin C. (That's far less than the U.S. recommended daily allowance of 75 to 90 milligrams—75 for women, 90 for men.) Native foods easily supply those 10 milligrams of scurvy prevention, especially when organ meats—preferably raw—are on the menu. For a study published with Kuhnlein in 2002, Fediuk compared the vitamin C content of 100-gram (3.55-ounce) samples of foods eaten by Inuit women living in the Canadian Arctic: Raw caribou liver supplied almost 24 milligrams, seal brain close to 15 milligrams, and raw kelp more than 28 milligrams. Still higher levels were found in whale skin and muktuk.

As you might guess from its antiscorbutic role, vitamin C is crucial for the synthesis of connective tissue, including the matrix of skin. "Wherever collagen's made, you can expect vitamin C," says Kuhnlein. Thick skinned, chewy, and collagen rich, raw muktuk can serve up an impressive 36 milligrams in a 100-gram piece, according to Fediuk's analyses. "Weight for weight, it's as good as orange juice," she says. Traditional Inuit practices like freezing meat and fish and frequently eating them raw, she notes, conserve vitamin C, which is easily cooked off and lost in food processing.

Hunter-gatherer diets like those eaten by these northern groups and other traditional diets based on nomadic herding or subsistence farming are among the older approaches to human eating. Some of these eating plans might seem strange to us— diets centered around milk, meat, and blood among the East African pastoralists, enthusiastic tuber eating by the Quechua living in the High Andes, the staple use of the mongongo nut in the southern African !Kung—but all proved resourceful adaptations to particular eco-niches. No people, though, may have been forced to push the nutritional envelope further than those living at Earth's frozen extremes. The unusual makeup of the far-northern diet led Loren Cordain, a professor of evolutionary nutrition at Colorado State University at Fort Collins, to make an intriguing observation.

Four years ago, Cordain reviewed the macronutrient content (protein, carbohydrates, fat) in the diets of 229 hunter-gatherer groups listed in a series of journal articles collectively known as the Ethnographic Atlas. These are some of the oldest surviving human diets. In general, hunter-gatherers tend to eat more animal protein than we do in our standard Western diet, with its reliance on agriculture and carbohydrates derived from grains and starchy plants. Lowest of all in carbohydrate, and highest in combined fat and protein, are the diets of peoples living in the Far North, where they make up for fewer plant foods with extra fish. What's equally striking, though, says Cordain, is that these meat-and-fish diets also exhibit a natural "protein ceiling." Protein accounts for no more than 35 to 40 percent of their total calories, which suggests to him that's all the protein humans can comfortably handle.

Wild-animal fats are different from other fats. Farm animals typically have lots of highly saturated fat.

This ceiling, Cordain thinks, could be imposed by the way we process protein for energy. The simplest, fastest way to make energy is to convert carbohydrates into glucose, our body's primary fuel. But if the body is out of carbs, it can burn fat, or if necessary, break down protein. The name given to the convoluted business of making glucose from protein is gluco-neogenesis. It takes place in the liver, uses a dizzying slew of enzymes, and creates nitrogen waste that has to be converted into urea and disposed of through the kidneys. On a truly traditional diet, says Draper, recalling his studies in the 1970s, Arctic people had plenty of protein but little carbohydrate, so they often relied on gluconeogenesis. Not only did they have bigger livers to handle the additional work but their urine volumes were also typically larger to get rid of the extra urea. Nonetheless, there appears to be a limit on how much protein the human liver can safely cope with: Too much overwhelms the liver's waste-disposal system, leading to protein poisoning—nausea, diarrhea, wasting, and death.

Whatever the metabolic reason for this syndrome, says John Speth, an archaeologist at the University of Michigan's Museum of Anthropology, plenty of evidence shows that hunters through the ages avoided protein excesses, discarding fat-depleted animals even when food was scarce. Early pioneers and trappers in North America encountered what looks like a similar affliction, sometimes referred to as rabbit starvation because rabbit meat is notoriously lean. Forced to subsist on fat-deficient meat, the men would gorge themselves, yet wither away. Protein can't be the sole source of energy for humans, concludes Cordain. Anyone eating a meaty diet that is low in carbohydrates must have fat as well.

Stefansson had arrived at this conclusion, too, while living among the Copper Eskimo. He recalled how he and his Eskimo companions had become quite ill after weeks of eating "caribou so skinny that there was no appreciable fat behind the eyes or in the marrow." Later he agreed to repeat the miserable experience at Bellevue Hospital, for science's sake, and for a while ate nothing but defatted meat. "The symptoms brought on at Bellevue by an incomplete meat diet [lean without fat] were exactly the same as in the Arctic . . . diarrhea and a feeling of general baffling discomfort," he wrote. He was restored with a fat fix but "had lost considerable weight." For the remainder of his year on meat, Stefansson tucked into his rations of chops and steaks with fat intact. "A normal meat diet is not a high-protein diet," he pronounced. "We were really getting three-quarters of our calories from fat." (Fat is more than twice as

calorie dense as protein or carbohydrate, but even so, that's a lot of lard. A typical U.S diet provides about 35 percent of its calories from fat.)

Stefansson dropped 10 pounds on his meat-and-fat regimen and remarked on its "slenderizing" aspect, so perhaps it's no surprise he's been co-opted as a posthumous poster boy for Atkins-type diets. No discussion about diet these days can avoid Atkins. Even some researchers interviewed for this article couldn't resist referring to the Inuit way of eating as the "original Atkins." "Superficially, at a macro-nutrient level, the two diets certainly look similar," allows Samuel Klein, a nutrition researcher at Washington University in St. Louis, who's attempting to study how Atkins stacks up against conventional weight-loss diets. Like the Inuit diet, Atkins is low in carbohydrates and very high in fat. But numerous researchers, including Klein, point out that there are profound differences between the two diets, beginning with the type of meat and fat eaten.

Fats have been demonized in the United States, says Eric Dewailly, a professor of preventive medicine at Laval University in Quebec. But all fats are not created equal. This lies at the heart of a paradox—the Inuit paradox, if you will. In the Nunavik villages in northern Quebec, adults over 40 get almost half their calories from native foods, says Dewailly, and they don't die of heart attacks at nearly the same rates as other Canadians or Americans. Their cardiac death rate is about half of ours, he says. As someone who looks for links between diet and cardiovascular health, he's intrigued by that reduced risk. Because the traditional Inuit diet is "so restricted," he says, it's easier to study than the famously heart-healthy Mediterranean diet, with its cornucopia of vegetables, fruits, grains, herbs, spices, olive oil, and red wine.

A key difference in the typical Nunavik Inuit's diet is that more than 50 percent of the calories in Inuit native foods come from fats. Much more important, the fats come from wild animals.

Wild-animal fats are different from both farm-animal fats and processed fats, says Dewailly. Farm animals, cooped up and stuffed with agricultural grains (carbohydrates) typically have lots of solid, highly saturated fat. Much of our processed food is also riddled with solid fats, or so-called trans fats, such as the reengineered vegetable oils and shortenings cached in baked goods and snacks. "A lot of the packaged food on supermarket shelves contains them. So do commercial french fries," Dewailly adds.

Trans fats are polyunsaturated vegetable oils tricked up to make them more solid at room temperature. Manufacturers do this by hydrogenating the oils—adding extra hydrogen atoms to their molecular structures—which "twists" their shapes. Dewailly makes twisting sound less like a chemical transformation than a perversion, an act of public-health sabotage: "These man-made fats are dangerous, even worse for the heart than saturated fats." They not only lower high-density lipoprotein cholesterol (HDL, the "good" cholesterol) but they also raise low-density lipoprotein cholesterol (LDL, the "bad" cholesterol) and triglycerides, he says. In the process, trans fats set the stage for heart attacks because they lead to the increase of fatty buildup in artery walls.

Wild animals that range freely and eat what nature intended, says Dewailly, have fat that is far more healthful. Less of their fat is saturated, and more of it is in the monounsaturated form (like olive oil). What's more, cold-water fishes and sea mammals are particularly rich in polyunsaturated fats called n-3 fatty acids or omega-3 fatty acids. These fats appear to benefit the heart and vascular system. But the polyunsaturated fats in most Americans' diets are the omega-6 fatty acids supplied by vegetable oils. By contrast, whale blubber consists of 70 percent monounsaturated fat and close to 30 percent omega-3s, says Dewailly.

Dieting is the price we pay for too little exercise and too much mass-produced food.

Omega-3s evidently help raise HDL cholesterol, lower triglycerides, and are known for anticlotting effects. (Ethnographers have remarked on an Eskimo propensity for nosebleeds.) These fatty acids are believed to protect the heart from life-threatening arrhythmias that can lead to sudden cardiac death. And like a "natural aspirin," adds Dewailly, omega-3 polyunsaturated fats help put a damper on runaway inflammatory processes, which play a part in atherosclerosis, arthritis, diabetes, and other so-called diseases of civilization.

You can be sure, however, that Atkins devotees aren't routinely eating seal and whale blubber. Besides the acquired taste problem, their commerce is extremely restricted in the United States by the Marine Mammal Protection Act, says Bruce Holub, a nutritional biochemist in the department of human biology and nutritional sciences at the University of Guelph in Ontario.

"In heartland America it's probable they're not eating in an Eskimo-like way," says Gary Foster, clinical director of the Weight and Eating Disorders Program at the Pennsylvania School of Medicine. Foster, who describes himself as open-minded about Atkins, says he'd nonetheless worry if people saw the diet as a green light to eat all the butter and bacon—saturated fats—they want. Just before rumors surfaced that Robert Atkins had heart and weight problems when he died, Atkins officials themselves were stressing saturated fat should account for no more than 20 percent of dieters' calories. This seems to be a clear retreat from the diet's original don't-count-the-calories approach to bacon and butter and its happy exhortations to "plow into those prime ribs." Furthermore, 20 percent of calories from saturated fats is *double* what most nutritionists advise. Before plowing into those prime ribs, readers of a recent edition of the *Dr. Atkins' New Diet Revolution* are urged to take omega-3 pills to help protect their hearts. "If you watch carefully," says Holub wryly, "you'll see many popular U.S. diets have quietly added omega-3 pills, in the form of fish oil or flaxseed capsules, as supplements."

Needless to say, the subsistence diets of the Far North are not "dieting." Dieting is the price we pay for too little exercise and too much mass-produced food. Northern diets were a way of life in places too cold for agriculture, where food, whether hunted, fished, or foraged, could not be taken for granted. They were about keeping weight on.

This is not to say that people in the Far North were fat: Subsistence living requires exercise—hard physical work. Indeed, among the good reasons for native people to maintain their old way of eating, as far as it's possible today, is that it provides a hedge against obesity, type 2 diabetes, and heart disease. Unfortunately, no place on Earth is immune to the spreading taint of growth and development. The very well-being of the northern food chain is coming under threat from global warming, land development, and industrial pollutants in the marine environment. "I'm a pragmatist," says Cochran, whose organization is involved in pollution monitoring and disseminating food-safety information to native villages. "Global warming we don't have control over. But we can, for example, do cleanups of military sites in Alaska or of communication cables leaching lead into fish-spawning areas. We can help communities make informed food choices. A young woman of childbearing age may choose not to eat certain organ meats that concentrate contaminants. As individuals, we do have options. And eating our salmon and our seal is still a heck of a better option than pulling something processed that's full of additives off a store shelf."

Not often in our industrial society do we hear someone speak so familiarly about "our" food animals. We don't talk of "our pig" and "our beef." We've lost that creature feeling, that sense of kinship with food sources. "You're taught to think in boxes," says Cochran. "In our culture the connectivity between humans, animals, plants, the land they live on, and the air they share is ingrained in us from birth.

"You truthfully can't separate the way we get our food from the way we live," she says. "How we get our food is intrinsic to our culture. It's how we pass on our values and knowledge to the young. When you go out with your aunts and uncles to hunt or to gather, you learn to smell the air, watch the wind, understand the way the ice moves, know the land. You get to know where to pick which plant and what animal to take."

"It's part, too, of your development as a person. You share food with your community. You show respect to your elders by offering them the first catch. You give thanks to the animal that gave up its life for your sustenance. So you get all the physical activity of harvesting your own food, all the social activity of sharing and preparing it, and all the spiritual aspects as well," says Cochran. "You certainly don't get all that, do you, when you buy prepackaged food from a store."

"That's why some of us here in Anchorage are working to protect what's ours, so that others can continue to live back home in the villages," she adds. "Because if we don't take care of our food, it won't be there for us in the future. And if we lose our foods, we lose who we are." The word Inupiat means "the real people." "That's who we are," says Cochran.

Critical Thinking

1. What kinds of diseases are on the increase among the Inuit and why?

2. Discuss the traditional high-protein, high-fat diet. How does this compare with the "balanced diet" most of us grew up with? What does this mean, according to Harold Draper?

3. Discuss the contrasting sources of vitamins A, D, and C between our diet and the diet of the Inuit. What is the advantage of eating meat and fish raw?

4. What is a "protein ceiling" and why? How did hunter-gatherers cope with the problem?

5. Where do the more healthful fats (monounsaturated and omega-3 fatty acids) come from? What are their benefits?

6. Why is it that Atkins-dieters are not really eating in an "Eskimo-like way"?

7. What are the differences between the subsistence diets of the Far North and "dieting"?

8. Were people of the Far North fat? Why not? In what ways did the old way of eating protect them?

9. How is the northern food chain threatened?

10. In what sense is there a kinship with food sources in the Far North that our industrial societies does not have and why? Why is it also a part of one's development as a person?

Create Central

www.mhhe.com/createcentral

Internet References

The Paleolithic Diet Page
www.paleodiet.com

The Institute for Intercultural Studies
www.interculturalstudies.org/main.html

Article   Prepared by: Elvio Angeloni, *Pasadena City College*

The Food Addiction

Paul J. Kenny

Learning Outcomes

After reading this article, you will be able to:

- Discuss the biological basis and evolutionary context of food addiction.

- Discuss the similarities between food addiction and drug addiction.

Would a rat risk dying just to satisfy its desire for chocolate?

I recently found out that in my laboratory, we gave rats unlimited access to their standard fare as well as to a mini cafeteria full of appetizing, high-calorie foods: sausage, cheesecake, chocolate. The rats decreased their intake of the healthy but bland items and switched to eating the cafeteria food almost exclusively. They gained weight. They became obese.

We then warned the rats as they were eating—by flashing a light—that they would receive a nasty foot shock. Rats eating the bland chow would quickly stop and scramble away, but time and again the obese rats continued to devour the rich food, ignoring the warning they had been trained to fear. Their hedonic desire overruled their basic sense of self-preservation.

Our finding mirrored a previous trial by Barry Everitt of the University of Cambridge—only his rats were hooked on cocaine.

So are the fat rats addicted to food? An inability to suppress a behavior, despite the negative consequences, is common in addiction. Scientists are finding similar compulsiveness in certain people. Almost all obese individuals say they want to consume less, yet they continue to overeat even though they know that doing so can have shockingly negative health or social consequences. Studies show that overeating juices up the reward systems in our brain—so much so in some people that it overpowers the brain's ability to tell them to stop eating when they have had enough. As with alcoholics and drug addicts, the more

they eat, the more they want. Whether overeating is technically an addiction, if it stimulates the same brain circuits as drug use, in the same way, then medications that dial down the reward system could help obese people to eat less.

Suspicious Hormones

Until the early 1990s, society viewed obesity solely as a behavioral disorder: overweight individuals lacked willpower and self-control. Since then, the view has changed dramatically, in the scientific community at least.

The first change in opinion arose from pioneering work by Douglas Coleman of the Jackson Laboratory in Bar Harbor, Me., and by Jeffrey Friedman of the Rockefeller University. Experiments with two strains of mice, both genetically prone to obesity and diabetes, determined what drove the mice to overeat. The researchers discovered that one strain had a genetic defect in fat cells that secrete a hormone called leptin. Mice, like humans, normally secrete leptin after a meal to suppress appetite and prevent overeating. The obese mice had a leptin deficiency—and an insatiable appetite. Researchers later found that obesity in the second strain of mice was caused by a genetic defect in their ability to respond to leptin and regulate its actions. The findings seemed to make it clear that hormones regulate appetite and therefore body weight. A hormonal imbalance could lead to overeating; indeed, obesity runs rampant in certain human families that have a genetic deficiency in leptin.

Two observations suggest that viewing obesity as a hormone disorder is too simplistic, however. First, only a small number of obese people in the U.S. and elsewhere have a genetic deficiency in appetite-related hormones. Second, we would expect blood tests of obese people to show either a lower level of hormones that suppress appetite or a higher level of hormones that increase appetite. Yet the reverse is true. Obese individuals generally have a paradoxically high level of appetite-suppressing hormones, including leptin and insulin.

This is where the concept of food addiction comes into play. Appetite-controlling hormones affect certain pathways of neurons—feeding circuits—in the hypothalamus. They also affect systems in the brain that control feelings of reward, which makes perfect sense. If you have not eaten for many hours, you will spend a great deal of time, effort, and money to obtain food—and it will taste very good! As the old adage says, "Hunger is the best sauce."

During periods of hunger, hormones heighten the reactivity of food-related reward circuits in the brain, particularly in the striatum. The striatum contains high concentrations of endorphins—chemicals that enhance feelings of pleasure and reward.

As you eat, your stomach and gut release appetite-suppressing hormones that decrease pleasure signals that are triggered by the striatum and other components of the reward system. This process makes food seem less attractive, and you may switch your activity away from eating and toward other pursuits. Appetite-regulating hormones control feeding, in part by modulating the pleasurable experience of consuming a meal.

Yet some modern, appetizing foods—dense in fat and sugar and often visually appealing—affect reward systems strongly enough to override the appetite-suppressing hormones, thus prompting us to eat. These foods activate our reward circuits more powerfully than leptin's ability to shut them down. All of us have experienced this effect: you have just finished a big dinner and could not possibly eat another bite. Yet when the chocolate cake appears, you can miraculously "find room" for one last morsel—one that happens to be the most calorie-laden of the day.

Therein lies the rub. We have evolved an efficient brain system to help maintain a healthy and consistent body weight by signaling when it is time to eat and when it is time to stop. But highly appetizing foods can often override these signals and drive weight gain.

Our body responds to the override by elevating the blood levels of appetite-suppressing hormones such as leptin and insulin higher and higher as body weight increases; yet, the hormones become progressively less effective as the body develops tolerance to their actions. Moreover, brain-imaging studies by researchers at Brookhaven National Laboratory and the Oregon Research Institute show that the brain's reward systems in overweight individuals respond weakly to food, even to junk food. These muffled reward circuits depress mood. How does an individual overcome this funk? By eating more delectable food to gain a temporary boost, thereby perpetuating the cycle. Obese individuals may overeat just to experience the same degree of pleasure that lean individuals enjoy from less food.

Obesity, it seems, is not caused by a lack of willpower. And it is not always caused by an imbalance in hormones. In some cases at least, obesity may be caused by hedonic overeating that hijacks the brain's reward networks. Like addictive drugs, overeating creates a feedback loop in the brain's reward centers—the more you consume, the more you crave, and the harder it is for you to satisfy that craving.

But does that make hedonic eating an addiction?

Tolerance and Relapse

Drugs of abuse, such as morphine, stimulate the brain's reward systems the way food does. Yet the similarities do not end there. When morphine is injected into the striatum of rats, it triggers binge-like overeating, even in rats that have been fed to satiety. This response shows that morphine and other opiates mimic the effects of neurotransmitters (brain chemicals) such as endorphins that are naturally produced in the brain to stimulate feeding behaviors.

We might expect, then, that drugs that block the action of endorphins could reduce hedonic overeating. Recent studies have shown that endorphin blockers do lessen the activation of reward circuits in humans and rodents that are presented with appetizing food—the subjects eat less. The blockers can also reduce heroin, alcohol, and cocaine use in human drug addicts, supporting the idea that common mechanisms regulate hedonic overeating and addictive drug use. Strikingly, rats that binge on food every day display behaviors that closely resemble withdrawal, a symptom of drug addiction, after they are treated with endorphin blockers. This behavior raises the remarkable notion that hedonic overeating can induce a drug-dependence-like state.

These discoveries add credence to the idea that overeating in some circumstances may share core features of drug addiction. We see the same similarities with another basic neurotransmitter: dopamine. All known addictive drugs lead to the release of dopamine into the striatum. Dopamine is central to motivation, spurring people to seek the drug. Most experts maintain that this action drives the development of addiction, although the precise mechanisms are hotly debated. It turns out that appetizing food also stimulates the release of dopamine into the striatum, motivating people to focus on obtaining and consuming food. Imaging studies reveal that the striatum of obese individuals shows low levels of a receptor that responds to dopamine, termed the dopamine D2 receptor (D2R). The same holds true for those suffering from alcoholism or from opiate, cocaine, or meth-amphetamine addiction.

We now also know that people who are born with reduced levels of D2R are at greater genetic risk of developing obesity and drug addiction. The condition results in lower levels of activity in the brain's reward systems, suggesting that these individuals may overeat just to obtain the same level of pleasure from food as those who do not have D2R deficits. These people also tend to have trouble learning to avoid actions that have negative consequences; brain systems involved in suppressing risky yet rewarding behaviors, such as consuming high-calorie food or using drugs, may not work as effectively.

Our lab study of rats backs up this idea. The obese rats that ate the cafeteria food regardless of warnings about being shocked had reduced levels of D2R in their striatum. Our study and others demonstrate that drug use in addicted rats and hedonic eating in overweight rats persist even when the animals face negative consequences. Many obese individuals struggle so badly with their poor food choices that they will voluntarily undergo potentially dangerous procedures, such as gastric bypass surgery, to help them control their eating. Yet very often they will relapse to overeating and gain weight.

This cycle of engaging in a bad habit that gives short-term pleasure, then attempting to abstain from it and eventually relapsing, sounds disturbingly like drug addiction. Given the latest research, it seems that obesity is caused by an overpowering motivation to satisfy the reward centers—the pleasure centers—of the brain. The hormonal and metabolic disturbances in obese individuals may be a consequence of weight gain rather than a cause.

New Treatments Possible

The similarities between obesity and addiction have led certain experts to say that the two conditions should be treated in the same manner. Some of them recommended that obesity be included in the most recent update to the Diagnostic and Statistical Manual of Mental Disorders—the bible of psychiatry that provides guidelines for diagnosing mental illnesses, known as the DSM-5. This proposal sparked lively debate among neuroscientists and psychiatrists, but arbiters for the DSM-5 ultimately dropped the idea, largely to avoid labeling obese people, in essence, as mentally ill.

Caution may have been warranted because despite the parallels, obesity and addiction differ in important ways. For example, if food is addictive, then surely it must contain some unique component that drives the addiction—the nicotine of junk food, if you will. Work by Nicole Avena of the University of Florida, the late Bartley Hoebel of Princeton University and others lends some credence to the idea that particular fats or sugars may be responsible. A small study by David Ludwig of Boston Children's Hospital suggests that highly processed, quickly digested carbohydrates could trigger cravings. But research overall indicates that no one ingredient stokes addiction-like behaviors. Rather the combination of fats and sugars, together with calorie content, seems to maximize food's "hedonic impact."

Other experts, including Hisham Ziauddeen, I. Sadaf Farooqi and Paul C. Fletcher of the University of Cambridge, do not think that tolerance and withdrawal occur in obese people the way they do in drug addicts. They argue that obesity and drug addiction are fundamentally different. This view is debatable, however. If obese individuals must eat more and more to overcome reduced activation of reward networks in the brain, that sounds a lot like tolerance. And weight loss can trigger negative mood and depression, much like that experienced by former addicts who try to practice abstinence, suggesting that withdrawal may be in effect.

Other experts have argued that the entire notion of food addiction is preposterous because we are all, in a sense, addicted to food. If we were not, we would not survive.

The difference in obesity, I would suggest, is that modern high-calorie foods can overwhelm our biological feedback networks in a way that other foods cannot. During millions of years of evolution, the major concern of humans was not suppressing appetite but hunting, collecting, or growing enough food to persist during lean times. Perhaps our feeding circuits are better at motivating food intake when we are hungry than they are at suppressing food intake when we are full. It is easy to imagine that the brain would regard overeating of high-calorie food as tremendously beneficial if it is unclear when food will again be available. Perhaps this behavior is no longer adaptive and could even be counterproductive in a world where food is bountiful.

The scientists who argue against an addiction model of obesity make reasonable points, and I also fear that the term "addiction" comes loaded with unhelpful preconceptions. Still, compulsive eating and compulsive drug use seem to share obvious features, most notably an inability to control consumption. It is up to scientists to determine if these similarities are superficial or stem from common, underlying alterations in the brain. More important will be determining whether the addiction model is useful. Unless it helps us design new treatment approaches, the debate is simply an academic exercise.

For an addiction model to have value, it should make accurate predictions about treatment options, including new medications. One example comes from Arena Pharmaceuticals, which recently obtained approval from the U.S. Food and Drug Administration to market a drug called Belviq for weight loss in obese or overweight adults. The drug stimulates a brain protein called the serotonin 2C receptor, which reduces the desire to consume nicotine in lab rats.

Another drug is rimonabant, which had been approved in Europe to help curb appetite in obese individuals. The drug exploits the well-known property of cannabis to increase desire for food—the so-called munchies. Cannabis activates a brain protein called the cannabinoid receptor 1, so researchers reasoned that inhibiting that receptor would decrease desire for food. Rimonabant does exactly that. A notable side effect is its ability to decrease tobacco users' desire to smoke. In rats, the drug also decreases the desire to use alcohol, opiates and stimulants such as cocaine.

As with all potentially therapeutic drugs, however, caution is required. Rimonabant has triggered depression and thoughts of suicide in some individuals. This finding led European authorities to suspend its use and prompted U.S. officials to not approve it. Why depression emerged is still unclear. Thus, although an addiction model of obesity could yield unexpected treatments, those modalities must be thoroughly scrutinized.

Before scientists can declare that overeating is or is not an addiction, they will have to identify precisely which networks and cellular adaptations in the brain drive compulsive drug use and then determine if the same mechanisms also motivate compulsive food intake. It is possible, even likely, that addiction networks for cocaine and for food operate in different parts of the brain yet use similar mechanisms. Scientists will also have to determine if common genetic variations, such as those that affect D2R, contribute to drug addiction and obesity. Identifying such genes may reveal new targets for medications to treat both disorders.

Even if scientists prove that obesity can stem from an addiction to food, and we find that anti-addiction medications can help people lose weight, obese individuals will have to struggle with one factor that seems now to be endemic in America: they will probably be surrounded by overweight family members, friends and co-workers who are still overeating, putting them in the same difficult environment they were in before. As we know from recovering drug addicts and alcoholics, environmental cues are a major cause of craving and relapse. Western society, saturated in fat and temptation, will make it hard for any obese person to quit.

Critical Thinking

1. Discuss the evidence that food addiction is much like alcohol and drug addiction.
2. Discuss the biological basis for addiction.
3. In what respects are modern appetizing foods conducive to addiction? What evidence is there that drugs of abuse have the same effect?
4. Discuss the effects of administering drugs that block the action of endorphins in treating drug addiction as well as food addiction.
5. Discuss the evidence that shows that dopamine plays a role in both drug and food addiction?
6. What is it about the modern diet that seems to trigger addiction, in other words, what is the "nicotine of junk food?"
7. In what ways are the symptoms of drug and food addiction similar?
8. Discuss the evolutionary context of food addiction.

Create Central

www.mhhe.com/createcentral

Internet References

Evolution and Medicine Network
http://evmedreview.com

The Paleolithic Diet Page
www.paleodiet.com

PAUL J. KENNY is an associate professor at the Scripps Research Institute in Jupiter, Fla. His laboratory investigates the mechanisms of drug addiction, obesity, and schizophrenia, as well as medications for these disorders.

Article　　　　　　　Prepared by: Elvio Angeloni, *Pasadena City College*

Curse and Blessing of the Ghetto

Tay-Sachs disease is a choosy killer, one that for centuries targeted Eastern European Jews above all others. By decoding its lethal logic, we can learn a lot about how genetic diseases evolve—and how they can be conquered.

JARED DIAMOND

Learning Outcomes

After reading this article, you will be able to:

- Discuss the genetic basis for Tay-Sachs disease.
- Explain why Tay-Sachs disease is so common among East European Jews.

Marie and I hated her at first sight, even though she was trying hard to be helpful. As our obstetrician's genetics counselor, she was just doing her job, explaining to us the unpleasant results that might come out of the genetic tests we were about to have performed. As a scientist, though, I already knew all I wanted to know about Tay-Sachs disease, and I didn't need to be reminded that the baby sentenced to death by it could be my own.

Fortunately, the tests would reveal that my wife and I were not carriers of the Tay-Sachs gene, and our preparenthood fears on that matter at least could be put to rest. But at the time I didn't yet know that. As I glared angrily at that poor genetics counselor, so strong was my anxiety that now, four years later, I can still clearly remember what was going through my mind: If I were an evil deity, I thought, trying to devise exquisite tortures for babies and their parents, I would be proud to have designed Tay-Sachs disease.

Tay-Sachs is completely incurable, unpreventable, and preprogrammed in the genes. A Tay-Sachs infant usually appears normal for the first few months after birth, just long enough for the parents to grow to love him. An exaggerated "startle reaction" to sounds is the first ominous sign. At about six months the baby starts to lose control of his head and can't roll over or sit without support. Later he begins to drool, breaks out into unmotivated bouts of laughter, and suffers convulsions. Then his head grows abnormally large, and he becomes blind. Perhaps what's most frightening for the parents is that their baby loses all contact with his environment and becomes virtually a vegetable. By the child's third birthday, if he's still alive, his skin will turn yellow and his hands pudgy. Most likely he will die before he's four years old.

My wife and I were tested for the Tay-Sachs gene because at the time we rated as high-risk candidates, for two reasons. First, Marie was carrying twins, so we had double the usual chance to bear a Tay-Sachs baby. Second, both she and I are of Eastern European Jewish ancestry, the population with by far the world's highest Tay-Sachs frequency.

In peoples around the world Tay-Sachs appears once in every 400,000 births. But it appears a hundred times more frequently—about once in 3,600 births—among descendants of Eastern European Jews, people known as Ashkenazim. For descendants of most other groups of Jews—Oriental Jews, chiefly from the Middle East, or Sephardic Jews, from Spain and other Mediterranean countries—the frequency of Tay-Sachs disease is no higher than in non-Jews. Faced with such a clear correlation, one cannot help but wonder: What is it about this one group of people that produces such an extraordinarily high risk of this disease?

Finding the answer to this question concerns all of us, regardless of our ancestry. Every human population is especially susceptible to certain diseases, not only because of its life-style but also because of its genetic inheritance. For example, genes put European whites at high risk for cystic fibrosis, African blacks for sickle-cell disease, Pacific Islanders for diabetes—and Eastern European Jews for ten different diseases, including Tay-Sachs. It's not that Jews are notably susceptible to genetic diseases in general; but a combination of historical factors has led to Jews' being intensively studied, and so their susceptibilities are far better known than those of, say, Pacific Islanders.

Tay-Sachs exemplifies how we can deal with such diseases; it has been the object of the most successful screening program to date. Moreover, Tay-Sachs is helping us understand how ethnic diseases evolve. Within the past couple of years discoveries by molecular biologists have provided tantalizing clues to precisely how a deadly gene can persist and spread over the centuries. Tay-Sachs may be primarily a disease of Eastern European Jews, but through this affliction of one group of people, we gain a window on how our genes simultaneously curse and bless us all.

The disease's hyphenated name comes from the two physicians—British ophthalmologist W. Tay and New York neurologist B. Sachs—who independently first recognized the disease, in 1881 and 1887, respectively. By 1896 Sachs had seen enough cases to realize that the disease was most common among Jewish children.

Not until 1962, however, were researchers able to trace the cause of the affliction to a single biochemical abnormality: the excessive accumulation in nerve cells of a fatty substance called G_{M2} ganglioside. Normally G_{M2} ganglioside is present at only modest levels in cell membranes, because it is constantly being broken down as well as synthesized. The breakdown depends on the enzyme hexosaminidase A, which is found in the tiny structures within our cells known as lysosomes. In the unfortunate Tay-Sachs victims this enzyme is lacking, and without it the ganglioside piles up and produces all the symptoms of the disease.

We have two copies of the gene that programs our supply of hexosaminidase A, one inherited from our father, the other from our mother; each of our parents, in turn, has two copies derived from their own parents. As long as we have one good copy of the gene, we can produce enough hexosaminidase A to prevent a buildup of G_{M2} ganglioside and we won't get Tay-Sachs. This genetic disease is of the sort termed recessive rather than dominant—meaning that to get it, a child must inherit a defective gene not just from one parent but from both of them. Clearly, each parent must have had one good copy of the gene along with the defective copy—if either had had two defective genes, he or she would have died of the disease long before reaching the age of reproduction. In genetic terms the diseased child is homozygous for the defective gene and both parents are heterozygous for it.

None of this yet gives any hint as to why the Tay-Sachs gene should be most common among Eastern European Jews. To come to grips with that question, we must take a short detour into history.

From their biblical home of ancient Israel, Jews spread peacefully to other Mediterranean lands, Yemen, and India. They were also dispersed violently through conquest by Assyrians, Babylonians, and Romans. Under the Carolingian kings of the eighth and ninth centuries Jews were invited to settle in France and Germany as traders and financiers. In subsequent centuries, however, persecutions triggered by the Crusades gradually drove Jews out of Western Europe; the process culminated in their total expulsion from Spain in 1492. Those Spanish Jews—called Sephardim—fled to other lands around the Mediterranean. Jews of France and Germany—the Ashkenazim—fled east to Poland and from there to Lithuania and western Russia, where they settled mostly in towns, as businessmen engaged in whatever pursuit they were allowed.

There the Jews stayed for centuries, through periods of both tolerance and oppression. But toward the end of the nineteenth century and the beginning of the twentieth, waves of murderous anti-Semitic attacks drove millions of Jews out of Eastern Europe, with most of them heading for the United States. My mother's parents, for example, fled to New York from Lithuanian pogroms of the 1880s, while my father's parents fled from the Ukrainian pogroms of 1903–6. The more modern history of Jewish migration is probably well known to you all: most Jews who remained in Eastern Europe were exterminated during World War II, while most of the survivors immigrated to the United States and Israel. Of the 13 million Jews alive today, more than three-quarters are Ashkenazim, the descendants of the Eastern European Jews and the people most at risk for Tay-Sachs.

Have these Jews maintained their genetic distinctness through the thousands of years of wandering? Some scholars claim that there has been so much intermarriage and conversion that Ashkenazic Jews are now just Eastern Europeans who adopted Jewish culture. However, modern genetic studies refute that speculation.

First of all, there are those ten genetic diseases that the Ashkenazim have somehow acquired, by which they differ both from other Jews and from Eastern European non-Jews. In addition, many Ashkenazic genes turn out to be ones typical of Palestinian Arabs and other peoples of the Eastern Mediterranean areas where Jews originated. (In fact, by genetic standards the current Arab-Israeli conflict is an internecine civil war.) Other Ashkenazic genes have indeed diverged from Mediterranean ones (including genes of Sephardic and Oriental Jews) and have evolved to converge on genes of Eastern European non-Jews subject to the same local forces of natural selection. But the degree to which Ashkenazim prove to differ genetically from Eastern European non-Jews implies an intermarriage rate of only about 15 percent.

Can history help explain why the Tay-Sachs gene in particular is so much more common in Ashkenazim than in their non-Jewish neighbors or in other Jews? At the risk of spoiling a mystery, I'll tell you now that the answer is yes, but to appreciate it, you'll have to understand the four possible explanations for the persistence of the Tay-Sachs gene.

First, new copies of the gene might be arising by mutation as fast as existing copies disappear with the death of Tay-Sachs children. That's the most likely explanation for the gene's persistence in most of the world, where the disease frequency is only one in 400,000 births—that frequency reflects a typical human mutation rate. But for this explanation to apply to the Ashkenazim would require a mutation rate of at least one per 3,600 births—far above the frequency observed for any human gene. Furthermore, there would be no precedent for one particular gene mutating so much more often in one human population than in others.

As a second possibility, the Ashkenazim might have acquired the Tay-Sachs gene from some other people who already had the gene at high frequency. Arthur Koestler's controversial book *The Thirteenth Tribe,* for example, popularized the view that the Ashkenazim are really not a Semitic people but are instead descended from the Khazar, a Turkic tribe whose rulers converted to Judaism in the eighth century. Could the Khazar have brought the Tay-Sachs gene to Eastern Europe? This speculation makes good romantic reading, but there is no good evidence to support it. Moreover, it fails to explain why deaths of Tay-Sachs children didn't eliminate the gene by natural selection in the past 1,200 years, nor how the Khazar acquired high frequencies of the gene in the first place.

The third hypothesis was the one preferred by a good many geneticists until recently. It invokes two genetic processes, termed the founder effect and genetic drift, that may operate in small populations. To understand these concepts, imagine that 100 couples settle in a new land and found a population that then increases. Imagine further that one parent among those original 100 couples happens to have some rare gene, one, say, that normally occurs at a frequency of one in a million. The gene's frequency in the new population will now be one in 200 as a result of the accidental presence of that rare founder.

Or suppose again that 100 couples found a population, but that one of the 100 men happens to have lots of kids by his wife or that he is exceptionally popular with other women, while the other 99 men are childless or have few kids or are simply less popular. That one man may thereby father 10 percent rather than a more representative one percent of the next generation's babies, and their genes will disproportionately reflect that man's genes. In other words, gene frequencies will have drifted between the first and second generation.

Through these two types of genetic accidents a rare gene may occur with an unusually high frequency in a small expanding population. Eventually, if the gene is harmful, natural selection will bring its frequency back to normal by killing off gene bearers. But if the resultant disease is recessive—if heterozygous individuals don't get the disease and only the rare, homozygous individuals die of it—the gene's high frequency may persist for many generations.

These accidents do in fact account for the astonishingly high Tay-Sachs gene frequency found in one group of Pennsylvania Dutch: out of the 333 people in this group, 98 proved to carry the Tay-Sachs gene. Those 333 are all descended from one couple who settled in the United States in the eighteenth century and had 13 children. Clearly, one of that founding couple must have carried the gene. A similar accident may explain why Tay-Sachs is also relatively common among French Canadians, who number 5 million today but are descended from fewer than 6,000 French immigrants who arrived in the New World between 1638 and 1759. In the two or three centuries since both these founding events, the high Tay-Sachs gene frequency among Pennsylvania Dutch and French Canadians has not yet had enough time to decline to normal levels.

The same mechanisms were one proposed to explain the high rate of Tay-Sachs disease among the Ashkenazim. Perhaps, the reasoning went, the gene just happened to be overrepresented in the founding Jewish population that settled in Germany or Eastern Europe. Perhaps the gene just happened to drift up in frequency in the Jewish populations scattered among the isolated towns of Eastern Europe.

But geneticists have long questioned whether the Ashkenazim population's history was really suitable for these genetic accidents to have been significant. Remember, the founder effect and genetic drift become significant only in small populations, and the founding populations of Ashkenazim may have been quite large. Moreover, Ashkenazic communities were considerably widespread; drift would have sent gene frequencies up in some towns but down in others. And, finally, natural selection has by now had a thousand years to restore gene frequencies to normal.

Granted, those doubts are based on historical data, which are not always as precise or reliable as one might want. But within the past several years the case against those accidental explanations for Tay-Sachs disease in the Ashkenazim has been bolstered by discoveries by molecular biologists.

Like all proteins, the enzyme absent in Tay-Sachs children is coded for by a piece of our DNA. Along that particular stretch of DNA there are thousands of different sites where a mutation could occur that would result in no enzyme and hence in the same set of symptoms. If molecular biologists had discovered that all cases of Tay-Sachs in Ashkenazim involved damage to DNA at the same site, that would have been strong evidence that in Ashkenazim the disease stems from a single mutation that has been multiplied by the founder effect or genetic drift—in other words, the high incidence of Tay-Sachs among Eastern European Jews is accidental.

In reality, though, several different mutations along this stretch of DNA have been identified in Ashkenazim, and two of them occur much more frequently than in non-Ashkenazic populations. It seems unlikely that genetic accidents would have pumped up the frequency of the same gene not once but twice in the same population.

It seems unlikely that genetic accidents would have pumped up the frequency of the same gene not once but twice in the same population.

And that's not the sole unlikely coincidence arguing against accidental explanations. Recall that Tay-Sachs is caused by the excessive accumulation of one fatty substance, G_{M2} ganglioside, from a defect in one enzyme, hexosaminidase A. But Tay-Sachs is one of ten genetic diseases characteristic of Ashkenazim. Among those other nine, two—Gaucher's disease and Niemann-Pick disease—result from the accumulation of two other fatty substances similar to G_{M2} ganglioside, as a result of defects in two other enzymes similar to hexosaminidase A. Yet our bodies contain thousands of different enzymes. It would have been an incredible roll of the genetic dice if, by nothing more than chance, Ashkenazim had independently acquired mutations in three closely related enzymes—and had acquired mutations in one of those enzymes twice.

All these facts bring us to the fourth possible explanation of why the Tay-Sachs gene is so prevalent among Ashkenazim: namely, that something about them favored accumulation of G_{M2} ganglioside and related fats.

For comparison, suppose that a friend doubles her money on one stock while you are getting wiped out with your investments. Taken alone, that could just mean she was lucky on that one occasion. But suppose that she doubles her money on each of two different stocks and at the same time rings up big profits in real estate while also making a killing in bonds. That implies more than lady luck; it suggests that something about your friend—like shrewd judgment—favors financial success.

What could be the blessings of fat accumulation in Eastern European Jews? At first this question sounds weird. After all, that fat accumulation was noticed only because of the curses it bestows: Tay-Sachs, Gaucher's, or Niemann-Pick disease. But many of our common genetic diseases may persist because they bring both blessings and curses (see "The Cruel Logic of Our Genes," *Discover,* November 1989). They kill or impair individuals who inherit two copies of the faulty gene, but they help those who receive only one defective gene by protecting them against other diseases. The best understood example is the sickle-cell gene of African blacks, which often kills homozygotes but protects heterozygotes against malaria. Natural selection sustains such genes because more heterozygotes than normal individuals survive to pass on their genes, and those extra gene copies offset the copies lost through the deaths of homozygotes.

So let us refine our question and ask, What blessing could the Tay-Sachs gene bring to those individuals who are heterozygous for it? A clue first emerged back in 1972, with the publication of the results of a questionnaire that had asked U.S. Ashkenzaic parents of Tay-Sachs children what their own Eastern European-born parents had died of. Keep in mind that since these unfortunate children had to be homozygotes, with two copies of the Tay-Sachs gene, all their parents had to be heterozygotes, with one copy, and half of the parents' parents also had to be heterozygotes.

As it turned out, most of those Tay-Sachs grandparents had died of the usual causes: heart disease, stroke, cancer, and diabetes. But strikingly, only one of the 306 grandparents had died of tuberculosis, even though TB was generally one of the big killers in these grandparents' time. Indeed, among the general population of large Eastern European cities in the early twentieth century, TB caused up to 20 percent of all deaths.

This big discrepancy suggested that Tay-Sachs heterozygotes might somehow have been protected against TB. Interestingly, it was already well known that Ashkenazim in general had some such protection: even when Jews and non-Jews were compared within the same European city, class, and occupational group (for example, Warsaw garment workers), Jews had only half the TB death rate of non-Jews, despite their being equally susceptible to infection. Perhaps, one could reason, the Tay-Sachs gene furnished part of that well-established Jewish resistance.

A second clue to a heterozygote advantage conveyed by the Tay-Sachs gene emerged in 1983, with a fresh look at the data concerning the distributions of TB and the Tay-Sachs gene within Europe. The statistics showed that the Tay-Sachs gene was nearly three times more frequent among Jews originating from Austria, Hungary, and Czechoslovakia—areas where an amazing 9 to 10 percent of the population were heterozygotes—than among Jews from Poland, Russia, and Germany. At the same time records from an old Jewish TB sanatorium in

Denver in 1904 showed that among patients born in Europe between 1860 and 1910, Jews from Austria and Hungary were overrepresented.

Initially, in putting together these two pieces of information, you might be tempted to conclude that because the highest frequency of the Tay-Sachs gene appeared in the same geographic region that produced the most cases of TB, the gene in fact offers no protection whatsoever. Indeed, this was precisely the mistaken conclusion of many researchers who had looked at these data before. But you have to pay careful attention to the numbers here: even at its highest frequency the Tay-Sachs gene was carried by far fewer people than would be infected by TB. What the statistics really indicate is that where TB is the biggest threat, natural selection produces the biggest response.

Think of it this way: You arrive at an island where you find that all the inhabitants of the north end wear suits of armor, while all the inhabitants of the south end wear only cloth shirts. You'd be pretty safe in assuming that warfare is more prevalent in the north—and that war-related injuries account for far more deaths there than in the south. Thus, if the Tay-Sachs gene does indeed lend heterozygotes some protection against TB, you would expect to find the gene most often precisely where you find TB most often. Similarly, the sickle-cell gene reaches its highest frequencies in those parts of Africa where malaria is the biggest risk.

But you may believe there's still a hole in the argument: If Tay-Sachs heterozygotes are protected against TB, you may be asking, why is the gene common just in the Ashkenazim? Why did it not become common in the non-Jewish populations also exposed to TB in Austria, Hungary, and Czechoslovakia?

At this point we must recall the peculiar circumstances in which the Jews of Eastern Europe were forced to live. They were unique among the world's ethnic groups in having been virtually confined to towns for most of the past 2,000 years. Being forbidden to own land, Eastern European Jews were not peasant farmers living in the countryside, but businesspeople forced to live in crowded ghettos, in an environment where tuberculosis thrived.

Of course, until recent improvements in sanitation, these towns were not very healthy places for non-Jews either. Indeed, their populations couldn't sustain themselves: deaths exceeded births, and the number of dead had to be balanced by continued emigration from the countryside. For non-Jews, therefore, there was no genetically distinct urban population. For ghetto-bound Jews, however, there could be no emigration from the countryside; thus the Jewish population was under the strongest selection to evolve genetic resistance to TB.

Those are the conditions that probably led to Jewish TB resistance, whatever particular genetic factors prove to underlie it. I'd speculate that G_{M2} and related fats accumulate at slightly higher-than-normal levels in heterozygotes, although not at the lethal levels seen in homozygotes. (The fat accumulation in heterozygotes probably takes place in the cell membrane, the cell's "armor.") I'd also speculate that the accumulation provides heterozygotes with some protection against TB, and that

that's why the genes for Tay-Sachs, Gaucher's, and Niemann-Pick disease reached high frequencies in the Ashkenazim.

Having thus stated the case, let me make clear that I don't want to overstate it. The evidence is still speculative. Depending on how you do the calculation, the low frequency of TB deaths in Tay-Sachs grandparents either barely reaches or doesn't quite reach the level of proof that statisticians require to accept an effect as real rather than as one that's arisen by chance. Moreover, we have no idea of the biochemical mechanism by which fat accumulation might confer resistance against TB. For the moment, I'd say that the evidence points to some selective advantage of Tay-Sachs heterozygotes among the Ashkenazim, and that TB resistance is the only plausible hypothesis yet proposed.

For now Tay-Sachs remains a speculative model for the evolution of ethnic diseases. But it's already a proven model of what to do about them. Twenty years ago a test was developed to identify Tay-Sachs heterozygotes, based on their lower-than-normal levels of hexosaminidase A. The test is simple, cheap, and accurate: all I did was to donate a small sample of my blood, pay $35, and wait a few days to receive the results.

If that test shows that at least one member of a couple is not a Tay-Sachs heterozygote, then any child of theirs can't be a Tay-Sachs homozygote. If both parents prove to be heterozygotes, there's a one-in-four chance of their child being a homozygote; that can then be determined by other tests performed on the mother early in pregnancy. If the results are positive, it's early enough for her to abort, should she choose to. That critical bit of knowledge has enabled parents who had gone through the agony of bearing a Tay-Sachs baby and watching him die to find the courage to try again.

The Tay-Sachs screening program launched in the United States in 1971 was targeted at the high-risk population: Ashkenazic Jewish couples of childbearing age. So successful has this approach been that the number of Tay-Sachs babies born each year in this country has declined tenfold. Today, in fact, more Tay-Sachs cases appear here in non-Jews than in Jews, because only the latter couples are routinely tested. Thus, what used to be the classic genetic disease of Jews is so no longer.

There's also a broader message to the Tay-Sachs story. We commonly refer to the United States as a melting pot, and in many ways that metaphor is apt. But in other ways we're not a melting pot, and we won't be for a long time. Each ethnic group has some characteristic genes of its own, a legacy of its distinct history. Tuberculosis and malaria are not major causes of death in the United States, but the genes that some of us evolved to protect ourselves against them are still frequent. Those genes are frequent only in certain ethnic groups, though, and they'll be slow to melt through the population.

We're not a melting pot, and we won't be for a long time. Each ethnic group has some characteristic genes of its own, a legacy of its distinct history.

With modern advances in molecular genetics, we can expect to see more, not less, ethnically targeted practice of medicine. Genetic screening for cystic fibrosis in European whites, for example, is one program that has been much discussed recently; when it comes, it will surely be based on the Tay-Sachs experience. Of course, what that may mean someday is more anxiety-ridden parents-to-be glowering at more dedicated genetics counselors. It will also mean fewer babies doomed to the agonies of diseases we may understand but that we'll never be able to accept.

Critical Thinking

1. How does the author describe Tay-Sachs disease?

2. What is the world-wide frequency of the disease? Who is most at risk and what is their frequency?

3. Are Jews more susceptible to genetic diseases than other human populations? Explain.

4. Discuss the genetic basis of the disease. (Do not bother with the chemical aspect.)

5. What evidence is there that Eastern European Jews have maintained a degree of genetic distinctness?

6. Discuss and evaluate the first three hypotheses on the origins of Tay-Sachs among the Ashkenazim. Note in particular the evidence for the founder effect among the Pennsylvania Dutch and the French Canadians.

7. Discuss the fourth hypothesis and the evidence for it. Why must we still call this a "speculative model"?

8. Describe the diagnostic possibilities of the Tay-Sachs story. What can we expect in the future with regard to genetic screening?

Create Central

www.mhhe.com/createcentral

Internet References

Evolution and Medicine Network
http://evmedreview.com
The Evolution & Medicine Review
http://evmedreview.com

Contributing editor **JARED DIAMOND** is a professor of physiology at the UCLA School of Medicine.

Article Prepared by: Elvio Angeloni

The Evolution of Diet

Ann Gibbons

Learning Outcomes

After reading this article, you will be able to:

- Discuss the popularity of the caveman or Stone Age diet.
- Discuss the "stew of misconceptions" regarding the Paleo diet.
- Discuss the question as to whether or not we are still evolving.
- Discuss the effect that eating meat and, later, food processing in general have had on humans.

It's suppertime in the Amazon of lowland Bolivia, and Ana Cuata Maito is stirring a porridge of plantains and sweet manioc over afire smoldering on the dirt floor of her thatched hut, listening for the voice of her husband as he returns from the forest with his scrawny hunting dog.

With an infant girl nursing at her breast and a seven-year-old boy tugging at her sleeve, she looks spent when she tells me that she hopes her husband, Deonicio Nate, will bring home meat tonight. "The children are sad when there is no meat," Maito says through an interpreter, as she swats away mosquitoes.

Nate left before dawn on this day in January with his rifle and machete to get an early start on the two-hour trek to the old-growth forest. There he silently scanned the canopy for brown capuchin monkeys and raccoonlike coatis, while his dog sniffed the ground for the scent of pig-like peccaries or reddish brown capybaras. If he was lucky, Nate would spot one of the biggest packets of meat in the forest—tapirs, with long, prehensile snouts that rummage for buds and shoots among the damp ferns.

This evening, however, Nate emerges from the forest with no meat. At 39, he's an energetic guy who doesn't seem easily defeated—when he isn't hunting or fishing or weaving palm fronds into roof panels, he's in the woods carving a new canoe from a log. But when he finally sits down to eat his porridge from a metal bowl, he complains that it's hard to get enough meat

for his family: two wives (not uncommon in the tribe) and 12 children. Loggers are scaring away the animals. He can't fish on the river because a storm washed away his canoe.

The story is similar for each of the families I visit in Anachere, a community of about 90 members of the ancient Tsimane Indian tribe. It's the rainy season, when it's hardest to hunt or fish. More than 15,000 Tsimane live in about a hundred villages along two rivers in the Amazon Basin near the main market town of San Borja, 225 miles from La Paz. But Anachere is a two-day trip from San Borja by motorized dugout canoe, so the Tsimane living there still get most of their food from the forest, the river, or their gardens.

I'm traveling with Asher Rosinger, a doctoral candidate who's part of a team, co-led by biological anthropologist William Leonard of Northwestern University, studying the Tsimane to document what a rain forest diet looks like. They're particularly interested in how the Indians' health changes as they move away from their traditional diet and active lifestyle and begin trading forest goods for sugar, salt, rice, oil, and increasingly, dried meat and canned sardines. This is not a purely academic inquiry. What anthropologists are learning about the diets of indigenous peoples like the Tsimane could inform what the rest of us should eat.

Rosinger introduces me to a villager named José Mayer Cunay, 78, who, with his son Felipe Mayer Lero, 39, has planted a lush garden by the river over the past 30 years. José leads us down a trail past trees laden with golden papayas and mangoes, clusters of green plantains, and orbs of grapefruit that dangle from branches like earrings. Vibrant red "lobster claw" heliconia flowers and wild ginger grow like weeds among stalks of corn and sugarcane. "José's family has more fruit than anyone," says Rosinger.

Yet in the family's open-air shelter Felipe's wife, Catalina, is preparing the same bland porridge as other households. When I ask if the food in the garden can tide them over when there's little meat, Felipe shakes his head. "It's not enough to live on," he says. "I need to hunt and fish. My body doesn't want to eat just these plants."

As we look to 2050, when we'll need to feed two billion more people, the question of which diet is best has taken on new urgency. The foods we choose to eat in the coming decades will have dramatic ramifications for the planet. Simply put, a diet that revolves around meat and dairy, a way of eating that's on the rise throughout the developing world, will take a greater toll on the world's resources than one that revolves around unrefined grains, nuts, fruits, and vegetables.

Until agriculture was developed around 10,000 years ago, all humans got their food by hunting, gathering, and fishing. As farming emerged, nomadic hunter-gatherers gradually were pushed off prime farmland, and eventually they became limited to the forests of the Amazon, the arid grasslands of Africa, the remote islands of Southeast Asia, and the tundra of the Arctic. Today only a few scattered tribes of hunter-gatherers remain on the planet.

That's why scientists are intensifying efforts to learn what they can about an ancient diet and way of life before they disappear. "Hunter-gatherers are not living fossils," says Alyssa Crittenden, a nutritional anthropologist at the University of Nevada, Las Vegas, who studies the diet of Tanzania's Hadza people, some of the last true hunter-gatherers. "That being said, we have a small handful of foraging populations that remain on the planet. We are running out of time. If we want to glean any information on what a nomadic, foraging lifestyle looks like, we need to capture their diet now."

So far studies of foragers like the Tsimane, Arctic Inuit, and Hadza have found that these peoples traditionally didn't develop high blood pressure, atherosclerosis, or cardiovascular disease. "A lot of people believe there is a discordance between what we eat today and what our ancestors evolved to eat," says paleoanthropologist Peter Ungar of the University of Arkansas. The notion that we're trapped in Stone Age bodies in a fast-food world is driving the current craze for Paleolithic diets. The popularity of these so-called caveman or Stone Age diets is based on the idea that modern humans evolved to eat the way hunter-gatherers did during the Paleolithic—the period from about 2.6 million years ago to the start of the agricultural revolution—and that our genes haven't had enough time to adapt to farmed foods.

A Stone Age diet "is the one and only diet that ideally fits our genetic makeup," writes Loren Cordain, an evolutionary nutritionist at Colorado State University in his book *The Paleo Diet: Lose Weight and Get Healthy by Eating the Foods You Were Designed to Eat.* After studying the diets of living hunter-gatherers and concluding that 73 percent of these societies derived more than half their calories from meat, Cordain came up with his own Paleo prescription: Eat plenty of lean meat and fish but not dairy products, beans, or cereal grains—foods introduced into our diet after the invention of cooking and agriculture. Paleo-diet advocates like Cordain say that if we stick to

the foods our hunter-gatherer ancestors once ate, we can avoid the diseases of civilization, such as heart disease, high blood pressure, diabetes, cancer, even acne.

That sounds appealing. But is it true that we all evolved to eat a meat-centric diet? Both paleontologists studying the fossils of our ancestors and anthropologists documenting the diets of indigenous people today say the picture is a bit more complicated. The popular embrace of a Paleo diet, Ungar and others point out, is based on a stew of misconceptions.

Meat has played a starring role in the evolution of the human diet. Raymond Dart, who in 1924 discovered the first fossil of a human ancestor in Africa, popularized the image of our early ancestors hunting meat to survive on the African savanna. Writing in the 1950s, he described those humans as "carnivorous creatures, that seized living quarries by violence, battered them to death . . . slaking their ravenous thirst with the hot blood of victims and greedily devouring livid writhing flesh."

Eating meat is thought by some scientists to have been crucial to the evolution of our ancestors' larger brains about two million years ago. By starting to eat calorie-dense meat and marrow instead of the low-quality plant diet of apes, our direct ancestor, *Homo erectus,* took in enough extra energy at each meal to help fuel a bigger brain. Digesting a higher quality diet and less bulky plant fiber would have allowed these humans to have much smaller guts. The energy freed up as a result of smaller guts could be used by the greedy brain, according to Leslie Aiello, who first proposed the idea with paleoanthropologist Peter Wheeler. The brain requires 20 percent of a human's energy when resting; by comparison, an ape's brain requires only 8 percent. This means that from the time of *H. erectus,* the human body has depended on a diet of energy-dense food—especially meat.

Fast-forward a couple of million years to when the human diet took another major turn with the invention of agriculture. The domestication of grains such as sorghum, barley, wheat, corn, and rice created a plentiful and predictable food supply, allowing farmers' wives to bear babies in rapid succession—one every 2.5 years instead of one every 3.5 years for hunter-gatherers. A population explosion followed; before long, farmers outnumbered foragers.

Over the past decade anthropologists have struggled to answer key questions about this transition. Was agriculture a clear step forward for human health? Or in leaving behind our hunter-gatherer ways to grow crops and raise livestock, did we give up a healthier diet and stronger bodies in exchange for food security?

When biological anthropologist Clark Spencer Larsen of Ohio State University describes the dawn of agriculture, it's a grim picture. As the earliest farmers became dependent on crops, their diets became far less nutritionally diverse than hunter-gatherers' diets. Eating the same domesticated grain every day gave early farmers cavities and periodontal disease rarely found in hunter-gatherers, says Larsen. When farmers began domesticating animals, those cattle, sheep, and goats became sources of milk and meat but also of parasites and new infectious diseases. Farmers suffered from iron deficiency and developmental delays, and they shrank in stature.

Despite boosting population numbers, the lifestyle and diet of farmers were clearly not as healthy as the lifestyle and diet of hunter-gatherers. That farmers produced more babies, Larsen says, is simply evidence that "you don't have to be disease free to have children."

The real Paleolithic diet, though, wasn't all meat and marrow. It's true that hunter-gatherers around the world crave meat more than any other food and usually get around 30 percent of their annual calories from animals. But most also endure lean times when they eat less than a handful of meat each week. New studies suggest that more than a reliance on meat in ancient human diets fueled the brain's expansion.

Year-round observations confirm that hunter-gatherers often have dismal success as hunters. The Hadza and Kung bushmen of Africa, for example, fail to get meat more than half the time when they venture forth with bows and arrows. This suggests it was even harder for our ancestors who didn't have these weapons. "Everybody thinks you wander out into the savanna and there are antelopes everywhere, just waiting for you to bonk them on the head," says paleoanthropologist Alison Brooks of George Washington University, an expert on the Dobe Kung of Botswana. No one eats meat all that often, except in the Arctic, where Inuit and other groups traditionally got as much as 99 percent of their calories from seals, narwhals, and fish.

So how do hunter-gatherers get energy when there's no meat? It turns out that "man the hunter" is backed up by "woman the forager," who, with some help from children, provides more calories during difficult times. When meat, fruit, or honey is scarce, foragers depend on "fallback foods," says Brooks. The Hadza get almost 70 percent of their calories from plants. The Kung traditionally rely on tubers and mongongo nuts, the Aka and Baka Pygmies of the Congo River Basin on yams, the Tsimane and Yanomami Indians of the Amazon on plantains and manioc, the Australian Aboriginals on nut grass and water chestnuts.

"There's been a consistent story about hunting defining us and that meat made us human," says Amanda Henry, a paleobiologist at the Max Planck Institute for Evolutionary Anthropology in Leipzig. "Frankly, I think that misses half of the story. They want meat, sure. But what they actually live on is plant foods." What's more, she found starch granules from plants on fossil teeth and stone tools, which suggests humans may have been eating grains, as well as tubers, for at least 100,000 years—long enough to have evolved the ability to tolerate them.

The notion that we stopped evolving in the Paleolithic period simply isn't true. Our teeth, jaws, and faces have gotten smaller, and our DNA has changed since the invention of agriculture. "Are humans still evolving? Yes!" says geneticist Sarah Tishkoff of the University of Pennsylvania.

One striking piece of evidence is lactose tolerance. All humans digest mother's milk as infants, but until cattle began being domesticated 10,000 years ago, weaned children no longer needed to digest milk. As a result, they stopped making the enzyme lactase, which breaks down the lactose into simple sugars. After humans began herding cattle, it became tremendously advantageous to digest milk, and lactose tolerance evolved independently among cattle herders in Europe, the Middle East, and Africa. Groups not dependent on cattle, such as the Chinese and Thai, the Pima Indians of the American Southwest, and the Bantu of West Africa, remain lactose intolerant.

Humans also vary in their ability to extract sugars from starchy foods as they chew them, depending on how many copies of a certain gene they inherit. Populations that traditionally ate more starchy foods, such as the Hadza, have more copies of the gene than the Yakut meat-eaters of Siberia, and their saliva helps break down starches before the food reaches their stomachs.

These examples suggest a twist on "You are what you eat." More accurately, you are what your ancestors ate. There is tremendous variation in what foods humans can thrive on, depending on genetic inheritance. Traditional diets today include the vegetarian regimen of India's Jains, the meat-intensive fare of Inuit, and the fish-heavy diet of Malaysia's Bajau people. The Nochmani of the Nicobar Islands off the coast of India get by on protein from insects. "What makes us human is our ability to find a meal in virtually any environment," says the Tsimane study co-leader Leonard.

Studies suggest that indigenous groups get into trouble when they abandon their traditional diets and active lifestyles for Western living. Diabetes was virtually unknown, for instance, among the Maya of Central America until the 1950s. As they've switched to a Western diet high in sugars, the rate of diabetes has skyrocketed. Siberian nomads such as the Evenk reindeer herders and the Yakut ate diets heavy in meat, yet they had almost no heart disease until after the fall of the Soviet Union, when many settled in towns and began eating market foods. Today about half the Yakut living in villages are overweight, and almost a third have hypertension, says Leonard. And Tsimane people who eat market foods are more prone to diabetes than those who still rely on hunting and gathering.

For those of us whose ancestors were adapted to plant-based diets—and who have desk jobs—it might be best not to eat as much meat as the Yakut. Recent studies confirm older findings that although humans have eaten red meat for two million years, heavy consumption increases atherosclerosis and cancer in most populations—and the culprit isn't just saturated fat or cholesterol. Our gut bacteria digest a nutrient in meat called L-carnitine. In one mouse study, digestion of L-carnitine boosted artery-clogging plaque. Research also has shown that the human immune system attacks a sugar in red meat that's called Neu5Gc, causing inflammation that's low level in the young but that eventually could cause cancer. "Red meat is great, if you want to live to 45," says Ajit Varki of the University of California, San Diego, lead author of the Neu5Gc study.

Many paleoanthropologists say that although advocates of the modern Paleolithic diet urge us to stay away from unhealthy processed foods, the diet's heavy focus on meat doesn't replicate the diversity of foods that our ancestors ate—or take into account the active lifestyles that protected them from heart disease and diabetes. "What bothers a lot of paleoanthropologists is that we actually didn't have just one caveman diet," says Leslie Aiello, president of the Wenner-Gren Foundation for Anthropological Research in New York City. "The human diet goes back at least two million years. We had a lot of cavemen out there."

In other words, there is no one ideal human diet. Aiello and Leonard say the real hallmark of being human isn't our taste for meat but our ability to adapt to many habitats—and to be able to combine many different foods to create many healthy diets. Unfortunately the modern Western diet does not appear to be one of them.

The latest clue as to why our modern diet may be making us sick comes from Harvard primatologist Richard Wrangham, who argues that the biggest revolution in the human diet came not when we started to eat meat but when we learned to cook. Our human ancestors who began cooking sometime between 1.8 million and 400,000 years ago probably had more children who thrived, Wrangham says. Pounding and heating food "predigests" it, so our guts spend less energy breaking it down, absorb more than if the food were raw, and thus extract more fuel for our brains. "Cooking produces soft, energy-rich foods," says Wrangham. Today we can't survive on raw, unprocessed food alone, he says. We have evolved to depend upon cooked food.

To test his ideas, Wrangham and his students fed raw and cooked food to rats and mice. When I visited Wrangham's lab at Harvard, his then graduate student, Rachel Carmody, opened the door of a small refrigerator to show me plastic bags filled with meat and sweet potatoes, some raw and some cooked. Mice raised on cooked foods gained 15 to 40 percent more weight than mice raised only on raw food.

If Wrangham is right, cooking not only gave early humans the energy they needed to build bigger brains but also helped them get more calories from food so that they could gain weight. In the modern context the flip side of his hypothesis is that we may be victims of our own success. We have gotten so good at processing foods that for the first time in human evolution, many humans are getting more calories than they burn in a day. "Rough breads have given way to Twinkies, apples to apple juice," he writes. "We need to become more aware of the calorie-raising consequences of a highly processed diet."

It's this shift to processed foods, taking place all over the world, that's contributing to a rising epidemic of obesity and related diseases. If most of the world ate more local fruits and vegetables, a little meat, fish, and some whole grains (as in the highly touted Mediterranean diet), and exercised an hour a day, that would be good news for our health—and for the planet.

On my last afternoon visiting the Tsimane in Anachere, one of Deonicio Nate's daughters, Albania, 13, tells us that her father and half-brother Alberto, 16, are back from hunting and that they've got something. We follow her to the cooking hut and smell the animals before we see them—three raccoonlike coatis have been laid across the fire, fur, and all. As the fire singes the coatis' striped pelts, Albania and her sister, Emiliana, 12, scrape off fur until the animals' flesh is bare. Then they take the carcasses to a stream to clean and prepare them for roasting.

Nate's wives are cleaning two armadillos as well, preparing to cook them in a stew with shredded plantains. Nate sits by the fire, describing a good day's hunt. First he shot the armadillos as they napped by a stream. Then his dog spotted a pack of coatis and chased them, killing two as the rest darted up a tree. Alberto fired his shotgun but missed. He fired again and hit a coati. Three coatis and two armadillos were enough, so father and son packed up and headed home.

As family members enjoy the feast, I watch their little boy, Alfonso, who had been sick all week. He is dancing around the fire, happily chewing on a cooked piece of coati tail. Nate looks pleased. Tonight in Anachere, far from the diet debates, there is meat, and that is good.

Science prevented the last food crisis. Can it save us again?

Critical Thinking

1. What kinds of health problems have indigenous groups experienced when abandoning their traditional diets?
2. Why is there no one ideal human diet?
3. What was the biggest revolution in the human diet and what have been some of its consequences?

Internet References

The Future of Food
 http://food.nationalgeographic.com/
Journal of Human Evolution
 http://www.journals.elsevier.com/journal-of-human-evolution/

ANN GIBBONS is the author of *The First Human: The Race to Discover Our Earliest Ancestors.*

Article   Prepared by: Elvio Angeloni, *Pasadena City College*

Ironing It Out

Sharon Moalem

Learning Outcomes

After reading this article, you will be able to:

- Discuss hemochromatosis in terms of its origins and its consequences.

- Explain why a deadly disease such as hemochromatosis would be bred into our genetic code.

Aran Gordon is a born competitor. He's a top financial executive, a competitive swimmer since he was six years old, and a natural long-distance runner. A little more than a dozen years after he ran his first marathon in 1984 he set his sights on the Mount Everest of marathons—the Marathon des Sables, a 150-mile race across the Sahara Desert, all brutal heat and endlesss sand that test endurance runners like nothing else.

As he began to train he experienced something he'd never really had to deal with before—physical difficulty. He was tired all the time. His joints hurt. His heart seemed to skip a funny beat. He told his running partner he wasn't sure he could go on with training, with running at all. And he went to the doctor.

Actually, he went to *doctors*. Doctor after doctor—they couldn't account for his symptoms, or they drew the wrong conclusion. When his illness left him depressed, they told him it was stress and recommended he talk to a therapist. When blood tests revealed a liver problem, they told him he was drinking too much. Finally, after three years, his doctors uncovered the real problem. New tests revealed massive amounts of iron in his blood and liver—off-the-charts amounts of iron.

Aran Gordon was rusting to death.

Hemochromatosis is a hereditary disease that disrupts the way the body metabolizes iron. Normally, when your body detects that it has sufficient iron in the blood, it reduces the amount of iron absorbed by your intestines from the food you eat. So even if you stuffed yourself with iron supplements you wouldn't load up with excess iron. Once your body is satisfied with the amount of iron it has, the excess will pass through you instead of being absorbed. But in a person who has hemochromatosis, the body always thinks that it doesn't have enough iron and continues to absorb iron unabated. This iron loading has deadly consequences over time. The excess iron is deposited throughout the body, ultimately damaging the joints, the major organs, and overall body chemistry. Unchecked, hemochromatosis can lead to liver failure, heart failure, diabetes, arthritis, infertility, psychiatric disorders, and even cancer. Unchecked, hemochromatosis will lead to death.

For more than 125 years after Armand Trousseau first described it in 1865, hemochromatosis was thought to be extremely rare. Then, in 1996, the primary gene that causes the condition was isolated for the first time. Since then, we've discovered that the gene for hemochromatosis is the most common genetic variant in people of Western European descent. If your ancestors are Western European, the odds are about one in three, or one in four, that you carry at least one copy of the hemochromatosis gene. Yet only one in two hundred people of Western European ancestry actually have hemochromatosis disease with all of its assorted symptoms. In genetics parlance, the degree that a given gene manifests itself in an individual is called penetrance. If a single gene means everyone who carries it will have dimples, that gene has very high or complete penetrance. On the other hand, a gene that requires a host of other circumstances to really manifest, like the gene for hemochromatosis, is considered to have low penetrance.

Aran Gordon had hemochromatosis. His body had been accumulating iron for more than thirty years. If it were untreated, doctors told him, it would kill him in another five. Fortunately for Aran, one of the oldest medical therapies known to man would soon enter his life and help him manage his iron-loading problem. But to get there, we have to go back.

Why would a disease so deadly be bred into our genetic code? You see, hemochromatosis isn't an infectious disease like malaria, related to bad habits like lung cancer caused by smoking, or a viral invader like smallpox. Hemochromatosis is inherited—and the gene for it is very common in certain populations. In evolutionary terms, that means we asked for it.

Remember how natural selection works. If a given genetic trait makes you stronger—especially if it makes you stronger before you have children—then you're more likely to survive, reproduce, and pass that trait on. If a given trait makes you weaker, you're less likely to survive, reproduce, and pass that trait on. Over time, species "select" those traits that make them stronger and eliminate those traits that make them weaker.

So why is a natural-born killer like hemochromatosis swimming in our gene pool? To answer that, we have to examine the relationship between life—not just human life, but pretty much all life—and iron. But before we do, think about this—why would you take a drug that is guaranteed to kill you in forty years? One reason, right? It's the only thing that will stop you from dying tomorrow.

Just about every form of life has a thing for iron. Humans need iron for nearly every function of our metabolism. Iron carries oxygen from our lungs through the bloodstream and releases it in the body where it's needed. Iron is built into the enzymes that do most of the chemical heavy lifting in our bodies, where it helps us to detoxify poisons and to convert sugars into energy. Iron-poor diets and other iron deficiencies are the most common cause of anemia, a lack of red blood cells that can cause fatigue, shortness of breath, and even heart failure. (As many as 20 percent of menstruating women may have iron-related anemia because their monthly blood loss produces an iron deficiency. That may be the case in as much as half of all pregnant women as well—they're not menstruating, but the passenger they're carrying is hungry for iron too!) Without enough iron our immune system functions poorly, the skin gets pale, and people can feel confused, dizzy, cold, and extremely fatigued.

Iron even explains why some areas of the world's ocean are crystal clear blue and almost devoid of life, while others are bright green and teeming with it. It turns out that oceans can be seeded with iron when dust from land is blown across them. Oceans, like parts of the Pacific, that aren't in the path of these iron-bearing winds develop smaller communities of phytoplankton, the single-celled creatures at the bottom of the ocean's food chain. No phytoplankton, no zooplankton. No zooplankton, no anchovies. No anchovies, no tuna. But an ocean area like the North Atlantic, straight in the path of iron-rich dust from the Sahara Desert, is a green-hued aquatic metropolis. (This has even given rise to an idea to fight global warming that its originator calls the Geritol Solution. The notion is basically this—dumping billions of tons of iron solution into the ocean will stimulate massive plant growth that will suck enough carbon dioxide out of the atmosphere to counter the effects of all the CO_2 humans are releasing into the atmosphere by burning fossil fuels. A test of the theory in 1995 transformed a patch of ocean near the Galápagos Islands from sparkling blue to murky green overnight, as the iron triggered the growth of massive amounts of phytoplankton.)

Because iron is so important, most medical research has focused on populations who don't get enough iron. Some doctors and nutritionists have operated under the assumption that more iron can only be better. The food industry currently supplements everything from flour to breakfast cereal to baby formula with iron.

You know what they say about too much of a good thing?

Our relationship with iron is much more complex than it's been considered traditionally. It's essential—but it also provides a proverbial leg up to just about every biological threat to our lives. With very few exceptions in the form of a few bacteria that use other metals in its place, almost all life on earth needs iron to survive. Parasites hunt us for our iron; cancer cells thrive on our iron. Finding, controlling, and using iron is the game of life. For bacteria, fungi, and protozoa, human blood and tissue are an iron gold mine. Add too much iron to the human system and you may just be loading up the buffet table.

In 1952, Eugene D. Weinberg was a gifted microbial researcher with a healthy curiosity and a sick wife. Diagnosed with a mild infection, his wife was prescribed tetracycline, an antibiotic. Professor Weinberg wondered whether anything in her diet could interfere with the effectiveness of the antibiotic. We've only scratched the surface of our understanding of bacterial interactions today; in 1952, medical science had only scratched the surface of the scratch. Weinberg knew how little we knew, and he knew how unpredictable bacteria could be, so he wanted to test how the antibiotic would react to the presence or absence of specific chemicals that his wife was adding to her system by eating.

In his lab, at Indiana University, he directed his assistant to load up dozens of petri dishes with three compounds: tetracycline, bacteria, and a third organic or elemental nutrient, which varied from dish to dish. A few days later, one dish was so loaded with bacteria that Professor Weinberg's assistant assumed she had forgotten to add the antibiotic to that dish. She repeated the test for that nutrient and got the same result—massive bacteria growth. The nutrient in this sample was providing so much booster fuel to the bacteria that it effectively neutralized the antibiotic. You guessed it—it was iron.

Weinberg went on to prove that access to iron helps nearly all bacteria multiply almost unimpeded. From that point on, he dedicated his life's work to understanding the negative effect that the ingestion of excess iron can have on humans and the relationship other life-forms have to it.

Human iron regulation is a complex system that involves virtually every part of the body. A healthy adult usually has between three and four grams of iron in his or her body. Most of this iron is in the bloodstream within hemoglobin, distributing oxygen, but iron can also be found throughout the body. Given that iron is not only crucial to our survival but can be a potentially deadly liability, it shouldn't be surprising that we have iron-related defense mechanisms as well.

We're most vulnerable to infection where infection has a gateway to our bodies. In an adult without wounds or broken skin, that means our mouths, eyes, noses, ears, and genitals. And because infectious agents need iron to survive, all those openings have been declared iron no-fly-zones by our bodies. On top of that, those openings are patrolled by chelators—proteins that lock up iron molecules and prevent them from being used.

Everything from tears to saliva to mucus—all the fluids found in those bodily entry points—are rich with chelators.

There's more to our iron defense system. When we're first beset by illness, our immune system kicks into high gear and fights back with what is called the *acute phase response*. The bloodstream is flooded with illness-fighting proteins, and, at the same time, iron is locked away to prevent biological invaders from using it against us. It's the biological equivalent of a prison lockdown—flood the halls with guards and secure the guns.

A similar response appears to occur when cells become cancerous and begin to spread without control. Cancer cells require iron to grow, so the body attempts to limit its availability. New pharmaceutical research is exploring ways to mimic this response by developing drugs to treat cancer and infections by limiting their access to iron.

Even some folk cures have regained respect as our understanding of bacteria's reliance on iron has grown. People used to cover wounds with egg-white-soaked straw to protect them from infection. It turns out that wasn't such a bad idea—preventing infection is what egg whites are made for. Egg shells are porous so that the chick embryo inside can "breathe." The problem with a porous shell, of course, is that air isn't the only thing that can get through it—so can all sorts of nasty microbes. The egg white's there to stop them. Egg whites are chock-full of chelators (those iron locking proteins that patrol our bodies' entry points) like ovoferrin in order to protect the developing chicken embryo—the yolk—from infection.

The relationship between iron and infection also explains one of the ways breast-feeding helps to prevent infections in newborns. Mother's milk contains lactoferrin—a chelating protein that binds with iron and prevents bacteria from feeding on it.

Before we return to Aran Gordon and hemochromatosis, we need to take a side trip, this time to Europe in the middle of the fourteenth century—not the best time to visit.

From 1347 through the next few years, the bubonic plague swept across Europe, leaving death, death, and more death in its wake. Somewhere between one-third and one-half of the population was killed—more than 25 million people. No recorded pandemic, before or since, has come close to touching the plague's record. We hope none ever will.

It was a gruesome disease. In its most common form the bacterium that's thought to have caused the plague (*Yersinia pestis*, named after Alexander Yersin, one of the bacteriologists who first isolated it in 1894) finds a home in the body's lymphatic system, painfully swelling the lymph nodes in the armpits and groin until those swollen lymph nodes literally burst through the skin. Untreated, the survival rate is about one in three. (And that's just the bubonic form, which infects the lymphatic system; when *Y. pestis* makes it into the lungs and becomes airborne, it kills nine out of ten—and not only is it more lethal when it's airborne, it's more contagious!)

The most likely origin of the European outbreak is thought to be a fleet of Genoese trading ships that docked in Messina, Italy, in the fall of 1347. By the time the ships reached port,

most of the crews were already dead or dying. Some of the ships never even made it to port, running aground along the coast after the last of their crew became too sick to steer the ship. Looters preyed on the wrecks and got a lot more than they bargained for—and so did just about everyone they encountered as they carried the plague to land.

In 1348 a Sicilian notary named Gabriele de'Mussi tells of how the disease spread from ships to the coastal populations and then inward across the continent:

Alas! Our ships enter the port, but of a thousand sailors hardly ten are spared. We reach our homes; our kindred . . . come from all parts to visit us. Woe to us for we cast at them the darts of death! . . . Going back to their homes, they in turn soon infected their whole families, who in three days succumbed, and were buried in one common grave.

Panic rose as the disease spread from town to town. Prayer vigils were held, bonfires were lighted, churches were filled with throngs. Inevitably, people looked for someone to blame. First it was Jews, and then it was witches. But rounding them up and burning them alive did nothing to stop the plague's deadly march.

Interestingly, it's possible that practices related to the observance of Passover helped to protect Jewish neighborhoods from the plague. Passover is a week-long holiday commemorating Jews' escape from slavery in Egypt. As part of its observance, Jews do not eat leavened bread and remove all traces of it from their homes. In many parts of the world, especially Europe, wheat, grain, and even legumes are also forbidden during Passover. Dr. Martin J. Blaser, a professor of internal medicine at New York University Medical Center, thinks this "spring cleaning" of grain stores may have helped to protect Jews from the plague, by decreasing their exposure to rats hunting for food—rats that carried the plague.

Victims and physicians alike had little idea what was causing the disease. Communities were overwhelmed simply by the volume of bodies that needed burying. And that, of course, contributed to the spread of the disease as rats fed on infected corpses, fleas fed on infected rats, and additional humans caught the disease from infected fleas. In 1348 a Sienese named Agnolo di Tura wrote:

Father abandoned child, wife husband, one brother another, for this illness seemed to strike through the breath and sight. And so they died. And none could be found to bury the dead for money or friendship. Members of a household brought their dead to a ditch as best they could, without priest, without divine offices . . . great pits were dug and piled deep with the multitude of dead. And they died by the hundreds both day and night. . . . And as soon as those ditches were filled more were dug. . . . And I, Agnolo di Tura, called the Fat, buried my five children with my own hands. And there were also those who were so sparsely covered with earth that the dogs dragged them forth and devoured many bodies throughout the city. There was no one who wept for any death, for all awaited death. And so many died that all believed it was the end of the world.

As it turned out, it wasn't the end of the world, and it didn't kill everyone on earth or even in Europe. It didn't even kill everyone it infected. Why? Why did some people die and others survive?

The emerging answer may be found in the same place Aran Gordon finally found the answer to his health problem—iron. New research indicates that the more iron in a given population, the more vulnerable that population is to the plague. In the past, healthy adult men were at greater risk than anybody else—children and the elderly tended to be malnourished, with corresponding iron deficiencies, and adult women are regularly iron depleted by menstruation, pregnancy, and breast-feeding. It might be that, as Stephen Ell, a professor at the University of Iowa, wrote, "Iron status mirror[ed] mortality. Adult males were at highest risk on this basis, with women [who lose iron through menstruation], children, and the elderly relatively spared."

There aren't any highly reliable mortality records from the fourteenth century, but many scholars believe that men in their prime were the most vulnerable. More recent—but still long ago—outbreaks of bubonic plague, for which there are reliable mortality records, demonstrate that the perception of heightened vulnerability in healthy adult men is very real. A study of plague in St. Botolph's Parish in 1625 indicates that men between fifteen and forty-four killed by the disease outnumbered women of the same age by a factor of two to one.

So let's get back to hemochromatosis. With all this iron in their systems, people with hemochromatosis should be magnets for infection in general and the plague in particular, right?

Wrong.

Remember the iron-locking response of the body at the onset of illness? It turns out that people who have hemochromatosis have a form of iron locking going on as a permanent condition. The excess iron that the body takes on is distributed throughout the body—but it isn't distributed *everywhere* throughout the body. And while most cells end up with too much iron, one particular type of cell ends up with much *less* iron than normal. The cells that hemochromatosis is stingy with when it comes to iron are a type of white blood cell called *macrophages*. Macrophages are the police wagons of the immune system. They circle our systems looking for trouble; when they find it, they surround it, try to subdue or kill it, and bring it back to the station in our lymph nodes.

In a nonhemochromatic person, macrophages have plenty of iron. Many infectious agents, like tuberculosis, can use that iron within the microphage to feed and multiply (which is exactly what the body is trying to prevent through the iron-locking response). So when a normal macrophage gathers up certain infectious agents to protect the body, it inadvertently is giving those infectious agents a Trojan horse access to the iron they need to grow stronger. By the time those macrophages get to the lymph node, the invaders in the wagon are armed and dangerous and can use the lymphatic system to travel throughout the body. That's exactly what happens with bubonic plague: the

swollen and bursting lymph nodes that characterize it are the direct result of the bacteria's subversion of the body's immune system for its own purposes.

Ultimately, the ability to access iron within our macrophages is what makes some intracellular infections deadly and others benign. The longer our immune system is able to prevent an infection from spreading by containing it, the better it can develop other means, like antibodies, to overwhelm it. If your macrophages lack iron, as they do in people who have hemochromatosis, those macrophages have an additional advantage—not only do they isolate infectious agents and cordon them off from the rest of the body, they also starve those infectious agents to death.

New research has demonstrated that iron-deficient macrophages are indeed the Bruce Lees of the immune system. In one set of experiments, macrophages from people who had hemochromatosis and macrophages from people who did not were matched against bacteria in separate dishes to test their killing ability. The hemochromatic macrophages crushed the bacteria—they are thought to be significantly better at combating bacteria by limiting the availability of iron than the nonhemochromatic macrophages.

Which brings us full circle. Why would you take a pill that was guaranteed to kill you in forty years? Because it will save you tomorrow. Why would we select for a gene that will kill us through iron loading by the time we reach what is now middle age? Because it will protect us from a disease that is killing everyone else long before that.

Hemochromatosis is caused by a genetic mutation. It predates the plague, of course. Recent research has suggested that it originated with the Vikings and was spread throughout Northern Europe as the Vikings colonized the European coastline. It may have originally evolved as a mechanism to minimize iron deficiencies in poorly nourished populations living in harsh environments. (If this was the case, you'd expect to find hemochromatosis in all populations living in iron-deficient environments, but you don't.) Some researchers have speculated that women who had hemochromatosis might have benefited from the additional iron absorbed through their diet because it prevented anemia caused by menstruation. This, in turn, led them to have more children, who also carried the hemochromatosis mutation. Even more speculative theories have suggested that Viking men may have offset the negative effects of hemochromatosis because their warrior culture resulted in frequent blood loss.

As the Vikings settled the European coast, the mutation may have grown in frequency through what geneticists call the founder effect. When small populations establish colonies in unpopulated or secluded areas, there is significant inbreeding for generations. This inbreeding virtually guarantees that any mutations that aren't fatal at a very early age will be maintained in large portions of the population.

Then, in 1347, the plague begins its march across Europe. People who have the hemochromatosis mutation are especially resistant to infection because of their iron-starved macrophages.

So, though it will kill them decades later, they are much more likely than people without hemochromatosis to survive the plague, reproduce, and pass the mutation on to their children. In a population where most people don't survive until middle age, a genetic trait that will kill you when you get there but increases your chance of arriving is—well, something to ask for.

The pandemic known as the Black Death is the most famous—and deadly—outbreak of bubonic plague, but historians and scientists believe there were recurring outbreaks in Europe virtually every generation until the eighteenth or nineteenth century. If hemochromatosis helped that first generation of carriers to survive the plague, multiplying its frequency across the population as a result, it's likely that these successive outbreaks compounded that effect, further breeding the mutation into the Northern and Western European populations every time the disease resurfaced over the ensuing three hundred years. The growing percentage of hemochromatosis carriers—potentially able to fend off the plague—may also explain why no subsequent epidemic was as deadly as the pandemic of 1347 to 1350.

This new understanding of hemochromatosis, infection, and iron has provoked a reevaluation of two long-established medical treatments—one very old and all but discredited, the other more recent and all but dogma. The first, bleeding, is back; the second, iron dosing, especially for anemics, is being reconsidered in many circumstances.

Bloodletting is one of the oldest medical practices in history, and nothing has a longer or more complicated record. First recorded three thousand years ago in Egypt, it reached its peak in the nineteenth century only to be roundly discredited as almost savage over the last hundred years. There are records of Syrian doctors using leeches for bloodletting more than two thousand years ago and accounts of the great Jewish scholar Maimonides' employing bloodletting as the physician to the royal court of Saladin, sultan of Egypt, in the twelfth century. Doctors and shamans from Asia to Europe to the Americas used instruments as varied as sharpened sticks, shark's teeth, and miniature bows and arrows to bleed their patients.

In Western medicine, the practice was derived from the thinking of the Greek physician Galen, who practiced the theory of the four humours—blood, black bile, yellow bile, and phlegm. According to Galen and his intellectual descendants, all illness resulted from an imbalance of the four humours, and it was the doctor's job to balance those fluids through fasting, purging, and bloodletting.

Volumes of old medical texts are devoted to how and how much blood should be drawn. An illustration from a 1506 book on medicine points to forty-three different places on the human body that should be used for bleeding—fourteen on the head alone.

For centuries in the West, the place to go for bloodletting was the barber shop. In fact, the barber's pole originated as a symbol for bloodletting—the brass bowl at the top represented the bowl where leeches were kept; the one at the bottom represented the bowl for collecting blood. And the red and white spirals have their origins in the medieval practice of hanging bandages on a pole to dry them after they were washed. The bandages would twist in the wind and wrap themselves in spirals around the pole. As to why barbers were the surgeons of the day? Well, they were the guys with the razor blades.

Bloodletting reached its peak in the eighteenth and nineteenth centuries. According to medical texts of the time, if you presented to your doctor with a fever, hypertension, or dropsy, you would be bled. If you had an inflammation, apoplexy, or a nervous disorder, you would be bled. If you suffered from a cough, dizziness, headache, drunkenness, palsy, rheumatism, or shortness of breath, you would be bled. As crazy as it sounds, even if you were hemorrhaging blood you would be bled.

Modern medical science has been skeptical of bloodletting for many reasons—at least some of them deserved. First of all, eighteenth- and nineteenth-century reliance on bleeding as a treatment for just about everything is reasonably suspect.

When George Washington was ill with a throat infection, doctors treating him conducted at least four bleedings in just twenty-four hours. It's unclear today whether Washington actually died from the infection or from shock caused by blood loss. Doctors in the nineteenth century routinely bled patients until they fainted; they took that as a sign they'd removed just the right amount of blood.

After millennia of practice, bloodletting fell into extreme disfavor at the beginning of the twentieth century. The medical community—even the general public—considered bleeding to be the epitome of everything that was barbaric about prescientific medicine. Now, new research indicates that—like so much else—the broad discrediting of bloodletting may have been a rush to judgment.

First of all, it's now absolutely clear that bloodletting—or phlebotomy, as it's known today—is the treatment of choice for hemochromatosis patients. Regular bleeding of hemochromatosis patients reduces the iron in their systems to normal levels and prevents the iron buildup in the body's organs that is so damaging.

It's not just for hemochromatosis, either—doctors and researchers are examining phlebotomy as an aid in combating heart disease, high blood pressure, and pulmonary edema. And even our complete dismissal of historic bloodletting practices is getting another look. New evidence suggests that, in moderation, bloodletting may have had a beneficial effect.

A Canadian physiologist named Norman Kasting discovered that bleeding animals induces the release of the hormone vasopressin; this reduces their fevers and spurs their immune system into higher gear. The connection isn't unequivocally proven in humans, but there is much correlation between bloodletting and fever reduction in the historic record. Bleeding also may have helped to fight infection by reducing the amount of iron available to feed an invader, providing an assist to the body's natural tendency to hide iron when it recognizes an infection.

When you think about it, the notion that humans across the globe continued to practice phlebotomy for thousands of years probably indicates that it produced *some* positive results.

If everyone who was treated with bloodletting died, its practitioners would have been out of business pretty quickly.

One thing is clear—an ancient medical practice that "modern" medical science dismissed out of hand is the only effective treatment for a disease that would otherwise destroy the lives of thousands of people. The lesson for medical science is a simple one—there is much more that the scientific community doesn't understand than there is that it does understand.

Iron is good. Iron is good. Iron is good.

Well, now you know that, like just about every other good thing under the sun, when it comes to iron, it's moderation, moderation, moderation. But until recently, current medical thinking didn't recognize that. Iron was thought to be good, so the more iron the better.

A doctor named John Murray was working with his wife in a Somali refugee camp when he noticed that many of the nomads, despite pervasive anemia and repeated exposure to a range of virulent pathogens, including malaria, tuberculosis, and brucellosis, were free of visible infection. He responded to this anomaly by deciding to treat only part of the population with iron at first. Sure enough, he treated some of the nomads for anemia by giving them iron supplements, and suddenly the infections gained the upper hand. The rate of infection in nomads receiving the extra iron skyrocketed. The Somali nomads weren't withstanding these infections *despite* their anemia: they were withstanding these infections *because of* their anemia. It was iron locking in high gear.

Thirty-five years ago, doctors in New Zealand routinely injected Maori babies with iron supplements. They assumed that the Maori (the indigenous people of New Zealand) had a poor diet, lacking iron, and that their babies would be anemic as a result.

The Maori babies injected with iron were seven times as likely to suffer from potentially deadly infections, including septicemias (blood poisoning) and meningitis. Like all of us, babies have isolated strains of potentially harmful bacteria in their systems, but those strains are normally kept under control by their bodies. When the doctors gave these babies iron boosters, they were giving booster fuel to the bacteria, with tragic results.

It's not just iron dosing through injection that can cause this blossoming of infections; iron-supplemented food can be food for bacteria too. Many infants can have botulism spores in their intestines (the spores can be found in honey, and that's one of the reasons parents are warned not to feed honey to babies, especially before they turn one). If the spores germinate, the results can be fatal. A study of sixty-nine cases of infant botulism in California showed one key difference between fatal and nonfatal cases of botulism in babies. Babies who were fed with iron-supplemented formula instead of breast-fed were much younger when they began to get sick and more vulnerable as a result. Of the ten who died, all had been fed with the iron-enhanced formula.

By the way, hemochromatosis and anemia aren't the only hereditary diseases that have gained pride of place in our gene pool by offering protection from another threat, and they're not all related to iron. The second most common genetic disease in Europeans, after hemochromatosis, is cystic fibrosis. It's a terrible, debilitating disease that affects different parts of the body. Most people with cystic fibrosis die young, usually from lung-related illness. Cystic fibrosis is caused by a mutation in a gene called CFTR; it takes two copies of the mutated gene to cause the disease. Somebody with only one copy of the mutated gene is known as a carrier but does not have cystic fibrosis. It's thought that at least 2 percent of people descended from Europeans are carriers, making the mutation very common indeed from a genetic perspective. New research suggests that, sure enough, carrying a copy of the gene that causes cystic fibrosis seems to offer some protection from tuberculosis. Tuberculosis, which has also been called consumption because of the way it seems to consume its victims from the inside out, caused 20 percent of all the deaths in Europe between 1600 and 1900, making it a very deadly disease. And making anything that helped to protect people from it look pretty attractive while lounging in the gene pool.

Aran Gordon first manifested symptoms of hemochromatosis as he began training for the Marathon des Sables—that grueling 150-mile race across the Sahara Desert. But it would take three years of progressive health problems, frustrating tests, and inaccurate conclusions before he finally learned what was wrong with him. When he did, he was told that untreated he had five years to live.

Today, we know that Aran suffered the effects of the most common genetic disorder in people of European descent—hemochromatosis, a disorder that may very well have helped his ancestors to survive the plague.

Today, Aran's health has been restored through bloodletting, one of the oldest medical practices on earth.

Today, we understand much more about the complex interrelationship of our bodies, iron, infection, and conditions like hemochromatosis and anemia.

What doesn't kill us, makes us stronger.

Which is probably some version of what Aran Gordon was thinking when he finished the Marathon des Sables for the second time in April 2006—just a few months after he was supposed to have died.

Critical Thinking

1. What is "hemochromatosis," why does it occur, and what are its consequences? What is its primary cause?

2. Why is iron important to humans?

3. Why does our iron set us up for biological threats?

4. Discuss the ways in which our bodies regulate iron in order to fight disease.

5. Discuss the way in which the bubonic plague killed its victims and why people with hemochromatosis were the more likely survivors.

6. How did hemochromatosis seem to get its start in Europe? How might the "founder effect" have played a role? How might the gene have increased over the centuries?

7. Why was bloodletting favored as a treatment over the millennia, then discounted, and now is back in favor in several respects?

8. What evidence is there that too much iron can be harmful?

9. Why is having two genes for cystic fibrosis harmful? Why is having one gene beneficial?

Create Central

www.mhhe.com/createcentral

Internet References

Evolution and Medicine Network
http://evmedreview.com

The Evolution & Medicine Review
http://evmedreview.com

Moalem, Sharon. From *Survival of the Sickest* (William Morrow, 2007). Copyright © 2007 by Sharon Moalem. Reprinted by permission of HarperCollins Publishers.

Article

Prepared by: Elvio Angeloni, *Pasadena City College*

Why We Help

MARTIN A. NOWAK

Learning Outcomes

After reading this article, you will be able to:

- Discuss the difficulty that biologists have had in making sense of the fact that selfless behavior is such a pervasive phenomenon.

- Discuss cooperation as the driving force of human evolution.

Last April, as reactors at Japan's Fukushima Daiichi nuclear power plant were melting down following a lethal earthquake and tsunami, a maintenance worker in his 20s was among those who volunteered to reenter the plant to try to help bring things back under control. He knew the air was poisoned and expected the choice would keep him from ever marrying or having children for fear of burdening them with health consequences. Yet he still walked back through Fukushima's gates into the plant's radiation-infused air and got to work—for no more compensation than his usual modest wages. "There are only some of us who can do this job," the worker, who wished to remain anonymous, told the Independent last July. "I'm single and young, and I feel it's my duty to help settle this problem."

Although they may not always play out on such an epic scale, examples of selfless behavior abound in nature. Cells within an organism coordinate to keep their division in check and avoid causing cancer, worker ants in many species sacrifice their own fecundity to serve their queen and colony, female lions within a pride will suckle one another's young. And humans help other humans to do everything from obtaining food to finding mates to defending territory. Even if the helpers may not necessarily be putting their lives on the line, they are risking lowering their own reproductive success for the benefit of another individual.

For decades biologists have fretted over cooperation, scrambling to make sense of it in light of the dominant view of evolution as "red in tooth and claw," as Alfred, Lord Tennyson so vividly described it. Charles Darwin, in making his case for evolution by natural selection—wherein individuals with desirable traits reproduce more often than their peers and thus contribute more to the next generation—called this competition the

"struggle for life most severe." Taken to its logical extreme, the argument quickly leads to the conclusion that one should never ever help a rival and that an individual might in fact do well to lie and cheat to get ahead. Winning the game of life—by hook or by crook—is all that matters.

Why, then, is selfless behavior such a pervasive phenomenon? Over the past two decades I have been using the tools of game theory to study this apparent paradox. My work indicates that instead of opposing competition, cooperation has operated alongside it from the get-go to shape the evolution of life on earth, from the first cells to Homo sapiens. Life is therefore not just a struggle for survival—it is also, one might say, a snuggle for survival. And in no case has the evolutionary influence of cooperation been more profoundly felt than in humans. My findings hint at why this should be the case and underscore that just as helping one another was the key to our success in the past, so, too, is it poised to be vital to our future.

From Adversary to Ally

I first became interested in cooperation back in 1987, as a graduate student studying mathematics and biology at the University of Vienna. While on a retreat with some fellow students and professors in the Alps, I learned about a game theory paradox called the Prisoner's Dilemma that elegantly illustrates why cooperation has so flummoxed evolutionary biologists. The dilemma goes like this: Imagine that two people have been arrested and are facing jail sentences for having conspired to commit a crime. The prosecutor questions each one privately and lays out the terms of a deal. If one person rats on the other and the other remains silent, the incriminator gets just one year of jail time, whereas the silent person gets slammed with a four-year sentence. If both parties cooperate and do not rat on each other, both get reduced sentences of two years. But if both individuals incriminate each other, they both receive three-year sentences.

Because each convict is consulted separately, neither knows whether his or her partner will defect or cooperate. Plotting the possible outcomes on a payoff matrix, one can see that from an individual's standpoint, the best bet is to defect and incriminate one's partner. Yet because both parties will follow that same line of reasoning and choose defection, both will receive the third-best outcome (three-year sentences) instead of the two-year sentences they could get by cooperating with each other.

The Prisoner's Dilemma seduced me immediately with its power to probe the relation between conflict and cooperation. Eventually my Ph.D. adviser, Karl Sigmund, and I developed techniques to run computer simulations of the dilemma using large communities rather than limiting ourselves to two prisoners. Taking these approaches, we could watch as the strategies of the individuals in these communities evolved from defection to cooperation and back to defection through cycles of growth and decline. Through the simulations, we identified a mechanism that could overcome natural selection's predilection for selfish behavior, leading would-be defectors to instead lend helping hands.

We started with a random distribution of defectors and cooperators, and after each round of the game the winners would go on to produce offspring who would participate in the next round. The offspring mostly followed their parents' strategy, although random mutations could shift their strategy. As the simulation ran, we found that within just a few generations all the individuals in the population were defecting in every round of the game. Then, after some time, a new strategy suddenly emerged: players would start by cooperating and then mirror their opponents' moves, tit for tat. The change quickly led to communities dominated by cooperators.

This mechanism for the evolution of cooperation among individuals who encounter one another repeatedly is known as direct reciprocity. Vampire bats offer a striking example. If a bat misses a chance to feed directly on prey one day, it will beg from its sated peers back at the roost. If it is lucky, one of its roost mates will share its blood meal by regurgitating it into the hungry bat's mouth. The vampires live in stable groups and return to the roost every day after hunting, so group members routinely encounter one another. Studies have shown that the bats remember which bats have helped them in times of need, and when the day comes that the generous bat finds itself in need of food, the bat it helped earlier is likely to return the favor.

What made our early computer simulations even more interesting was the revelation that there are different kinds of direct reciprocity. Within 20 generations the initial tit-for-tat strategy had given way to a more generous strategy in which players might still cooperate even if their rival defected. We had, in essence, witnessed the evolution of forgiveness—a direct-reciprocity strategy that allows players to overlook the occasional mistake.

In addition to direct reciprocity, I later identified four more mechanisms for the evolution of cooperation. In the several thousand papers scientists have published on how cooperators could prevail in evolution, all the scenarios they describe fall into one or more of these five categories.

A second means by which cooperation may find a foothold in a population is if cooperators and defectors are not uniformly distributed in a population—a mechanism termed spatial selection. Neighbors (or friends in a social network) tend to help one another, so in a population with patches of cooperators, these helpful individuals can form clusters that can then grow and thus prevail in competition with defectors. Spatial selection also operates among simpler organisms. Among yeast cells, cooperators make an enzyme used to digest sugar. They

do this at a cost to themselves. Defector yeast, meanwhile, mooch off the cooperators' enzymes instead of making their own. Studies conducted by Jeff Gore of the Massachusetts Institute of Technology and, independently, by Andrew Murray of Harvard University have found that among yeast grown in well-mixed populations, the defectors prevailed. In populations with clumps of cooperators and defectors, in contrast, the cooperators won out.

Perhaps one of the most immediately intuitive mechanisms for the evolution of selflessness concerns cooperation among genetically related individuals, or kin selection. In this situation, individuals make sacrifices for their relatives because those relatives share their genes. Thus, although one may be reducing one's own direct reproductive fitness by assisting a relative in need, one is still fostering the spread of those genes the helper shares with recipients. As 20th-century biologist J.B.S. Haldane, who first mentioned the idea of kin selection, put it: "I will jump into the river to save two brothers or eight cousins," referring to the fact that our siblings share 50 percent of our DNA, whereas our first cousins share 12.5 percent. (It turns out that calculating the fitness effects of kin selection is a rather complicated task that has misled many researchers. My colleagues and I are now engaged in an intense debate about the underlying mathematics of kin selection theory.)

The fourth mechanism that fosters the emergence of cooperation is indirect reciprocity, which is quite distinct from the direct variety that Sigmund and I studied initially. In indirect reciprocity, one individual decides to aid another based on the needy individual's reputation. Those who have a reputation for assisting others who fall on hard times might even find themselves on the receiving end of goodwill from strangers when their own luck takes a turn for the worse. Thus, instead of the "I'll scratch your back if you scratch my mine" mentality, the cooperator in this situation might be thinking, "I'll scratch your back, and someone will scratch mine." Among Japanese macaques, for example, low-ranking monkeys that groom high-ranking ones (which have good reputations) may better their own reputations—and hence receive more grooming—simply by being seen with the top brass.

Last, individuals may perform selfless acts for the greater good, as opposed to abetting a single peer. This fifth means by which cooperation may take root is known as group selection. Recognition of this mechanism dates back to Darwin himself, who observed in his 1871 book *The Descent of Man* that "a tribe including many members who . . . were always ready to aid one another, and to sacrifice themselves for the common good, would be victorious over most other tribes; and this would be natural selection." Biologists have since argued fiercely over this idea that natural selection can favor cooperation to improve the reproductive potential of the group. Mathematical modeling by researchers, including me, however, has helped show that selection can operate at multiple levels, from individual genes to groups of related individuals to entire species. Thus, the employees of a company compete with one another to move up the corporate ladder, but they also cooperate to ensure that the business succeeds in its competition with other companies.

One for All

The five mechanisms governing the emergence of cooperation apply to all manner of organisms, from amoebas to zebras (and even, in some cases, to genes and other components of cells). This universality suggests that cooperation has been a driving force in the evolution of life on earth from the beginning. Moreover, there is one group in which the effects of cooperation have proved especially profound: humans. Millions of years of evolution transformed a slow, defenseless ape into the most influential creature on the planet, a species capable of inventing a mind-boggling array of technologies that have allowed our kind to plumb the depths of the ocean, explore outer space and broadcast our achievements to the world in an instant. We have accomplished these monumental feats by working together. Indeed, humans are the most cooperative species—supercooperators, if you will.

Given that the five mechanisms of cooperation occur throughout nature, the question is: What makes humans, in particular, the most helpful of all? As I see it, humans, more than any other creature, offer assistance based on indirect reciprocity, or reputation.

Why? Because only humans have full-blown language—and, by extension, names for one another—which allows us to share information about everyone from our immediate family members to complete strangers on the other side of the globe. We are obsessed with who does what to whom and why—we have to be to best position ourselves in the social network around us. Studies have shown that people decide on everything from which charities to sponsor to which corporate start-ups to fund based in part on reputation. My Harvard colleague Rebecca Henderson, an expert on competitive strategy in the business world, notes that Toyota gained a competitive edge over other car manufacturers in the 1980s in part because of its reputation for treating suppliers fairly.

The interplay between language and indirect reciprocity leads to rapid cultural evolution, which is central to our adaptability as a species. As the human population expands and the climate changes, we will need to harness that adaptability and figure out ways to work together to save the planet and its inhabitants. Given our current environmental track record, our odds of meeting that goal do not look great. Here, too, game theory offers insights. Certain cooperative dilemmas that involve more than two players are called public goods games. In this setting, everyone in the group benefits from my cooperation, but all else being equal, I increase my payoff by switching from cooperation to defection. Thus, although I want others to cooperate, my "smart" choice is to defect. The problem is that everyone in the group thinks the same way, and so what begins as cooperation ends in defection.

In the classic public goods scenario known as the Tragedy of the Commons, described in 1968 by the late ecologist Garrett Hardin, a group of livestock farmers who share grazing land allow their animals to overgraze on the communal turf, despite knowing that they are ultimately destroying everyone's resource, including their own. The analogies to real-world concerns about natural resources—from oil to clean drinking water—are obvious. If cooperators tend to defect when it comes to custodianship of communal assets, how can we ever hope to preserve the planet's ecological capital for future generations?

All for One

Thankfully, not all hope is lost. A series of computerized experiments conducted by Manfred Milinski of the Max Planck Institute for Evolutionary Biology in Plön, Germany, and his colleagues have revealed several factors that motivate people to be good stewards of the commons in public goods games. The researchers gave each subject €40 and had them play a game via computer in which the object was to use the money to keep the earth's climate under control. Participants were told that for each round of the game, they had to donate some of their money into a common pool. If at the end of 10 rounds there was €120 or more in the common pool, then the climate was safe and the players would go home with the money they had left over. If they raised less than €120, then the climate would break down and everyone would lose all their money.

Although the players often failed to save the climate, missing the mark by a few euros, the investigators observed differences in their behavior from round to round that hint at what inspires generosity. The researchers found that players were more altruistic when they received authoritative information about climate research, indicating that people need to be convinced that there really is a problem to make sacrifices for the greater good. They also acted more generously when they were allowed to make their contributions publicly rather than anonymously—that is, when their reputation was on the line. Another study by researchers at Newcastle University in England underscored the importance of reputation by finding that people are more generous when they feel they are being watched.

These factors come into play every month when I receive my home's gas bill. The bill compares my household's consumption with both the average household gas consumption in my neighborhood outside Boston and that of the most efficient homes. Seeing how our usage stacks up against our neighbors' motivates my family to use less gas: every winter we try to lower the temperature in the house by one degree Fahrenheit.

Evolutionary simulations indicate that cooperation is intrinsically unstable; periods of cooperative prosperity inevitably give way to defective doom. And yet the altruistic spirit always seems to rebuild itself; our moral compasses somehow realign. Cycles of cooperation and defection are visible in the ups and downs of human history, the oscillations of political and financial systems. Where we humans are in this cycle right now is uncertain, but clearly we could be doing a better job of working together to solve the world's most pressing problems. Game theory suggests a way. Policy makers should take note of indirect reciprocity and the importance of information and reputation in keeping defectors in check. And they should exploit the capacity of these factors to make better cooperators of us all in the mother of all public goods games: the seven-billion-person mission to conserve the rapidly dwindling resources of planet Earth.

Critical Thinking

1. Discuss the claim that selfless behavior abounds in nature.
2. Why has it been difficult for biologists to "make sense" of the fact that selfless behavior is such a pervasive phenomenon?
3. How does the Prisoner's Dilemma allow scientists to probe the relation between conflict and cooperation? What did the computer simulation show?
4. Using examples, describe the five ways in which cooperation may take hold in a group. Why does the author think these mechanisms may have been the driving force in the evolution of life on earth from the beginning?
5. How and why have humans become the "most helpful of all"?
6. How do the examples of game theory, the Tragedy of the Commons, computerized experiments, and the author's gas bill all provide us with a better understanding of how to preserve the planet's ecological capital?
7. How do evolutionary simulations show cooperation to be intrinsically unstable?
8. What can policymakers learn from game theory?

Create Central

www.mhhe.com/createcentral

Internet References

American Anthropologist Association
www.aaanet.org

Living Links
www.emory.edu/LIVING_LINKS/dewaal.html

MARTIN A. NOWAK is a professor of biology and mathematics at Harvard University and director of the Program for Evolutionary Dynamics. His research focuses on the mathematical underpinnings of evolution.

Nowak, Martin A. From *Scientific American*, Vol. 306, No. 7, July, 2012, pp. 34-39. Copyright © 2012 by Scientific American, a division of Nature America, Inc. All rights reserved. Reprinted by permission.

Article   Prepared by: Elvio Angeloni

Don't Swallow Them

CAROLINE WILLIAMS

Learning Outcomes

After reading this article, you will be able to:

- Discuss the misconceptions regarding having to drink eight glasses of water a day, the effect of sugar on children's behavior, the role of antioxidants in our health, the various methods of detoxification and the relationship between being overweight and early death.

- Discuss the pros and cons of the "evolutionary discordance hypothesis."

1. Drink Eight Glasses of Water Per Day

It's the myth that just won't go away. Almost everyone thinks they don't drink enough water, but the idea that we all should drink lots of it—eight glasses per day—is based on no scientific data whatsoever.

No one really knows where the eight-glasses idea comes from. Some blame the bottled water industry but plenty of doctors and health organisations have also promoted it over the decades. The source might be a 1945 recommendation by the US National Research Council (NRC) that adults should consume 1 millilitre of water for each calorie of food, which adds up to about 2.5 litres per day for men and 2 litres for women.

According to Barbara Rolls, a nutrition researcher at Penn State University and author of the 1984 book *Thirst*, this amount is about right for people in a temperate climate who aren't exercising vigorously. And 1.9 litres is what you'll get from drinking eight 8-ounce glasses of water—the 8 × 8 rule—as per the US version of the myth.

What most people don't realise, though, is that we get a lot of that water from our food, as the NRC pointed out at the time. Foods contain water and are broken down chemically

into carbon dioxide and more water. So if you are not sweating buckets you need only about a litre a day—and 1.2 litres is what you will get from the eight 150-millilitre glasses recommended by the UK's health service.

But any talk of glasses is misleading because there is no need to drink pure water. The fluids that people drink anyway, including tea and coffee, can provide all the water we need, says Heinz Valtin, a kidney specialist at Dartmouth Medical School in Lebanon, New Hampshire, who has reviewed the evidence (*Regulatory Integrative and Comparative Physiology*, vol 283, p R993).

According to the myth, however, caffeinated drinks don't count because they are diuretic, stimulating the body to lose more water than it gets from the drink. Not true. A comparison of healthy adults in 2000 found no difference in hydration whether they got their water from caffeinated drinks or not (*Journal of the American College of Nutrition*, vol 19, p 591). Even one or two mildly alcoholic drinks will hydrate you rather than dehydrating you.

Hydrophilics respond by saying that pure water is better than other drinks. Even this claim is arguable, but the crucial point is that if you are a healthy individual already drinking enough tea, milk, juice or whatever, there is no evidence that swigging down water as well will achieve anything other than making you go to the bathroom all the time.

The final aspect of this myth is that we need to force ourselves to drink because by the time we are thirsty we are already seriously dehydrated. Not so. Rolls showed nearly 30 years ago that we get thirsty long before there is any significant loss of bodily fluids. It takes less than a 2 percent rise in the concentration of the blood to make us want to drink, while the body isn't officially regarded as dehydrated until a rise of 5 percent or more.

So relax and trust your body. Don't force yourself to gulp down gallons of water if you don't want to—that can be dangerous—just drink the beverage of your choice whenever you're thirsty.

2. Sugar Makes Children Hyperactive

Every parent has seen it happen: take a group of young children, add sugar, then stand back and watch them bounce off the walls. But although many parents will find it hard to believe, sugar does not cause hyperactivity.

A 1996 review of 12 blinded studies, where no one at the time knew which kids had received sugar and which a placebo, found no evidence to support this notion. This is true even for children with ADHD or whose parents consider them to be sensitive to sugar (*Critical Reviews in Food Science and Nutrition,* vol 36, p 31).

In fact, one of these studies concluded that the sugar effect is all in parents' minds. Parents and their 5-to 7-year-old "sugar-sensitive" children were split into two groups. The parents of one group were told their children had been given a large dose of sugar, while the others believed their kids were in the placebo group. In reality, all the children had been given sugar-free food. But when the parents watched their offspring at play afterwards, those who thought their kids were in the sugar group were more likely to rate their behaviour as hyperactive (*Journal of Abnormal Child Psychology,* vol 22, p 501).

Having said all that, sugar does affect kids' brains, although in a surprising way. In one study, David Benton, a psychologist at Swansea University in the UK, found that in the half-an-hour or so after having a glucose drink, 9 to 11-year-old schoolchildren were better able to concentrate on tasks and scored higher in memory tests (*Biological Psychology,* vol 78, p 242). That's the opposite of hyperactivity, one characteristic of which is an inability to concentrate.

But don't start plying your kids with sugary drinks—as the study notes, the performance boost may not last long. Non-sugary meals that help the body maintain a constant supply of glucose to the brain are better.

So perhaps what parents' mistake for hyperactivity at parties is just sugar-fuelled kids focusing hard on having fun. "Provision of energy is clearly going to increase the possibility of energy expenditure," says Andrew Scholey, who studies glucose and cognitive enhancement at Swinburne University in Melbourne, Australia.

3. Antioxidant Pills Help You Live Longer

It seems blindingly obvious. As our cells metabolise the food we eat, they produce rogue molecules called free radicals that wreak havoc. Over a lifetime, the damage they do slowly builds up and may cause all kinds of degenerative diseases. Luckily, though, many chemicals can act as antioxidants that mop up free radicals. Plus, eating vegetables rich in antioxidants seems to reduce the risk of degenerative diseases. So popping pills packed with antioxidants must surely help stave off these diseases too?

That's what some scientists started thinking from the 1970s onwards. The Nobel prizewinning chemist Linus Pauling enthusiastically promoted high doses of vitamins without waiting for the evidence, the public lapped it up and a whole new industry sprang up to meet demand.

Then, in the 1990s, the results of rigorous trials of some of the most popular supplements, including beta carotene, vitamin E and vitamin C, started to come in. Study after study has found that while these substances do work as antioxidants in the test tube, popping the pills does not provide any benefit.

On the contrary, some studies suggest that they are harmful. A 2007 review of nearly 70 trials involving 230,000 people concluded that not only do antioxidant supplements not increase lifespan, but that supplements of beta carotene and vitamins A and E actually seem to increase mortality (*Journal of the American Medical Association,* vol 297, p 842).

Why? Perhaps because high levels of free radicals tell cells to ramp up their own built-in antioxidant defences, says Barry Halliwell, a biochemist at the National University of Singapore. He thinks these internal defences are far more effective than the antioxidants we get from food. So by taking supplements we may be deactivating a first-rate defence mechanism and replacing it with a poorer one (*Nutrition Reviews,* vol 70, p 257). "Free radicals in low amounts also play useful roles," Halliwell says.

If this is right, the benefits of vegetables may have nothing to do with antioxidants. One suggestion is that vegetables are beneficial because they are mildly poisonous—a little poison may activate protective mechanisms that ward off disease.

In the meantime, the antioxidant juggernaut rolls on. No one seems keen to abandon the idea that antioxidant supplements are good for you.

We live in a toxic world. You're breathing in lead as you read this. Your next meal will contain everything from natural poisons to pesticides and pollutants. As a result, the human body is a veritable cesspit of suspect chemicals. The last US National Report on Human Exposure to Environmental Chemicals found potentially concerning levels of dozens of undesirable substances, including heavy metals, dioxins, PCBs and phthalate plasticisers, in the blood and urine of Americans.

The question is, what can we do about it? According to popular wisdom, we need to "detox" to get rid of these poisons in our body, and there is no shortage of advice on the best way to accomplish this. But do any of these detox plans actually work? And is detoxing really good for us?

For a start, we are already doing it all the time, with the help of our livers, kidneys, and digestive systems. Most of the toxic chemicals we consume are broken down or excreted, or both, within hours.

However, it can take weeks, months or even years to get rid of some substances, especially fat-soluble chemicals such as dioxins and PCBs.

4. Our Bodies Can and Should Be Detoxed

If we take these in faster than our bodies can get rid of them, levels build up in our bodies.

Many detox programmes promote a period of consuming only fluids and no solid food, but this will make virtually no difference to levels of chemicals that have built up over years. "For many of these it will take between six and 10 years of zero exposure to get rid of one-half of the amount stored in our fat tissues," says Andreas Kortenkamp, a toxicologist at Brunel University in London. "That is not achievable, because, unfortunately, there is no zero exposure."

What's more, fasting or dieting releases fat-soluble chemicals into the blood, rather than eliminating them from the body. One study found the level of organochlorines and pesticides in blood shot up by 25 to 50 percent after people lost a lot of weight quickly (*Obesity Surgery*, vol. 16, p. 1145). Animal studies show that this increases the level of compounds in tissues like the muscles and brain, where they can do more harm than in fat.

This sudden flood of chemicals could even cause the kind of problems detoxers are trying to avoid, says Margaret Sears, an environmental health researcher at the CHEO Research Institute in Ottawa, Canada. "These chemicals have toxic effects as endocrine disruptors that paradoxically affect energy levels and appetite, potentially contributing to yo-yo weight loss and gain," she says. Plus there's no guarantee that chemicals released from fat will actually leave the body—some will end up back in storage.

With chemicals that the body does eliminate rapidly, such as phthalates, a short fast will lower levels. It's not clear that this does you any good, though. As soon as you start eating again, says Kortenkamp, levels go back to where they were.

For these reasons, Sears recommends what she calls a "life-long detox," which involves eating as healthily as possible and avoiding chemicals in the home and workplace as much as you can. But Kortenkamp isn't convinced that even that will help much. "Only regulatory action that reduces exposures will work. Individual avoidance strategies are but a drop in the ocean," he says.

That said, you can greatly reduce your exposure to toxic chemicals like nicotine and alcohol. There is also one way

of speeding up the removal of many fat-soluble toxic chemicals that is supported by scientific evidence—producing milk (*Lipids*, vol 36, p 1289). While it is possible for women to induce lactation without giving birth—and even for men to lactate—the milk-yourself detox method is probably unlikely to catch on.

5. Being a Bit Overweight Means You Will Die Sooner

Let's be clear—being seriously obese is bad for your health. A body mass index of over 40 increases the risk of type 2 diabetes, heart disease, and certain cancers and increases the risk of dying from any cause by up to 29 percent. This is not a health myth.

But carrying just a few extra pounds, far from being a one-way ticket to an early grave, seems to deter the grim reaper, according to a recent review of nearly a hundred studies involving nearly three million people. The review, led by Katherine Flegal of the US Centers for Disease Control in Hyattsville, Maryland, reported earlier this year that being "overweight"—defined as having a body mass index (BMI) of 25 to 29—seems to have a protective effect, with a 6 percent reduction in death risk compared with people with a BMI of between 18.5 and 25. Those with BMIs over 35, however, have a higher risk (*JAMA*, vol. 309, p. 71).

It isn't clear why being overweight might protect against an early death. Perhaps carrying a few extra pounds in reserve helps the body fight off illness or infection. Perhaps overweight people are more likely to receive medical attention. Or perhaps some of those counted as "normal" had lost weight due to serious illnesses.

Whatever the reason, Flegal says her finding is not a green light to eat all the pies. Overweight people might be more likely to develop diseases that affect the quality of life, for instance. Even so, it seems that a little bit of flab may not be the crime against health it has always been made out to be.

6. We Should Live and Eat Like Cavemen

Our bodies didn't evolve for lying on a sofa watching TV and eating chips and ice cream. They evolved for running around hunting game and gathering fruit and vegetables. So, the myth goes, we'd all be a lot healthier if we lived and ate more like our ancestors.

This "evolutionary discordance hypothesis" was first put forward in 1985 by medic S. Boyd Eaton and anthropologist Melvin Konner, both of Emory University in Atlanta, Georgia (*NEJM*, vol 312, p 283). In it they claimed that while our genes haven't changed for at least 50,000 years, our diets and lifestyles have changed greatly since the advent of agriculture 10,000 years ago, and it has all happened too quickly for us to evolve to deal with it. This, they argued, is the reason why diabetes, heart disease and cancers are rife. If we could only exercise more and eat like hunter-gatherers, we'd be fitter, happier and healthier.

In recent years, the Stone Age or "paleo" diet based on these ideas has become very popular. It involves eating game, fish, fruit, vegetables and nuts, and avoiding grains, dairy, legumes, oils, refined sugars, and salt. Some aspects, such as exercising more and eating less highly processed grains and sugars, agree with the latest evidence. But others, such as ditching grains, legumes and dairy, do not. And the underlying rationale is flawed.

The idea that there was some evolutionary sweet spot 50,000 years ago just isn't true, says Marlene Zuk, an evolutionary biologist at the University of Minnesota in Saint Paul, who has written a book debunking the paleo lifestyle. Our ancestors were not perfectly adapted to their lifestyles, and we have adapted to our agricultural diet.

For instance, many people have extra copies of genes for digesting the starch found in grains. The ability to digest milk as an adult—lactose tolerance—has also evolved independently in several populations.

Another criticism is that we don't know for sure what our ancestors ate. They definitely didn't eat anything like the animals and plants we eat today, which have been transformed beyond recognition by selective breeding. Last but not least, it's not clear that ancient hunter-gatherers really were that much healthier than the rest of us (*The Lancet*, vol 381, p 1211).

Evolution, after all, doesn't care if we drop dead once we've raised our children and grandchildren.

The original proponents of the discordance hypothesis still stand by their idea, but they have revised it in light of the latest evidence. Eaton and Konner now include low-fat dairy products and whole grains in their recommended foods (*Nutrition in Clinical Practice,* vol 25, p 594).

Critical Thinking

1. Critically assess the notion that we should be drinking eight glasses of water a day.
2. Discuss the effect of sugar on children's behavior.
3. Discuss the role of antioxidants in our health and what we can do to promote them.
4. Discuss the merits of various methods of detoxification.
5. Review the evidence for the relationship between being overweight and early death.
6. Discuss the pros and cons of the "evolutionary discordance hypothesis."

Internet References

Evolution and Medicine Network
http://evmedreview.com

The Paleolithic Diet Page
http://www.paleodiet.com

CAROLINE WILLIAMS is a freelancer based in Surrey, UK.

Article   Prepared by: Elvio Angeloni, *Pasadena City College*

The Evolution of Inequality

DEBORAH ROGERS

Learning Outcomes

After reading this article, you will be able to:

- Discuss the egalitarian nature of our hunter-gatherer ancestors before 5,000 years ago.

- Discuss the transition from egalitarian hunter-gatherer societies to the distinctive inequality that exists in modern times.

H umans lived as egalitarians for tens of thousands of years. As unequal society arose, its instability caused it to spread, argues anthropologist Deborah Rogers.

For 5000 years, humans have grown accustomed to living in societies dominated by the privileged few. But it wasn't always this way. For tens of thousands of years, egalitarian hunter-gatherer societies were widespread. And as a large body of anthropological research shows, long before we organised ourselves into hierarchies of wealth, social status and power, these groups rigorously enforced norms that prevented any individual or group from acquiring more status, authority or resources than others.

Decision-making was decentralised and leadership ad hoc; there weren't any chiefs. There were sporadic hot-blooded fights between individuals, of course, but there was no organised conflict between groups. Nor were there strong notions of private property and therefore any need for territorial defence. These social norms affected gender roles as well; women were important producers and relatively empowered, and marriages were typically monogamous.

Keeping the playing field level was a matter of survival. These small-scale, nomadic foraging groups didn't stock up much surplus food, and given the high-risk nature of hunting—the fact that on any given day or week you may come back empty-handed—sharing and cooperation were required to ensure everyone got enough to eat. Anyone who made a bid for higher status or attempted to take more than their share would be ridiculed or ostracised for their audacity. Suppressing our primate ancestors' dominance hierarchies by enforcing these egalitarian norms was a central adaptation of human evolution, argues social anthropologist Christopher Boehm. It enhanced cooperation and lowered risk as small, isolated bands of humans spread into new habitats and regions across the world, and was likely crucial to our survival and success.

How, then, did we arrive in the age of institutionalised inequality? That has been debated for centuries. Philosopher Jean-Jacques Rousseau reasoned in 1754 that inequality was rooted in the introduction of private property. In the mid-19th century, Karl Marx and Friedrich Engels focused on capitalism and its relation to class struggle. By the late 19th century, social Darwinists claimed that a society split along class lines reflected the natural order of things—as British philosopher Herbert Spencer put it, "the survival of the fittest." (Even into the 1980s there were some anthropologists who held this to be true—arguing that dictators' success was purely Darwinian, providing estimates of the large numbers of offspring sired by the rulers of various despotic societies as support.)

Birth of Hierarchy

But by the mid-20th century a new theory began to dominate. Anthropologists including Julian Steward, Leslie White and Robert Carneiro offered slightly different versions of the following story: Population growth meant we needed more food, so we turned to agriculture, which led to surplus and the need for managers and specialised roles, which in turn led to corresponding social classes. Meanwhile, we began to use up natural resources and needed to venture ever further afield to seek them out. This expansion bred conflict and conquest, with the conquered becoming the underclass.

More recent explanations have expanded on these ideas. One line of reasoning suggests that self-aggrandising individuals who lived in lands of plenty ascended the social ranks by exploiting their surplus—first through feasts or gift-giving, and later by outright dominance. At the group level, argue anthropologists Peter Richerson and Robert Boyd, improved coordination and division of labour allowed more complex societies to outcompete the simpler, more equal societies. From a mechanistic perspective, others argued that once inequality took hold—as when uneven resource-distribution benefited one family more than others—it simply became evermore entrenched. The advent of agriculture and trade resulted in private property, inheritance, and larger trade networks, which perpetuated and compounded economic advantages.

It is not hard to imagine how stratification could arise, or that self-aggrandisers would succeed from time to time. But none of these theories quite explain how those aiming to dominate would have overcome egalitarian norms of nearby communities, or why the earliest hierarchical societies would stop enforcing these norms in the first place. Many theories about the spread of stratified society begin with the idea that inequality is somehow a beneficial cultural trait that imparts efficiencies, motivates innovation and increases the likelihood of survival. But what if the opposite were true?

In a demographic simulation that Omkar Deshpande, Marcus Feldman and I conducted at Stanford University, California, we found that, rather than imparting advantages to the group, unequal access to resources is inherently destabilising and greatly raises the chance of group extinction in stable environments. This was true whether we modelled inequality as a multitiered class society, or as what economists call a Pareto wealth distribution—in which, as with the 1 percent, the rich get the lion's share.

Counterintuitively, the fact that inequality was so destabilising caused these societies to spread by creating an incentive to migrate in search of further resources. The rules in our simulation did not allow for migration to already-occupied locations, but it was clear that this would have happened in the real world, leading to conquests of the more stable egalitarian societies—exactly what we see as we look back in history.

In other words, inequality did not spread from group to group because it is an inherently better system for survival, but because it creates demographic instability, which drives migration and conflict and leads to the cultural—or physical—extinction of egalitarian societies. Indeed, in our future research we aim to explore the very real possibility that natural selection itself operates differently under regimes of equality and inequality. Egalitarian societies may have fostered selection on a group level for cooperation, altruism and low fertility (which leads to a more stable population), while inequality might exacerbate selection on an individual level for high fertility, competition, aggression, social climbing and other selfish traits.

So what can we learn from all this? Although dominance hierarchies may have had their origins in ancient primate social behaviour, we human primates are not stuck with an evolutionarily determined, survival-of-the-fittest social structure. We cannot assume that because inequality exists, it is somehow beneficial. Equality—or inequality—is a cultural choice.

Critical Thinking

1. In what respects were hunter-gatherers egalitarian before 5,000 years ago and why?

2. What have been the various theories of the past that have been put forth to explain inequality? What was the opposing theory developed by the mid-20th century?

3. How did agriculture perpetuate and compound economic advantages for some?

4. Why did inequality spread from group to group in spite of the fact that it is inherently destabilizing?

5. How do egalitarian societies contrast with those with inequality with regard to the process of selection?

6. What can we learn from all of this, according to the author?

Create Central

www.mhhe.com/createcentral

Internet References

Living Links
www.emory.edu/LIVING_LINKS/dewaal.html
Society for Historical Archaeology
www.sha.org

DEBORAH ROGERS is an affiliated researcher at Stanford University's Institute for Research in the Social Sciences and directs the Initiative for Equality.